INTERNATIONAL AND ICC ARBITRATION

Conference papers and source materials

Editors

John Uff
Director

Elizabeth Jones
Solicitor of the Supreme Court

Centre of Construction Law & Management
King's College, London

1990

Published in Great Britain by
Centre of Construction Law and Management,
King's College, University of London,
The Old Watch House, Strand,
London WC2R 2LS.
071 873 2446
071 872 0210 (Fax)

Printed by The Eastern Press Ltd., Reading.

ISBN 0-9514866-1-6

Preface

For too long there has been a scarcely-veiled tension between arbitrators, arbitral institutions, and writers about arbitration, across that geographically short and intellectually large divide, the Channel. The reasons are easy enough to see. At least within recent decades international arbitrations in mainland Europe have tended to be few in number; large in scale; conducted under the auspices of institutions; procedurally administered by "civilian" processes. The writers on the subject have in the main been scholars, and the language of discourse has been French. By contrast, arbitrations in England have been numerous; smaller in size, as regards the amounts involved and the length of the proceedings; less liable to be initiated through institutions than *ad hoc*; conducted by procedures which are either recognizably "common law" in nature or so informal as to bear no resemblance to any national judicial process; the writers, so far as there are any, have been participants not professors; and the language has in the main been English.

Differences of this kind will always exist. Written on a larger scale they could be seen at once by any observer of the debates leading to the formulation of the UNCITRAL model law on arbitration. These debates were of a high standard, and marked by an exceptional degree of cultural magnanimity. At the same time it was evident that the participants shared no common view of what arbitration was, or how it might or should be conducted. Yet, although they spoke a different language of arbitration, there remained a willingness to listen, learn and to accommodate.

Regrettably, this spirit had for a long time been absent in exchanges between the two European arbitral communities. More than one observer has remarked upon and regretted that arbitration has tended to generate a kind of forensic chauvinism. It must be said that until quite recently this has been a feature of relationships between the International Chamber of Commerce and those writers and thinkers who are within its cultural orbit, and participants in the arbitral process on this side of the Channel.

Happily, sincere efforts made on both sides to eliminate this short-sighted and deadening set of preconceptions have recently borne fruit. Nowhere more conspicuously than in the conference of which these papers are the record. From time to time it is said, not entirely in jest, that in the arbitration industry – and make no mistake, it is now an industry – there will soon be more arbitration conferences than arbitrations. What is printed in this work shows that the *Conference on International and ICC Arbitration:*

1989 was worth while. Nothing bland; complacent; general. Rather, sharp-edged; sceptical; focused. Although the immediate aims of the Conference and its aftermath might at first sight seem parochial to readers in the countries of, say, eastern Europe or the Pacific rim, I believe that anyone concerned in arbitration can profit greatly from works such as this, and build upon them. For those immediately concerned the ice is now thoroughly broken. We must now take our common aims, if diverse methods, for granted.

Sir Michael J. Mustill
Lord Justice of Appeal
December 1990

Contents

General Introduction

The Conference on International and ICC arbitration took place at King's College London on 21st and 22nd September 1989. This was the Second Annual Conference of the Centre of Construction Law and Management. This volume contains the full proceedings of the conference, revised and edited, together with additional material: Mr. B. Vigrass contributed an additional paper dealing with the work of the London Court of International Arbitration; and the paper by Prof. Abrahamson has been enlarged, and re-written. The conference proceedings including the topics of debate are reviewed by the Editors in Paper 2, which discusses the major current issues in international arbitration.

The proceedings commence with the keynote address delivered by Lord Wilberforce, which is accompanied by the Editors' review paper. The succeeding papers are arranged in the following sections:

- Organisation and Status of the ICC
- Features of ICC and international arbitration
- Particular issues in international arbitration
- United Kingdom attitude to international arbitration.

The conference was conducted in plenary session throughout, with discussion and debate following presentation of the papers. In addition to the papers the Appendix contains some essential source material, including the ICC Arbitration Rules.

A particular feature of the conference was a demonstration arbitration conducted in accordance with normal ICC practice using documentation previously distributed to the conference delegates. A panel of arbitrators, all of whom had extensive experience of ICC proceedings, gave directions and then heard oral argument on certain preliminary issues. The arbitrators then formulated and delivered their award. A full set of this documentation is included in the first Appendix, with the parties' written submissions presented to the arbitrators, and the arbitrators' considered award. These documents may form a useful precedent for preparation and drafting in international arbitration,and the award offers a valuable insight into the working of an experienced tribunal.

The Centre of Construction Law expresses its gratitude to all those involved in the conference, the contributors and delegates, and to the organisers and sponsors, IBC Legal Studies and Services Limited. A full list of contributors is set out in the following pages. In addition to those whose contributions are listed, the Centre would wish particularly to acknowledge the invaluable help of Pauline Gale, Manager of the Centre of Construction Law, who assisted throughout the organisation of the conference and subsequent preparation of the papers for publication; and of Caroline Roldanus who undertook the bulk of the conference organisation on behalf of IBC. Thanks are also due to Jacqui Bausch, Director of IBC, for whose support and encouragement we are greatly indebted. We would like to acknowledge the continuing support and advice of Jane Belford and Andrew Prideaux of Chancery Law Publishing Ltd, who have given us the benefit of their considerable expertise in helping to publish this work.

Finally, the Centre of Construction Law and Managaement continues to depend on encouragement and support from colleagues at King's College London. We are grateful to them for having so readily welcomed the development of a new subject in the academic sphere.

1st November 1990

JFU
EAJ

Centre of Construction Law & Management,
The Old Watch House,
King's College,
London WC2R 2LS

List of Contributors

Conference Chairman: The Hon. Sir Robin Auld, FKC, Judge of the High Court of Justice

Keynote Speaker: The Rt. Hon. the Lord Wilberforce, former Lord of Appeal in Ordinary

Participants

Professor Max W. Abrahamson, BA, LLB, FCIArb, Visiting Professor, King's Centre of Construction Law and Management.

Stephen Bond, Secretaire General ICC Cœur d'Arbitrage, Paris.

Professor Phillip Capper, MA, BA, Masons Professor of Construction Law, King's Centre of Construction Law and Management. Special Adviser on Construction Law, Masons.

Lawrence Collins, Solicitor, Partner Herbert Smith, General Editor, Dicey and Morris, Conflict of Laws.

Paul Darling, BA (Oxon) BCL (Oxon), Barrister.

Michael Davis, Solicitor, Partner, Herbert Smith.

Anthony Edwards, Solicitor, Partner, Freeman & Co.

The Rt.Hon. Sir Edward Eveleigh, former Lord Justice of Appeal, International arbitrator.

Martin Harman, Solicitor, Partner Masons.

J. Martin Hunter, MA(Cantab), FCIArb, Solicitor, Partner Freshfields, joint author of *Law of Practice of International Commercial Arbitration*.

Elizabeth Jones, MA, LLB, ACIarb Solicitor, Group Legal Adviser, Highpoint plc.

David Kemp QC. Practising Barrister and arbitrator.

Humphrey LLoyd, QC, MA, LLB, practising Barrister and arbitrator. Co-editor in chief of *The International Construction Law Review*.

David Marks, Barrister, former Editor of *Rowlatt on Principal and Surety*.

Vivian Ramsey, BA, CEng, MICE, Barrister.

Peter Rowland, BA, LLB, FCA, FCIArb, Barrister.

David Sarre, Arbitration consultant, ICC United Kingdom.

Anthony Thompson QC, MA (Oxon), former Chairman of Bar European Group, co-chairman European Banking Law Commission of the Union Internationale des Avocats.

Professor J. F. Uff, QC, PhD, CEng, FICE, FCIArb, Director, King's Centre of Construction Law and Management.

Professor Ian N. Duncan Wallace, QC, Visiting Professor, King's Centre of Construction Law and Management, Barrister.

Dr. J. Gillis Wetter, Solicitor-Royal, Sweden.

Jeremy Winter, LLB, solicitor, Partner, Baker & McKenzie specialising in International construction law.

Table of statutes

Table of cases

Part I

Introduction

Keynote Address 1

Lord Wilberforce

I would like to highlight some areas in the general field of arbitration, in international arbitration, and in ICC arbitration, which have seemed to me interesting and important during the 10 years in which I have been actively engaged in arbitration matters. I am not sure that my career has been well organised. I started as an advocate, middled as judge, and finished as an arbitrator. The process might have been better if it had been reversed. I certainly would have been a better judge if I had first had experience as an arbitrator; and I am sure that I would have been a better advocate if I had first been a judge. I am sure, however, of one thing, that a former judge cannot become a good arbitrator without considerable adjustment to his ideas. On this I can rely only on my own experience and give my own views.

Let me start with arbitration itself: this legal, or as I prefer to call it, para-legal concept. For most of my professional life it has been regarded rather patronisingly by judges as a kind of unlisted security. It was regarded as a minor subject in the law exams; all you had to know was the existence of section 4 of the Arbitration Act 1889. Mr. Quintin Hogg, as he then was, was able to write what was almost a leading book on the subject in his spare time. This is to be compared to the years during which *Mustill and Boyd* was in gestation. Arbitration was *ex hypothesi*, of second order: for anything important you had to go to the courts. An arbitrator was not of himself entitled to sit at the high table. Even so experienced a man as Monsieur Badinter, the French Minister of Justice, a very few years ago was content to describe arbitration as "filling a gap".

The change since then, in the last 10 years, or perhaps one ought to say since the first oil crisis, 15 years, has been extraordinary. Arbitration now has a full quotation and is regarded as a form of dispute settlement of equal status with the other two, litigation and conciliation. The great arbitrators are as well know, if not better known, internationally, than the great judges. The reasons for this are very easy to find. They can be summed up by saying that we live in a much more complicated world. Before 1939 trade was conducted between a limited number of reasonably solvent Western nations or their colonies and under a small number of governing laws. Construction contracts in particular were generally organised in accordance with the colonial system, the governing law being that of the colonial power. Finance and borrowing contracts were similarly drawn up in typically legal forms with default provisions easily enforceable under the same law. Then, a slim volume could encompass the whole law and jurisprudence of the subject. Of course there was then international arbitration. The ICC itself is over 60 years old. The American Arbitration Association is even older, and so also is the London Court of Arbitration.

Since World War II, what a change has occurred. We now have 160 nations, hostile to colonial regimes, all wanting their own distinctive law. Legal systems and sub-systems multiply. The international legal world is not just diversified, it is multi-cultural. Across the cultural divide we find three main philosophies; the industrial nations first, the state capitalised governments second and the developing world third. We have all of these and interacting different cultures, different sub-systems, and different philosophies, all trying to enter into the same kind of work.

Development contracts have become much more ambitious and more long-term. They inevitably involve sub-contractors of different nationalities under different laws. We have the involvement of governments and state agencies. We have the use in one country, developed or less developed, of technologies derived from another country, with all the complications of rights of access and protection. We have financial structures which are vulnerable to currency changes, inflation, moratoria or blocking devices. We have had perhaps the most significant event in our time with the first oil crisis in the early 1970's. This produced an economic disturbance which has been fatal to long term contracts, to the solvency of developing countries as customers for construction projects, and to traditional jurisprudence. All of this, and I have only very briefly summarised what is well-known, gives a strong and competitive edge to international arbitration, particularly to institutional arbitration. Litigation in the classical style could not compete in that world. Let us now look at some facets of this situation.

As regards the choice of forum, litigation has problems with large international companies and their international subsidiaries. Who are you to sue, where are you to sue? A Dutch company might contract with a UK company to erect a plant in Kuwait. Proceedings about the uranium cartel were brought in the United States, United Kingdom, France, Canada, Australia, and probably other countries too. If you are owed money by a government you do not want to have to sue in its courts. The Government on the other hand will not be sued anywhere else. A forum chosen by the ICC, or named in an ICC arbitration clause, may be acceptable to everybody. That the ICC does meet this particular demand is shown by the interesting fact that 16% of parties to ICC arbitration are governmental or quasi-governmental entities.

As regards choice of law, we know how the courts handle this question. It is one of the delights for judges, a real intellectual pleasure to try to solve the problems of conflicts. But it may not give a good result for the parties. The judges produce their result and the parties then have to live with it. On the contrary, the ICC Rules (see Art. 13(3)) are much more flexible, and I, as an arbitrator, have found them to give good results. This is an interesting and important problem, discussed further in the paper of Mr Davis.

The enforcement of arbitration awards is, I suggest, easier and more effective than the enforcement of judgments of the courts. It is true that within Europe the 1968 Convention works effectively as between the parties to it, but we must all know of cases where the process of execution abroad is slow, technical, expensive and ineffective. The judgment of the International Court of Justice in the early 1950's against Albania is still unsatisfied. But in arbitration the New York Convention of 1958 is broadly accepted and it is claimed that 90% of ICC awards are accepted and paid. The ICC, we know, pays a good deal of attention to enforceability of awards (see Art. 13(2)); and the Court does scrutinise awards in draft form from this angle. But there do remain problems, a few which I now outline.

First the Tribunal itself. In litigation you know what you are getting. If you choose the Commercial Court you know you are getting a very professional competent trial body. In arbitration you have a say; you have your own choice, but is that a good thing? Usually the parties each nominate their own arbitrator. How often they come to regret their choice. I have been involved as a party arbitrator in a long case. At the close of that case, when we were discussing our award and the amount of damages, I and the distinguished English QC who was the other party-arbitrator, realised that we were advocating the case of the opposite party, not of the one by which we were nominated. Of course, it cancelled out so that the parties never knew what had happened. If you are going to be independent (and we felt that was our duty) that is the result which may occur.

Then the Chairman: there may be long negotiations before he is agreed upon. In the end there may have to be a choice by the ICC and this is a tremendous gamble. I have more than once been amazed that people, commercial companies of great size, are willing to entrust the decision of large, often multi-million dollar sums, to so haphazard a process, which can lead (I do not say generally or often does) to a horrifyingly unadapted personality.

We must bear in mind that arbitrations vary tremendously in character. Construction contracts are not homogeneous with commercial contracts generally, that is commercial contracts between business men of comparable economic power. Construction contracts are quite different from them, so the considerations which apply to the latter do not necessarily apply to the former. The case for selected and recognisably expert arbitrators may be far greater in relation to construction contracts. Are we happy with the trend, which other contributors detect, towards the selection of legally expert arbitrators rather than those competent in the subject? Should we leave this job of selection to the ICC? Mr Sarre's paper contains valuable advice on this point.

Second, on a slightly more reflective level we may consider the question of bias, or rather lack of independence. I refer not to the possession of an interest in the proceedings, which rarely occurs, but a doctrinal or cultural bias which few people are without, and for which indeed they may have been nominated in the first place. Ought we to try to exclude this? or on the contrary, is its existence, properly balanced and controlled, of the essence of arbitration? Are we happy about the way in which the ICC handles these questions? Are we in Britain too complacent about this question of independence?

Third, the question of procedure. We can contrast with the tight rules of court which exist in all countries the flexible rules of the ICC (see Art.

11) which broadly leave questions of procedure to the Tribunal and the parties. Is this in the parties' best interests? Does it work well when you have arbitrators coming from different legal systems? Proliferation of pleadings can be a great menance and discovery a monstrous evil. Oral arguments may get out of hand. Can they be controlled? All these matters need to be discussed. My own belief is that, except in cases where you have a strong-minded single arbitrator, the parties are better served by some positive institutional direction such as the ICC Rules or the rules of the London Court of International Arbitration. See further the papers of Mr Thompson and Mr Sarre.

Fourth, the question of finality. Has the 1979 Act and the House of Lords created a satisfactory position. I was not a member of the House of Lords in the *Nema* case, or in any of the decisions in this area. Are we happy with the use of exclusion agreements, which are fully allowed in construction cases, particularly since our courts have accepted Article 24 of the ICC Rules as having the effect of an exclusion agreement? Or do we think, particularly where we are dealing with third world countries, that more liberal access to the court would be appropriate. Mr Wallace offers a powerful paper on this subject.

Fifth, the use of precedent. Where does arbitration stand in this regard? Of course it is not bound by the strong rules that still – *pace* Lord Denning – exist in English law. Every ICC arbitration is indeed unique in its tribunal and unique in its subject matter. The ICC moreover has an understandable reluctance to publish too readily individual awards. But we know that precedents are looked for and are followed in international arbitration. ICC awards or parts of them are published in the *Year Book* and in *Clunet*, commented on in *Dalloz* or *Arbitration International*. They are referred to in text books, particularly in *Craig*, *Park* and *Paulsson*. Experienced arbitrators have their own collections of decisions, the tools of their trade, like the clinical notes of surgeons. We seem indeed to be getting near to the European conception of jurisprudence, useful but not binding. Is this a good thing? This, of course, overlaps to some extent with the argument for greater access to the courts, so that a visible jurisprudence may be established.

These are some of the points that need to be discussed. Behind them all lies the broad question as to where English policy stands as regards international arbitration. Have we got a policy at all? Personally I think that we should have a comprehensive Act covering both domestic and international arbitration. We should not adopt the UNCITRAL Model Law; we should open the doors to the courts somewhat. Harmonization is not an end in itself. We should have our own distinctive stance, but we must await the final report of the Mustill Committee on these questions.

I conclude with one thought, a keynote if you like. Arbitration is not second-class litigation, nor ought the tendency to be for it to become more and more judicialised. Do judges and ex-judges indeed play too great a role in it? Ought we to be looking more for practical men, trained in arbitration, or for more professors in the job. Arbitration is an art in its own right, equal and parallel to litigation but of distinct standing. It is an essentially practical art which must be shaped according to the type of dispute with which it is concerned.

Arbitration is an evolving art, never frozen in the text of rules. The history of the evolution of the ICC Court of Arbitration since 1920, a fascinating story, shows this. Arbitration, both domestic and international, should have confidence in itself. It is indeed self-confidence that has made the ICC the successful institution that it undoubtedly is.

2 Current issues in International Arbitration

The Editors

Synopsis

This is a review of issues of current importance in the field of international arbitration, emerging from the written papers and the conference debates. It is cross-referenced to the conference papers, where further more detailed material will be found.

Introduction

The subject of this conference is international arbitration with two particular points of emphasis: first, the bulk of the papers and discussion comes from English lawyers variously experienced in international arbitration but essentially rooted in the common law system; secondly, the ICC arbitration system is taken as the role model for international arbitration, and much of the detailed consideration in the papers is centred on ICC procedure. While these points of emphasis may be seen as limiting, they may also be regarded as placing this conference in a clear practical context. Arbitration of any kind is or should be an essentially practical medium, which has no other justification than its utility. If it does not work in practice, no amount of theory will revive it; and if it does work, those who explore the theoretical basis should exercise caution that over-exposure of the roots does not damage a flourishing tree. These two points of emphasis may also be seen as providing a bridge between the common law on the one hand, as representing a substantial and vigorous element of the world's legal systems, and the ICC on the other hand, being in practical terms the most successful international arbitration institution, which for historical reasons has developed largely from civil law origins. If, as this conference has sought to demonstrate, these two elements can co-operate successfully, the consequences for international arbitration under a variety of systems are favourable, indicating new possibilities for the removal of artificial barriers and the achievement of genuine free trade between the nations.

This paper now proceeds to consider 12 issues which may be seen as representative of the general and particular questions which will continue to arise for discussion and solution, now and in the future.

1. International arbitration compared to multi-state litigation

Disputes which involve a number of different national interests[1] necessarily involve potential competition between different systems for their resolution. The question of applicable law is generally capable of resolution by reasonably ascertainable means,[2] whether the dispute is subject to arbitration or court proceedings. The essential differences between the alternative systems is that multi-state litigation necessarily involves either the choice of one particular state as the forum, with the real possibility of perceived bias on the part of parties who are foreign to that state; or proceedings taking place in a number of different states with the considerable problems of overlap and recognition.

Against this, international arbitration offers the real advantages of a forum which, although necessarily rooted in one jurisdiction[3] can reflect the international character of the dispute through its procedure and particularly through the composition of the tribunal. Thus, international arbitration offers a convenient and comprehensive solution to most of the problems which arise from competition between interested states. The arbitration process is subject to well-known disadvantages in terms of sanctions and enforceable powers, compared to courts. However, the enforcement of orders or judgments from a particular state court in other states poses similar problems. And in regard to the enforcement of awards, the New York Convention in particular has brought about a transformation in the effectiveness of the international arbitration process,[4] and the view is expressed that enforcement of arbitration awards in different countries is now more effective than the enforcement of judgments of national courts.[5] In the particular context of the ICC, there is an additional element in that the secretariat undertakes, with some measure of success, to persuade parties to comply voluntarily.[6]

In the result, while there will remain certain particular advantages in submission to a national court,[7] where there is actual or potential conflict regarding the forum or the procedure to be adopted, international arbitration offers an infinitely adaptable solution, capable of meeting the reasonable needs and expectations of the parties in regard to national balance, and the international arbitration system is itself sufficiently underpinned by recognised conventions to render the process generally effective. It may be added that the advent of the UNCITRAL model law, and its spreading

1 The term "international arbitration" as such has no fixed meaning: see Paper 23.
2 See Paper 19.
3 But see discussion below on *lex mercatoria*.
4 See Paper 4.
5 See Paper 1.
6 See Papers 3 and 7.
7 For example, the Commercial Court in London undertakes a material volume of international cases within its particular areas of expertise.

influence is an indicator that international arbitration is to be regarded as the normal means of resolving international trade disputes.

It should be observed that the present international arbitration institutions have grown out of and remain geared to a comparatively small volume of business. With the rapid growth of international trade throughout the world, and the particular and potentially vast growth within the EC, the adequacy of the present institutions has to be kept under review. There does not presently exist an international system capable of dealing with volumes of commercial business comparable to those transacted by many national courts. If, as appears possible and even likely, there is a considerable growth of international arbitration business, this may dictate the need for solutions of a new order of magnitude.

2. The ICC and other means of international arbitration

While ad hoc international arbitrations are possible, they pose serious problems in terms of cohesion as well as procedures and enforcement. In practical terms, an administrative system as part of the arbitration agreement is highly desirable. The ICC system and those of other bodies such as the Stockholm Chamber of Commerce and the London Court of International Arbitration will provide the basic framework for successful administered arbitration.

The issues which arise in terms of the general suitability and effectiveness of the ICC and similar bodies are twofold. First, within the present framework of international trade disputes, can the existing procedures be improved so as to encourage and require speedy, cheap and satisfactory resolution of international commercial disputes? The answer to this question is undoubtedly that there is ample room for improvement.[8] However, the task of changing rules and procedures which have already gained a measure of international acceptance and credence should not be underestimated. It might be said that under any particular arbitration system there is a huge disparity between different arbitrations conducted under the same rules, and ranging from arbitrations which are regarded as highly efficient and satisfactory to the opposite extreme. In short, arbitration is heavily dependent on the individual capabilities and approach of those involved, particularly the representatives of the parties and, of course, the arbitrators themselves. Thus, the view could be taken that the function of an arbitration system is to provide the means of efficient arbitration and, so far as possible, to encourage the appointment of the most suitable persons for the task. It may be that the choice between different international arbitration systems may safely be left to market forces and the development of a healthy degree of commercial competition between those who offer their systems. Parties are not unaware of the fact that arbitration institutions are to a large degree financed by the arbitrations which they attract, and this ought to be a sufficient fillip to improvement.

The second question that arises in relation to existing arbitration systems, is whether they are able to accommodate necessary changes. The growth

8 See, particularly, Paper 4.

of international trade since World War II has been remarkable.[9] But the likelihood is that trade in the future, particularly in the construction field, and especially within the EC, will be largely international. The question is, therefore, whether the existing institutions can accommodate not merely further degrees of change, but potentially vast increases in the volume of disputes. It might be said that the success of the international arbitration system to date has been based on treating each case with a high degree of individual attention which, for example, no national court system could provide. Could the international arbitration system respond to such a demand? It may be that in the future, wholly new institutions may be needed, drawing where necessary on the accumulated expertise of the existing ones.

3. Judicial review and the role of national courts

This has been regarded as a matter of the highest importance in the United Kingdom, such that the domestic law was radically changed by the Arbitration Act 1979 for the express purpose of bringing English law into line with other major trading nations in severely restricting appeals. Whether this course was justified is a matter which is still open to debate.[10] In the context of the apparent desire to achieve uniformity, it may be remarked that practically none of the major trading nations of the West have opted for the convenient course of adopting the UNCITRAL model law, either generally or for international arbitration. The variations that exist between arbitration law in different countries, although surmountable in practice, can operate as a material disadvantage to international arbitration. Attention has been drawn to the disparities in the rules applicable to misconduct by arbitrators.[11] Disparity in mandatory procedural rules applying in different countries can lead to a situation in which, for example, a claim is statute-barred in one country but not in another. Clearly, some body of generally accepted procedural law would be desirable.

A further consequence of the lack of appeal, is the absence of judicial precedent to guide arbitrators. This problem is particularly acute where an issue of law is known to recur in arbitrations, but where there exists no means of bringing the matter before a competent court, even for the purpose of offering guidance.[12] A limited volume of arbitration material is published in the journals and yearbooks, but this is generally insufficient to establish any workable jurisprudence. Perhaps a more systematic procedure for publishing material from international awards could be devised, but the problems are immense, not the least being that of confidentiality.

4. Multi-party disputes

The lack of workable procedures permitting the joinder of parties into arbitrations is a particular weakness of the system, especially in regard to

9 See Paper 1.
10 See Papers 1, 23 and particularly 21.
11 See Tupman, ICLQ, vol. 38, 36.
12 See further below under Time Bar Clauses.

construction disputes, which normally involve more than two parties. Court procedures can readily be tailored to accommodate these problems, but since arbitration must be based on agreement, there is no ready means of importing these systems into the arbitration process.

Some limited types of dispute may successfully be conducted between three or more parties, such as those involving two or more claimants in joint venture, or two or more defendants having similar interests in the dispute. The system cannot, however, accommodate three or more parties in situations where separate disputes are involved, for example, where the "third" party has a separate contract with one of the two primary parties to the arbitration, such as a sub-contractor or a design professional. Nor can the system accommodate cross-claims between parties other than the primary parties. Where related disputes arise, it is often possible to appoint the same tribunal in all the disputes, with the possibility of concurrent or consecutive hearings. However, this requires a degree of co-operation between the parties, and in practice this can readily break down, for example, by one party refusing to appoint as arbitrator the person appointed in another dispute.

Despite these difficulties, if the volume of international arbitration were to increase markedly, the lack of effective multi-party procedures would be a very serious impediment to the efficient disposal of disputes. The only practical way of achieving a satisfactory procedure would appear to be through an international convention or, in relation to the European Community, a directive to apply throughout the Member States.[13]

5. The ICC Court and Secretariat

The role and constitution of the ICC Court has given rise to some concern by users, who regard the procedure for scrutinising awards as creating potential problems. It has been emphasised[14] that the role of the Court in regard to scrutiny relates to the form of the award from the point of view of enforceability, and not to its substance. Considering the origins of the ICC in the civil law systems, it is perhaps surprising that a more active involvement in the arbitral process is not found. This may be the result of the influence of common law jurists or, more probably, a positive intention to leave the decisions solely to the arbitrators chosen by the parties.

Among criticisms which have been levelled at the ICC is the lack of support given to appointed arbitrators, both in terms of practical and secretarial assistance and in terms of advice in resolving procedural problems. These matters are addressed in Paper 7, by the Secretary-General of the ICC.

With regard to the appointed arbitrators, a number of questions arise. Are three arbitrators (or indeed any other number) preferable to one? Under ICC arbitrations, three arbitrators sometimes find themselves dealing with comparatively modest disputes as against the common law tradition of using

13 The European Commission is currently (1990) undertaking a review of liability and procedures in the construction industry with a view to some form of harmonisation.
14 See Papers 6 and 7.

one arbitrator whatever the sum in issue. The advantage of using a panel of three, is that it gives the opportunity of achieving an appropriate national or cultural balance.[15] A further question that arises is the extent to which arbitrators are independent or at least disinterested.[16] It should be recognised that arbitrators and parties under different systems do not operate under the same traditions or expectations. Where party-appointed arbitrators are known or seen to uphold the interests of their appointing party, a fair balance can still be maintained. A problem arises if one of the party appointed arbitrators is independent and disinterested, but the other is not. This is a compartively rare occurrence.

6. Terms of reference and the role of pleadings

This subject is dealt with in Paper 8. Common lawyers and civil lawyers tend to polarise in their attitude towards terms of reference and pleadings, not simply in regard to their utility, but on the question of defining the issues to be determined. Under the common law system, pleadings are regarded as a first step in defining the issues which, however, will not become crystallised until after full discovery of documents; and the final determination of the issues may not be attempted until after the conclusion of the hearing.[17] Conversely, the ICC rules envisage "pleadings" in the form of the Request for Arbitration and the Defence, which are generally intended to embody sufficient particulars to make it possible for the arbitrators then to define the issues arising at the very outset, and before investigation of the case starts. The contrast between these two systems is discussed in Papers 8, 10 and 22.

7. Jurisdiction and amendments

The ICC Rules contain useful provisions whereby the Court or the arbitrators can determine certain questions relating to jurisdiction.[18] Other problems concerning jurisdiction, however, can arise as a result of the ICC Rules, from the requirement to define the issues to be determined in the terms of reference.[19] The problem arises if one of the parties wishes to introduce new or different claims or contentions. In an arbitration where the procedure is such that the issues develop and do not become defined until the hearing, such amendments pose little problem. However, the effect of Article 16 of the ICC Rules appears to be to limit amendments without the consent of the other party, which will often not be forthcoming in practice.[20] The utility of terms of reference in this particular regard is addressed in Paper 4. While terms of reference undoubtedly have some attraction and usefulness, not least in giving the parties an early opportunity to reconsider

15 See further Paper 8.
16 See Papers 1 & 11.
17 See further Paper 4.
18 See Art. 8.3 and 8.4.
19 See generally Paper 9.
20 But see Paper 7, where the question is addressed by the Secretary General of the ICC.

the subject of the arbitration, a strong case can be made out for avoiding rigidity and the problems which can arise if amendments are restricted.

8. Time bar clauses with particular reference to FIDIC

The particular question which has arisen under the FIDIC form of contract, Third Edition, is whether, in order to prevent the time bar under Clause 67 applying, it is necessary to serve a Request for Arbitration within the meaning of the ICC Rules. The matter has been considered at some length elsewhere.[21] A number of decisions have been rendered by ICC arbitral tribunals going both ways. The problem has now been cured by amended wording in the Fourth Edition of the form of contract. The question that arises, however, is what steps are open to the ICC in regard to this type of problem.

No machinery exists under the ICC Rules for the Court itself to render a decision, nor for the Court to express any opinion regarding preference for one decision against another which is inconsistent. Furthermore, the arbitral system generally prevents such matters being brought before a court of competent jurisdiction. Even if the matter could be brought before a court, the question would then arise to what extent arbitrators, *a fortiori* in different countries, were bound by such decision. It is thought that the administering body (in this case the ICC) must be the appropriate body to resolve such issues, should they occur again. Since the extent of the powers of the Court are comparatively undefined, it is suggested that there is sufficient scope within existing rules for the court to refuse to approve a decision which is fundamentally inconsistent with another award previously approved by the Court. In this sense, the Court would be required to determine the matter for itself. While the possibility of challenge to such a course of action exists, the alternative of approving inconsistent awards in different cases, could also lead to challenge.

It is suggested that, in the absence of any regular or systematic process of judicial review, any international arbitration body needs to include sufficient and express powers to deal with this type of problem. This would involve either the creation of an effective record system in regard to awards which have been approved, so as to promote consistency or, alternatively, a limited and specific right of appeal would need to be created in order to give the administering body the power to render (and promulgate) decisions as appropriate.

9. Bonds and guarantees

These form a significant element in the operation and financing of major construction projects, particularly in the international field. The law and practice has developed rapidly in recent years as a result of the adoption of on-demand bonds. These matters are considered in Papers 13 and 14. The ICC has attempted to regulate practices through promulgating their own

21 See Wallace, *Construction Contract: Principles and Policies in Tort and Contract*, Chap. 18 and see also Paper 16 of this volume.

rules.[22] However, a number of fundamental problems remain which are, at least in part, susceptible of regulation by contract.

Perhaps the most fundamental question, on which the law and the relevant contractual instruments are usually silent, is what happens to funds paid over as a result of a valid call on a bond after the account position between the parties to the underlying contract has been finally determined by arbitration or process of law. It is usually assumed that there is a duty to bring this money into account, so that any balance will be repaid to the contractor. But the position under English law is unclear. Neither is it clear for what purposes the employer is entitled to apply the bond money, assuming there is a duty to account for the balance. Is the permissible use limited to proper claims under the underlying contract, or does it extend, for example, to payment of costs and other expenses connected with the underlying matter of complaint? These are ultimately matters of private agreement between the parties to the underlying contract, and it is highly desirable that the terms of that contract should cover these questions. It is a matter of regret that the standard forms of contract provide for the giving of bonds, but not for consequences such as those mentioned.

A further procedural matter which is also capable of being dealt with in the underlying contract, is the jurisdiction of arbitrators appointed to deal with disputes which may be the same as or at least connected with those which gave rise to the call on the bond. Ordinarily, such arbitrators will have no jurisdiction over the bond itself since, although given under a requirement contained in the underlying contract, the bond involves contracts between other persons. It is frequently the case, where a bond has been called and paid, that the contractor will ask the arbitral tribunal to consider the validity of the call, and to make protective interlocutory orders.[23] The parties may agree in the underlying contract to give the tribunal jurisdiction in relation to the bond monies, for example, by giving power to direct that part or all of the funds should be brought into a designated account. As pointed out in Paper 14, the absence of provisions regulating the bond proceeds may render the express provisions of the underlying contract meaningless.

While the law applicable to bonds will not permit any restriction on their calling, save in the most exceptional circumstances, and while prospective employers continue to ask for this form of security with little or no regulation, the possibility of limiting abuses of the system through arbitration procedures must remain an attractive option. Appropriate provisions will need to be drafted at the time that the underlying contract is made. It is appropriate that at this time, neither party should seriously contemplate the possibility of acting unfairly, and ought in principle to agree readily to any future arbitral tribunal being given appropriate jurisdiction.

10. Procedure, evidence and oral hearings

One of the great strengths of the ICC system is the disparity of procedures which can be accommodated within the rules. Papers 10 and 11 deal with

22 See Paper 14 and Part VI – Appendix.

23 See Craig Park & Paulsson, *ICC Arbitration*, para. 26.05; *Sperry International Trade* v. *Government of Israel* 532 F Supp 901 (SDNY 1982).

procedure and evidence, and Paper 22 with the common law approach to ICC arbitration. Against these views, Paper 12 offers a radical interpretation of the ICC rules, confirming the wide variety of procedures possible under the rules.

The question of evidence and documents is fundamental to the progress of an arbitration. It should be recognised that the result of the arbitration and therefore the resolution of the dispute is likely to depend to a material degree on the evidence which the parties produce. Thus, it should not be assumed that "procedure" is simply a matter of how the proper resolution of the arbitration is arrived at: it is a fundamental part of the dispute. While the arbitrators are given ample powers under the ICC rules to determine the procedure, it is important, in regard to matters such as discovery of documents, that this should reflect the reasonable expectations and wishes of the parties. For example, if parties are unused to oral evidence and discovery, these should generally not be imposed upon them merely because a lawyer from the common law system is appointed as neutral chairman. It could be argued that such matters are of sufficient importance that they need to be covered expressly by the rules. Conversely, the ICC rules are designed to operate in such a wide variety of circumstances, that all possibilities could not be encompassed, and specific rules would tend to restrict the arbitrator's discretion. If the rules are to continue to provide virtually unfettered discretion in terms of procedure, it creates a positive burden on the arbitrators to ensure that the procedure adopted is compatible with the reasonable expectation of the parties.

11. Lex mercatoria

The place of *lex mercatoria* in arbitrations conducted under the auspices of the ICC is a major issue raised in discussion and touched on in more than one of the papers. One of the arguments of advocates of *lex mercatoria* is that a body of international commercial law can be built up using published extracts from past awards given in arbitration proceedings[24] under ICC Rules. But the concept of *lex mercatoria* is treated with great suspicion by most Anglo-Saxon lawyers:

> "We doubt whether a *lex mercatoria* even exists in the sense of an international commercial law divorced from any state law; or at least that it exists in any sense useful for the solving of commercial disputes".[25]

It is not clear whether the objection to something which is intended to represent "internationally accepted principles of law governing contractual relations"[26] is based on the argument that "so far as the old *lex mercatoria* now exercises any influence on the course of commercial business it does so by virtue of having been received into the law of individual states through the medium of judicial decision and to a lesser degree through being

24 Schmitthof, *Export Trade* at 601.

25 Mustill and Boyd, *Commercial Arbitration* at 81.

26 *Deutsche Schatbau- und Tiefbohrgesellschaft mbh* v. *The R'as Al Kharmah National Oil Co. and Shell International Petroleum Co.Ltd.* CA [1987] 2 Lloyd's Rep. 246.

embodied in legislation".[27] This is a neat circle which ends logically with the application of national law in the *Deutsche Schatbau* case. The Court of Appeal decided in favour of the powers of the arbitrator to adopt "a common denominator of principles underlying the laws of various nations governing contractual relations".[28]

The attitude of English common lawyers is that contracts are incapable of existing in a vacuum and are devoid of all legal effect unless they can be attached to some system of private law. Vast and complex systems of conflicts of law rules have been built up with precisely the aim of discovering which private law system governs a particular transaction. Perhaps this is a counsel of perfection which ignores commercial realities, such as cost. Before a dispute is to be resolved, must the parties in a transaction concluded without the aid of lawyers and with the minimum of formalities, be expected to indulge in lengthy and costly proceedings to establish the applicable law? Is not the theory of floating or delocalised arbitration not more attractive and more practical? The judgment in the *Bank Mellat* case[29] bears out the common law attitude that English law "does not recognise the concept of arbitral procedures floating in the trans-national firmament unconnected with any municipal system of law".[30] This attitude will be relevant to foreign companies deciding upon a seat for their arbitrations and a law to govern them, particularly given decisions such as the *Nema*.[31]

For a more detailed exposition of *lex mercatoria* see Paper 17. For adverse comment see Paper 21.

12. The attitude of English law to international arbitration

The United Kingdom has a clear and perceived interest in attracting international arbitration to London and other UK venues and equally in playing a full part in international disputes abroad. This interest is reflected in the changes to UK domestic arbitration law and in the careful consideration given to the UNCITRAL model law.[32] It is generally surprising that greater recognition of international arbitration does not exist under English law. It would be appropriate if the starting point for any such consideration were the real possibility of parties exercising a positive choice as to the venue of their arbitration, including the possibility of selecting more than one location. It is obviously desirable that there should be a high degree of uniformity, at least throughout the major trading nations of the West, and also sufficient degree of recognition of the international arbitration process to engender confidence in parties who choose to take their disputes to a particular country. The United Kingdom has not chosen to move in this direction, but it may be that the European Community will seek to tackle the problem, at least in the limited context of the European construction industry.

27 Mustill and Boyd, *Commercial Arbitration* at 81.
28 Sir John Donaldson MR.
29 *Bank Mellat v Hellinki Techiniki SA* [1984] QB 291.
30 *Ibid.* at 301.
31 *Pioneer Shipping Ltd.* v. *BTP Tioxide Ltd. The Nema* [1982] AC 724.
32 See Paper 23, generally.

Statistics relating to the use of the United Kingdom as a venue for international arbitration[33] indicate less use than either France or Switzerland. Conversely, however, statistics indicate that in terms of the choice of arbitrators of other nationalities, the United Kingdom ranks alongside Switzerland and significantly ahead of France. While no sweeping conclusions should be drawn from the obviously limited data (in this case dealing only with ICC arbitrations over a limited period of time) one possible conclusion is that, while English professionals have retained the respect of foreign nationals, the United Kingdom as a venue for international arbitration has not.

Conclusions

International commercial arbitration must now be regarded as an institution of major economic importance, which contributes in a material degree to the free and effective flow of trade and commerce. The ICC is a major part of this system. While its rules and procedures rightly call for serious debate, it remains without doubt the most successful international arbitration institution, and a model for others to follow.

In the particular field of construction, international arbitration is a particular necessity, since there is generally little chance of the parties agreeing upon submission to any particular national court. As international commerce in general and construction in particular, grow in volume and importance, it is vital that the arbitration process should be made as efficient and effective as possible. A balance clearly needs to be drawn between specific rules and powers, and the discretion to be given to the arbitrators, and this balance needs to be kept under review.

It is vital for all arbitration institutions to keep in tune with developments and with evolution in the needs and expectations of users. Some apparently intractable problems exist, but it is important that these be kept under review. It is suggested that the existing arbitration institutions, including the ICC, may not have the flexibiity to accommodate a large increase of workload, such as is likely to be generated by the European construction industry within the European Community. Either new procedures must be found to accommodate this workload, or other institutions must be created to ensure an efficient and effective through-put of disputes. Generally, there is a need for harmonization of national systems so as to eliminate as far as possible the effect of a particular venue. Each potential arbitration centre can then compete, principally in terms of the professional and commercial services which it offers to international arbitrations.

33 See Paper 5.

Part II

Organisation and Status of the ICC

Arbitration of international commercial disputes under the auspices of the ICC 3

Stephen R Bond

Synopsis

In this paper the Secretary-General of the ICC International Court of Arbitration describes the characteristics of international arbitration under the auspices of the ICC, including the operation of the ICC and its Secretariat.

Introduction

The International Chamber of Commerce was founded in 1919 with the objective of promoting international commerce. It was found immediately that ensuring respect for and execution of international contracts in a foreign country was a major requirement of businessmen contemplating the investment of human, technical and financial resources abroad. This is so because in their domestic commercial activities businessmen can rely on familiarity with known behaviour and practices and, if a dispute must be resolved, on the national law and courts. However, in international business they face a number of additional uncertainties, problems, risks and fears ranging from dealing in a foreign language with people whose cultural background, customs, laws and business practices are less well known than their own, to selecting foreign lawyers to deal with a foreign judicial process about whose neutrality and independence they may have doubts. Consequently, the ICC's international arbitration system was established four years later, in 1923.

Since its inception, ICC arbitration has been specifically tailored to handle international disputes. Indeed, it is our view that the continual increase in the volume and complexity of international trade and investment makes it more important than ever before to have in place neutral and effective means of resolving disputes which may arise from these transactions. While it is technically possible to submit a purely domestic dispute to ICC arbitration, the fact is that the ICC deals virtually exclusively with international commercial arbitration. I would add that "international arbitration" should not be understood as necessarily meaning that the parties are of more than one nationality or located in more than one country. Often they are not. However, in these cases, the contract between them which is the subject of the arbitration is almost always one which is related to an international commercial matter in one way or another.

This dedication in principle and practice to international arbitration is fundamental in shaping the structure, procedures and working methods of ICC arbitration. In particular, it accounts for those features of ICC arbitration aimed at ensuring the neutrality, independence and expertise necessary for the ICC to carry out its responsibilities. Also, bearing in mind the additional complexities and difficulties which international commercial arbitration can entail both in the arbitration and enforcement process, ICC arbitration is geared and designed to produce an arbitral award that, by virtue of its procedural and substantive soundness, will compel defendants to honour it and will resist efforts before national tribunals to have it annulled.

Therefore, if certain of the particular features of ICC arbitration appear as unusual or unnecessary in the context of more familiar domestic litigation or arbitration practice, it should be remembered that international arbitration in general and ICC arbitration in particular, have many special features. In ICC arbitration, these may be vital to the success of an international arbitration, success being measured not by the mere rendering of an award, but by a party obtaining satisfaction on that award.

Statistics

In 1989, 305 requests for arbitration were filed with the ICC. The total caseload of the ICC varied between 673 and 700 cases at any one time and involved claims and counterclaims totalling at least $10 billion. The largest category of cases was that of claims ranging from $1 million to $10 million, this group comprising some 34% of new cases submitted But the ICC is not simply for huge cases. In 1989 some 5% of the cases submitted were far below $5.000. About 45% of the cases submitted were for amounts below $1 million.

The 1989 breakdown of these cases by economic sector was as follows:

Sales and supplies	26%
Distribution	9%
Commission	4%
Construction	20%
Engineering	1%
Research	0.4%
Licencing	5%
Know How	5%
Transfer of technology	4%
Technical assistance	2%

High technology	2%
Banking	3%
Financing	3%
Consultancy	2%
Marketing	2%
Management	1%
Maintenance	1%
Various services	0.4%
Labour	0.4%
Transportation	3%
Company law	0.4%
Mergers and take-overs	0.4%
Joint ventures	5%
Total	100%

The ranking of cases by economic sector has remained fairly steady over the past several years. Other points of general interest are that, during the past years:

- about one-sixth of the cases submitted involved governmental or para-statal entities.
- approximately one-quarter of the parties were from developing countries.
- many parties (100 in 1989) from developing countries were claimants in ICC arbitrations.

A number of ICC cases involve both claimants and defendants from developing countries or exclusively parties from Eastern Europe and developing countries. All of this reflects an increasing resort to ICC arbitration by developing countries and means that these countries and have a stake in the integrity of ICC arbitration, a factor which contributes, I believe, to the high proportion of ICC awards voluntarily complied with or upheld by national courts when challenged.

Fundamental characteristics of ICC arbitration

A. Universality

This brief statistical overview has highlighted a key feature of ICC arbitration, its universality. The ICC is available for any kind of international dispute so that public, semi-public and private parties from every country are free to agree to turn to ICC arbitration in relation to any kind of contract. International Chamber of Commerce cases are handled under all systems of law; the main ones being civil law, common law and Islamic Law; in different languages, mostly English, French, German and Spanish but also Arabic and Japanese. In 1989 ICC arbitrations involved parties from some 90 countries, ranging from Algeria to Zaire; ICC arbitrations took place in some 32 countries, including developing countries, and arbitrators from some 41 countries, including 21 developing countries, participated in ICC cases.

B. Neutrality and impartiality

Obviously the ICC Court could not effectively maintain a meaningful policy of universality if parties were fearful that ICC arbitration was biased in any manner whatsoever, whether on grounds of nationality or the political or economic system of the party or any other basis. From the outset, it has been a hallmark of ICC arbitration that it is completely impartial as between the parties concerned. This has been reflected in Article 2 (6) of the Rules of the Court of Arbitration, which requires that when the Court itself must appoint an arbitrator, the sole arbitrator or the chairman of an arbitral tribunal shall be chosen from a country other than those of which the parties are nationals, unless the parties otherwise agree. The ICC Court and Secretariat are both aware that unwavering neutrality is one of the ICC's greatest assets and are determined that their every action be consistent with this principle.

C. Party autonomy

Stemming both from the precepts of universality and from the consensual nature of arbitration, both the ICC Court's Rules and practice permit the parties the largest possible freedom in selecting their counsel, arbitrators, the place of arbitration, the governing law, the language and (subject to any mandatory provisions of the forum) the procedural law. In this sense, ICC arbitration is similar to ad hoc arbitration.

With respect to the number and selection of arbitrators, the parties are free to decide on one or three arbitrators. If a panel of three is agreed upon, each party may propose an independent arbitrator and, if the parties are agreed upon such a procedure, the arbitrators or the parties themselves may agree on a chairman. The Court has no established lists of arbitrators from which the parties or the Court are required to select an arbitrator. The Court appoints arbitrators only when the parties have not appointed them or otherwise provided for their appointment.

D. Administered arbitration

International Chamber of Commerce arbitration is administered or supervised arbitration, as opposed to ad hoc arbitration. Indeed ICC arbitration is probably the most highly supervised system for international arbitration, the most important elements of this supervision and administration being the regular screening of the development of each case by the ICC Secretariat and Court, the requirement that in each arbitration the arbitral tribunal establishes Terms of Reference which must then be presented to the ICC Court, and scrutiny of the arbitral awards by the ICC Court. Thus, unlike most other arbitral institutions, the ICC International Court of Arbitration has a role not only in shaping the arbitral proceedings where the parties have not been able to agree on such matters as the number and identity of the arbitrators and the place of arbitration, but the ICC also supervises the actual application of its Rules by the arbitral tribunal. The objective of combining both party autonomy and a highly supervised system is precisely to have ICC arbitration offer simultaneously to the parties the advantages of both ad hoc and institutional arbitration.

Examining more closely the administered and supervised aspects of ICC arbitration, what is the nature of the regular screening of the development of each case? After an arbitral tribunal has been established, the arbitrators have two months to draft the Terms of Reference. Before the expiry of the two months, the case is presented by the Secretariat to the Court's Committee, for examination and possible extension of the time-limit. Once the Terms of Reference become effective the arbitrators have six months to render their award. The Court's supervision during this second stage of the proceedings aims at ensuring that the arbitrators do not delay the rendering of the award without good reason. Therefore, before the expiry of the six-month period, the case is presented to the Court by the Secretariat, giving an account of where the arbitrators are in the arbitration process and when they expect to deliver the draft award for the Court's scrutiny. Where circumstances so justify, the Court prolongs the time for rendering the award by three months, and where there are good reasons for it at the expiry of the first prolongation, another three-month period is accorded and so on. Once the original six-month deadline has expired, the arbitral proceedings will generally be examined at least every three months. Once a draft award has been given to the Court by the arbitrators, the Court scrutinises the award, a process which will be considered later.

Consequently each case is reviewed both by the Secretariat and the ICC Court every two months until the Terms of Reference have been signed and thereafter each case is reviewed by them every three months until the award is drafted. Arbitrators who cannot justify a delay can ultimately be replaced so that the case may be conducted to a conclusion.

Institutional components

It will readily be seen that an institution that wishes to exercise effective, meaningful supervision over an arbitral system that features universality and party autonomy, while maintaining absolute neutrality and impartiality between the parties, has a hard task. It is precisely the need to meet these high standards that has shaped the rules, practice and institutional elements of the ICC.

A. The Secretariat

The Secretary-General of the ICC Court has overall responsibility for the activities of the Secretariat, in particular as regards the handling of the individual cases. A General Counsel has responsibility for legal research and information. The heart of the Secretariat's operations is what are called the teams. Each new case which comes to the Secretariat is assigned to a team, which consists of a Counsel (*i.e.* an attorney), an assistant to the Counsel (some of whom are also lawyers) and a secretary. In 1985, because of the ever-increasing caseload and the desire to render improved service, a fifth team was added to the Secretariat. The Counsel are selected not only for their intellectual and legal qualities but also with a view to ensuring that the Secretariat has access to as many languages and national legal systems as possible.

The Secretariat is composed of some 25 persons, comprising some 10 nationalities. In the past few years there has been an increased emphasis on the role of the staff in assisting the Court, parties, and arbitrators. This covers matters such as defining issues, furnishing answers to procedural and substantive questions related either to a particular arbitration or in general, interpreting the Rules of the Court and providing information on practices that have developed in the handling of ICC arbitrations. The Secretariat is thus prepared to offer objective advice and assistance to parties, counsel and arbitrators at all times, before, during and after a particular case. I believe that those who avail themselves of the support of the Secretariat will agree that it is of great utility and benefit.

The Secretariat also has the responsibility of preparing every matter upon which the International Court of Arbitration must render decisions under ICC Rules, such as:

- the existence or non-existence of a prima facie agreement between the parties to arbitrate;
- the number of arbitrators, the place of arbitration and the identity of the sole arbitrator or chairman (where the parties cannot agree on these points);
- action regarding deadlines or extensions of time;
- fees to be paid to the arbitrators;
- matters arising out of the scrutiny of partial or final awards.

The Secretariat thus serves as the main channel of communication between the ICC Court and the parties, their counsel and the arbitrators.

B. The Court and the National Committees

The term "Court" of Arbitration is misleading. The ICC Court has no judicial power and does not itself render any award. Neither parties nor their lawyers appear before the Court, whose function is simply to organise and to supervise appropriate arbitral proceedings for each specific international dispute which the parties have agreed to submit to ICC arbitration. It is the arbitral tribunal set up in a given case that will exercise the judicial power throughout the proceedings.

The International Court of Arbitration, which is distinct from the Secretariat, has been designed to fulfill its international role and functions. The present Chairman of the ICC Court, is French. The Vice-Chairmen of the Court are from Egypt, India, Japan, Mexico, Sweden, Switzerland and the United States. Counting the seven Vice-Chairmen and the 44 other Court members, some 11 members of the Court come from common law countries, five from Arab countries, and the balance from countries having one variety or another of civil law systems. The Court members are not ICC employees. They are independent professionals, all with a strong legal background, serving a three-year renewable mandate on the Court. They are not remunerated for their Court activities.

In June 1989, the ICC Council approved the addition of the word "international" to the name of the ICC Court of Arbitration in order to bring clearly into evidence the international vocation of the Court, in its composition as well as in its approach to the arbitrations submitted to it.

Being within the ICC family, Court members have a keen practical knowledge of international trade and investment. Indeed, the members of the Court are appointed by the various ICC National Committees, which themselves are entities representing local business with international commercial interests. The entire ICC Court structure is thus not only completely independent of government control and support, but is designed to bring to bear the expertise and experience of those who know and understand both international commerce and international commercial law.

The Court meets in plenary session once a month to consider awards and challenges to arbitrators. The Committee of the Court (three persons) meets twice a month to decide on administrative matters and awards by consent. Thus, the Committee handles more or less routine matters in order to free the monthly plenary sessions to concentrate on complex and difficult cases that may require extensive discussions. Of course, whenever there is an actual or potential interest of a Court member in a particular matter, whether personal, financial or otherwise, that Court member does not receive the documents related to the matter and leaves the room when it is discussed.

The International Court of Arbitration itself fulfills four main tasks. First, it ensures that before it initiates an ICC arbitration there exists a prima facie agreement between the parties to arbitrate under the ICC Rules. Any disagreement by the parties as to the validity of such a prima facie agreement will be turned over to the arbitral tribunal for its decision. Second, the Court will supervise and where necessary decide on the composition of the arbitral tribunal. The Rules provide that the Court must be informed of any facts which might bring into question the independence of each arbitrator. The Court may refuse to confirm arbitrators proposed by the parties if there is an apparent lack of independence, which does occasionally happen. Failing agreement of the parties within a reasonable period of time, the Court will decide whether the case will be referred to a sole arbitrator or to a three-member tribunal and which of the 59 National Committees of the ICC will be asked to propose either the sole arbitrator or the chairman of a three-member arbitral tribunal, or a co-arbitrator on behalf of a defaulting party. While fulfilling these duties the Court and National Committees will aim at ensuring the independence and the competence of the arbitrators and the neutrality of the arbitral tribunal. The Court is free to reject a person so proposed if there is a question as to his competence or suitability for the case at hand. The ICC Rules also provide that, in appropriate circumstances and where the parties agree, the ICC may select a chairman or a sole arbitrator from a country where no ICC National Committee exists. The Court will also decide on challenges to arbitrators by a party, on removal of arbitrators for violation of their duties, and will replace missing arbitrators.

Third, failing an agreement of the parties the Court will determine the place of arbitration for each case, taking account of all elements desirable for smooth proceedings and execution of the awards. Fourth, the Court, having confirmed or completed the steps required to enable an arbitral tribunal to handle the case, will supervise the proceedings conducted by the tribunal.

Failing agreement of the parties and subject to the mandatory provisions of the law of the place of arbitration, it is the arbitral tribunal, exercising its judicial power, that decides on the applicable law and on the language of the proceedings. The tribunal will examine the case, clarify the scope of the dispute, decide on hearings and expertise, present to the Court partial or final awards in draft and, after examination by the Court and approval as to their form, render these awards.

There is a fifth responsibility of the ICC Court which has an importance not always understood or appreciated. This is the determination of the fees of arbitrators, using as a basis the scales and guidelines set forth in the ICC Rules. In this delicate area, the ICC serves as a buffer between the parties and the arbitrators. Indeed, it is ICC policy to refuse to accept fee arrangements between arbitrators and parties. This is because such arrangements could, on the one hand, inhibit the complete neutrality and independence of the arbitrator, and on the other hand give an arbitrator too much leverage to extract exorbitant fees from a party who is reluctant to antagonise him by arguing about the matter. While some arbitrators express doubts about this policy, by and large we believe that it is most useful in protecting the interests of all concerned.

Particular features of ICC arbitration

Terms of Reference

Terms of Reference must be established, pursuant to Article 13 of the Rules, before arbitrators may deal with the merits of the case. Most importantly, the Terms of Reference must include a summary of the parties' respective claims and a definition of the isues to be determined. The Terms of Reference must be signed by the Arbitral Tribunal and at least one of the parties. Usually both parties sign. Should only one of the parties sign, the document is submitted to the Court for approval, and a brief period, usually 15 days, is set for the other party to sign, failing which the Terms of Reference nevertheless become operative.

The establishment of Terms of Reference is, as far as I am aware, unique to the Arbitration Rules of the ICC. Lawyers encountering Terms of Reference for the first time, especially those from common law jurisdictions, are sometimes puzzled as to its *raison d'être* and meaning. In fact, the Terms of Reference constitute for the ICC both an invaluable means of assisting the parties and the arbitrators and of ensuring meaningful supervision over the arbitration.

Terms of Reference should be seen in their context in international commercial arbitration. This often involves parties and arbitrators of several nationalities with differing legal training and background who are compelled to deal with inherently complex subjects, under legal systems with which they are not all equally familiar. Thus, while this feature of ICC arbitration sometimes raises questions from those whose arbitration experience tends to be in the domestic sphere, praise is heard for Terms of Reference, for some or all of the following reasons:

Technical reasons

(a) The Terms of Reference provide a means to bring order to what is often an incoherent and incomplete set of initial pleadings, permitting the arbitral tribunal to establish a rational structure and organization for the future path of the entire arbitration. Terms of Reference, for example, result in pulling together complex claims and counterclaims into a single document, making it easier for all concerned to deal with the issues. Where all of the parties sign the Terms of Reference, the document can also be used to record definitively agreement by the parties on such matters as applicable law, the language of the arbitration, the extent that discovery and cross-examination of witnesses will be permitted, and a variety of other procedural matters.

(b) The signature of Terms of Reference marks the end of the period during which the initial claims and counterclaims can be introduced, thus preventing defendants from raising new claims as a dilatory tactic. After signature, the Terms of Reference may be amended only with the agreement of all parties.

(c) Examination of the Terms of Reference helps the ICC Court to ensure that the arbitration will be conducted in accordance with the ICC Arbitration Rules.

(d) Terms of Reference make clear to the arbitral tribunal on what issues it must render a decision. A comparison of the Terms of Reference with the draft award helps the arbitrator to ensure not only that he has ruled on the issues raised by the parties, but also that he does not go outside those issues, where the award would be subject to annulment before a national court. The Terms of Reference also make it easier to assess whether additional claims made by a party after an award has been rendered are to be considered as having already been covered by the award, or are indeed new claims to be resolved in a new arbitration.

(e) Terms of Reference assist the ICC Court in scrutinising the award pursuant to Article 21 to make sure that the tribunal has rendered a decision on all points submitted to it and has not gone beyond the mandate accorded to it by the parties.

Psychological advantages

(a) The meeting of the arbitral tribunal and the counsel/parties that generally is held for the purpose of establishing the Terms of Reference is often similar in effect to a "pretrial conference" or even a "mini-trial", permitting the parties to assess as objectively as possible the strengths and weaknesses of their case. It is found that the process of establishing Terms of Reference frequently leads to agreement on subsidiary issues or points and sometimes to settlement of the entire case. Indeed, most of the amicable settlements reached in ICC cases occur around the time of establishment of the Terms of Reference.

(b) Even where no settlement is reached, the process of establishing the Terms of Reference serves an important educational function when parties are from diverse legal and national backgrounds, permitting the counsel and arbitrators to have a common understanding of the claims and issues at stake.

Legal advantages

(a) Many Arab or Latin American countries do not accept the validity of a clause agreeing to submit a future dispute to arbitration. Unless there is a specific reservation on the point, signature of the Terms of Reference by all of the parties can constitute a "compromise" whereby the parties agree to have an existing dispute submitted to arbitration. This helps protect an arbitral award which must be enforced in such countries against annulment on the grounds of failure to agree to arbitrate the dispute. In other cases, signature of the Terms of Reference can cure possible jurisdictional defects in the original arbitration clause.

(b) The signature of Terms of Reference has been cited by a US District Court as an element proving the participation of a foreign governmental entity in a foreign arbitration. It was held that under the US Foreign Sovereign Immunities Act the entity had waived its immunity from suit in the United States, even though it had not appeared in the arbitration which followed signature of the Terms of Reference.

Scrutiny of draft award

This is perhaps the most important, and at the same time the most misunderstood, aspect of the supervisory and administrative character of ICC arbitration. Article 21 of the Rules of the ICC International Court of Arbitration provides that the Court may lay down modifications as to the form of the award and, without affecting the arbitrator's liberty of decision, may also draw his attention to points of substance. It may be of interest to give some detail of the procedures, implications and practical consequences of Article 21.

When a draft award is sent to the Secretariat by the arbitrators, the responsible Counsel will do a preliminary examination of the award, verifying such matters as the calculation of damages (lawyers are notoriously bad at arithmetic) , the internal consistency of the award, typographical or linguistic errors and any problems relating to the form of the award. The Secretariat will often contact a member of the Court to act as the "Rapporteur" for an award. The Rapporteur is selected with a view either to being someone conversant with the applicable substantive law or having expertise in the area of law involved (*e.g.* construction, sale of goods, etc.) or both. The Rapporteur, often working with the responsible Counsel, will generally prepare a written report on the award which will summarise the issues at hand and the reasoning and conclusions of the arbitrators. The Rapporteur will look not only at matters of form but also substance, just as would a national court faced with a request to annul an arbitral award. The Rapporteur's report would therefore look at such matters as whether anything in the award is *ultra petita* or is in conflict with any rules of public policy of the applicable law or the law of the state where the award is rendered or might have to be enforced. Any inconsistency in reasoning is noted. Such persistently difficult matters as the determination of the rate of interest used for any damages due are examined. Of course, the Rapporteur cannot and does not go beyond the award itself and the Terms of Reference to review the decision of the arbitrators on such points as the veracity of witnesses or the assessment of evidence.

The Court members attending a plenary session have before them any written report on the award, and also listen to the oral summary of the Rapporteur. The Court members will also have received, via private courier some 10 days before the session, the text of all of the awards to be considered that day. If the Court considers that a draft award has grave defects it will not approve it, but rather will send it back to the arbitral tribunal, drawing its attention to the difficulties found by the Court. While a few commentators have expressed concern that scrutiny of draft awards takes away from the independence of the arbitrators, the process provides assurance to parties from different countries as to the impartiality and effectiveness of an arbitral award. Moreover, in every instance in which this procedure has been challenged before national courts as infringing upon the freedom of decision of the arbitrators, except in one Turkish case several years ago, the ICC procedure universally has been upheld. This is no doubt because, as the wording of Article 21 itself makes clear, the arbitrators retain complete freedom to accept or reject the points of substance that the Court may draw to their attention.

Scrutiny of the draft award can thus be characterised as a "quality control" process. It allows the International Court of Arbitration to draw the attention of the arbitral tribunal to those points which might constitute weaknesses in the award in the view of a state court likely to be requested to enforce it. In fact, though perfectly free to make up their minds and absolutely entitled to have the final word except for matters of form, the arbitrators generally pay great attention to the remarks of the International Court of Arbitration. The experience of the ICC indicates that in the rare cases where a state court has annulled an ICC award or refused to enforce it, the International Court of Arbitration had generally drawn the attention of the arbitral tribunal to the relevant points when scrutinising the draft award.

The carefully exercised scrutiny by the Court during the arbitral proceedings can thus significantly increase the probability that the validity and the enforcement of ICC awards will be upheld by state courts. This is important in achieving the practical result which the ICC International Court of Arbitration considers its best service to international business. This is that, failing an amicable settlement, the dispute should be terminated by an ICC award appearing so definitely enforceable that it will be honoured by the losing party without further discussion. In terms of offering the greatest possible likelihood that its arbitral awards will be enforceable, there can be no question as to the value of scrutiny of awards. Indeed, it is estimated that some 90% of ICC awards are honoured voluntarily by the losing party. Of the other 10%, the vast majority are ultimately enforced after an exequatur procedure or after the failure of efforts to have the award annulled by a national court.

The future

In 1985 the ICC initiated a broad ranging review and analysis of the Court, including its methods of operations, its Rules, the cost to the users and the working patterns of the Court and its Secretariat. The results of these studies, and of certain measures the ICC had instituted prior to them, have lead to significant reforms in various aspects of ICC arbitration. The ICC has taken major and costly steps to provide the human and material resources needed to ensure not only that the system does not become clogged but also to enable the Secretariat to increase the rapidity of its handling of the cases at every stage of the arbitral process. The Secretariat of the Court now consists of some 25 persons, including nine lawyers. Word-processing facilities have been installed, as well as computer facilities.

Regarding the duration of ICC arbitrations, considerable progress has been made in ensuring that no ICC arbitration take longer than is legitimately warranted by the circumstances of each particular case. A number of measures have been put into place toward this end. First, there is the all-important question of attitude. Just as arbitrators should "manage" their arbitrations and whenever necessary exercise their authority to this end, the Secretariat is encouraged to do no less. The Secretariat acts on the premise that neither it nor the arbitrators can be passive players, routinely requesting or granting extensions of time and simply waiting for Terms of Reference and an award to appear in the fullness of time. The opportunities presented by the ICC screening procedures are being used to ensure that arbitrators are aware of the importance of establishing schedules leading to a final award within a reasonable time, given the particular circumstances of the case.

A request for arbitration that arrives in the ICC should be on the way to the defendant within one week at the most. National Committees are now aware that they must assure themselves that the arbitrators they propose have the time available to devote to the arbitration.The Secretariat and the Court are vigorous in refusing to appoint as chairman or sole arbitrators persons who have demonstrated themselves to be excessively slow or otherwise unqualified to exercise the heavy responsibilities entailed in this work. Although the ICC has no power to refuse to appoint arbitrators who are nominated by the parties, the ICC can, and will in appropriate cases, remove arbitrators who fail to meet their responsibilities under the ICC rules, including the duty to advance the arbitration in a timely manner. The ICC will not select as the situs of an arbitration a country where the relevant law permits constant resort to the courts to the detriment of the arbitral process, although again the ICC cannot prevent parties from selecting such places.

The results of these measures are beginning to be felt. A good percentage of Terms of Reference are now completed within the two-month period provided for in the ICC Rules. We are seeing more awards rendered within one year after the arbitral panel is constituted. It is reported that arbitrators are now quite aware of the importance the ICC places on avoiding unwarranted delay. Of course, it would be wrong to give the impression that the ICC is in favour of speed at any price. As Article 26 of the ICC Rules provides "the Court of Arbitration shall make every effort to make sure that the award is enforceable at law" and neither this fundamental objective nor the important protections provided for by the ICC Rules should be sacrificed in a drive to achieve speed. Moreover, some cases are simply too complex to expect a speedy resolution. The point is simply that the ICC is actively and successfully endeavouring to ensure that unwarranted delay has no place in ICC arbitration.

Costs

Significant changes have been made regarding the costs of ICC arbitration since 1986. The changes consist of the following:

1. Staggering the payment of the advance on costs, so that instead of 100% being requested at the commencement of the case, now 50% (25% from each party) is requested before the arbitrators become seized with the case, and the second 50% requested before the Terms of Reference become operative and the arbitrators enter into the merits.
2. Placing a ceiling on the formerly open-ended scale of administrative expenses, so that for a $50 million case these expenses amount to $50,500 and remain at this sum for larger claims.
3. Bank guarantees will be accepted from a party which has paid in cash 50% of the costs and must thereafter cover all or part of the advance on costs due from a defaulting party.
4. The initial advance on costs to be sent with a request for arbitration is fixed at $2000, to be paid exclusively by the claimant, all of which is credited against the claimant's share of the administrative expenses.

The overall result of these changes is to make the payment of costs for an ICC arbitration far less burdensome for the parties. We also took into account that, by facilitating the payment of the arbitration expenses, delays caused by difficulties which some parties experience in meeting the costs would be greatly decreased.

Another factor in the cost of an arbitration, perhaps the largest factor, is the fees of the arbitrator. The ICC does not remunerate arbitrators solely on the basis of how many hours they work as we see no reason to use a system that creates a disincentive for rapid work. The ICC Court sets the fees for arbitrators, taking into account not only hours worked, but also the complexity of the proceedings and the rapidity and quality of the arbitrator's work. While a few arbitrators criticize this aspect of ICC arbitration because their usual hourly rates are not guaranteed, we believe that the overall result is one which encourages efficient, competent work at reasonable fees from the point of view of the parties as well as of the arbitrators.

The Rules

The ICC Rules were last revised in 1987. The amendments, which came into force on 1 January 1988, do not alter the basic system of ICC arbitration, but are aimed rather at increasing further the efficiency and effectiveness of ICC arbitration by *inter alia*:

1. Eliminating ambiguities in certain provisions of the Rules such as the method of selecting arbitrators by the ICC Court (Art. 2(6) of the amended Rules), the computing of periods of time specified by the Rules or set by the Court (Art. 6(4)) and the joint responsibility of parties for the advance on costs (Art. 9(2)).

2. Reducing delays by reinforcing the provisions related to selection of arbitrators by the ICC Court (Art. (6)), the challenge of arbitrators (Art. 2(8) and (9)), and the replacement of arbitrators by the Court (Art. 2 (10), (11) and (12)), including a provision which makes clear that resignation by an arbitrator does not take effect unless and until accepted by the Court (Art. 2 (10)).

3. Strengthening the universality of ICC arbitration by permitting the ICC Court under certain circumstances to select the sole arbitrator or the chairman of an arbitral tribunal from countries without an ICC National Committee (Art. 2(6)).

4. Establishing more clearly the responsibility of arbitrators to disclose matters possibly affecting their independence vis-à-vis the parties (Art. 2(7)).

5. Eliminating discrepancies between English and French texts (Article 9) and other disparities (Arts. 13(2) and 18(2)).

Appendices II and III to the ICC Rules of Arbitration have been adjusted to reflect the amendments to the main body of the Rules. The amended ICC Rules of Arbitration govern arbitrations which commence on or after 1 January 1988. It is intended to undertake an extensive review of the balance of the ICC Rules. This process will probably take a minimum of three to four years to complete. The objective will be to ensure that the ICC will continue to be capable of handling its growing caseload with despatch and certainty accompanied by an increasingly legalistic attitude on behalf or the parties and their legal advisers.

Aids and alternatives to arbitration

Through its long experience with international commercial arbitration, the ICC has endeavoured to develop methods which can lead to the most efficient resolution of disputes. This has led to the development of certain alternatives to arbitration, which are considered in the following paragraphs.

Conciliation

When a dispute arises between the parties to a contract, they usually first try to negotiate. Failure to reach an agreement usually causes them to look towards outside elements which might enable them to reach a solution.

This involves conciliation, which can be seen as an alternative to arbitration, or as the groundwork to arbitration in the event that conciliation fails. ICC conciliation is optional, and requires the agreement of the parties even where a conciliation clause is included in the contract. Agreements resulting from conciliation are enforceable against the parties, by separate legal action. In the absence of an agreement, however, the conciliation process itself is not enforceable.

Conciliation may be the ideal way to settle disputes when it appears that the parties will respect the outcome of conciliation. Moreover, conciliation is well suited to parties who, like certain sovereign states, cannot or do not wish to submit themselves to a binding jurisdiction, whether that of another state or of an arbitral tribunal. Because of the non-binding nature of conciliation, a party does not compromise its position because it agrees to the transaction; the party is not judged by anyone. It may be more acceptable to perform the agreed result without being forced by the threat of a writ of execution, as in the case of an arbitral sentence. Conciliation clearly benefits from the same level of confidentiality as arbitration. This is an important element of its attraction.

In commencing ICC conciliation proceedings in a given dispute, the Secretary-General of the International Court of Arbitration appoints a conciliator; he is a national of a country different to that of the parties. The conciliators are personalities well known in the business community. According to the revised ICC Conciliation Rules which came into force on 1 January 1988, conciliators receive remuneration for their services. The conciliation proceedings may be either written or oral according to the parties' choice. If written, the parties commence by exchanging notes. The conciliator then invites the parties to a meeting. If the proceedings are oral, the parties may appear in person or by representatives. Each party presents his case and answers the conciliator's questions. The conciliator tries to create an atmosphere favourable to reaching an agreement. An essential factor for success in the conciliation proceedings is the personal attendance of the parties, or of a representative having full power to reach an agreement. The parties representative may be of any nationality or profession. The parties may also be assisted by counsel of their choice, without restrictions.

Conciliation may bring about one of the three following results:

1. Settlement of the dispute: the conciliator notes in his minutes the agreement reached, which is signed by both the the parties and the conciliator.
2. Basis for an agreement: the conciliator gives recommendations to the parties, on which they are asked to settle the dispute within a certain time period.
3. Failure of the attempt at conciliation: if the dispute is not settled, the parties remain free to submit it either to arbitration or to any competent court if they are neither bound by an arbitration clause nor have made an agreement to arbitrate after the dispute arose (compromis). In the event that conciliation fails, nothing said or written during conciliation proceedings may in any way jeopardize the rights of the parties in future arbitral or judicial proceedings. In addition, a person who has served as a conciliator may not be appointed as arbitrator for the same dispute.

The costs of the conciliation proceedings are calculated in each case on the basis of the amount in controversy. Each party bears half of the costs. When a dispute is not settled by conciliation and then goes on to ICC arbitration, half of the amount paid for conciliation is credited towards the costs of the ICC arbitral proceeding. The most recent practice shows that the requests for conciliation are few, some eight in the last year, and insignificant in amount when compared with the requests for ICC arbitration.

The International Arbitration Commission of the ICC formed a working group in 1985 to examine the reasons for the decline in conciliation and to suggest ways to render this method of dispute resolution more popular. The group's working thesis was that conciliation is a method of dispute resolution worthy of more widespread use. It appeared necessary to create a climate more favourable to conciliation, and to provide parties with a clear and simple means of settlement requiring no further resort to judicial or arbitral bodies. The group considered that there was particular need for conciliation services provided by an independent organization, and available to the parties at the opportune moment. An initiative from an outside organization may avoid causing the parties to feel they are compromising their positions. The tendency, at least in western countries, seems to be that a party who suggests conciliation has ulterior motives, such as delaying an eventual arbitration. Even though this attitude is difficult to overcome, the ICC must take it into consideration. Choosing the right moment is important because an ill-timed intervention may destroy the chances of reaching an agreement.

In a recent case the Secretariat of the Court took a well-timed initiative. Two parties, one Asian and one European, came to the ICC Secretariat in Paris at the suggestion of the Secretariat. They arrived at an amicable agreement within one and a half days in a dispute over large sums of money in relation to the performance of a public works project in the Middle East. We feel that the ICC's offer of conciliation to the parties, the use of its offices and a secretary, and the calm and neutral atmosphere of our organization contributed to the satisfactory resolution of the dispute. Nor was the satisfaction of the parties tarnished by the ICC's low administrative fees.

Technical expertise

Many disputes submitted to arbitration are nothing more than the consequences of technical difficulties which were not resolved in a timely fashion. The ICC Rules of Technical Expertise offer the means of rapidly determining the cause or causes of such problems before the progress of the project could destroy or conceal the evidence, and to provide the parties with the relevant facts for an amicable agreement, or to establish the evidentiary basis for future judicial or arbitral proceedings. Requests to the ICC for the nomination of experts result from a variety of difficulties arising in the performance of international contracts. Some recent examples illustrate this fact:

1. In the course of constructing and furnishing a hotel in Iraq, a German company encountered payment problems. Because of a disagreement between the supplier and the client in regard to supplemental payments for electrical work, plumbing and air-conditioning, the two parties agreed to seek the opinion of a technical expert.
2. A Soviet factory owner complained that factory valves obtained from a Polish supplier failed to conform to the contract. In an arbitration proceeding brought by the Polish supplier against the Italian manufacturer, the arbitral tribunal requested the International Centre for Technical Expertise to appoint an expert to evaluate the engineering standards of the valves.
3. A North African company bought from a European company a turnkey freezer system for fish. Allegedly, production capacity was below that contracted for, some of the machines were secondhand, and the seller had not performed his obligation to train the buyer's personnel. The buyer requested an expert's appraisal as to whether the seller fulfilled all the conditions of the contract.

These examples show how an expert appraisal proceeding is used to determine the conformity to contractual specifications of products supplied or services rendered. In the majority of the cases, the parties turn to expert appraisers when differences have already arisen. In these cases, the decision or recommendation of the expert enables the parties to avoid immediate recourse to arbitration or judicial proceedings. The opinion of the expert serves as a basis for negotiation between the parties who, in the majority of cases, reach an amicable agreement. The advantages are obvious: the parties save time and avoid the constraints of judicial or arbitral proceedings which most often hinder contractual relations. In other cases the expert supervises the proper delivery of contract goods or the progress of construction so that he may intervene before any technical difficulties create a dispute between the parties. When a dispute arises, the parties may authorise the expert to recommend appropriate measures to fulfill the purposes of the contract.

An ICC expert appraisal proceeding may be requested where the parties have agreed, preferably in the contract, that recourse to expert appraisal is available. The request may be made jointly by all the parties to the contract, or where the parties have agreed to such recourse in the contract, by any one of the parties. The request must set out the facts and the subject of the appraisal requested. The expert is chosen mutually by the parties or by the ICC. In the latter case the President of the ICC chooses an expert who is neutral with respect to the nationality or domicile of the parties. After hearing the parties, the expert renders his conclusions under the authority granted him by the parties. If the parties have so agreed, the expert may also give recommendations and may supervise the contract performance. The parties must then decide whether they will be bound by the findings of the expert.

In cases where the preservation of evidence is crucial, it is important to appoint the expert immediately. If the role of the expert is well defined in the petition, the ICC can normally appoint the expert within a few weeks. The Centre does not itself employ experts. They are appointed on an ad hoc basis and are remunerated according to the nature of their expertise and the services required. Due to the worldwide organization of the ICC, experts are readily available in many countries. This helps reduce delays resulting from selection and reduces travel expenses.

It is important to distinguish expert appraisal from arbitration. The determinations of the expert are not legally binding on the parties but may be helpful as predetermined evidence or even as presumptions of law in certain legal systems. During its 10 years existence the Centre has gathered experience from some 70 cases. The number of requests for an expert has increased significantly in recent years. The Centre is increasingly co-operating with other organizations such as the International Experts Organization (ORDINEX) and INTEREXPERT, which help to find experts. In the area of public works the Centre works with FIDIC to find qualified experts. Co-operation may also prove possible with national organizations.

Pre-arbitral referee procedure

A working party constituted under the ICC Commission on International Arbitration has concluded that a procedure inspired by the French institution known as *juge des référés* could offer a viable dispute resolution mechanism. Accordingly, a set of Pre-arbitral Referee Procedure Rules approved by the Commission on International Arbitration was adopted by the Council of the ICC came into force on 1 January 1990. The appointed referee may, on request of the party, make a provisional decision, which is not to affect the substantive rights of the parties, just as the French *juge des référés* is often asked to make urgent decisions such as ordering payments to be made issuing injunctions and taking conservatory measures. Just as in the *juge des référés* system, the Referee under the ICC Rules does not participate in the decision on the substance, for which another jurisdiction remains competent.

The Pre-arbitral Referee Procedure is an innovation which will have connections with the Centre for Technical Expertise. Experience shows that international business transactions may call for urgent decisions to be taken during the performance of a contract. This is particularly the case in construction contracts and industrial plant sales, which may encompass questions both of a technical and legal nature. In the field of construction and civil engineering for instance the FIDIC Conditions of Contract give the engineer extensive powers to make decisions during the performance of a contract, decisions which the contractor is bound to respect. If the contractor is dissatisfied with the engineer's decision he may refer the matter to arbitration. Following the 1977 amendment to Clause 67 in the FIDIC Conditions of Contract, it is no longer necessary for parties to await completion of a contract before taking a dispute to arbitration. Construction contracts based on other general conditions may not have any provision at all as to whether arbitration is allowed during the performance of the contract. In the absence of clear stipulations, reference of a dispute to arbitration often causes on-site activity to be suspended until an award is given. When work does continue during arbitration proceedings it cannot later be undone. If activity is halted, both parties will suffer considerable costs due to the time spent idle.

The lively discussion during recent years on abuse of guarantees payable on first demand is another example of the need for a procedure whereby quick decisions can be taken with a binding effect upon the parties. The traditional arbitration procedure is often regarded as too slow for these needs.

Conclusion

The resolution of international commercial disputes will continue to be a major activity of the ICC. The accumulated experience and wisdom of the ICC in this domain will continue to be applied to help prevent and, where necessary, to resolve such disputes as effectively as possible. The working methods and procedures of the Court and its Secretariat are flexible enough to be able to take into account any constructive comment or criticism. The next few years will see an intensive study and possible redrafting of the Rules for ICC arbitration. Timely comments are therefore welcome.

4 The ICC in the Context of International Arbitration

J Gillis Wetter

Synopsis

This paper reviews the international arbitration process including arbitration institutions. The ICC, its arbitration system and rules are examined critically and particular problems are identified. It is concluded that all arbitration institutions must adapt to modern market demands in order to remain viable.

I. Basic features of international arbitration

It is appropriate to restate at the outset the objectives and fundamental conditions of international commercial arbitration, and particularly those which differ from domestic arbitration or which have a special dimension in the international sphere.

Final resolution of international business disputes

The renowned Indian lawyer, Fali S Nariman, in a recent speech[1] appropriately stated as follows:

> "Though litigation is compulsory and arbitration is consensual, both are judicial processes of an adversarial character. That is why arbitration has always been regarded as quasi-judicial."

The ultimate objective of international arbitration is the same as that of litigation, that is, to constitute a mechanism for the final resolution of international business disputes. It is consensual in the sense that the mechanism cannot be imposed on anybody without agreement by contract,

1 4 *Arbitration International* 1988, 311.

in advance or when a dispute has arisen. But all other elements of arbitration are as compulsory as those of the ordinary judicial process.

Reasons for prescribing arbitration in lieu of litigation

In the domestic context, there is a clear choice between arbitration and proceedings before courts in the relevant jurisdiction. But in the international sphere, the courts of at least two nations can always compete for supremacy and often have overlapping jurisdiction. Lack of trust in the courts of a foreign system, linguistic diversity and the absence of effective enforcement procedures applicable to foreign judgments have combined in motivating businessmen to opt for arbitration of their transnational disputes. The reasons for this choice are, first, that the composition of an international arbitral tribunal *per se* is a combination of several domestic elements; secondly a single language familiar to both parties is employed; and thirdly awards are enforceable virtually everywhere under the New York Convention and other treaties.

We should not lose sight of the fact that the starting-point in any discussion of arbitration must be its relative advantages or disadvantages in comparison with the sole available alternative, which is litigation before the courts of one state. The latter will always be alien to one party at least.

Party influence on the tribunal

Traditionally, for the reasons stated, the right of each party to appoint one member of the customary panel of three arbitrators has been viewed as fundamental and inalienable. This is so despite the fact that a significant proportion of ICC arbitrations, and many other proceedings, are conducted by a sole arbitrator, and the fact that such appointments are technically impossible in most multi-party disputes. The appointment by parties of a tribunal member of their choice enhances trust in the tribunal, in the sense that each party may feel confident that at least one of the decision-makers will be sympathetic to his cause and receptive to his argument. The universal view, outside the United States, is, that all arbitrators should be impartial and independent. Indeed, Mr Nariman in his speech quoted earlier said that "standards of behaviour expected of arbitrators are no less stringent than those demanded of judges; in fact arbitrators are expected to behave a shade better since judges are institutionally insulated by the established court-system, their judgments being also subjected to the corrective scrutiny of an appeal."[2]

Competence of tribunal

Closely linked with the right of each party to appoint one arbitrator is the notion that an arbitral tribunal should possess greater competence and

2 *Ibid.* 311–12.

expertise to decide relevant disputes than may be expected of a court of law. The "club justice" dispensed by some lay commodity panels or other narrowly specialised arbitration bodies has its roots in the same desire by parties to be judged by their peers. In international arbitration, perhaps unfortunately, the requirement for competence in the subject-matter on the part of arbitrators has been deeply eroded in favour of the appointment of legally trained arbitrators. This trend has acquired a further dimension as a consequence of the emergence of lawyers whose main activity lies in the realm of arbitration so that increasingly they take on the appearance of professional arbitrators. Such arbitrators are, of course, fundamentally different from full-time lay arbitrators who specialise in particular commercial fields. As a result, we have lost a desirable emphasis on industry or trade-orientated expertise among arbitrators. But we have gained the first fruits of a distinct effort to eliminate or modify national procedural divergences and practices and to provide in their stead a relatively uniform and highly professional international arbitral process.

Flexibility as compared to court procedures

The international arbitral process is characterised by a flexibility greater than that prevalent in most national courts. Its basic features affect the time and location of the proceedings, the nature and format of presentations of evidence, as well as of argument as to fact and law, and the relationship between the disputants and the tribunal.

Procedural safeguards

While the flexibility and informality expected in an international arbitration are essential features of the process, so equally are the requirements of what in the United States is referred to as due process. This refers to those strict and inalienable principles which protect the integrity of proceedings, and to legal rights, such as equality of the parties, *audiatur et altera pars* and the impartiality and independence of the tribunal. Any serious breach of these safeguards invalidates the award and nullifies the process.

Speed and economy

Promoters of international arbitration traditionally have placed speed and economy high on the list of the virtues of arbitration as compared to litigation. Very many users have been deeply disappointed in suffering from a lack of both. Proceedings in disputes which are other than simple and straightforward are rarely completed in less than two years. Total costs can reach a figure of US $ 500,000 or even up to one million dollars even when the amount at issue is no more than two or three times that amount. The only realistic correctives to these unfortunate developments would seem to be universal adoption of the principle that costs follow the event and, in addition, rules on market-related interest on outstanding debts. Neither of these is yet a general rule in international arbitration.[3]

Speed is, however, a most desirable feature. The arbitral process is helped by the fact that, in distinction to courts, ad hoc arbitral tribunals have no accumulated case loads. Nevertheless, arbitrators should regard it as important to avoid overcrowding their own personal calendars, to prevent dilatory tactics by any party or lawyer, and to achieve timely processing at all stages of an arbitration. It is through such efforts that a much-desired economy may be achieved.

II. The role of conventions, national laws, rules and arbitration institutions

Conventions

Leaving aside the ICSID Convention, which creates a special supra-national arbitral regime for private investments in developing countries, the most significant treaty is the New York Convention of 1958. By making arbitral awards enforceable in large parts of the world it is the single most important pillar on which the international arbitration edifice rests; indeed it is difficult to see that international arbitration would exist without it or equivalent bilateral or multilateral treaty provisions. Lord Justice Mustill is correct in saying that the New York Convention "perhaps could lay claim to be the most effective instance of international legislation in the entire history of commercial law".[4]

The New York Convention defines the concept of an arbitration agreement, taking into account that the process is based exclusively on contract. It further spells out in detail and exhaustively on what grounds enforcement of an award may be refused. It is only in that context, and thus in a negative sense, that the Convention deals with the heart of arbitration, *i.e.* procedural rules and practices.

National laws

The essential problems affecting arbitration are regulated by national laws. Thus, paradoxically, so-called international arbitral proceedings are not in the ultimate analysis international at all but domestic in a strict legal sense, even though several jurisdictions may apply different rules and standards to international and domestic proceedings.

The national character of each proceeding constitutes the greatest weakness of the international arbitral process and is also the source of most problems encountered in the field. The only unification effort that has been made is the UNCITRAL Model Law which, however, was not conceived

3 See Wetter, "Interest as an element of damages in the arbitral process", *International Financial Law Review*, December 1986; Hunter and Triebel, "Awarding interest in international arbitration", 6 Jour Int Arb 1 March 1989, 8–23.

4 Mustill, "Arbitration: history and background", 6 Jour Int Arb, 2 June 1989, 43–56 at 49.

as a convention and, while undoubtedly useful as a reference guide, is not likely to be adopted by many of the nations in which the most important proceedings have so far been conducted. Indeed, in Lord Justice Mustill's words, "the cause of harmonisation might not unkindly be said to be going backwards rather than forwards".[5]

Hand in hand with the law goes the ingrained habits and procedural practices of the legal practitioners who handle arbitrations in each country. Vital procedural elements vary widely and depend on the location of the proceedings. These include discovery and inspection; format of pleadings and other written submissions; admissibility of evidence, depositions, examination of witnesses; expert testimony and oral argument. The only specific and almost universal domestic requirement which has not been permitted to permeate the international arbitral process has been the monopoly of local lawyers. In only a very few jurisdictions, such as Singapore, has the contrary gained acceptance.[6]

Institutional and non-institutional rules

The multiplicity of procedural rules and practices governing arbitration proceedings is, to some extent, modified by the influence of an emerging corps of legally trained professional international arbitrators. More important as an element of international unification are arbitration rules. Institutional rules serve two purposes: to regulate and fortify the arbitration institution itself and to clarify, modify or fill gaps in national legal systems. Among non-institutional rules, the UNCITRAL Arbitration Rules are by far the most important and have gained widespread acceptance.

A basic difficulty is created by the uncertainty which prevails as to the permissible outer limits of what rules may provide, *i.e.* to what extent national laws are mandatory and may not be varied by agreement (the relevant rules being incorporated into contracts by reference). This difficulty is aggravated by the fact that many matters which are deemed to be governed by national procedural law (as defined by the *lex arbitri*) are often wrongly understood by parties to be governed by substantive law. This has frequently been the experience of foreigners in England, where the scope of procedural law is seen as surprisingly large, covering such matters as limitation of actions, quantum of damages, interest and validity of guarantees.[7] Few institutional rules are comprehensive and their inherent usefulness in resolving important and often recurring problems varies considerably.

Arbitration institutions

Throughout the world, numerous institutions exist whose sole object is to administer international arbitrations. Indeed, their proliferation in recent

5 Mustill, *ibid.* at 54.

6 See Polkinghorne, "The right of representation in a foreign venue", 4 *Arbitration International* (1988), 333–39.

7 See with regard to interest Hunter and Triebel, *ibid.* at 13, where it is said that in England, post-award interest is treated as a procedural matter governed by English law and that in the absence of an express contractual stipulation, the liability to pay pre-award interest is determined by the proper law of the contract while the period and the rate to be applied are determined by English law and are not a matter for an arbitral tribunal's discretion.

years has created a measure of confusion. The object of this paper is not to present a comparative, analytical survey of the leading arbitration institutions, all of which, for historical reasons, have distinct characteristics and to some extent serve different markets.[8] The present subject of discussion is one of the oldest of these institutions, the International Court of Arbitration of the ICC (ICC Court) as it was renamed in June 1988. Among the institutions, the ICC Court handles the largest number of international cases. It currently receives about 300 requests for arbitration each year. As Lord Justice Mustill remarks, "the number of disputes actually handled was and remains small, by comparison with the total of ad hoc arbitrations conducted throughout the world. The importance of the Institute [the ICC Court] has, however, consisted more of what it has been prepared to offer than it is actually called upon to provide".[9]

Before reviewing various specific aspects of the ICC Court, it is appropriate to note that it is an administering institution which engages in rather far-reaching involvement in actual arbitration proceedings. Yet, it offers relatively little support to arbitration tribunals, either administratively or intellectually. Thus, the ICC Court does not provide office facilities and staff support in actual proceedings except to a negligible extent. Similarly, arbitrators faced with complex procedural problems (whether or not they must be resolved with reference to local law and practice or to previous practice among ICC tribunals) are not likely to obtain high-powered and truly experienced guidance from the executive arm of the ICC Court, *i.e.* the Secretariat, much less legal research or office staff support. This is not to say that the Secretariat does not engage in considerable efforts to assist both tribunals and parties on a daily basis. The statement is a value judgment as to available capacity and level of experience and its use. Overall, therefore, the most striking feature of the relationship between the ICC Court and the arbitral tribunals working under its auspices is the restraints of the essentially negative, controlling functions of the institution and its simultaneous lack of substantive, constructive support.

III. The ICC Court and the ICC rules

Caveat

Only a person who has devoted most of his work over a long period of time to any particular institution is capable of giving fully informed and meaningful comments on its performance and viability and the need for reform. The present writer is not in that position. On the other hand, anybody who is or has been so intimately connected with an institution may inevitably lose the distance and detachment required to discern negative characteristics and desirable improvements. Too often, unswerving support for an institution is wrongly assumed to require refutation of any criticism

8 An attempt at such an analysis was made 10 years ago and remains essentially valid today, see Wetter, *The International Arbitral Process: Public and Private* (1979), 119–254, especially 234–43.

9 Mustill, *ibid.* at 48.

and insistence on the preservation of the existing order at any cost. In fact, dynamic change and adaptation to new circumstances is the sole means of survival and growth in the business world.

Organization of the ICC Court and Secretariat

The ICC Court proper, like any other public or private institution, has many features which are antiquated holdovers of the past. Among them is the unwieldy size of the ICC Court (making it resemble a small parliament), to which each of the National Committees may appoint a member. The ICC Court is composed of no less than 51 people (having grown from 30 in 1977), including five Vice-Presidents. However, a quorum of six suffices. In reality, a limited number of members (reportedly 15–20, including those from Australia, Brazil, Canada, India, Israel, Lebanon, Morocco, Pakistan, Senegal and the United States), and predominantly residents of Paris and nearby cities, attend its sessions. The members of the ICC Court receive no remuneration. While this feature may be seen as a laudable contribution of public service by those concerned, it will also be realised that it limits the attraction of the posts, since the workload is quite heavy.

The Secretariat was thoroughly reorganised less than a decade ago and, as a result of that work and subsequent changes, now consists of a Secretary-General, a General Counsel and seven so-called counsel, each assisted by a secretary. The counsel, or case administrators, are typically of different nationalities, relatively inexperienced at their start of tenure and tend to stay for four or five years before they leave to accept better paid positions with law firms or establish their own practice. As a result, the Secretariat has a short institutional memory; events and cases fall into universal oblivion in five or at most seven years. The heaviest burden of work falls on the Chairman and select, active members of the Court and of course on the staff of the Secretariat, which, apart from the legally trained nine members, consists of 14 persons. The only direct contacts that any arbitrator or party or legal adviser may have with the ICC Court is with the Secretariat. It is solely with this group of persons that any outsider deals. Yet most of those individuals are relatively transient and not vested with decision-making power except in routine matters.

Much of the frustration from time to time experienced by arbitrators and users stems from the anonymous character and total insulation of the ICC Court from any direct relationship with tribunals, parties and their legal advisers. Dissatisfaction with the qualifications of the Secretariat's staff members also contributes. Although the ICC Court determines a number of matters of considerable consequence in adversarial proceedings, no person affected by its decisions is allowed to plead before it and most often its decisions are not motivated. Some continental, Scandinavian and other lawyers may accept such an order without protest because it resembles the procedures and practices of national administrative courts with which they are familiar. Among others it may and sometimes does create a feeling of exasperation as well as fear and suspicion of the unknown; whispers of Star Chamber justice are overheard. Only a fundamental restructuring of the ICC Court itself and the organization of its work, and a thorough revision of the standards of recruitment and the level of remuneration of the Secretariat staff members could bring about a meaningful change of these conditions. Neither has, reportedly, been contemplated.

The ICC Rules

The current ICC Rules of 1975 have been amended on several occasions, most recently as of 1 January 1988, and have been supplemented with Internal Rules (which also have been amended). The changes made in the Rules have been viewed as acutely necessary, *e.g.* to permit successive payments of deposits. Significantly, they have not been the product of a sustained and systematic review of basic procedural issues arising in arbitration. As a result, the regulatory system as a whole now has the appearance of a complex patchwork which is difficult to grasp by an occasional user. More important is the fact that fundamental gaps and obscurities remain in the original basic rules. The ICC Court prides itself in the fact that the number of ICC cases in the 11 years between 1977 and 1989 (*i.e.* 3,000) virtually equalled the number of cases in the preceding 54 years (*i.e.* 3,500) and that the complexity and amounts in dispute also have increased dramatically. In 1988, 45 per cent of the cases involved US $ 1-10 million and 8.3 per cent over US $ 10 million. Yet, 15 years of such extensive and unique experience has not prompted any truly meaningful revision of those parts of the Rules which pertain to the conduct of the arbitration by those immediately concerned, *i.e.* the arbitrators and the parties. Nor has the ICC Court articulated (except indirectly in occasional, informal speeches and articles by members of the Secretariat) the rules, principles and standards it applies in the determination of matters such as prima facie jurisdiction, challenge actions, award review policies and arbitrator fee levels.[10] This is the more remarkable as during the same time period other rules have come into being or been updated and other institutions have been created, both of which provide fertile grounds for comparative studies.

Reference may be made in this context to one particular aspect of the ICC Rules which significantly influences the time and cost of proceedings.[11]

> "The arbitration proceeding commences with a request for arbitration. There are two schools of thought with regard to its scope and significance. Under one theory, the request for arbitration is a document which merely identifies the parties, the cause of action[12] and the claim in an extremely summary fashion and contains only those elements which are required to set in motion the formation of a tribunal and the running of time (similar to an English writ or an American summons). The response to such a request for arbitration has no

10 The recent observation is certainly correct that the "secrecy of the process (in regard to challenge actions) in many arbitral regimes remains troublesome", Tupman, "Challenge and disqualification of arbitrators in international commercial arbitration", 38 ICLQ (1989) 26–52, at 51.

11 Text quoted from Wetter, "The Conduct of the Arbitration", 2 *Journal of International Arbitration*, June 1985, 1–38, at 12–13.

12 The term "cause of action" is used here in the same general sense as in Brownlie, "Causes of Action in the Law of Nations", 50 *British Yearbook of International Law* (1979) 13.

specific name, and we may simply call it the response. Its scope and contents of course normally mirror those of the request.

"The other theory is that the initial request for arbitration should be merged with the full claim. This is the position taken, *e.g.*, by the ICC Rules which provide that the request shall contain 'a statement of the Claimant's case'.[13] In addition, such a document shall be accompanied by the relevant documentary evidence relied upon by the claimant. The response (the so-called 'Answer') then necessarily becomes correspondingly comprehensive.[14] One important aspect of such a procedure is that although the claimant usually has unlimited time at his disposal for preparing his request for arbitration (unless the underlying arbitration ageement or substantive contract contains restrictive time limits), the respondent must reply within 30 days and will be granted a delay by the Secretariat only 'in exceptional circumstances'.

"The UNCITRAL Arbitration Rules provide for a 'notice of arbitration' which is conceived to be of the simplified kind referred to initially but which may, at the option of the claimant, be expanded so as to 'include' what is referred to as a 'statement of claim'.[15] The latter, which if not included in the notice of arbitration will necessarily be the next pleading submitted, comprises a statement of facts supporting the claim, the points at issue and the relief or remedy sought and may include documentary evidence or a reference thereto.[16]"

It is submitted that the ICC Rules ought to be amended so as to mirror the provisions of the UNCITRAL Arbitration Rules, Article 3. Such a reform would alleviate the unfair burden presently placed on defendants and also make the Rules endorse a procedure which is almost universally accepted internationally as convenient and fair.

Degree of involvement of the ICC Court

The extent to which the ICC Court becomes involved in arbitration proceedings is and has always been controversial, both in a purely factual sense and in regard to its propriety. What is the role of the ICC Court?[17]

First, to the ICC Court's necessarily inherent functions obviously belong determinations as to whether or not it has prima facie jurisdiction under an existing arbitration agreement, as provided in paragraph 12 of the Internal Rules. These are properly characterised as decisions of an administrative nature. Secondly, the ICC Court takes final decisions under Article 2 paragraph 13 of the Rules as to the appointment, confirmation, challenge or replacement of an arbitrator. Thirdly, the ICC Court takes note of the terms of reference in each case and approves them if they have not been signed by all concerned. Fourthly, the ICC Court determines the deposits to be paid and fixes the remuneration of the arbitrators. Fifthly, the ICC Court reviews and approves the text of awards. Each of these activities of the ICC Court will be discussed below.

13 See Art. 3.2 of the Rules for the ICC Court of Arbitration (1975).
14 See Art. 4.1 of the ICC Rules.
15 See Art. 3 of the UNCITRAL Arbitration Rules.
16 See Art. 18 of the UNCITRAL Arbitration Rules.
17 See generally the recent article by Antoine Kassis, "The questionable validity of arbitration and awards under the Rules of the International Chamber of Commerce", 6 Jour Int Arb 2, June 1989, 79–100, and materials cited therein.

Degree of involvement of the Secretariat

Although ICC arbitration tribunals are essentially *ad hoc* bodies whose members have exclusive responsibility, and legal liability, in respect of all jurisdictional, procedural and substantive matters, Article 6 of the ICC Rules provides for an extraordinary degree of involvement on the part of the Secretariat in the proceedings. Thus, one copy of every pleading and written statement submitted by the parties is to be supplied to the Secretariat and, in practice, copies of all papers and communications (except those between the arbitrators) are required so to be submitted. This filing requirement is expensive as it extends to telex and fax messages and serves no ostensible purpose except to create (i) a backlog of references for specific cases where actions by the ICC Court might be required (such as in regard to challenges of arbitrators, extensions of time limits, etc.) and (ii) a permanent archive at the disposal of the parties after the case has been closed. If consistently read, analysed, understood, and made retrievable by attentive, informed and truly experienced staff, these materials of course would provide an unequalled guide to the suitability of the performing (or non-performing) arbitrators. The papers are reported by the Secretariat itself to be systematically used for these purposes in the pending 700 cases, which is one of many indications of the great ambitions and awesome workload of the Secretariat.

Procedure in ICC arbitrations: influence of the applicable national law and of the ICC Rules

In all ICC arbitrations, relatively greater influence is exercised by national procedural laws and practices than by the ICC Rules. This is due in part to the exigencies of territorial sovereignty, but in very large measure due also to the silence of the ICC Rules on many crucial matters, such as the full sequence of a regular proceeding, manner of presentations of evidence and notably oral testimony, the choice between written and oral argument, the distinction between decisions, interim (separate) awards and final awards and amendments of claims. Article 11 of the Rules in sweeping terms gives the parties, if they agree, or otherwise the tribunal, the power to settle all such procedural matters. But by doing so, the Rules create not only a theoretical flexibility, but they also accord a much wider role to national law and practices than would otherwise be the case. If the parties have chosen the locale, they have presumably taken this consequence into consideration or must at least bear responsibility for it. If they have not, the selection by the ICC Court of the locale will carry with it additional legal and practical dimensions. Thus, for example, a claim may become barred by a statute of limitation which in the selected venue is regarded as procedural and mandatory in character; witnesses may or may not be subpoenaed; evidence (including expert evidence) may be regarded as inadmissible, and cross-examination or dissenting opinions may be allowed or forbidden, etc. In short, the entire proceeding normally will take on the colour of the locale unless both sides and the chairman share a different common attitude to the proper manner of procedural conduct.

It should be stressed that diversity is not *per se* to be avoided; it is the unexpected, and elements of surprise are undesirable in any international business context, because they may be viewed as inequitable and unjust.

Particular problems

Initial determination of jurisdiction

The initial determination of jurisdiction is a necessary feature of any institution and the manner of its actual exercise by the ICC Court does not call for extensive comment. It has been discussed notably in respect of multi-party arbitrations in which the ICC Court has assumed such jurisdiction even in cases where no explicit arbitration agreement has been executed by one or several parties.[18] In any event, paragraph 12 of the Internal Rules seems to regulate the topic adequately. It reads:

> "Where there is no prima facie arbitration agreement between the parties or where there is an agreement but it does not specify the ICC, the Secretariat draws the attention of the Claimant to the provisions laid down in Article 7 of the Rules of Arbitration. The Claimant is entitled to require the decision to be taken by the Court of Arbitration.
>
> "This decision is of an administrative nature. If the Court decides that the arbitration solicited by the Claimant cannot proceed, the parties retain the right to ask the competent jurisdiction whether or not they are bound by an arbitration agreement in the light of the law applicable.
>
> "If the Court of Arbitration considers prima facie that the proceedings may take place, the arbitrator appointed has the duty to decide as to his own jurisdiction and, where such jurisdiction exists, as to the merits of the dispute."

Challenge actions

One notable advantage of institutional arbitration, as distinct from purely *ad hoc* proceedings, is the rule that the institution decides on challenge actions, even if such determinations are not final at law in the jurisdiction where the proceedings take place or an award is enforced. The practices of the ICC Court in this regard have recently been extensively described by its Secretary-General.[19] As mentioned earlier, the ICC Court does not articulate or publish the norms applied by it, on the theory that no precedents should be created in the field and that every decision must be based on the particular facts of each case. The validity of this attitude can be disputed on two grounds. First, looked at from the point of view of those directly involved in any challenge proceeding, Mr. Michael Tupman's recent remarks are pertinent:

18 See Jarvin, "Analysis of arbitration clauses in the light of the practice of the International Chamber of Commerce", unpublished paper presented at a Conference in Geneva, 24–25 February 1989; Bond, "Multi-party arbitration in the experience of the ICC Court of Arbitration", unpublished paper presented at a Conference in Stockholm, 29–30 May 1989.

19 Bond, "The selection of ICC Arbitrators and the requirement of independence", 4 Arb Int 300–10, 1988.

> "On the one hand, an arbitral institution has a legitimate interest in preserving the confidentiality of its internal administration, and in ensuring that challenges are disposed of expeditiously so as not to delay an award on the merits. On the other hand, a party which challenges in good faith might lose confidence in the arbitral process if there is no explanation whatsoever why its arguments were not persuasive. Perhaps there could be a middle way for some reasons to be communicated, though not a detailed written decision with findings of fact and law."[20]

Secondly, in a broader perspective, it may be said that every institution active in the field has a moral duty to contribute to the rational development of the law so as to narrow the scope of prevailing uncertainty. Also, such an institution should not insulate itself from public scrutiny lest its credibility be at some point jeopardised.

Independence and impartiality are increasingly important requirements on which prospective arbitrators and counsel often experience legitimate doubt, and for this reason alone the ICC Court should share its experience on a regular basis with the international arbitration community.

Terms of reference

One of the most controversial and debated relics of the past in the ICC Rules is the requirement that the arbitrators and the parties must agree on a definition of the dispute at their first meeting. It was prompted by the rule obtaining in France at the time that an arbitration agreement entered into before a dispute arose was invalid, a notion which unfortunately still persists in some jurisdictions, notably in South America. Although this reason has long since disappeared in France, the ICC Court still regards terms of reference as indispensable for the dual purpose of establishing a basis (i) for fixing deposits in relation to stated monetary claims (this is denied by the Secretariat as being a rationale) and (ii) for reviewing the award for compliance with the stipulations in the document concerning claims and issues to be decided.

The Terms of Reference should indicate with precision the issues in dispute. However, a former First President of France's highest court remarked at an ICC Conference in Paris some years ago, that he had never decided a case in which the issues could be defined before argument was closed. Additional rationales for the existing system are often cited, one being that it is useful for the parties and the tribunal to meet at an early point (an objective which evidently can be achieved anyway) and another being that the process of negotiating Terms of Reference sometimes leads to settlement (which is correct).

The troubling aspect of the practice is the time and thus the expense that the exercise entails, mostly without conferring tangible benefits in the sense of advancing a resolution of the case. A second problem is that the ICC Rules do not contain a provision for amendments of claims; hence neither party can amend its claims as fixed in the Terms of Reference without the approval of the tribunal and the other party. In some jurisdictions this

20 Tupman, *ibid.* at 49.

is not an acceptable procedural rule, especially not in arbitration where the expense of commencing a second proceeding may be prohibitive.

It is said that there are many supporters of terms of reference even among common law lawyers. However, the fact that no other arbitral institution, no other arbitration rules, and, to the writer's knowledge, no *ad hoc* tribunals require terms of reference is sufficient proof that the notion is misconceived and that the requirement should be abolished in the interest of both economy and justice. A useful substitute would be rules on pre-trial meetings, modelled, *e.g.*, on note 4 to Article 15 of the UNCITRAL Arbitration Rules, adopted by the Iran-United States Claims Tribunal which provides that "the arbitral tribunal may make an order directing the arbitrating parties to appear for a pre-hearing conference."[21] The Internal Guidelines of the Tribunal suggest that the following matters may be on the agenda of a pre-trial meeting:[22]

> "The following list is illustrative of the matters which may be considered at the pre-hearing conference held pursuant to Note 4 to Article 15 of the Tribunal Rules, and the arbitral tribunal may in its discretion determine to consider additional, or fewer, matters at the pre-hearing conference:
>
> clarification of the issues presented and the relief sought;
>
> identification of any issues to be considered as preliminary questions;
>
> status of and settlement discussions;
>
> whether any further written statements, including any reply or rejoinder, is requested by the arbitrating parties or required by the arbitral tribunal (see Tribunal Rules, Article 22);
>
> fixing a schedule for submission by each arbitrating party of a summary of the documents or lists of witnesses or other evidence it intends to present (see Tribunal Rules, Article 24, para. 2);
>
> fixing a schedule for submission of any documents, exhibits or other evidence with the arbitral tribunal may then require (see Tribunal Rules, Article 24, para. 3);
>
> whether voluminous and complicated date should be presented through summaries, tabulations, charts, graphs or extracts in order to save time and costs;
>
> desirability of appointing an expert by the arbitral tribunal, and if so the expert's qualifications and terms of reference; whether the arbitrating parties intend to present experts, and, if so, the qualification of and the areas of expertise to be covered by any such expert;
>
> determining what documentary evidence will require translation;
>
> fixing a schedule of hearings;
>
> other appropriate matters."

Fees

The ICC Court has become sufficiently concerned about the voicing of diverse views on its determination of arbitrator fees to establish a committee to examine the matter. Paragraph 18 of the Internal Rules provides:

21 Final Tribunal Rules of Procedure, 3 May 1983, quoted from 2 *Iran–US Claims Tribunal Reports* 419.

22 Quoted from 1 *Iran–US Claims Tribunal Reports* 98; the typographical errors therein have not been corrected.

"In setting the arbitrator's fees on the basis of the scale attached to the ICC Rules of Arbitration, the Court of Arbitration takes into consideration the time spent, the rapidity of the proceedings and the complexity of the dispute, so as to arrive at a figure within the limits specified or, when circumstances require, higher or lower than those limits (Art. 20 (3) of the ICC Rules of Arbitration)."

Evidently, only wide and first-hand experience and full statistics can bear out whether or not that rule is implemented in accordance with its literal wording. However, it is rare to meet an ICC arbitrator who is not convinced that the main yardstick used by the ICC Court is the amount at issue, rather than time spent, or the complexity of the case, or the skill in bringing it to a fast conclusion, and that a global sum is then split among the arbitrators in the proportions 40–30–30%, in panels of three.

In some countries, the practice of relating fees of lawyers directly to amounts in dispute on a regressing scale is normal and even more or less obligatory; in others neither regulatory bodies, nor clients accept such a notion. It is often advocated by the ICC that fixed fees provide an incentive to arbitrators to proceed swiftly and prevent them from wasting time. The answer is that men and women whose work habits are influenced by such considerations should not be appointed as arbitrators by the ICC Court. In the writer's opinion, fees should be related to time, complexity and skill. The reason for this is not moral but pragmatic. While a system based on percentage fees has the advantage of making the fees of the tribunal relatively predictable, it will not attract arbitrators of the highest calibre to take on any but the largest cases, and hence it automatically creates tiers of second-rate and third-rate arbitrators for lesser cases. Cases involving amounts in dispute of 5–10 million US dollars nowadays often fall into the latter category because the time necessarily required to resolve them in a proper fashion results in fees which on an hourly basis are unacceptably low. Recently, one chairman of an ICC tribunal was seen to work day and night, seven days a week, for very many months, render a US $ 15 million award and receive a fee equivalent to US $ 35 an hour. Of course, examples of the opposite, unjustified windfalls, also exist. Such a system is absurd and can only contribute to a decline in the quality of the justice dispensed under the auspices of the institution which fails to recognise that it operates in a competitive market, where arbitrators have other options to employ their skills.

International arbitration is an expensive process. It is, for that reason, not suitable for disputes or contracts which do not involve substantial sums of money. If parties insist on acquiring a luxury in a commercial context, they must realise that it has an inevitable price in relation to the inherent complexity of the problems at issue and the time reasonably required by qualified experts to resolve them in full-scale arbitral proceedings. The alternative is to resort to litigation; but on average the saving is only 30–35% on the cost of the tribunal and the arbitration institution, not taking into account the added cost of an appeals process and other negative features already referred to. Transnational litigation is generally even more costly than international arbitration, and will carry the same or even greater risks. The truth that must be realised by businessmen, therefore, is that there is no cheap and safe way of resolving disputes under international contracts, except by settlement.

Time of processing

The time required to process a case largely depends on the parties and their counsel as well as on the management of the proceedings by the tribunal and particularly its chairman. In the ICC system, two additional elements are added, *i.e.* the Terms of Reference procedure (which may take anything from two months to several years) and the approval of awards procedure (which as a minimum takes six weeks and may extend to six months if an award must be sent back and forth between the ICC Court and the tribunal several times). The negative impact of these added delays as compared to the immediacy of an ad hoc proceeding must be weighed against the general and specific advantages of institutional arbitration. In any event its importance varies widely in individual cases.

Advance review of awards

Article 21 of the ICC Rules reads:

> "Before signing an award, whether partial or definitive, the arbitrator shall submit it in draft form to the Court. The Court may lay down modifications as to the form of the award and, without affecting the arbitrator's liberty of decision, may also draw his attention to points of substance. No award shall be signed until it has been approved by the Court as to its form."

Article 21 should be read with Article 22 of the Internal Rules of the ICC Court (which came into force on 1 March 1980). This provision reads as follows:

> "When it scrutinizes draft arbitral awards in accordance with Article 21 of the ICC Rules of Arbitration, the Court of Arbitration pays particular attention to the respect of the formal requirements laid down by the law applicable to the proceedings and, where relevant, by the mandatory rules of the place of arbitration, notably with regard to the reasons for awards, their signature and the admissibility of dissenting opinions."

Apart from the terms of reference, the topic of the scope of the ICC Court's scrutiny and approval of awards is the most controversial one in the ICC system (see most recently the article by Kassis quoted *ante*.) There is nothing inherently wrong in the concept that an arbitral institution should exercise quality control over a product that bears its name. There is no reason to believe that expert eyes may not see flaws in the output of other experts and that a collective effort and double checking is not to be preferred to the preservation of error. The great size and unique diversity of the ICC Court certainly makes it an unequalled body of informed and devoted arbitration experts. The problem is that for decades the allegation has been made that the ICC Court exceeds its powers as defined in Article 21 and assumes the role of an appeal court or "super arbitrator". This is of course neither possible at law (and that issue is particularly sensitive in France) nor acceptable to a tribunal mindful of its integrity under the applicable *lex arbitri* because it would violate the basic constitution and structure of the ICC Court system.

In the case of *Bank Mellat* v. *GAA Development Construction Company*,[23] Steyn J referred to an instance in which a draft award was not approved by the ICC Court and the tribunal was asked "to provide it with a strengthened motivation of two issues raised in the award." The Secretariat in a letter produced before the High Court asserted that "this request concerned a matter of form, not of substance" and that "the [ICC] Court's request fell within the power conferred to it under art. 21 of its Rules which states that it may lay down modification as to the form of the award'". Steyn J had the following to say on the intervention by the ICC Court in that arbitration:

> "The communication from the ICC Court to the arbitrators was not placed before me, and that is perfectly understandable. But it is clear from secondary evidence that it related to the reasoning of the majority in support of their decision on the merits, and the reasoning in support of the award of interest. . . . It will be recalled that in the ICC Secretariat's letter of 31 July 1987 the view was expressed that the amendments to the draft majority award were matters of form rather than substance within the meaning of Article 21 of the ICC Rules. In a careful and helpful speech Mr. David Hunt, Q.C., for Bank Mellat, contended that the contrary was the case. It is sometimes difficult to draw the line between amendments of form and substance. Without deciding the question I will assume that the amendments which the majority made to their draft award must rank as matters of substance."

It is believed that the ICC Court at times is forced to intervene in a manner which is difficult to reconcile with the restrictive language of Article 21 and that this is caused by the submission of clearly deficient draft awards. Hence the real problem is the selection of arbitrators, and especially chairmen, confirmed or made by the ICC Court itself. It is from that angle that the problem should be attacked and resolved. If it persists, then the deeper roots of it must be sought elsewhere, such as in the fee structure or in the workings of the institution at large.

At the same time, it should be stressed that if as a result of the review process many awards are in fact improved and fortified, it is reasonable to acknowledge that the quality control of the ICC Court is useful. But usefulness may not be the proper criterion to apply in an overall assessment when legal principles of autonomy of tribunals and inalienable procedural rights of parties are at issue. For the integrity of the tribunal is undoubtedly violated, and as Kassis points out, another problem is that the review process may be said to infringe upon the parties' right of defence.[24]

Article 21 refers to "awards, partial or definitive" but does not encompass "decisions". Very many determinations of the utmost importance may be made in the course of an arbitral proceeding in the form of decisions which are not styled awards. There exist unarticulated rules within the ICC Court which purport to define matters which must be decided in the form of an award, so as not to escape the advanced scrutiny of the ICC Court. Their validity under the relevant *lex arbitri* is questionable. This is, as intimated earlier, one point on which a revision of the Rules would seem to be desirable.

23 [1988] 2 Lloyd's Rep. 44.
24 Kassis, *ibid.* at 88–89.

Assistance in enforcement endeavours

Once an award had been rendered, it is issued in the name of the ICC Court. Formerly, the winning party was by and large left on its own to enforce it against the losing party. In recent times, the Secretariat has reportedly increased its activities in support of voluntary compliance by parties with awards, *e.g.*, by requesting information as to enforcement, addressing communications to the losing party and the National Committee as well as entertaining contacts with the arbitral tribunal. Such active support by the ICC Court in favour of securing performance of awards by recalcitrant parties undoubtedly enhances the attractiveness of the institution to potential users.

IV. Financial aspects

The following two paragraphs are passages included in a review of the ICC Court published 10 years ago[25]

> "The ICC is an institution legally classified under French law as a foreign association. It has a permanent staff of about 70 persons; its budget for fiscal year 1977 was French Francs 14,658,322 (including a surplus of F F 162,822).
>
> "The accounts of the ICC Court are not kept separate from those of the ICC, and therefore the economics of the arbitration activities cannot be fully presented. However, administrative charges in 1977 amounted to F F 5,645,704. By year-end, a sum of F F 38,313,958 was held as arbitration deposits. Interest collected on those deposits is not credited to the parties but absorbed as income by the ICC. The greater part of the figure of F F 1,446,325 shown as interest income was derived from arbitration deposits. On the assumption that two thirds of the income from seminars and publications (F F 1,043,028 and 968,293, respectively), and 90 per cent of the said interest were related to the arbitration activities, the profit on the arbitration business was over F F 7 million. The total income of the ICC in 1977 being F F 14,658,322, arbitration activities thus accounted for almost 50 per cent thereof."

Those figures were verified as correct at the time by the ICC. It has not proved possible for the writer to obtain from the ICC Court updated figures for the fiscal year 1988. Bank guarantees have been accepted in approximately 40 of the presently pending cases, which might have somewhat reduced interest income. However, it must be assumed that the position remains essentially the same as it was 11 years ago, *i.e.* that a very substantial proportion of the total income of the ICC is derived from arbitration activities.

Therefore, the ICC as an institution is in all likelihood vitally dependent on the revenues of the activities of the ICC Court. Consequently the conduct and prospects of the latter should be of the greatest concern to the ICC.

V. Conclusions

In opting for international arbitration as the appropriate means of resolving future disputes under contracts, parties must exercise a choice as to whether

25 Wetter, *ibid.* 151–52.

they wish to provide for institutional or non-institutional arbitration and in the latter case for the possible incorporation of rules and the designation of an appointment authority. They should also specify a locale, the governing substantive law and the language of the proceedings.

There are obvious advantages to institutional arbitration, in which the ICC Court has the largest international caseload. First and principal among them is the administrative support given in the formative stage of a proceeding, *i.e.* until the tribunal has been constituted. But clearly, a mere appointing authority is capable of performing the same essential functions with equal ease at lesser cost. A second advantage lies in the incorporation of rules, to the extent that they are deemed to be adequate. But again the UNCITRAL Arbitration Rules or other rules can be incorporated (as they are, or modified) without engaging the services of an administering authority. A third advantage lies in the mechanisms offered by institutions for the challenge and removal of arbitrators, but it should be appreciated that courts in most jurisdictions reserve to themselves the exclusive right of ultimate determination of challenge actions. A fourth advantage to parties and arbitrators alike is the financial administration undertaken by institutions, which relieves the arbitrators of potential embarrassment and clerical work and, if properly carried out, provides proper security to them. A fifth advantage is the weight accorded to the award when endorsed by the institution itself, being a large and reputable organization compared to the tribunal itself, composed of a single arbitrator, or three arbitrators, however prominent. In this context, the actual quality control exercised by the ICC Court is distinctly unique. A sixth advantage is the assistance of the institution in securing compliance with awards by losing parties.

Each contracting party must consider whether these advantages, and possibly others, in their aggregate are worth, first, the price tag which is attached to them in the form of administrative expenses and other cost items; secondly, the additional time required for institutional as compared to non-institutional arbitration; and thirdly, the restraints inherent in any particular system as administered by the institution in question.

The market place, *i.e.* those who draw contracts, from time to time will determine which of the two principal alternatives they prefer. Unfortunately the arbitration business is not like other businesses, because comparative statistics exist neither of contract clauses nor of non-institutional arbitrations. Hence it is impossible for anybody to make even an informed guess as to market shares or trends. It is, however, often said these days that there is a marked increase of purely *ad hoc* cases. While a reliable scholarly analysis cannot be made, it is believed that all institutions, and not the least the ICC Court, must improve their products and engage in aggressive marketing of them to preserve their relative shares of the total arbitration market.

The ICC Court and the system of arbitration administered by it should have much to gain from a strong and immediate effort to modernise and streamline both the ICC Rules and the organization itself so as to create an attractive, alert and intellectually and practically minded institution well fit to continue to take on the increasingly complex tasks of administering the resolution of international commercial disputes in the entire world.

The legacy of history is important, but adaptation to our own time, its accelerating pace of constant change and movement, and rapid internationalisation is of even greater urgency. In fact, it may be a condition for survival.

5 ICC United Kingdom: and its role in arbitration

David Sarre

Synopsis

This paper describes the process of nomination and appointment of arbitrators where the ICC in Paris call on the services of ICC United Kingdom. The procedures and criteria applied are described. Statistics are given regarding the use of UK personnel and the demand for the United Kingdom as a venue for international arbitration.

Introduction

A fundamental of the ICC arbitration system is that the parties have considerable freedom of choice. For example, in the selection of arbitrators, no list is imposed on the parties; nor for that matter is a list provided. It is also a basic principle, in the words of Article 7 of the Rules, that: "Every arbitrator appointed or confirmed by the Court must be and remain independent of the parties . . .". The parties nominate; the Court confirms or appoints. It is, therefore, possible for the Court to refuse to confirm a nomination made by a party, or even by both parties, but in practice this is extremely rare.

How does the Court proceed when it has to appoint an arbitrator? There are three situations:

- if there is to be a sole arbitrator, and the parties do not agree a nomination;
- if there is to be a tribunal of three, and one of the parties fails to make a nomination of a co-arbitrator;
- if there is to be a tribunal of three, and the two co-arbitrators fail to agree a nomination for chairman.

In any of these situations the Court almost always seeks the assistance of one of the ICC's 57 National Committees. In deciding which National

Committee should be invited to make a nomination the Court takes into account several factors, including the following:

- the nationality of the parties;
- the place of arbitration;
- the law of the contract (if known);
- the language of the contract;
- the language likely to be used in the arbitration;
- the history of nominations made by national committees;
- and, of course, the nature of the dispute.

If the appointment to be made is that of a co-arbitrator, the Court will normally invite a nomination from the National Committee corresponding to the nationality of the party which has failed to nominate. If the appointment is that of a sole arbitrator or of a chairman, unless the parties agree otherwise, it will invite a proposal from a National Committee of a country different from that of the parties and, usually, different from that of the nationality of a co-arbitrator. This is to say, the Court looks for an arbitrator with a "neutral" nationality.

ICC United Kingdom

How does the National Committee deal with such an invitation and in particular, how does the British National Committee, ICC United Kingdom, deal with it?

This begins with receipt of a letter from the Secretariat. The letter is more or less in a standard form and a simulated example is attached, (Annex 1), together with a Summary of the Dispute. These call for close study in order to understand the niceties of how the terms of the invitation come about and to understand the basis on which national committees are required to play their part in the ICC arbitration system.

Also attached are ICC United Kingdom's Guidelines for its Arbitration Consultant with regard to the making of nominations of Arbitrators (Annex II). Although it is hoped that the intentions behind the Guidelines are mainly clear, it may be useful to emphasise and clarify some of the provisions.

Paragraph 1: It is not a committee which makes the decision as to who should be nominated; that is the function of the Arbitration Consultant. He is not, however, uncontrolled or unsupervised. For, as can be seen from paragraph 4, if someone who has not previously acted as an ICC arbitrator is to be nominated, at least two members of the Arbitration Panel are to be consulted. Arbitration Panel is perhaps a misnomer. It is in effect a committee which oversees the Arbitration Consultant in the discharge of his responsibilities. It is chaired by Sir Michael Kerr,[1] the other members being three Queen's Counsel and five solicitors. The Panel meets once a year when the Consultant makes a report, particularly on the nominations made in the course of the year. Preserving the confidentiality required in ICC arbitrations, the identity of parties is not disclosed even to members

1 Now Mr Justice Steyn.

of the Panel. The information on which the Consultant based his choice of arbitrator is given, for example:

- the nature of the dispute;
- the amount involved;
- the place of arbitration;
- governing law (if known);
- language of the arbitration;
- (in the case of a tribunal of three) the co-arbitrators

At the meeting, discussion mainly centres on the criteria applied and the weight given to them in the making of each nomination. It is also understood that outside the meeting members discuss invididuals with the Consultant in confidence, their qualities, or lack of them. In this connection, the Consultant is also assisted in forming his opinions by confidential discussions with the Secretary-General and other colleagues in the Secretariat, and with practitioners who from time to time give feedback as to how arbitrators have fulfilled their function.

Paragraph 2(a) of the Guidelines is important. It reads: "the nature and extent of the individual's knowledge and experience (whether as lawyer or otherwise) of commercial law and practice and the conduct of business in and beyond the United Kingdom;". An individual, however intellectually gifted, if insular in his legal cultural outlook is not a candidate for nomination by ICC United Kingdom to be an ICC arbitrator.

Paragraph 2(g): Increasingly it is considered desirable to take account of the identity and likely style of the lawyers involved. Are they highly-experienced, litigation lawyers very familiar with a particular style and tradition of advocacy? If this applies to the representation of one party, does this apply to the other also? Maybe the advocates on one side have little experience of international commercial arbitration, even perhaps little experience of international business transactions. What may be needed is a chairman or an arbitrator who can be firm, and maybe tough, with one side, but very patient and understanding with the other. Not all candidates have such qualities.

Nominations by ICC United Kingdom in the past five years

The figures set out in Annex III need to be understood for what they are. They show the involvement of ICC United Kingdom in the making of nominations. A nomination does not necessarily lead to an appointment. The choice of the place for the arbitration does not necessarily mean that the arbitration went ahead, there or anywhere else.

Nominations sometimes do not lead to appointments because the parties, between one meeting of the Court and another, agree between themselves on the sole arbitrator or chairman. In this situation it is the policy of the Court to accept the nomination agreed by the parties in preference to that made by a National Committee.

Assuming the nomination does lead to an appointment, this does not necessarily mean that the arbitration takes place. The fact that an arbitral tribunal is constituted can itself prompt a claimant to withdraw the Request, either because the case is settled or for some other reason. Thus, in Annex III, "107 nominations" does not mean that 107 British arbitrators were appointed. Similarly, "55 arbitrations . . . to be in London" means that of the 107 for which ICC United Kingdom was invited to make a nomination, for 55 of them London was to be the place of the arbitration. Whether these ever took place or not is another matter. It will be appreciated that these figures do not reveal how many ICC arbitrations were to be in London or how many British arbitrators were appointed. These are matters we shall now consider.

Nominations by ICC United Kingdom in the international context

Place of arbitration

Article 12 of the ICC Rules states: "The place of arbitration shall be fixed by the Court, unless agreed upon by the parties". This notwithstanding, it is remarkable how parties, and their legal advisers, have over recent years increasingly recognised the importance of the choice of the place of arbitration. This phenomenon was first pointed out by Craig, Park and Paulsson.[2] The figures reveal a clear picture:

	Place chosen by Parties (%)	Fixed by Court (%)
1980	52.2	46.6
1988	79.4	20.6

The choice of place may, in effect, determine the outcome of the case. In ICC Case no. 4491 between a Finnish corporation and an Australian one, London was to be the place of arbitration, specified in the arbitration clause. The case involved royalty payments allegedly not made and the purported cancellation of the relevant agreement in 1976. In 1982 the licensor initiated arbitration. The arbitrator found that because the arbitration was taking place in England, the English Limitation Act applied. So, even assuming that Finnish law was the applicable law and there was no comparable limitation rule under that system, the arbitrator felt obliged to apply the English six-year limitation period, barring all claims arising before 1976, which effectively meant all claims.

In a recent article on "How to draft an arbitration clause"[3] Stephen Bond, when commenting on some of the oddities revealed in clauses that came across his desk in 1987, pointed out that if an arbitration clause refers to the ICC "of" Paris, or "in" Paris, this will be interpreted by the Court as an indication of the intended place of arbitration, unless another *situs* is clearly indicated in the clause. This rule of interpretation is applied consistently. When for example a clause refers to the ICC "of" Geneva or "in" London this is similarly interpreted as being the choice of place for the arbitration. Some figures relating to the place of arbitration are shown in Annex IV.

2 *International Chamber of Commerce Arbitration*, 1984 (2nd ed. 1990).
3 6 Jour Int Arb 2, 65–78.

Nationality of Arbitrators

The Court in effect appoints all arbitrators, either by confirming the appointment of an individual nominated by one or both parties or, in the absence of such nomination, by itself appointing an individual. Parties are free to choose arbitrators of any nationality, including their own. When appointments are being confirmed or made the Court has regard to the following in regard to the proposed arbitrator's:

- nationality;
- residence; and
- other relationships with the countries of which the parties or the other arbitrators are nationals.

When the Court has to appoint a sole arbitrator or the chairman of a tribunal of three its appointee, unless the parties agree otherwise, will be of a different nationality from theirs. Some figures relating to the nationality of arbitrators are shown in Annex IV.

Attention is drawn to the numbers and percentages of arbitrators whose nationality is different from that of the party nominating him. There is no obvious explanation as to why there is such a significant difference in the percentage of French arbitrators nominated by non-French parties as compared with the Swiss and British. It is also remarkable how the nomination of non-national arbitrators by claimants on the one hand and defendants on the other is very similar in respect of all three nationalities. Again no obvious explanation presents itself.

Applicable law

In Stephen Bond's article on drafting an arbitration clause referred to above, he reports that of the 178 contracts which in 1987 came across his desk, 75% contained a choice of law clause, either specifically or by reference such as "the law of the seller's country". Also of interest, he points out, is the rarity of clauses which authorise the tribunal to resolve the dispute on the basis of equity, amiable composition, *ex aequo et bono*, or with the arbitrators acting as mediators. In 1987 only some nine clauses (3%) incorporated anything of this kind. No clause in 1987 mentioned *lex mercatoria*.

Referring to Annex III which gives some details of nominations made by ICC United Kingdom, it will be seen that in 28 (26%) of the 107 cases there was no choice of law clause. It will be seen that this corresponds very closely with the 25% noted by Stephen Bond across the international spectrum for 1987. One can therefore conclude that the cases referred to ICC United Kingdom are in line with the general trend.

Advice by ICC United Kingdom

The enquirers

These range from the small businessman to partners in specialist firms of solicitors. The majority, however, are at neither end of this range. Lawyers and engineers in industry and solicitors constitute the main clientele. Occasionally foreign lawyers have made enquiries, usually about possible arbitrators, usually British, but not always.

The enquiries

At the contract stage, these range from those made by a businessman who for example has a well-developed UK business which is about to expand internationally, with the appointment of agents in different countries. He wishes to discuss the pros and cons of arbitration and the different forms of arbitration that might be suitable. The Arbitration Consultant aims to offer objective advice in what he believes is the best interest of the enquirer. He does not try to "sell" ICC arbitration, if that does not seem to be the best form of arbitration for the circumstances, considered objectively. In this context the place of arbitration is often discussed, and the question of governing law. Much the same kind of discussion takes place with lawyers in business or in practice, other than those in the specialist firms. The last-mentioned rarely make enquiries at the contract negotiation stage.

At the dispute stage, there are more enquiries from practising solicitors, many of whom may have considerable experience in commercial work and indeed in arbitration, but have not acted before in an ICC arbitration. These enquirers usually want clarification of such things as the detail and form required for the Request for Arbitration. They also ask about costs, for they do not find the Schedules that accompany the Rules easy to understand; nor does the Arbitration Consultant.

At this more sophisticated level enquiriers also ask about the place of arbitration likely to be fixed by the Court, if not agreed by the parties; or they may ask for views on the venue suggested by the other side. The Arbitration Consultant can give only very tentative advice on the first line of enquiry. On the second he can often refer the enquirer to literature on, for example, a recent change in the law in a particular country or a reported case which shows the attractiveness, or otherwise, of the venue suggested.

Lastly, the Arbitration Consultant is asked about possible candidates for nomination by a party as a co-arbitrator, as a sole arbitrator or as a chairman; and he is sometimes asked to comment on names proposed by the other side. The response to such enquiries is more or less on standard lines: the ICC does not have lists or panels of arbitrators, nor does ICC United Kingdom; but given reasonable information about the case in question the Arbitration Consultant can give, never a single name, but the names of two or three individuals who have acted as arbitrator in similar cases. There can be a difficulty in this area, for if the parties fail to agree a sole arbitrator or a chairman, ICC United Kingdom might be the National Committee invited by the Court to make a nomination. In such a situation he either declines to discuss the matter further or gives the names of two or three individuals, keeping in mind other "possibles" for use in case of need.

There have been some enquiries by foreign lawyers regarding possible arbitrators, usually British, but not invariably so. It should be made clear that enquiries as to possible arbitrators are not confined to ICC arbitrations. In the past five years a total of some 250 enquiries have been dealt with.

Technical expertise

Although not relating directly to arbitration, there is another service provided by the ICC which can be useful in avoiding a dispute having to go to arbitration and which may assist the arbitral process itself. The Rules of The International Centre for Technical Expertise provide essentially for the appointment of an independent expert on the application of one or both parties to a contract, when a difference of opinion on a technical matter is anticipated.

As National Committees can become involved, and as ICC United Kingdom through the Arbitration Consultant has been involved on four occasions in the first five years, it is appropriate to mention the service here. The four instances called for experts to undertake the following:

- to go to South America to give an opinion on welding work on an off-shore drilling-rig;
- to go to North Africa to give an opinion on the operation of a plant producing milk products;
- to go to North Africa to observe the commissioning of a petrochemical plant;
- to go to North Africa to observe the commissioning of a sugar refining plant.

Annex I

Letter received by ICC United Kingdom from Secretariat of ICC Court of Arbitration inviting nomination.

1234/PT

The Big Corporation (USA) v. *Another Big Corporation (Netherlands)*

Dear Sir,

The Court of Arbitration at its regular sessions on ....

decided to invite the ICC United Kingdom to propose a nominee who could act as sole arbitrator for the subject case.

I would be grateful to receive your proposal before .... if possible, so that the Court can consider it at its next session. Your proposal should be accompanied by the curriculum vitae of your nominee.

Article 2.7 of the Rules of the Court provides that the arbitrators appointed by the Court, acting either on the nomination of a party or on the nomination of a National Committee, must be "independent of the parties", and remain so during the arbitration.

Accordingly you should provide the Court with your written assurance of the independence of any individual you nominate. You should also obtain and send to the Court the written assurance of your nominee. Any facts or circumstances that might raise questions about the appearance of the complete independence of your nominee should be disclosed to the Court in writing.

The nominee should be made aware of the mandatory nature of the time-limits imposed under the Rules of the Court for submitting the Terms of Reference and sending the Award so that appropriate commitment of time made by him.

XYX has been confirmed as the place of arbitration.

(OR – XYX has been fixed by the Court as the place of arbitration.)

Arbitrator's fees may vary between US$ .... and US$ ....

(average US$ ....)

If you need any further information, please feel free to
call upon me.
Yours sincerely,

Peter Tucker
ICC Court of Arbitration
Secretariat
Enc: Summary of the dispute
1234PT
The Big Corporation (USA) v. *Another Big Corporation (Netherlands)*
Characteristics of the dispute
By an agreement dated ......, as amended, Defendant agreed to sell and Claimant agreed to buy ..... (quantity of goods, deliverable over stated period, price formula .....) .....
Claimant alleges that Defendant failed to deliver ......
Respective positions of the Parties
– Claimant seeks damages of not less than ...., together with declaration that ....
– Defendant: No response received as at ....
Applicable law:
Language used in the file: English and Dutch
Setting in motion of the procedure:
Contractual provision:
(Arbitration and other relevant clauses quoted)
Desiderata of parties:
– Number of arbitrators: Sole arbitrator (both parties)
– Claimant: Sole arbitrator should be familiar with the practices of the ...... industry
– Defendant: Sole arbitrator should be a lawyer with great experience of international trade law

Annex II

ICC United Kingdom

Nomination of Arbitrators – Guidelines for Arbitration Consultant

Nominations in response to requests by the ICC Court of Arbitration are to be made on behalf of ICC United Kingdom by the Arbitration Consultant in accordance with the following guidelines:

1. Each nomination will be made on the basis that in the opinion of the Arbitration Consultant the nominee is a person competent and suitable for the particular appointment

2. In forming such an opinion the Arbitration Consultant will take into account the following factors:

(a) the nature and extent of the individual's knowledge and experience (whether as lawyer or otherwise) of commercial law and practice and the conduct of business in and beyond the United Kingdom;

(b) the nature and extent of the individual's experience in a judicial or quasi-judicial capacity (including that as arbitrator) in and outside the United Kingdom;

(c) the individual's linguistic abilities;

(d) the individual's usual place of residence;

(e) having regard to the place of arbitration and the likely duration of the arbitral proceedings, the health of the individual;

(f) where the nomination is for the chairman of an arbitral tribunal, the identity and qualifications of the other members of the tribunal; and

(g) such other factors as the case may require.

3. No person will be excluded or omitted from consideration as a possible nominee on the grounds of race, sex, religion or professional qualifications

4. When the Arbitration Consultant is considering the nomination of an individual who has not previously acted as arbitrator under the auspices of the ICC Court of Arbitration, before making such nomination the Arbitration Consultant will consult not less than two members of the Arbitration Panel established by ICC United Kingdom.

5. The Arbitration Consultant will maintain lists of those nominated as arbitrators and, in the light of information available to him, of those British Nationals who have been appointed by a party or by parties to an arbitral proceeding.

6. At least once each year the Arbitration Consultant will report to the Arbitration Panel on the nominations and on the lists referred to in paragraph 5. The Arbitration Consultant will be at liberty to disclose the names and qualifications of any persons whose names are on such lists to such persons as appear to him to have a legitimate interest in the information, always provided that no such disclosure infringes the rules and practice of the ICC Court of Arbitration as to the confidentiality of arbitration proceedings.

7. The Arbitration Consultant will not during the period of his appointment act as arbitrator, counsel, expert or in any other capacity in an arbitration under the auspices of the ICC Court of Arbitration or in any other form of arbitration

8. No individual who is a member of the Arbitration Panel of ICC United Kingdom or of any committee or working-party will be disqualified or otherwise inhibited from acting in any arbitration proceedings under the auspices of the ICC Court of Arbitration as arbitrator, counsel, instructing solicitor, expert or otherwise. If consulted by the Arbitration Consultant regarding the nomination of an arbitrator for a particular proceeding, the individual so consulted will be under an obligation to disclose any interest he may have in the proceedings.

Annex III

Appointment of Arbitrators

Nominations by ICC United Kingdom

1 October 1984 – 1 September 1989

107 nominations:

44 chairmen
60 sole arbitrators
3 co-arbitrators

107 arbitrations:

55 to be in London:
– for 37, agreed by parties;
– for 18, fixed by Court
20 to be in Paris:

– for 17, agreed by parties;
– for 3, fixed by Court
9 to be in Geneva
– for 8, agreed by parties;
– for 1, fixed by Court

and the other 23 elsewhere, from Copenhagen to Chicago to Katmandu.
107 arbitrations:

English law 25
silent 28

Annex IV

Place of Arbitration

In the nine years (1980–88) the place was determined for 1933 ICC arbitrations.

The three countries most frequently chosen were:

France – 646: Switzerland – 525: United Kingdom – 191

Choices by the parties and by the Court were as follows:

France		Switzerland		United Kingdom	
Parties	Court	Parties	Court	Parties	Court
478	165	455	70	142	49

France was chosen as the venue for 33.5% of all cases worldwide
Switzerland ,, ,, ,, ,, ,, ,, 27.0% ,, ,, ,, ,,
United Kingdom ,, ,, ,, ,, ,, ,, 10.0% ,, ,, ,, ,,

In each of the five years (1984-88) the details were as follows:

	France		Switzerland		UK	
	Parties	Court	Parties	Court	Parties	Court
1984	52	6	68	7	11	3
1985	59	16	51	7	18	10
1986	73	8	64	4	18	7
1987	71	15	53	1	20	6
1988	70	9	63	3	16	4

	France		Switzerland		United Kingdom	
	Parties	Court	Parties	Court	Parties	Court
1984	52	6	68	7	11	3
1985	59	16	51	7	18	10
1986	73	8	64	4	18	7
1987	71	15	53	1	20	6
1988	70	9	63	3	16	4

Broken down yearly figures for 1980–83 are not available but the yearly average for the two periods 1980–83 and 1985–86 can be calculated, with the following results:

	France		Switzerland		United Kingdom	
	Parties	Court	Parties	Court	Parties	Court
1980–83	38.25	28.5	41.5	12	9.75	4.75
1984–88	65	10.2	59.8	4.4	16.6	6

Annex V

Nationality of arbitrators

In the nine years (1980–88) 4,160 arbitrators were appointed.

French, Swiss and British arbitrators were the most frequently appointed, details being shown in the following Table:

Chosen by:

	Claimant	Defendant	Jointly	Court	Total
French	286(134)	199(96)	73	205	763
Swiss	150(116)	106(82)	126	361	743
British	119(90)	61	153	433	766

It is to be noted that the nationality of arbitrators most frequently appointed as a result of nomination by one of the parties was:

French – 485: Swiss – 256: British – 219

The number in brackets in the Table is the number of arbitrators nominated by a party of a different nationality from that of the nominee.

It is also to be noted that the percentages of non-national arbitrators were in descending order: Swiss, British and French, thus:

150 Swiss arbitrators nominated by Claimants: 115 (77.3%) by non-Swiss claimants

106 Swiss arbitrators nominated by Defendants: 82 (77.66%) by non-Swiss Defendants

119 British arbitrators nominated by Claimants: 90 (75.63%) by non-British Claimants

100 British arbitrators nominated by Claimants: 76 (76%) by non-British Defendants

286 French arbitrators nominated by Claimants: 134 (46.85%) by non-French Claimants

199 French arbitrators nominated by Defendants: 96 (48.24%) by non-French Defendants.

A View from the ICC Court of Arbitration 6

Martin Hunter

Synopsis

In this paper the author, who is a UK member of the ICC Court of Arbitration, gives a view of the workings of the ICC Court, covering the different activities by which the Court supports and controls the international arbitration process.

Introduction

It is perhaps unfortunate that the body charged with the supervisory and administrative role in relation to the ICC system of arbitration is called a "court". The *Shorter Oxford English Dictionary* gives several definitions of the word including "A clear space enclosed by walls or surrounded by buildings"; "The place where a sovereign resides and holds state, attended by his retinue"; and "A court of judicature, or law". The ICC's Court of Arbitration, now called the International Court of Arbitration, is none of these things. It is an administrative body which has the function of performing the specific tasks allocated to it by the ICC Rules. These are:

- determining the number of arbitrators (where the parties have not agreed); confirming and appointing arbitrators; and deciding on challenges of arbitrators (Art. 2);
- determining on a provisional basis the existence or otherwise of a prima facie agreement to arbitrate (Arts. 7 and 8.3);
- fixing the amount of the advance on costs (Art. 9);
- fixing the place of arbitration (where the parties have not agreed) (Art. 12);
- "approving" the terms of reference where a party refuses to sign them (Art. 13.3.);
- fixing the arbitrator's fees and expenses and the ICC's administrative costs (Art. 20.2);
- scrutinising awards (Art. 21);
- dealing with requests for joinder of claims between the same parties (Internal Rules, Art. 13);

– dealing with requests for extensions of time limits where provided for in various places in the Rules.

It is not my intention today to discuss these functions in detail. For those who wish to study them further a good deal of relevant information is given in Stephen Bond's paper. There is a succinct and useful summary in the judgment of Mr Justice Steyn in *Bank Mellatt* v. *GAA Development Construction*,[1] and a more extended account in Chapter 2 of *International Chamber of Commerce Arbitration*.[2] Incidentally, I believe that a second edition of this excellent work will be available shortly.

Rather, it is my purpose to describe the way in which the Court performs its functions on a day-to-day basis and to try to share with you some of my personal impressions of the operation of the Court. I am pleased to have this opportunity, because as I travel around I find a certain amount of misunderstanding and hostility which arises largely because – in accordance with its own Internal Rules (Art. 3) – the Court operates behind closed doors. I have taken the slightly unusual step of presenting this paper in the first person singular specifically in order to emphasise that it contains my own personal perspective of the work of the Court. These views may not be shared by other members of the Court – or indeed by the Secretariat – and are in no way authoritative.

The Court is currently composed of 52 members. The number is made up by 44 delegates from countries which have National Committees affiliated to the ICC, plus the President and seven Vice-Presidents. Under Article 1 of the Internal Rules the President and the Vice-Presidents are appointed by the Council of the International Chamber of Commerce directly. The national delegates are appointed by the Council on the nomination of the relevant National Committees. In practice the nominations by National Committees are reviewed by the "bureau" of the Court, comprising the President and Vice-Presidents, before the Council makes the appointments. The term of a Court member's appointment is for three years, which is renewable. Many of you will know that my predecessor, Gerald Pointon of Herbert Smith's Paris Office, was in fact the UK member for some 13 years, for which I admire him greatly as the work is considerably time-consuming. He made a massive contribution during his term of office. Members of the Court receive no fee for their work and may not be appointed directly by the Court to act as sole arbitrator or chairman of a tribunal. With the exception of the President and Vice-Presidents (who may not act as arbitrator or even as counsel in any ICC case) members of the Court may be appointed as sole arbitrator or chairman of a tribunal by agreement of the parties. They may also serve as party-nominated arbitrators, subject to confirmation by the Court in the normal manner under Article 5 of the Internal Rules. Under Article 6 of the Internal Rules members of the Court must notify the Secretariat where they have any direct or indirect interest in an ICC arbitration, in which event they withdraw when the case comes before the Court and the Secretariat ensures that the documents relating to such a case are excluded from their dossiers before they are sent out by courier.

Basically, members participate in the work of the Court in two separate ways; at the plenary sessions and at the committees.

1 [1988] 2 Lloyd's Rep 44.
2 Craig, Park and Paulson (Oceana) 1984.

Plenary sessions

Plenary sessions are held monthly as required by Article 1.2 of the Rules. These currently take place on the third Thursday of each month. Incidentally, this is an important fact which arbitrators and practitioners should know, because if you just miss one plenary session you may have an unnecessary delay of nearly a month. Plenary sessions start at 2 pm and continue sometimes until 7 or 8 pm. I am personally fortunate in having a cut-off point, in that the airline timetables for most of the year require me to leave by around 6.15 pm in order to catch the last flight back to London. Of the total of 52 members, the average attendance figure is around 20. Not surprisingly, the majority of regular attenders are those members who reside in Paris – although there are a number, such as myself, who come regularly from other nearby European countries; and we see the members who live in other continents perhaps two or three times a year. The Rules do permit the appointment of alternates (Internal Rules, Art. 2), but so far as I am aware this is rarely if ever done.

The working languages of the Court are English and French, and members are expected to be able to read documents in both languages, although not necessarily with equal facility. They may speak at the plenary sessions in either language, and simultaneous translation is provided. Some arbitrations are, of course, conducted in other languages. There are always a number of arbitrations in German each year, and occasional cases in Arabic, Italian or Spanish. In these cases, the documents to be placed before the Court are translated either into English or French. The cost of these translations is not charged directly to the parties, but is paid out of the ICC funds.

The agenda for the plenary sessions is divided into three sections, known as Parts A, B and C.

Part A

Any challenges to arbitrators under Article 2 of the Rules are dealt with at the beginning of Part A of the agenda, as are decisions on questions concerning the prima facie existence of an agreement to arbitrate. These items are followed by scrutiny under Article 21 of the Rules of the "Part A awards". These are awards considered by the Secretariat to meriting full consideration by the Court at a plenary session, assisted by a rapporteur. The rapporteurs appear to be selected on a somewhat ad hoc basis by the Counsel in charge of the file. I am not sure how much consultation there is within the Secretariat about who should be the rapporteur for a particular case. Presumably knowledge of the applicable law and/or the subject matter of the dispute play a large part – although I have had several *lex mercatoria* cases! Incidentally, according to my count only 12 of the 52 members of the Court are common lawyers by background, and of those less than half attend the plenary sessions on a regular basis. In practice you receive a telephone call from one of the Counsel, perhaps 10 days or two weeks before the plenary session, inviting you to prepare a report. If you are able to do it, the papers are sent by courier and you are expected to submit a written report on the award in time for the session, and then to supplement that report by an oral presentation. Any points on the award are then debated, and the President invariably permits the rapporteur to have the last word before he presents a summary of the consensus of the meeting. I do not recall a vote being necessary on whether or not an award should be approved, although I suppose in theory this could happen. Where a final award is approved, the Court fixes the costs of the arbitration in accordance with Article 20.2 of the Rules.

The information required for the purposes of Article 18 of the Internal Rules is presented by the Secretariat, which normally makes a recommendation as to the figures - although the rapporteur will sometimes give his or her view separately. The factors to be taken into account are the maximum and minimum amounts provided in the scale, which depend on the amount in dispute; time spent; rapidity; and complexity. Although the arbitrators' fees can be fixed outside the maximum and minimum figures this happens only rarely and, accordingly, the amount in dispute clearly has the greatest influence. It is now widely considered that the essentially *ad valorem* based system sometimes produces some odd results in that, on the one hand, some arbitrators have to do an enormous amount of work for a relatively small fee but, on the other hand, other arbitrators occasionally receive a totally unjustifiable "windfall".

The whole question of arbitrators' fees is now the subject of a review by a working party which was, I believe, established partly as a result of my own comments early in 1988 when I first saw how the system operated. It is my hope that the worst features of the *ad valorem* system, which are seen both at the "top" and "bottom" ends of the scale will be at least ameliorated if not eliminated altogether. However, I am personally not in favour of a basis solely related to time spent, for two reasons. The first is that I feel there should be a positive incentive for arbitrators not to sit back comfortably whilst the parties (or their lawyers) over-litigate a case at great length. The second is that, by contrast with the ambience of a well-controlled office, it is difficult to achieve a consistent basis for time-recording when arbitrators come from such a wide variety of backgrounds. A questionnaire was sent out to a number of arbitrators and practitioners, seeking their views. If you have not received one and would like to present your views, please write to Mr Benjamin Davies at the ICC Headquarters in Paris. He is one of the counsel, and is the secretary of the Working Group.

Part B

Part B of the agenda for the plenary sessions involves scrutiny of awards which have been examined by the committees (which meet twice in each month) to which I shall refer later, and is – in most cases – the granting of formal approval by the Court under Article 21 of the Rules on the recommendation of a committee. Part B only contains awards of a rather uncontroversial nature, where the Secretariat and the relevant committee had no doubts as to its approval.

Part C

Part C of the agenda, which rarely requires discussion, comprises notification to the Court of any urgent decisions taken by the President, which must be reported to the Court under Article 1.3 of the Rules, and copies of any material relating to proceedings in national courts affecting ICC arbitrations.

Article 21: Withholding of Approval

It may be of particular interest for arbitrators to be aware that there are two forms of withholding of approval by the Court under Article 21 where matters of "form" are involved. The first is where there is some relatively minor technical defect; for example, where the calculations are manifestly wrong, or – which happens surprisingly often – the arbitrator fails to deal with the question of costs properly in accordance with Article 20 of the Rules. In these cases, the Court gives its "approval subject to . . .", and the award need not be re-submitted to the Court if the Secretariat is satisfied with the revised draft.

The second type of case is where the Court perceives some rather more fundamental defect of form, particularly where the defect may affect the validity or enforceability of the award. In such cases the award is returned to the arbitrator "not approved" with a letter from the Secretariat explaining the reason and asking the arbitrator to take into consideration the relevant point and to re-submit the award for reconsideration by the Court. Occasionally a procedural defect is revealed by the award and the Court will require this to be remedied before approval is given. I stress, of course, the point that "approval" by the Court under Article 21 relates solely to matters of form. Matters of substance may be drawn to the arbitrator's attention but, as is clear from the wording of Article 21, the arbitrator's liberty of decision is unrestrained and approval of an award cannot be withheld by the Court because it does not agree with the substance of an award. This aspect of scrutiny of awards is often overlooked by critics, who attack the system on the basis that the Court runs the risk of becoming some form of appellate tribunal before which the parties have no right of representation. In the *Bank Mellat* case, to which I referred earlier, Mr Justice Steyn remarked that the dividing line between matters of form and matters of substance may be narrow. This was in the context of the Court requesting the tribunal to provide further reasoning in connection with some particular issues. But the Court only regards its comments on reasoning to be a matter of form where there is no (or no adequate) motivation given for a particularly decision, which may result in the award being invalid or unenforceable in some legal systems. Where there is reasoning but it seems to be defective or (as is more often the case) unintelligible, the Court's comments are categorised as relating to questions of substance, and not a basis for the withholding of approval under Article 21 of the Rules.

Other Decisions

Decisions of the Court on challenge of arbitrator and on the prima facie existence of an agreement to arbitrate are somewhat different, but when these questions arise the parties are each given an opportunity to make written submissions to the Court, and to reply to each other's submissions. On a challenge of an arbitrator the parties do not see the arbitrator's comments, which are withheld on the ground that arbitrators must be able to make their comments freely.

Even if it were necessary or desirable, the sheer volume of cases that must be processed each month makes it totally impracticable for hearings to take place at which the parties would be able to make oral submissions to the Court.

Committees of the Court

The second way in which members of the Court participate in its work is attendance at the committee meetings. These take place twice in each month. One of the committee meetings is on the day preceding the plenary session. The committees are attended by the chairman and two members of the Court. Normally, one of the members comes from a common law jurisdiction and one from a civil law jurisdiction. The Secretary-General of the Court, the General Counsel and the other counsel of the Secretariat are also present. Being much smaller gatherings, the pace tends to be quicker. As in the case of plenary sessions, the committee members will have received a dossier of the relevant papers about a week before the meeting. Incidentally, these dossiers are usually substantial. They are contained in a lever-arch file about three or four inches thick. As in the case of plenary sessions, the meetings start at 2 pm and go on as long as necessary – although they do not usually take as long as the plenary sessions. The counsel in charge of each case on the agenda makes an oral presentation to the committee, which discusses the action to be taken and makes its decision. Typically, a committee will spend much of the meeting dealing with decisions on the place of arbitration; the number of arbitrators; confirmation (or otherwise) of arbitrators nominated by the parties, after consideration of their declarations of independence; appointment of sole arbitrators, or chairman of three-member tribunals; fixing (or subsequent adjustment of) the advance on costs and matters such as joinder of arbitrations and extending time limits.

Under Article 11 of the Internal Rules the committees are empowered to take decisions on all matters except questions relating to the removal of arbitrators under Article 2 of the Rules and approval of awards under Article 21 of the Rules.

If the committee cannot reach a unanimous decision the matter must be referred to the next plenary session of the Court. This has not happened in my experience, although I understand that it does occasionally occur. The Court is notified of decisions taken by the committees by means of an addendum to the minutes of the plenary sessions.

The question of who takes the decisions leads me to mention one particular point which raises its head from time to time when I talk to practitioners. There is the question of the role of the Secretariat. Because the Secretariat deals with all communications with the outside world many people receive the impression that the Secretariat takes the decisions. I can state emphatically that this is not the case. It is true that initial action under Article 7 is taken by the Secretariat on its own initiative, but the claimant has the right to request that the matter should be put before the Court. It is also true that the Secretariat makes comments and recommendations on matters which are before the Court for decision (except when a rapporteur has been appointed). But in my experience the Secretariat is always mindful of the fact that it does not take the decisions, and that its role in the sessions of the Court – and in the committees – is to provide the factual matrix for the members of the Court.

General impressions

My overall impression, having been a member of the Court for a little more than a year and a half, is one of satisfaction – and surprise. My sense of satisfaction arises from the fact that I have found the work extremely interesting, and it has given me an entirely new perspective on international arbitration. The enhancement of my understanding of the way in which the Court functions from the inside has helped me to perform my more accustomed function as a representative of the parties with great effectiveness, certainly in the procedural context. It has also taught me a number of lessons – both "do's" and "don'ts" – in the context of my less frequent role of acting as an arbitrator in ICC cases. I have also gained satisfaction from seeing at first hand that, behind its closed doors, the Court is not the capricious or amateurish body that I had sometimes thought it to be when looking at it from the outside.

Scrutiny of Awards

This leads me to the elements which have surprised me. The first cause for surprise is to find that the ICC can find so many people to undertake so much work for no remuneration. In my own case it is neither her nor there, because in effect my firm supports work that I do on a *pro bono* basis. But many members of the Court are academics or sole practitioners who could use the time that they devote to the work of the Court in a way in which they might be financially rewarded. The other point which surprised me greatly was just how bad some of the awards are which come before the Court for scrutiny. If I ever had doubts as to the necessity for a system of scrutiny of awards (and terms of reference, without which scrutiny could not play any meaningful role), those doubts were dispelled by studying the draft awards which come before the Court. Sometimes they do not decide the issues that the tribunal was mandated to decide; they reveal serious procedural irregularities; and they are sometimes written in language so obscure that it is impossible to discern the reasoning behind them.

Where these defects involve matters of form, the Court can in effect insist on defects being remedied by holding approval. However, the Court has no direct sanction when the arbitrator has made a decision of substance which is manifestly wrong, which occasionally happens. Sometimes, in my frustration, it makes me feel that the Court should have wider powers in relation to the substance of awards. However, any such powers would indeed run the risk of the Court exercising a judicial function, which it clearly should not exercise without the right of parties to be present and be represented. The only course available to the Court is the *ex post facto* remedy of drawing particular instances to the attention of National Committees for further reference, and to exhort them more generally to be careful to nominate arbitrators of high quality. I do not mean to suggest, of course, that the bad awards constitute a large proportion of the awards which come before the Court; of course not. There are many good awards, but the bad ones are highlighted in my memory.

I do not think that the criticisms we hear of the system of scrutiny of awards is justified. I think that such a system is necessary in ICC arbitration, and that it works reasonably well both in theory and in practice under the Rules. I am also convinced that it is necessary for scrutiny to be performed behind closed doors, and that no injustice arises from it. I believe that most of the criticism is based on a lack of understanding of Article 21 of the Rules, and how the Court approaches its obligations under the Rules in practice. It is a very superficial approach to argue that the Court acts as a form of appellate tribunal. It does not, because all decision making on the merits of a dispute remain entirely in the hands of the arbitral tribunal.

However, I am more uneasy about the practice in relation to the other major functions of the Court on matters which may affect the parties' substantive rights. These are, first, challenge of arbitrators and, secondly, decisions as to the prima facie existence of an arbitration agreement.

Challenge of Arbitrators

I have already explained that it would be impracticable for such matters to be dealt with at an open hearing of the Court, at which the parties would have the right to be represented. That would be out of the question, given the context of the operation of the Court. Nonetheless, whilst I have no doubt that these matters can be decided adequately on the basis of written submissions from the parties, it does concern me that these decisions fall within the "behind closed doors" ambit. They are decisions which can have a very important effect on the rights of the parties. The dismissal of a challenge of an arbitrator, or chairman, in whom the challenging party has no confidence may be a correct decision, but it may be one which destroys the confidence of the party in the arbitration system. Furthermore, once he has challenged an arbitrator and failed, the party who has made the challenge will fear that the arbitrator will be prejudiced against him. This may equally be the case when a challenge is submitted to a national court and rejected, but at least the challenging party has his day in court. Under the present ICC practice he does not even know, sometimes, whether his challenge has been rejected on the merits or because it was made out of time. I do not think that this issue has yet arisen under Article 3 of the LCIA Rules (on which the ICC Rule was modelled) but it will be interesting to discover what line the LCIA Court takes on this point.

Existence of Arbitration Agreement

A decision by the Court that a prima facie arbitration agreement does not exist can be a serious matter for the claimant, in that it throws him back on the pursuit of remedies in national courts – very often the courts of the defendant. Sometimes this kind of case is not straightforward, particularly when there are related corporate entities involved in a dispute. The party which signed the arbitration agreement may be a worthless subsidiary by the time the dispute arises. The Court frequently sees arguments in favour of joining non-signatories to the arbitration agreement based on *alter ego* principles, or where it is alleged that another corporate entity has become a party by its conduct. Equally serious can be the case when the Court does allow a case to go forward for a decision by the arbitral tribunal under Article 8.3 of the Rules. In my time on the Court I have seen several attempts by claimants to join the signatory of the arbitration agreement personally, even though he has signed it expressly in his capacity as the duly authorised representative of a corporate entity. If such cases go forward to the arbitral tribunal under Article 8.3 tremendous pressure is put on that individual, particularly as arbitral tribunals rarely award a total indemnity as to costs – even though a party has succeeded in arguing that he was never a proper party to the arbitration. It is not easy for the Court to steer a course between, on the one hand, allowing the matter to go forward so that the tribunal can decide its own jurisdiction and, on the other hand, the manifest undesirability of allowing a party to suffer the expense and other pressures of being dragged before an arbitral tribunal where he has not signed the arbitration agreement. I believe that the Court, as currently constituted, and under its present leadership, takes a responsible and pragmatic approach to this difficult question. But it is not easy, and the fact that it is necessarily done behind closed doors makes the whole exercise more difficult.

Conclusion

In making these remarks, I am conscious that it is easy to raise doubts and not so easy to suggest solutions. In general, I am satisfied that the system is operated as fairly and effectively as it can be in relation to Article 2, Article 7 and Article 8.3. However, I would like to see some mechanism devised so that it could be done more openly if only in the sense that the parties would be given the reasons for decisions of the Court which may have a fundamental effect on their remedies – just as arbitrators in ICC cases are required to give reasons for their decisions.

7 Post-conference review of ICC arbitration

Stephen Bond

Synopsis

In this paper the Secretary-General of the ICC comments on the conference and the papers submitted. A response is given to certain criticisms of the ICC system. Overall, it is concluded that the papers submitted demonstrate the viability of the ICC system which, however, remains open to constructive and practical criticism.

Introduction

This conference has a special significance. Not too many years ago it would have been inconceivable to have a two-day conference in London on ICC arbitration at the initiative of the English themselves and with speakers and participants representing the cream of the English arbitration scene. The "case-stated" procedure had in effect until 1979 resulted in the ICC Court rarely situating arbitrations in London. Notwithstanding the quality of English jurists, the ICC UK was rarely called upon by the ICC Court to propose arbitrators. So too, the ICC was generally perceived in England as a species, not too high on the evolutionary scale, of a civil law approach to arbitration that was to be avoided whenever possible.

Today's situation represents a sea-change. The 1979 Act and its interpretation by the English courts have removed all barriers to the selection by the ICC Court of England as an arbitration *situs*. The ICC United Kingdom is sought out whenever possible so that the full talent of the English legal profession can be brought to bear in ICC arbitrations. United Kingdom parties frequently have resort to ICC arbitration. Indeed, they have generally been among the top five users of ICC arbitration in the past several years.[1]

Certainly, some of this change in the relations between the United Kingdom and ICC arbitration represents enlightened self-interest on everyone's behalf. But, happily, more than that is at play. I believe that mutual

1 See Paper 5, which provides more detail on these points.

respect and understanding has also developed and deepened. This is not to say that there is now an uncritical, blind acceptance (far from that), but rather there now exists an appreciation borne of experience that the world of international commercial arbitration and the needs of international commerce are varied and complex enough to allow for, (indeed, to require), different approaches, and splendid isolation is no longer to anyone's advantage. So too, on the human level I could not wish for closer or better relations between the ICC United Kingdom, English jurists and the personnel of the ICC Secretariat.

The ICC approach to international arbitration

The papers submitted for this conference not only provide a rich fund of knowledge and experience to be examined and learned from, but also, inevitably prompt questions that must be addressed. Accordingly, this paper will deal with aspects of ICC arbitration about which most comment is heard, at this conference and elsewhere. Paper 4, which appears to contain the only real criticism of ICC arbitration is given particular attention. Comment is especially called for with regard to the overriding question of whether the present system of ICC arbitration is outdated; or whether it remains a viable institution offering unique solutions in the constantly evolving and increasingly complex world of international commercial arbitration.

Since its inception, ICC arbitration has been specifically tailored to handle international disputes. This dedication in principle and practice to international arbitration is not merely a slogan or a vague philosophy but, rather, has been and remains fundamental in shaping the structure, procedures and working methods of ICC arbitration. In particular, it accounts for those unique features aimed at ensuring the neutrality, independence and expertise necessary for the ICC to carry out its responsibilities.

This is so because we believe that the international element present in over 95% of the approximately 300 cases we receive yearly (and about 20–25% of these cases are international construction cases) adds a qualitatively different aspect to commercial disputes. Even within a relatively homogeneous area such as the European Community, those who have commercial dealings with each other across national borders do not necessarily get along, often misunderstand each other and very quickly can revert to nationalistic and aggressive attitudes when disagreeements arise. Imagine then the challenge inherent in creating a dispute resolution system that can gain and hold the respect, confidence and trust of parties from the more than 100 different countries that have used ICC arbitration over the past decade.

This challenge can only grow in the years to come as economic relations between and among parties from every part of the world increase in number, breadth and complexity. More than ever before business people will face the additional uncertainties, problems, risks and fears that arise from dealing in a foreign language with people whose cultural background, customs, laws and business practices are different from their own and, occasionally but inevitably, resolving the disputes that arise between them. The ICC also bears in mind the additional complexities and difficulties which international commercial arbitration can entail both in the arbitration proceedings and the enforcement process. Thus, ICC arbitration is geared and designed to produce an arbitral award that, by virtue of its procedural and substantive soundness, will compel defendants to honour it and will resist efforts before national tribunals to have it annulled.

Accordingly, certain features of ICC arbitration not present in domestic or other international arbitration systems exist because they have been and continue to be considered as important to the success of an international arbitration, success being measured not by the mere rendering of an award, but by a party obtaining satisfaction on that award whatever the nationalities of the parties, the relevant legal systems or the place of arbitration.

This, then, is the context in which it is important to bear in mind the relevance of the over 6,500 requests for arbitration that have been filed with the ICC since its founding. Namely, the present day ICC system has not been created out of whole cloth by theoreticians and then frozen in time. It is continually tested and retested by experience and shaped by those with immediate, real expertise in the field, practitioners and national courts as well. Over the years, elements that have been found to be lacking have been dropped and others modified or added as necessary.

The past 15 years have been ones of constant re-examination and change, including the major redrafting of the ICC Rules in 1975, the addition of the Internal Rules in 1980, the total revamping of the Secretariat (which will lead in 1990 to the completion of computerised systems for case-management and retrieval of ICC jurisprudence), modifications in the system of costs and payments in 1986 and the incorporation of various amendments into the Rules in 1988. To this must be added the valuable work charged to the ICC's Commission on International Arbitration on such subjects related to the ICC Arbitration rules as dissenting opinions and partial awards[2] the model arbitration clause, etc.

In sum, then, we see ICC arbitration as a dynamic, evolving system determined to maintain its place in the forefront of international arbitration by providing exceptional services to those who place their confidence in it. Its special features are ones which have proven their usefulness in the past and which, unless and until experience shows us otherwise, appear to be at least of equal importance for the future.

Overview of ICC arbitration

How can ICC arbitration best be characterised? In Paper 4 it is seen as "the restraints of the essentially negative, controlling functions of the institution and its simultaneous lack of substantive, constructive support." Lord Justice Mustill is quoted writing that "the importance of the [ICC Court] has, however, consisted more of what it has been prepared to offer than it is actually called upon to provide," and the view is expressed that the ICC "offers relatively little support to arbitration tribunals, either administratively or intellectually." Paper 4 concludes with the warning that

2 Dealt with by a working group chaired by Martin Hunter.

"the legacy of history is important, but adaptation to our own time, its accelerating pace of constant change and movement and rapid internationalization is of even greater urgency. In fact, it may be a condition for survival."

On the other hand, Paper 17 quotes the late Professor Schmitthof as stating that the ICC "is the most important institution for the arbitral settlement of international trade disputes. It is widely used and enjoys the confidence and respect of businessmen all over the world and is also frequently resorted to in East West Trade." And in presenting Paper 20 Sir Edward Everleigh expressed the view that "the record of the ICC in relation to arbitrations since 1923 has been such as to attract the greatest respect." The general attitude of speakers at the conference is reflected in the full paragraph from Lord Justice Mustill's article, which is as follows:

> "The aftermath of the First World War saw the rise of idealistic internationalism. This provided fertile soil for the growth of an international spirit in the field of commercial arbitration. Two features may be particularly mentioned. The first was the inauguration of the International Chamber of Commerce, with its associated Court of Arbitration. The number of disputes actually handled was and remains small, by comparison with the total of ad hoc arbitrations conducted throughout the world. The importance of the Institute has, however, consisted more of what it has been prepared to offer than it is actually called upon to provide. Participants in large commercial ventures can stipulate in their contracts arbitration under the auspices of the ICC hoping, in the great majority of cases correctly, that their relationships will not involve a fight, but knowing that if unhappily this should come to pass there will be a standing body of proven independence ready and able to furnish the structure for an orderly resolution of the dispute. Furthermore, the ICC has in recent years made strenuous efforts to the benefit of the international community in general, to ameliorate the tensions which could have been detected to exist between itself, with an intellectual foundation rooted in the mainland European concepts of arbitration, and the more pragmatic approach of the common lawyers. Recent concentration on practical issues, rather than debate on overworked theoretical questions, have created a climate in which the serious problems which face international commercial arbitration today can be faced in a truly ecumenical intellectual spirit."

What accounts for the different perceptions of ICC arbitration expressed in Paper 4? Most speakers stated views based on their experience. Paper 4, on the other hand, has a largely theoretical approach to ICC arbitration. This has led to errors of fact and perception, a tendency to give credence to "allegations" unsupported by evidence, a dismissal of "usefulness" as a proper criteria by which to judge procedures, and the assertion that arbitration is "not suitable for disputes or contracts which do not involve substantial sums of money" and that the only persons worthy of being arbitrators are those whose work habits are in no way influenced by monetary considerations. In short, Paper 4 ignores the age-old insight that "the best is the enemy of the good." It can, rather, be understood as an examination of ICC arbitration not in comparison with other arbitral institutions or in light of what the international business community has a right to expect of international arbitration, or taking into account what is realistically possible, but rather in comparison to a utopian arbitration system. Nonetheless, Paper 4 provides a useful agenda to comment on a number of points concerning ICC arbitration and the balance of this paper will do so.

The ICC International Court of Arbitration

As the world of international commerce has expanded and the appeal of international arbitration along with it, so has the ICC Court. In 1989 parties from 90 countries were involved in the requests for arbitration registered with the ICC. The Court now has members from virtually every economic, social and political system.

The ICC Court stands as a unique contribution to international arbitration. It meets once a month in plenary session and twice a month in committee. To every decision of the Court (including whether an arbitration cannot continue because of lack of prima facie agreement to arbitration, challenges of arbitrators, the scrutiny of draft awards, the place of arbitration, the number of arbitrators, the arbitrators' fees, etc.) the international composition of the Court brings to the parties involved (who are generally of different nationalities) an assurance of the neutrality, impartiality and independence of the decision-making body as well as an expertise unsurpassed by any other arbitral system.

The Court's present membership of 51 allows it to ensure that it will be possible to have the 48 members of the Court who must sit each year with the President or a Vice-President of the Court at the 24 Committee meetings of the Court held each year. These committees sessions were instituted in 1980 in order to meet the greatly increased caseload of the ICC.

The Court members have a heavy workload, but this has not prevented the Court from attracting members of world renown in legal and arbitration circles. For example, the two new Vice-Presidents named to the Court in June 1989 are Fali S Nariman of India and Toshio Sawada of Japan. The UK Court member is Martin Hunter, who provides an "insider's view" of the work of the Court at this conference.[3] No one familiar with the ICC Court would recognise this body from the description in Paper 4, which speaks essentially of its "unwieldy size" and the "limited attractiveness" of the post of Court member. These comments are not borne out by the facts. In the discussion of the ICC Court in Paper 4 certain essential questions are not addressed. For example, are the purposes and objectives of the ICC Court in question and if not, is there another arbitral institution that does a superior job of bringing international expertise to bear on international arbitration? Is there another arbitration system that has better adjusted to the "rapid internationalization" of international commerce and arbitration? The reader interested in such questions will have to look elsewhere, particularly to other papers presented at this conference.

The Secretariat of the Court

Composed of 25 persons (including nine lawyers) of eight different nationalities, the Secretariat assures the preparation of the Court session and is there

3 Paper 6.

to offer objective advice and assistance to parties, counsel and arbitrators at all times, before, during and after a case. The utility of the Secretariat can perhaps best be summed up by the following quote from a letter by an attorney in a completed case to the ICC Counsel in charge of the file:

> "The procedure, schedules and guidance provided by the ICC was exceptional throughout the proceeding. I want to thank you for your kind and helpful direction at various critical points in the proceeding. Although I hope my clients will not need to proceed to arbitration in the future, I certainly will recommend the ICC procedure to them if they are in need of it. Again, my thanks to you and everyone at the ICC who helped bring this dispute to a sensible conclusion."

It might be added that this was a case where a losing defendant in a case for tens of millions of dollars had failed to honour the award until, at the request of the claimant, I wrote to the defendant reminding it of the legal and moral obligations it undertook when it agreed to ICC arbitration. A few weeks subsequent to this letter, the matter was disposed of to the claimant's satisfaction. This result, I firmly believe, would not have been reached in an *ad hoc* arbitration because, as my letter to the defendant pointed out:

> "Even beyond the legal requirement incumbent upon the defendant, there is yet another reason why we urge you to honour the award. Namely, the ICC Court of Arbitration is an institution which is utilized by a variety of parties, including governments, public and private entities and individuals, coming from a wide range of countries. The same entities can be and often are involved in ICC arbitrations sometimes as claimants and sometimes as defendants. The party which has lost an ICC arbitration today may be a winning party in an ICC arbitration tomorrow. It would certainly not be in the interest of a party to act in a manner that could derogate from the integrity of ICC arbitration and thus possibly damage its ability to enforce an award in its favour which it might win in another arbitration."

I can think of no other international arbitral institution with a higher ratio of staff to cases or which has multilingual attorneys of five or more nationalities responsible for the administration of the cases submitted to it.

The work of the Secretariat can, of course, be improved, and the ICC is investing substantial time and money to do so. For example, over the past decade the size of the Secretariat has almost tripled. By the end of 1990 computerised systems for case-management and retrieval of ICC jurisprudence will be in place, a revised Handbook of Secretariat Procedures will be completed, etc. Turnover of Secretariat personnel will never be ended, but the ICC is doing its utmost to ensure that a well qualified staff has all possible means to fulfil with distinction its responsibilities.

The ICC Rules

The philosophy behind the ICC Rules is that they must strike an appropriate balance between, on the one hand, setting out with clarity the roles and powers of the parties, the institution and the arbitral tribunal and on the other hand allowing the parties and the arbitral tribunal sufficient flexibility to conduct arbitrations involving parties and arbitrators of different nationalities and legal systems of every imaginable sort, often mixed together in the same arbitration. We believe that, in general, the present rules accomplish this well. As the distinguished former ICC Secretary General Yves Derains has written:

> "It may be a paradox, but to state that all arbitrations conducted under the ICC Rules are similar would be as inaccurate as to state that they are all different. It is true that all ICC arbitrations are governed by the same rules and supervised by the same Court of Arbitration to which the terms of reference must be communicated. The Court scrutinizes all awards before notifying the parties. However, an ICC arbitration in London which follows the common law procedure, with discovery of documents and examination and cross-examination of witnesses by counsel, has very little in common with an ICC arbitration in Vienna, which follows civil law procedure, with no discovery of documents and possibly no witnesses at all."

The suppleness of the ICC Rules, which provide a structure while avoiding becoming a Procrustean bed, is carefully analysed in Paper 23, where it is stated: "one of the more significant features of the [ICC] Rules is their flexibility and adaptability"; and "the most important feature of the Rules which I identify is the facility which they provide for the swift and efficient resolution of a dispute". Paper 8 also notes that the Rules "are an amalgam of both civil and common law systems".

Thus, to argue as does Paper 4 that the rules contain "fundamental gaps and obscurities", and that because of their silence on various subjects "national procedural rules and practices" influence an arbitration more that do the ICC Rules, is to miss the essential point that the Rules are designed precisely to establish only a basic framework so that in each arbitration there can be established the procedural elements best suited to the particular mix of parties, arbitrators and issues at hand. How is this done?. The key is Article 11 of the ICC Rules which provides that:

> "The rules governing the proceedings before the arbitrator shall be those resulting from these Rules and, where these Rules are silent, any rules which the parties (or, failing them, the arbitrator) may settle, and whether or not reference is thereby made to a municipal procedural law to be applied to the arbitration."

A clear hierarchy is thus established whereby apart from matters covered by the ICC Rules themselves (such as Article 19 which permits the chairman alone to render a decision where there is no majority) the parties may agree upon the procedure and where they cannot do so the arbitrators may. Pursuant to Article 11, all of these procedural rules may be established independently of any municipal procedural law (except, obviously, for those rare instances where mandatory principles are contained in the relevant procedural law.) The scope of Article 11 is fully understood in Paper 9 as well as in Paper 19, which explains the freedom of local legal constraints intended by Article 11. The canvas on which those procedural elements desired by the parties/arbitrator are set down is, in general, the Terms of Reference.

Terms of Reference

Terms of Reference (TOR) must be viewed in the context of international commercial arbitration, which generally involves parties and arbitrators of several nationalities with differing legal training and background who are compelled to deal with inherently difficult subjects under legal systems with which they are not all equally familiar. Thus, while this feature of ICC arbitration often raises questions by those whose arbitration experience tends to be in the domestic sphere, we generally hear praise of the utility of Terms of Reference for a number of reasons which are set out in Paper 3.

Paper 4 refers to the TOR as a "relic" which should be "abolished", and states that:

> "The ICC Court still regards Terms of Reference as indispensable for the dual purpose of establishing bases for (i) fixing deposits in relation to stated monetary claims (this is denied by the Secretariat as being a rationale) and (ii) reviewing the award for compliance with the stipulations in the document concerning claims and issues to be decided."

In my view the author of Paper 4 was closer to the truth in 1985 when he wrote:

> "The reason why [TOR] have been kept is not the fact they may facilitate enforcement in some cases, nor even the need to affirmatively determine the amounts in dispute which are so important for purpose of fixing deposits and fees but primarily the desirability in many cases to bring order to an incoherent, incomplete and bewildering set of initial pleadings and allow the tribunal, preferably with the concurrence of both parties, to structure the subsequent proceedings in a rational manner. The necessity for the tribunal and the parties to meet for the purpose of drawing up the terms of reference also brings indirect benefits, not the least of which is an opportunity for the parties to seriously consider a settlement."[4]

It would be useful here to correct a misunderstanding sometimes encountered about amending Terms of Reference. It is sometimes said that TOR are too restrictive because claims incorporated into them cannot thereafter be amended. However, Article 16 of the ICC Rules makes it clear that the agreement of the parties is needed only for new claims or counterclaims which are not already within the limits fixed by the TOR. Thus, an increase or decrease in an amount already claimed does not require the agreement of the parties, nor does the addition of new "issues to be decided" so long as they relate to claims already contained in the TOR.

As to the abolition of TOR, my own view is that this would be a serious error given the many benefits of TOR. One could, of course, imagine a drafting of the relevant rules which would more clearly set out what TOR should contain and what their legal nature is. The Secretariat is preparing, as part of a Handbook for Arbitrators, several model TORs so as better to illustrate to arbitrators how to use TOR to their full advantage.

The confidential nature of certain ICC procedures and decisions

As with every other arbitral institution of which I am aware, the Court members of the ICC, who make the various decisions called for under the

4 Wetter, "The conduct of the arbitration", Jour Int Arb No. 2 (1985), 7 at 22.

Rules, do their utmost to avoid any confusion between their administrative role and the jurisdictional role of the arbitral tribunal, which decides the claims on their merits. While the ICC Rules and practice ensure that, on the various administrative decisions to be taken, the parties are accorded an opportunity to present their point of view, neither the parties nor their counsel ever appear in person to argue before the ICC Court. So too, as with virtually every other arbitral institution, the reasons for certain decisions of the ICC Court (especially those relating to the constitution of the arbitral tribunal, such as challenges) are not communicated to the parties. For reasons not clearly articulated, it is asserted in Paper 4 that this creates exasperation, fear and suspicion, insofar as the ICC Court is concerned.

It is difficult to understand why the ICC is singled out for these criticisms except that its vast caseload requires it to put into practice what other arbitration systems provide for in theory. For example, of all the other international arbitral systems that decide on challenges, I am not aware of a single one with rules calling for the communication of the reasons for such decisions. Indeed, when the London Court of International Arbitration totally revised its Rules in 1985 it apparently took as its model in this area the ICC Rules, incorporating almost verbatim the ICC's provisions about such decisions being administrative in nature and the reasons for the decision not being communicated. It should not be forgotten that the reasons for the challenge are set out in writing by the challenging party, and all concerned are accorded an opportunity to comment. The issues on which the ICC Court makes its decision are, therefore, well known.

The new Rules for the Court of Arbitration of the Stockholm Chamber of Commerce have an equivalent procedure to that of the ICC prima facie procedure which appears to work essentially in the same way as that of the ICC, namely, written submissions of the views of the parties are followed by a decision of the three member Board of the Arbitration Institute. The reasons for the ICC's policy in regard to challenges, apparently convincing to other arbitral institutions, include encouraging a frank and full communication from the members of the arbitral tribunal and discouraging litigation before national courts, while at the same time avoiding practices or procedures that would tend to make of the Court a "jurisdictional" body instead of the administrative body it is. National courts have repeatedly upheld the ICC's challenge procedure, including the refusal to communicate the reasons. No constructive suggestions for improvement of the challenge process in international commercial arbitration (including the ICC system) have been put forward.

Arbitrators' fees

The provisions of the ICC Rules relating to the fixing of arbitrators fees are similar to the comparable provision (Section 30) in the newly revised Rules of the Arbitration Institute of the Stockholm Chamber of Commerce, except that the Stockholm Rules do not explicitly take into account "the rapidity of the proceedings" as do the ICC Rules.

The fees are decided upon by the ICC Court, which consists of practising lawyers with experience as counsel and arbitrators, so that it can be said that the ICC rules are applied as intended That the ICC has been relatively successful in this endeavour is given support by Paper 8, the only other paper to deal with arbitrators' fees. Paper 8 states that:

> "*experience* shows that the fee payable by the ICC's to arbitrators are broadly reasonable. Certainly there are few people, to my knowledge who have declined to serve as an ICC arbitrator as a matter of principle because the fees are too low. Experience also shows that the costs of ad hoc arbitration can be at least as high as ICC arbitration (even including the ICC's administration fees)." (emphasis added)

Notwithstanding this general support which exists for the ICC fee system, the conclusions of the ICC Court's working group on arbitrator fees (not yet available) will be examined with care by the Court, which is fully cognizant of the importance of according fees that are fair and reasonable from the point of view of both arbitrators and parties alike.

Scrutiny of the draft award by the ICC Court

Scrutiny of the draft award by the ICC Court is criticised by Paper 4. Strangely enough, in all those decades, except for a Turkish judgment some 12 years ago, now essentially reversed[5] and a case reported in the Syrian Administrative Courts, national courts seem not to have been aware of, let alone convinced, of this alleged deficiency in the ICC Rules and have, conversely, given support to ICC awards in numerous decisions, several of which have directly addressed the point. Paper 20 on "The attitude of the English courts to ICC arbitration" deals with this subject and quotes extensively from the decision which most closely touches on the scrutiny of awards, namely *Bank Mellat* v. *GAA Development*.[6]

Paper 4 contains a brief quote from this decision, but the main discussion on the point at issue is not included. It would be worthwhile repeating part of the omitted passages:

> "The supervision function which is germane to the issues in the present case is the [ICC] court's power of scrutiny of awards before they are published. That power exists because the ICC system, the most truly international of all arbitral systems, provides for the conduct of arbitrations in most countries of the world, and the members of a three man tribunal frequently come from different continents, or at least from different countries, with fundamentally different legal systems. It is regarded as the first imperative of the ICC system that awards rendered under it should be enforceable. It has been pointed out that something like 90 per cent of ICC awards are voluntarily complied with and that ICC award have a good record of enforcement in National Courts... . The system of scrutiny of awards by the *Court contributes to the enforceability of ICC awards.*" (emphasis added.)

Comments in a similar vein have recently been made by the highest jurisdiction in New Zealand, the Court of Appeals, in a case involving what

5 See Tekinay, "The Turkish situation in the field of international commercial arbitration", *International Business Law Journal* (1989), No. 2.
6 [1988] 2 Lloyd's Rep. 44.

was said to be the largest ever construction project in that country.[7] By a unanimous decision the Court sustained the finality of an ICC Arbitral Award, citing the *Bank Mellat* case with approval. Judge Barker, in his concurring opinion referred to the importance of the existence of "well-respected and established international arbitration regimes, such as ICC . . .". Judge McMullin noted that "the whole process of arbitration under ICC Rules is one which imposes its own safeguards against erroneous awards by the adoption of processes whereby the appointment of the arbitrator and any award which he makes is subject to supervision."

Paper 6 addresses ICC arbitration from the point of view of a Court member. I shall, therefore, discuss only two other elements related to the Court itself and to scrutiny of the draft award. First, the opinion is sometimes voiced that if the ICC would take care to appoint only good arbitrators there would be no need to scrutinise the award. However, experience shows that in a complex international commercial arbitration involving parties from more than one country, the chairman or sole arbitrator is often not a national of the state whose substantive law is applicable to the dispute. This is so either because the determination of the applicable national law is made by the arbitral tribunal itself (this decision should not and cannot be prejudged by the ICC Court when selecting the chairman or sole arbitrator) or because the requirement of a "neutral" chairman precludes a national of the state whose substantive law is applicable. Similarly, an arbitrator selected for his expertise in the applicable substantive law may not be fully knowledgeable about mandatory provisions of procedural law of the state of the situs of the arbitration. There will, therefore, always be occasions when scrutiny of the award is appropriate, irrespective of the experience or quality of the tribunal. Even Homer has been known to nod, but not to acknowledge the fact.

Scrutiny of the draft award is also important because the autonomy accorded the parties in an ICC arbitration means that the sole arbitrator or chairman is often selected by the parties themselves or, as the case may be, by the co-arbitrators. During 1989 this occurred in nearly 30% of the cases before the ICC Court. In such instances, it is not for the ICC Court to decide for itself that a person selected by the parties or the arbitrators does not have the requisite expertise for the job. It should not be forgotten in this regard that in virtually all arbitral tribunals composed of three persons it is the parties which have proposed the majority of the tribunal.

Conclusions

The papers submitted at this conference demonstrate that ICC arbitration is a system fully capable of meeting and overcoming the increasingly complex and difficult issues inherent in today's international commercial arbitration.

This is not to say that the ICC system is complacent or that improvements are not sought. Both the ICC Court and its Secretariat are continually seeking and putting into effect ameliorations to the Rules, procedures and

7 *CB/New Zealand Ltd.* v. *Badger BV and Chiyoda Chemical Co. Ltd.* (CA 185/88).

work methods. The broad appeal of ICC arbitration to parties from so many countries and the outstanding record of compliance with ICC awards both voluntarily and, when necessary, through the support of national courts is concrete evidence of the continuing adaptability and acceptability of ICC arbitration. The continuing support of the ICC is shown by the fact that some 81% of the cases brought before the ICC in 1989 related to contracts concluded in 1980 or thereafter and 47 of the cases relate to contracts concluded from 1985 or thereafter.

Constructive criticism is not only accepted but encouraged by the ICC. However, it is always necessary to endeavour to strike a balance between the successes and the perceived problems of ICC arbitration in the context of international arbitration as a whole. It must also recognise that international arbitration, an institution called into being in order to meet the needs of international commerce and investment, cannot fail to be less pragmatic and realistic than international commerce itself lest it becomes completely irrelevant. The ICC stands ready, as Lord Justice Mustill observed,[8] to concentrate "on practical issues rather than debates on overworked theoretical questions" and thus to build for the future.

8 See ante p. 81.

Part III

Features of ICC and international arbitration

Particular features of the ICC Rules of Arbitration 8

Humphrey LLoyd

Synopsis

This paper reviews the procedures involved in an ICC arbitration with particular emphasis on the ICC Rules relating to appointment of arbitrators and what in the English system are called "the Pleadings". The matters which should be covered in the Terms of Reference are set out in some detail and useful practical hints are given.

Introduction

This short paper is intended to highlight particular aspects of the ICC Rules of Arbitration[1]. It is worth emphasising that the ICC Rules of Arbitration are concerned with all types of commercial arbitration from the simple to the complex. A construction arbitration can be at times quite complex and is certainly representative of a species of arbitrations arising out of complex and long-term contracts, but is not *sui generis*.

Construction arbitrations occupy only about a quarter (by number) of those that are commenced annually at the ICC, but they provide more than that amount towards the costs of the ICC.

Some years ago an attempt was made to devise a set of rules for construction arbitrations. The working party was pleased with the result but the Commission on International Arbitration felt that it would depart too much from the philosophy, as it was understood, of ICC arbitration for such rules to be adopted even though special rules for maritime arbitrations had been adopted (upon which these draft rules had been modelled). Part of the disquiet also related to my first topic, namely, who would be the arbitrators. There was, and still is, a feeling that construction arbitrations call for arbitrators of the same background and calibre as other complex commercial arbitrations.

1 See Part VI – Appendices.

Appointment of arbitrators

Contrary to popular belief, the arbitrator or arbitrators in an ICC arbitration are appointed by the Court of Arbitration. I shall assume in my discussion that the tribunal comprises three people. Construction arbitrations under ICC Rules are sometimes conducted by a sole arbitrator but this is relatively uncommon. It has, however, much to commend it, not least in the saving of time and money. Parties cannot be blamed for not wishing to agree on a sole arbitrator in an arbitration agreement which is to refer future disputes to arbitration: who knows that the dispute will be in the circumstances in which it comes to be arbitrated. Nevertheless, the parties might perhaps reconsider the position more frequently rather than as a gut reaction, assuming that three arbitrators will be appointed. If the tribunal appointed is one of three obviously independent people then history shows that it is unlikely that the chairman will be a dissentient (although it has happened) and serious consideration ought to be given to inviting the two arbitrators originally nominated by the parties to step down and for the arbitration to proceed with the chairman as sole arbitrator.

The International Court of Arbitration of the ICC requires a high standard of impartiality in its arbitrators. The declarations require to be made by arbitrators that have been strengthened. An arbitrator is now required to declare either:

> "I am independent of the parties and intend to remain so: to the best of my knowledge, there are no facts and circumstances, past and present, that might be of such a nature as to call into question my independence in the eyes of the parties."

or

> "I am independent of the parties and intend to remain so: however . . . in consideration of Article 2, paragraph 7 of the Rules of Arbitration I wish to call your attention to the following facts or circumstances which might be of such a nature as to call into question my independence in the eyes of the parties . . .".

Arbitrators are required to resolve any doubt in favour of disclosure. They are also required to disclose to the court and to the parties any facts or circumstances which might arise between their appointment or confirmation by the court and notification of the Final Award could call into question the arbitrator's independence.

Having said that, arbitrators tend to be put forward by the parties as those likely to show understanding about the parties' case and, consistent with impartiality, to be sympathetic to it. In practice one expects an arbitrator nominated by the parties to see that his co-arbitrators are aware of that party's case, but to fall far short of being an advocate of the party or in any way of prejudicing his independence of mind and decision. Arbitrators nominated by parties regularly rule against the party who nominated them. It is not unknown for an arbitrator nominated by a party to write a dissenting award against the interests of that party, notwithstanding that his co-arbitrators are in favour of that party!

This is not the place to go into the question of degrees of impartiality. However, it should be noted that parties advised by American lawyers tend to be hypersensitive about issues of impartiality.

Who should be nominated?

The Court of Arbitration will only appoint as chairman an arbitrator who already has experience of ICC arbitrations. The same rule ought to be followed in the majority of cases by a party putting forward an arbitrator for confirmation by the Court. At the outset of an ICC arbitration, a party must be aware that he is, as it were, entering a different world from a domestic or national arbitration in which a different language is spoken, possibly both literally as well as figuratively. The ICC Rules are an amalgam of both civil and common law systems. Although the differences between the two systems are now perhaps less marked and although in many cases the differences are ones of means rather than ends, they can be most pronounced at the outset of an arbitration. For example, it is virtually unheard of in the civil law systems for an arbitrator to be other than a person who has legal qualifications and is almost certainly likely to be a lawyer in practice – but perhaps not in private practice. He might be a company lawyer or an industrialist.

This must be taken into account by a claimant in selecting an arbitrator. A person who puts forward a non-lawyer as an arbitrator is frequently at a disadvantage (unless the dispute is so highly technical that the co-arbitrators are going to eat out of that arbitrator's hand). In the majority of cases no confident view can be taken about what the real issues in the case are likely to be as opposed to those perceived initially. For this reason a party should think very hard before selecting a person other than a practising lawyer as an arbitrator in an ICC arbitration. If the arbitration does require matters of technical expertise then there is power to appoint an expert. A list is maintained by the ICC in Paris of arbitrators put forward by FIDIC and various national bodies. This is not always as up to date as it should be and in the case of this country contains some remarkable omissions. It should be treated very carefully. It does, however, have the advantage of setting out the age of some prospective arbitrators - not an unimportant consideration!

How is an arbitrator appointed?

A party should obviously first approach his prospective appointee to see whether he is willing to be an arbitrator. There is no use nominating somebody who will decline the appointment. That person will almost certainly require to know about the amount at stake and the likely duration of the dispute since the fees payable by the ICC may be insufficient for some arbitrators. In this connection it is perhaps worth mentioning that such experience as there is shows that the fees payable by the ICC's two arbitrators are broadly reasonable. Certainly there are few people, to my knowledge, who have declined to serve as an ICC arbitrator as a matter of principle because the fees are too low.

Experience also shows that the costs of *ad hoc* arbitration can be at least as high as ICC arbitration (even including the ICC's administration fees). There is also an "open-endedness" about many ad hoc or other administrative arbitrations *e.g.* under the UNCITRAL rules where the arbitrators may maintain constant demands for increasing deposits (on account of their fees and expenses). The ICC is conscious that its system is criticised for being expensive and there is reluctance to increase the amount of the deposits unless it is warranted.

The arbitrators do not, however, take charge until the file is sent to them. That does not take place until the pleadings are closed and the deposits paid or guarantees set up.

Pleadings

The Statement of Case should not be like an English Statement of Claim. A party should present it as if it was his last opportunity to set out his case in full – unlikely but nevertheless it will lead to a clear and vocal presentation of the case. It should deal with all known and tenable defences to the claim. It need not annexe all supporting documents – in the case of construction arbitrations it is probably quite undesirable to do so. It must, however, annexe the contract and the principal documents relied on *e.g.* the relevant instructions and notices required by the contract.

If the claim is based upon a contract incorporating the FIDIC Conditions and if Clause 67 of the FIDIC Conditions is applicable then the Statement of Case must show that the procedure set out in Clause 67 has been followed, *viz.* that the Engineer has been requested to make a decision on the claim or claims being presented in the arbitration; that he has either decided adversely or has failed to decide; and that the party is within the relevant time limits. Note that in relation to FIDIC Conditions 2 and 3 there is a difference of opinion as to what constitutes an effective commencement of the arbitration. To be on the safe side one ought to file the request for arbitration within the 90-day period. Do not forget that under the ICC Rules the arbitrators decide such matters of jurisdiction: see Article 8.

Unless the dispute is to be referred to a sole arbitrator the Court of Arbitration needs to know whether a party agrees on three arbitrators, and if so, the name of the arbitrator to be appointed at an early date. A defendant's answer should deal with this part of the Request for Arbitration and ask for more time to deliver the substantive defence. The Court of Arbitration is relatively generous in relation to extensions of time, at least until the arbitrators are appointed after which the matter lies within their jurisdiction. Similarly, arbitrators are generous, providing that the substantive defence is known by the date of the terms of reference or, if issue has been taken as to jurisdiction, then that point is clearly established. The arbitrators may well not require a pleading on the merits to be filed until their jurisdiction over the claim or the admissibility of the claim has been determined.

The Answer should deal fully with all the defences to the claim and set out any counterclaim.

Similarly a Counterclaim should be presented as if it were a claim (which of course it is and like defences has to be summarised in the Terms of Reference – see Article 13.1(c). Article 5.2 permits a Reply to the Counterclaim which is a defence.

There is no provision for a reply to the answer or for a rejoinder and the Tribunal's permission will (in the absence of agreement) need to be obtained for this or for any other pleading. Practice in ICC arbitrations (and in certain instances the mandatory law) requires equality so that if a reply is permitted to the defence, a defendant should be able to serve a further pleading. Frequently these pleadings are best replaced by written submissions unless required to raise claims (see above).

Amendments must not be assumed to be permissible; see Article 16. Hence it is desirable to draw up wide Terms of Reference since Article 16 requires the agreement of the parties (and the Tribunal). Requests for particulars and discovery are all best dealt with in the Terms of Reference. It is usually not worthwhile attempting to write in provisions of a White Book[2] nature as the effective sanctions available tend to be few.

Terms of Reference

These notes cannot, in the nature of things, be exhaustive and it is hoped that they will provide the basis for discussion. In approaching this topic I have made certain assumptions.

First it is assumed that in principle the necessary preliminaries to the drafting of the Terms of Reference have taken place (*e.g.* the parties have set out their respective cases in written form by way of statement of case and defence, the arbitral tribunal has been constituted, and that there is no challenge to the arbitral tribunal – although its jurisdiction may be in question). The Terms of Reference have to be drawn up on the basis of the documents and in the light of the parties most recent submissions (whatever that means).

Secondly, the question of drafting is approached on the assumptions that the Terms of Reference are required to fulfil the following practical purposes:

1. to establish the actual mission of the arbitral tribunal as a result of ascertaining the likely true issues;
2. to establish which of these issues may be regarded as fundamental or of a preliminary nature, *e.g.*:
   (a) those which call into question the existence or extent of the arbitrators' jurisdiction to determine a particular claim or defence;
   (b) those which it is sensible from the point of view of time and money to determine before other issues.

It must not be forgotten that the Court of Arbitration may scrutinise any award submitted to it for approval to see whether the award resolves the issues described in the Terms of Reference. It naturally follows that for the purpose of enforcement it is essential for the party who considers that it will obtain a benefit from the award to make certain that nothing occurs when the Terms of Reference are drawn up which could have the effect of prejudicing enforcement of the subsequent award.

2 *The Supreme Court Practice 1988* (Sweet & Maxwell and Stevens & Sons).

The Terms of Reference should not be a long or elaborate document. They should be drafted with clarity and brevity. It is good practice to circulate them to the parties for comment before a final draft is presented.

I shall approach the question of drafting the Terms of Reference having regard to each of the sub-paragraphs in Article 13. It is also now customary and good practice to follow the same order in the Terms of Reference.

A. Names of the parties

As a preliminary, it is essential not to forget to put the country of the parties in the heading of the proceedings. Otherwise the ICC are liable to return the Terms of Reference or the award for the information to be provided.

The full names of the parties are required. This is clearly of importance where the parties are individuals but it may well be of considerable interest to ascertain the precise nature of a corporate or state body or joint venture so that it is properly described. This may require, on occasion, investigation of the contract to see who was the true contracting party. In one recent case the first issue which the arbitrators had to decide was the effect of documents which included an invitation to tender issued by:

> "the Government of the . . . Republic, through the National . . . Authority . . ." resulting in a contract which began: "This Agreement is made the day of 19 . . . between the Government of the . . . Republic represented by the Director General of the National . . . Authority (hereinafter called "the Purchaser") of the one part and . . . Limited (hereinafter called "the Contractor") of the other part".

Getting the name wrong, like having the wrong party, may lead to the award being unenforceable.

The description tends to be forgotten (in French *qualités* – a narrower term) but may be important: does the claimant actually or legally exist?

If a party claims that the tribunal has no jurisdiction it should be made clear in this section that the inclusion of the name of a party is without prejudice to that party's contentions.

B. Addresses

Note that these are not necessarily the addresses of the parties but the addresses "to which notifications or communciations arising in the course of the arbitration may validly be made". However, it is good practice to include the true residence or seat of a party as well as the address for the purposes of Article 13.1(b).

It is essential but not always remembered that the address should be full and should be accompanied by the numbers of the relevant telephone, telex and fax/telecopier.

Furthermore, it is good practice to identify by name the individual who has responsibility for handling the communication.

It is now quite customary to name under this section the party's legal representative also and to designate that party as the person who has authority to give and receive notifications or communications. But is that authority exclusive? The municipal law may prevent delegation to a lawyer; see below.

Some Terms of Reference also go further and make provision for what is to happen if the nominated representative of the party ceases to have that party's authority. This should only be done if requested by a party as it adds complications to the Terms of Reference.

If both the party and a representative are named in this section then it should be made clear to which of the two a notification or communication, if sent, will be deemed to have been validly made. For this reason, it is not necessary to provide for copies of notifications or communciations to be sent (unless of course both parties so require it).

C. Summary of the parties' respective claims

It is here desirable to refer back to the beginning of Article 13.1 to emphasise that the Terms of Reference are to be drawn up "in the light of [the parties] most recent submissions", *i.e.* what the parties have last said. What the parties first said may therefore need to be revised or restated in the light of what the other party said or in the light of second (and possibly better) thoughts. Parties should be discouraged from taking the opportunity to re-argue their case in the Terms of Reference in the belief that they will influence the tribunal. "Claims" here include the principal assertions by way of defence.

It must not be forgotten that the inclusion of the party's claim in the Terms of Reference does not mean that the other party accepts them. This is made clear in Section 4.9 (p.41) of the ICC *Guide to Arbitration* but is sometimes overlooked, and sometimes may need to be expressly declared.

For this reason it is sometimes desirable to allow or request the parties to draw up a description of their own claims. This may be done where the tribunal can rely on the parties (or their legal representatives) to do so in accordance with the spirit of Art. 13.1(c). The danger in this course lies in the fact that it thereafter becomes difficult for the tribunal to edit the claims to remove unnecessary material and otherwise to produce a summary. On the other hand there is more likely to be agreement about this section if a party does not challenge a description of its claim.

However, Article 13.1(c) does require the claims to be summarised, but they must state amounts then claimed by the parties.

Amounts claimed by way of "interest, loss of profit, loss of goodwill, damages for amounts, expenses, taxes and legal expenses", should be included, all of which arbitrators and the ICC Court of Arbitration should know the financial extent (and thus measure the gravity) of each party's claims.

D. Definition of the issue

This is generally considered to be the most delicate section. The manner in which it is drafted may be used to obtain the attitude of the Tribunal to the disposition of the case.

First, it is highly desirable, as already stated, that all fundamental or preliminary issues be clearly identified and prominently and clearly set out. Secondly, any issues the determination of which is likely to lead to other issues not being effective ought also to be identified at this stage.

On the other hand it is not necessary to provide an exhaustive catalogue of all issues (or sub-issues) that may conceivably arise on the parties' claims as they are presently framed. If it is clear that there are no fundamental or preliminary issues it may be quite adequate to provide a brief summary of the major areas of inquiry.

Incorporation of the pleadings:

Where the issues are set out in broad terms it is sometimes desirable to state quite clearly that the true issues are those which arise from the pleadings including any amendments that may be made with the permission of the Tribunal. This enables a degree of flexibility to be introduced and serves as a reminder to the parties that the issues which the arbitrators will actually determine will not necessarily be those defined at the initial meeting resulting in the Terms of Reference but may well be ones which emerge as a result of further investigations of the facts (by the arbitrators under Art. 14.1), as a result of the appointment of experts (under Art. 14.2), as a result of hearings on preliminary or fundamental issues, or as a result of further information becoming available both on a voluntary or involuntary basis.

E. The arbitrator/s full name/s, description/s and addresses

Curiously, one would have thought that this section would have come earlier in the list in Article 13.1. Ideally it ought to be close to the addresses of the parties so as to provide a "directory".

It is not clear why a description of an arbitrator should be provided: it is however customary to state whether an arbitrator has been nominated by a party.

Obviously the addresses, telephone, telex and fax/telecopier information should be fully set out so as to avoid the possibility of communications going astray.

In those cases where the tribunal has been constrained to appoint a secretary the position of that person should be defined in this section. In the writer's view a secretary is unnecessary and can lead to the parties having doubts as to whether there is not a second (or fourth) arbitrator.

F. The place of arbitration

This will be either the place agreed by the parties (perhaps in the contract) or the place fixed by the Court under Article 12. It does not of course follow that hearings have to be held at the place of arbitration. The contract or the parties' agreement may deal with this expressly or by implication but the designation of the place of arbitration by the Court carries no such implication. Every arbitration has to have a seat and the award must be valid in accordance with the law of the seat of the arbitration. That law may, for example, require arbitrations to be held at the place in order to be valid or for the arbitrators to meet at that place in order for the award to be valid or for at least an award to be signed at that place to ensure its validity.

G. Procedural rules

Although not essential it is desirable here to state whether or not the tribunal has power to act as an amiable compositeur.

This section can cause great difficulty since its existence can be used as an opportunity by warring parties to have a battle about the procedure to be adopted. If the parties agree a procedure acceptable to the Tribunal (or vice versa) then of course that procedure should be recorded in this section. In the nature of things a procedure can never be exhaustive and is likely only to set out some rudimentary elements.

However, a popular and adequate formula generally adopted is to leave the procedure to the arbitrators. This is commended as a means of avoiding argument. It has also the advantage, amongst other things, of "de-nationalising" an arbitration to the maximum extent permissible and this gives the tribunal maximum flexibility. Precisely how the tribunal will exercise its power will be a matter for it to determine once the Terms of Reference have been signed and it is free to proceed to hear the claims in respect of which deposits have been paid pursuant to Article 9.4. It is of course customary to give such directions in anticipation of approval under Article 9.4.

On the other hand certain matters of procedure could usefully be determined at this stage, *e.g.* the language in which the proceedings will be held, whether translations are to take place, whether there is to be a written official record short-hand/steno note of the proceedings. (The latter would only normally be required if requested by the parties and at their own expense.)

In general, very careful consideration should be given to incorporating more than outline or general procedural rules in the Terms of Reference. For example, to set out the procedure that is to be followed in the next few months, even if it is agreed, may only be suitable for the most simple case and ought in any event to be contained in a separate procedural direction. In cases of any complexity it is generally better to leave it to the tribunal to determine what procedure should be followed in the light of its selection of the principal issues.

H. Other particulars

The contents of this section will be completed with two purposes in mind: first, whether particulars are required to make the arbitral award enforceable; secondly, and probably in practice more frequently, those particulars that might be regarded as "helpful" by the Court of Arbitration or the arbitrator. (The reference to the Court of Arbitration" is not wholly clear.)

Those particulars which fall into the first category will be ones which almost certainly will arise as a result of specific local requirements.

Particulars that should be regarded as helpful may be categorised as follows:

Applicable law: If there is agreement as to the applicable law it is desirable to record it in the Terms of Reference. If there is no agreement or only partial agreement then the extent of the disagreement ought also to be recorded although this almost certainly will have appeared earlier in the summary of the claims and the definition of the issues.

Language: If the language of the arbitration has not already been dealt with, it should be set out here.

Arbitrators' powers: It is certainly desirable that if the arbitrators are to have specific powers, as agreed by the parties, they should be set out here. It is also useful to give the chairman of a tribunal of three people power to decide interlocutory questions either of his own or in conjunction with another member of the tribunal, in cases of urgency and where neither party nor any arbitrator requires that the matter should be decided by the tribunal as a whole.

This is particularly desirable where the three arbitrators live in different places and it is likely that the interlocutory or procedural matters may have to be dealt with after a hearing. Nevertheless, it also has value where the submissions are made in writing.

Time limits: It is desirable to record that time limits are to be treated as having been observed if the chairman receives a letter or notice. Requests for extension of time ought also to be dealt with: normally time will only be extended if the chairman receives an application before the relevant time limit has expired.

Validity of appointment: It is sometimes desirable to record that the parties agree that the tribunal has been validly appointed; this need not go as far as requring the parties to waive their rights of challenge under Article 2.7 or their rights under Article 2.8.

Interim or partial award: Sometimes there is doubt as to whether the Tribunal has power to make an interim or partial award as the ICC Rules do not make this crystal clear. This should be recorded here.

Administrative matters: It is desirable also to record if a party has taken responsibility for arranging a venue or other administrative matters; it is also desirable to record the procedure for the exchange of further pleadings, written submissions, witness statements, etc.

Awards

For the money paid the ICC system confers two substantial advantages:

an experienced administration;
scrutiny of the award which is in turn likely to lead to an enforceable award (although this cannot always be guaranteed).

It is, therefore, one of the features of the ICC system that the arbitrator's award has no effect until it has been scrutinised, approved and published by the Court of Arbitration. Delays occur at this stage but they can frequently be overcome by arbitrators submitting their award in draft at the Secretariat, taking into account any observations of the Secretariat and then submitting for approval an award signed by all parties but with the date left blank. In this way if the award is approved by the Court of Arbitration it will be dated by the Secretariat and issued at once: this can save up to three weeks delay for otherwise the award will have to be circulated amongst all the arbitrators before it is issued. This course cannot always be followed.

An award is scrutinised in two ways: first the Counsel in charge of the case or some other member of the Secretariat will examine the award to see whether there are any mistakes or other matters which should be corrected or brought to the attention of the Court of Arbitration. Secondly, a member of the Court of Arbitration will scrutinise the award as well. Although the deliberations of the court are confidential and secret we may assume that the Court of Arbitration would be concerned about the following matters:

Does the award deal with all the issues set out in the Terms of Reference?

Does it state the tribunal's decision on those issues? Here the dispositive part of the award should be checked against the reasoning so as to ensure that all matters which are required to be decided are declared to be decided.

Does it give reasons for all these decisions? The manner in which and the extent to which reasons are given will vary from arbitration to arbitration. Reasons may be required to ensure that an award is enforceable. Reasons may be required also to demonstrate that the procedure which was followed is one which is not contrary to the parties' agreement or to rules of public policy. Above all reasons are required so as to demonstrate to the parties (in particular a party against whom a decision is being made) that all the issues have been considered by the tribunal and that the parties, whether satisfied or not, should have confidence in the decision and indeed in the ICC system.

Conclusion

ICC arbitration contains a number of features peculiar to itself alone, not least the process of scrutiny referred to in the last section of this paper and also (*inter alia*) in Paper 4 where the point is made that the scrutiny processes are not sufficiently thorough or efficient.

The other processes described are largely derived from the civil law systems and therefore foreign to common lawyers although the device of the Terms of Reference may well be thought advantageous rather than the contrary.

9 Powers and Jurisdiction of the Arbitral Tribunal

Paul Darling and Vivian Ramsey

Synopsis

In this paper the authors have examined two of the more problematic aspects of modern commercial arbitration, the problem of procedure and the interpretation of the agreement to arbitrate, and the problems caused by multi-party arbitration. Case studies of the latter are given and the attitude of the ICC in particular is examined.

Introduction

Arbitration under the ICC Rules usually derives from an arbitration clause contained in the underlying contract. That contract may provide limits to the right to arbitration, either in terms of time limits or by way of conditions precedent to the right to arbitration.

Although the jurisdiction and powers of the Arbitral Tribunal derive from the underlying contract incorporating the ICC Rules, the Terms of Reference define the jurisdiction and powers of the arbitrators.

Extent of the arbitrators' power and jurisdiction

This needs to be considered in two stages. The first stage is to review the powers and jurisdiction that are expressly provided for under the agreement to arbitrate in the underlying contract. The second stage is then to consider the powers and jurisdiction under the Terms of Reference, to see the extent to which these have added to or limited the powers or jurisdiction under the agreement to arbitrate.

Agreement to arbitrate

An example of an agreement to arbitrate under the ICC Rules is given in Condition 67 of the FIDIC Standard Forms (Second Edition). That Clause makes provision for an initial reference to the Engineer followed by arbitration. In summary:

> disputes or differences are first referred to and settled by the Engineer;
> time limits are set down for such steps as the Engineer's decision, for the time within which claims to arbitration are to be communicated and for the time within which matters are to be referred to arbitration;
> all disputes or differences in respect of which the decision of the Engineer has not become final and binding are finally settled under the Rules of Conciliation and Arbitration of the ICC Rules.

The jurisdiction of the arbitrator depends, therefore, upon proper initial references to the Engineer and then upon the final reference to arbitration in compliance with time limits for disputes and differences where the decision of the Engineer has not become final and binding.

The powers of the Arbitral Tribunal derive from the ICC Rules. These are supplemented or limited by the provisions of Condition 67. That condition, for instance, gives full power to open up, review or revise any decision, opinion, direction, certificate or valuation of the Engineer. On the other hand, it limits the Tribunal from entering on the reference until after completion of the Works and as set out above, limits references which have not strictly complied with the initial dispute process.

Terms of Reference

The Terms of Reference in an ICC Arbitration forms a useful formal definition of jurisdiction drawn up by the parties and the arbitrator (or arbitrators) and signed by the parties.

Under Article 13 (1) (d) and (g) of the ICC Rules, the Terms of Reference expressly has to include both a definition of the issues to be determined and particulars of the applicable procedural rules.

In this way, the Arbitral Tribunal's jurisdiction is generally defined by the Terms of Reference, subject to several important points.

The first is the question of whether the Tribunal has jurisdiction at all. Under Article 8(3) of the ICC Rules, if one of the parties raises a plea concerning the existence or validity of the agreement to arbitrate, then the matter proceeds in two stages. Initially, the ICC Court has to be satisfied of the *prima facie* existence of the arbitration agreement. If so, then it decides that the arbitration shall proceed.

At that second stage, a decision as to the Arbitrator's jurisdiction is taken by the Arbitral Tribunal itself. Where this occurs, it is suggested that the Arbitral Tribunal can adopt several different procedures. One possibility would be for it to determine the jurisdiction at the Terms of Reference meeting prior to drawing up Terms of Reference. This seems to be difficult given the importance of the Terms of Reference in giving the Arbitral Tribunal power to proceed (subject to costs payment). However, it can be argued that if the Tribunal does not have jurisdiction it should not draw up Terms of Reference.

A second way of proceeding, which again is not usually adopted, is to draw up Terms of Reference limited to determining the question of jurisdiction.

The difficulty is that this assumes that a second, or "contingent", Terms of Reference can be drawn up.

The final possibility, and the one most usually adopted is to include the question of jurisdiction as one of the issues to be determined in the full Terms of Reference. The Tribunal can then proceed by way of a partial or final award to determine the issue of jurisdiction.

Whatever the Tribunal decides as to its jurisdiction under Article 8 (3), a party will, subject to any agreement expressly or impliedly to accept that decision, still retain a challenge to an award if, contrary to its contentions, the Tribunal determines that it does have jurisdiction.

If a point of jurisdiction is available to a party but is not taken in the Terms of Reference then that party may be taken to have waived its right of objection. This is particularly so where that party has signed the Terms of Reference rather than deciding to refuse to sign and thereby bringing in the default procedure of Article 13 (2) of the ICC Rules.

The second point raises the question of the extent to which the claims of either party can alter after the Terms of Reference. Under Article 16 of the ICC Rules, the parties may make new claims or counterclaims before the Arbitrator on condition that these remain "within the limits fixed by the Terms of Reference" or are specified in a rider to that document. This gives an express ability to "make new claims". It is often done by amending the Request for Arbitration or Answer to the Request. The potential amendment can raise a challenge and the Tribunal then has to determine the limits fixed by the Terms of Reference. It is open to the parties to incorporate their own provision in the Terms of Reference giving some other express right. This can, however, cause problems in the relationship of such a provision to Article 16.

The powers of the Arbitral Tribunal contained in the Terms of Reference are thus of major importance. Besides the normal directions there are three matters that can be and should be dealt within the Terms of Reference:

- Whether or not the Tribunal is given the role of an amiable compositeur (see Arts. 13 (1) (g) and 13 (4)): the parties may wish to adopt a particular process for conciliation, and it is suggested that the role of the Tribunal should be fully defined and distinguished from that of Arbitrator.
- Whether or not the Tribunal has the power to make interim or partial awards. In the absence of an express power, it is arguable that the Tribunal has such power. The argument centres upon the requirement for "the Award" and the distinction between "partial" and "definitive" awards apparent in Article 21.
- Whether or not the parties may amend, substitute or add new claims in excess of the powers in Article 16 as dealt with above.

Generally under Article 11 of the ICC Rules, the rules governing the proceedings are those resulting from the ICC Rules and, where these Rules are silent, "any rules which the parties (or, failing them, the Arbitrator) may settle". There is therefore a wide ability for the Arbitral Tribunal to add new powers or rules governing the proceedings. The difficulty is evidently to detract from such powers.

Problems of multi-party disputes

As with so many arbitration provisions there is currently no express provision in the ICC Rules to indicate that they contemplate multi-party disputes.

Disputes between more than one party can arise in several ways although generally there are the following ways by which more than one party may become involved.

First, two or more parties may contract with another party. This is common where there is a joint venture party. Provided that the joint venture parties pursue a common cause and appoint one party to represent the joint venture then no problem arises and the dispute can be dealt with in the usual way.

Secondly, a party may have a dispute with two or more parties, each of which has an independent agreement incorporating an ICC Arbitration Clause. This may occur where, for instance, an Employer has a main contract with one party and a guarantee with another or where a contractor has a main contract and a sub-contract. In such cases problems arise in the following ways:

- Where by agreement or under Article 2 (5) there are three Arbitrators, Article 4 (1) provides that each party can chose an Arbitrator and one can either be appointed by the Court or agreed by the parties under Article 2 (4). If there are more than two parties and they do not agree on an Arbitrator the rules break down.
- There is no provision for cross claims between Defendants or Claimants.
- There is no provision for different rules or powers to apply to different parties in the combined arbitration.
- The place or law or language of the arbitrations may vary.

Thirdly, a party may have a dispute with two or more parties but have an agreement incorporating an ICC Arbitration Clause with some, but not all, of these parties. It cannot bring the dispute outside the ICC Arbitration Clause within the procedure and this can lead to a case proceeding both in the courts and in an ICC arbitration. This can result in inconsistent findings.

Although there are no express provisions in the ICC Rules there are many cases which have more than one party. Of course, this may happen by consent. What happens, though, if a Claimant puts in a request for arbitration which names more than one party as Defendant?

The practice of the ICC Court

At the Stockholm Conference on Multi-Party Arbitration (29–30 May 1989) Stephen Bond, the Secretary-General of the ICC International Court of Arbitration dealt with the practice of the ICC Court.

The initial stage, he said was to apply Article 7 of the ICC Rules to determine whether or not there was, prima facie, an agreement to arbitrate under the ICC Rules. Once the Court has decided that the dispute can go forward in a single arbitration, he dealt with the practice of the ICC Court as to how to constitute the Arbitral Tribunal. In summary the position is as follows:

- Where there is a sole arbitrator then Article 2 (3) of the ICC Rules can be applied. The parties can be given a chance to agree upon a nomination and otherwise, in default of agreement, the ICC Court will appoint one.
- Where a sole arbitrator is not called for, the ICC Court has not construed the ICC Rules as requiring more than three arbitrators. Rather, the Court requires that one arbitrator be named for all the Claimants and one arbitrator be named for all the Defendants. Multiple Defendants are first offered the opportunity to propose by joint agreement one arbitrator. In default of such agreement the Court selects and appoints one.

Whilst Stephen Bond accepted that the ICC Rules did not explicitly set out the procedure for such an appointment, he said that the ICC Court has not taken the lack of explicit provision to be an indication that the ICC Rules are not made or intended for multi-party arbitration.

The basis for this pragmatic approach to the problem lies in provisions of Article 3 of the Statutes of the Court and Article 26 of the ICC Rules. It therefore considers that it must act for defaulting multiple defendants and it does so, Stephen Bond said:

> ". . . in light of Article 3 of its Statute . . . which gives the Court 'all the necessary powers' to ensure the application of its Rules and also of Article 26 of the ICC Rules which states, *inter alia*, that 'In all matters not expressly provided for in these Rules, the Court of Arbitration . . . shall act in the spirit of these Rules.'"

It is suggested that Articles 3 and 26 do not necessarily give the ICC Court the power to act. Article 3 of the Statutes of the Court provides:

> "Functions and Powers
>
> The function of the Court of Arbitration is to ensure the application of the Rules of Conciliation and Arbitration of the International Chamber of Commerce, and the Court has all the necessary powers for that purpose. It is further entrusted, if need be, with laying before the Commission on International Arbitration any proposals for modifying the Rules of Conciliation and Arbitration of the International Chamber of Commerce which it considers necessary."

The provision of Article 3 indicates strongly that the Court of Arbitration does not have the power to modify the ICC Rules by simply making new ad-hoc rules. Indeed it expressly provides for laying before the Commission proposals for modifying the ICC Rules. That shows that the Court must follow that procedure to exercise its function and powers under Article 3. That procedure therefore leads to a modification of the Rules and does not lead to ad hoc rules.

The second provision relied upon is Article 26 of the ICC Rules which provides:

> "In all matters not expressly provided for in these Rules, the Court of Arbitration and the arbitrator shall act in the spirit of these Rules and shall make every effort to make sure that the award is enforceable at law."

It is evident that multi-party arbitration is "not expressly provided for in these Rules". It is suggested that the purpose of the general rule is not to permit new ad hoc rules to be made upon a major provision such as multi-party arbitration but to permit the Court or the arbitrator to interpret the Rules in the spirit rather than the letter of the Rules. In other words, it is there to assist in the construction of the existing Rules.

Examples of multi-party arbitrations

Despite the evident difficulty in the express provisions of the ICC Rules or Statutes it is only in a few Court cases that the problems of multi-party ICC Arbitration have surfaced.

In *Arab Republic of Egypt* v. *Westland Helicopters Ltd.* (Cour de Justice, Geneva 26 November 1982; Tribunal Federal 16 May 1983), Westland as Claimant commenced an ICC Arbitration against six parties.

Westland had entered into an agreement with AOI (a company formed by the Governments of four Arab States including Egypt) to create a jointly owned company (ABH) to construct military helicopters. The contracts between Westland and AOI and ABH contained ICC Arbitration Clauses.

After Egypt signed the peace treaty with Israel in 1979, the other three Arab States dissolved AOI. Egypt announced that AOI would continue and Westland commenced an ICC Arbitration against all four states, AOI and ABH.

The ICC appointed an arbitrator on behalf of all six defendants, as a member of a Tribunal of three arbitrators, in default of any agreement. Egypt and AOI challenged this and brought proceedings before the Cour de Justice, Geneva to determine that it was not bound to arbitrate and in addition to challenge the Arbitral Tribunal for partiality.

On the appointment of the Arbitral Tribunal, the Court stated that the contractually agreed-upon method of selecting arbitrators under the ICC Rules had been complied with by the ICC Court of Arbitration. In giving reasons it said:

> "In this case, the parties have submitted themselves to the Rules of the ICC and these have been applied, in particular, as has been seen, concerning the method of nomination of the arbitrators. One cannot claim that the application of such Rules gave to Westland a preponderant influence. The ICC system offers all guarantees and in any case more than others, since the parties only propose arbitrators, who are named by the Court of Arbitration of the ICC. The Arab Republic of Egypt is wrong when it claims that it has the right to be represented on the tribunal. The arbitrator, even if designated by one party is not the agent of that party, nor his representative."

That, evidently, supports the ICC Court's contention that it can appoint arbitrators for a defaulting multiple party.

More recently, (5 May 1989) the Cour d'Appel de Paris had a similar problem to consider in *BKMI Industrieen Lagen GmbH* v. *Dutco Construction Co. Ltd.* In that case BKMI had agreed to construct a cement plant in Oman. BKMI, therefore, entered into a consortium agreement with Siemens and Dutco for the execution of the project.

That consortium agreement provided that all disputes should be settled by ICC Arbitration. In 1986 Dutco commenced an ICC Arbitration naming both BKMI and Siemens as defendants. BKMI and Siemens contended that Dutco should have commenced separate ICC arbitrations against BKMI and Siemens.

The ICC Court, following the usual practice, found the prima facie existence of an ICC Agreement and called upon BKMI and Siemens to nominate jointly one arbitrator. The Arbitral Tribunal in the end consisted of an arbitrator nominated by Dutco, an arbitrator nominated (under protest and without prejudice) by BKMI and Siemens jointly and a Chairman appointed by the ICC Court.

The Arbitral Tribunal made a partial award in May 1988 finding that the proceedings were properly commenced and that the Arbitral Tribunal had been properly constructed.

The Court of Appeal in Paris upheld that award on the grounds that the parties had agreed to multi-party arbitration and that Article 2 (4) of the ICC Rules was therefore to be interpreted as meaning that the two Arbitrators to be nominated by the claimant and the defendant were to be nominated one by the claimant or claimants, the other by the defendant or defendants.

This decision was evidently based upon the Court's finding that the consortium agreement indicated that the parties had agreed to multi-party arbitration. The indications were contained in the following:

1. the arbitration clause which expressly provided for three arbitrators;
2. the multi-party nature of the contract which envisaged disputes potentially including all three parties;
3. the specific requirement providing that "all disputes" be submitted to arbitration.

Again this supports the ICC Court's practice. The case, however, has been appealed to the Cour de Cassation. It is suggested that the case, in any event, only indicates that where the parties agree, then a multi-party ICC arbitration can take place. Such an agreement can be and often is made at the time of the arbitration. Here it was held to have been made at the time of the contract. The one difference though is that where a party agrees at the time of the arbitration, it also agrees the method for appointment of arbitrators. Here, the method was imposed in order to put the parties' contractual intention into effect.

It is considered that if a case concerning multi-party arbitration without consent should arise between three independent parties (for example, employer, contractor and sub-contractor in a building contract), neither the agreement to arbitrate nor the ICC Rules could justify such multi-party proceedings. It is, therefore, appropriate for the ICC Court to consider whether express provision is made in the ICC Rules for multi-party arbitration, so that in all cases the procedure is clear.

Conclusion

The problems highlighted by this paper are already seriously felt in international arbitration and are likely to become more pressing as international trade becomes increasingly complex. The ICC rules in particular, with their pragmatic approach to multi-party arbitrations could be said to leave something to be desired, as could Clause 67 of FIDIC.

Written and oral evidence in international arbitration 10

David Kemp

Synopsis

This paper compares the different procedures employed in ICC arbitration and the English courts for the presentation of evidence and particularly the different attitudes on the continent to what is known here as discovery of documents.

Introduction

I have, in this paper concentrated on construction disputes and in particular on those of a complex and lengthy nature. Where the subject matter of the litigation falls within a narrow compass or where the relevant issue in dispute is a short point of law, some of what I have to say may not apply.

The attitude of the English courts

Before turning to the procedures appropriate in a complex construction arbitration, I shall consider briefly the attitude of English courts to written evidence and argument. English courts still maintain the traditional procedures of oral evidence and oral argument. But these are no longer exclusive procedures.

The courts have long required pre-trial exchange of expert evidence. Recently the courts have been empowered to require pre-trial exchange of statements of factual evidence. In 1986 RSC Rule 382A empowered the Chancery Division, the Commercial Court, the Admiralty Court and the Official Referees to require such exchange. In 1988 this power was extended to all Divisions of the High Court. The power is extensively used by Official Referees in construction disputes.

After an experimental period in which parties were encouraged, but not compelled, to file skeleton written arguments in appeals to the Court of

Appeal, this is now a mandatory requirement.[1] I quote below some passages from this Practice Direction, since they emphasise one of the main points which I wish to make in this paper:

> "A very important element in the working party's strategy . . . is that time spent in Court will be shortened if the members of the court who are going to hear the appeal are able to do effective pre-reading. This can only be done if, well in advance of the hearing, the Court has details of the points which are going to be argued and the authorities which are going to be cited. For that reason the keystone of the new system is that skeleton arguments will no longer be optional, but will be required for all civil appeals (other than appeals heard with exceptional urgency). So far as timing is concerned, in all cases . . . skeleton arguments must be lodged not less than four weeks before the date on which the hearing is scheduled to begin.
>
> "Requiring the skeleton arguments to be lodged well before the appeal hearing has three main advantages. First and foremost, the judges can do really effective pre-reading and thus save a considerable amount of time which would otherwise be spent reading aloud in Court . . ."

Legal submissions in arbitration proceedings

In introducing these sensible procedures the English court followed what had long been the practice in English domestic arbitrations and in international arbitrations, such as those held under ICC Rules. That practice has generally been to require all evidence, both expert and factual, to be put in writing, to be exchanged between the parties and to be submitted to the tribunal well before the oral hearing. It has also been the practice to require full submissions (not merely skeleton arguments) to be likewise exchanged and submitted to the tribunal.

Such requirements have two main purposes: first to avoid the parties being taken by surprise, second to save time and costs by reducing oral evidence and oral argument to the bare minimum.

For this procedure to work satisfactorily, it is essential that before the start of the oral hearing the tribunal should have thoroughly read and appreciated the evidence and the submissions. It is also important that the parties' legal advisers should be confident that the tribunal has mastered the material before it. The intention behind the procedure is that there should be no need to have the written evidence and submissions read aloud at the hearing. But if an advocate is not confident that the tribunal, or some member of it, has mastered the material, he may well spend considerable time reading extracts from the written evidence or repeating what is already set out in the written submissions.

I believe that a complex construction arbitration can only be kept within reasonable bounds if at the start of the arbitration the tribunal provides:

- that the scope and function of written and oral evidence and of written and oral submissions are clearly defined;
- that the parties are to be strictly limited to presenting their evidence and submissions within such defined ambit;

1 See Practice Direction (Court of Appeal Presentation of Arguments) [1989] 1 WLR 281.

- that discovery and presentation of documents are to be limited to documents that are clearly material;
- that a core bundle of documents of limited size is to be prepared and submitted to the tribunal no later than the time when final factual witness statements are submitted; and
- above all that all written material is to be submitted to the tribunal at least six weeks before the start of the oral hearing.

I make the assumption that arbitrators are conscientious and will do their best to read all the papers and master their contents. But there is a limit to an arbitrator's powers of comprehension: the procedural directions must take account of the practical constraints under which he works. The oral hearing will have to be fixed for a period or periods during which the tribunal and Counsel are available. In an important arbitration there may well be three arbitrators and four Counsel to be considered, and it may be difficult to find suitable dates. There will probably have to be some compromise in fixing the dates. If an arbitrator is a practising lawyer, he is likely to have other professional commitments with which the hearing must be co-ordinated. He is unlikely to be certain of having a definite clear period immediately before the hearing during which he can master the papers. When the initial directions are given, he is unlikely to know the extent of the documentation which will be submitted to him.

In such circumstances I strongly contend that a period of at least six weeks should be allowed before the hearing date to enable an arbitrator to be sure of time in which to master the papers. He may have numerous and lengthy witness statements to read and digest. He may have extensive correspondence and contractual documents to study. It is significant that the Court of Appeal requires four weeks merely to study the skeleton argument and to read the relevant authorities : and its members are free of the varied and uncertain commitments which attend a practising lawyer.

Fixing a timetable

As soon as the Terms of Reference have been settled pursuant to Article 13 of the ICC Rules, an estimate should be made of the probable length of the oral hearing and a period or periods fixed for the hearing. The procedural directions should be structured so that the last document to be submitted to the tribunal should be submitted at least six weeks before the start of the hearing. If a suitable timetable cannot be devised to allow for this, the start of the hearing must be altered to accommodate this requirement.

Such a timetable will not be popular with the parties' legal advisers. It means that preparation of the case will have to be completed six weeks before the hearing. Counsel will press for the final documents to be submitted much later. But such pleas should be firmly rejected. Otherwise it is quite possible that the hearing will start without the tribunal having mastered the documentation and much of the benefit of the pre-trial submission of evidence and argument will be wasted.

Depending upon the number of witnesses and the scope of their evidence, it may be desirable to impose some limit on the time to be allowed for cross-examination and re-examination. Whether such a limit should be imposed and, if so, its extent can best be determined by the tribunal after all documentation has been submitted to it. A meeting for procedural directions can be arranged to determine this question shortly before the hearing date.

Similarly some limit should probably be imposed on oral submissions, supplemental to the written submissions.

Discovery and presentation of documents

It is not the practice and it is generally undesirable in an ICC construction arbitration to order general discovery such as is ordered by an English court. The parties will already in the Request for Arbitration and in the Answer to the Request have set out much of the documentation on which they rely. It usually suffices to leave it to the parties to make voluntary discovery of such documents as the other party requests and to apply, if necessary, to the tribunal for an order to disclose a particular document or a particular class of documents. The parties should be strongly discouraged from presenting unnecessary documentation to the tribunal. It may be necessary, for example, to disclose to the other party site minutes, drawings, internal memoranda, wage sheets etc., but such documents should not be submitted to the tribunal unless they are really material. In my experience thousands of pages of documents are unnecessarily submitted to the arbitrators and are never referred to throughout the arbitration. The parties should be warned that the presentation of unnecessary documents may result in the party responsible being severely punished in costs.

The Contract should usually be presented as a separate bundle. In addition a core bundle of limited size should be prepared containing documents which will undoubtedly be referred to and which are essential to an understanding of the dispute. If a core bundle cannot be agreed, it should be prepared by the Claimant and any extra documents required by the Respondent can be contained in a separate supplemental bundle. An agreed bundle or bundles of relevant correspondence should be presented. It is often convenient if the parties in an appendix to their written submissions indicate any documents other than those in the core bundle to which the tribunal's attention is particularly directed.

It will usually be right to provide that there be simultaneous exchange of statements of witnesses of fact, to avoid the possibility of evidence in reply being modified in the light of the other party's evidence. With regard to expert evidence, the appropriate procedure is likely to depend upon the position as revealed in the pleadings. Sometimes it will be appropriate to provide for simultaneous exchange, but more often it will probably be appropriate to provide for sequential exchange. The exchange of written submissions should not take place until the parties have completed the exchange of expert and factual evidence. The exchange should then be sequential. There is, of course, no standard form of procedural directions to provide for evidence and submissions. I append below a specimen form of directions for this purpose.

Conclusion

In any large construction dispute, one of the problems is that of controlling the enormous quantity of relevant paper. It is in many ways easier to do this in an arbitration where, for example, ICC rules apply, than in English court proceedings. The two sets of procedures are, however, becoming more similar rather than less, as indicated above.

Appendix

By [date] the Claimants shall serve any expert evidence on which they rely.
By [date] the Respondents shall serve any expert evidence in reply on which they rely.
By [date] the Claimants shall serve any expert evidence on which they rely in response to the Respondents' expert evidence.
By [date] each party shall serve a written statement of the evidence of any witness of fact which that party intends to call at the hearing.
By [date] each party shall serve a written statement of any witness of fact, whose evidence supplements or amplifies any previous witness statement, where such supplement or amplification is occasioned by the service of the other party's witness statements. Such supplemental or amplifying evidence may include, if necessary, statements from witnesses in respect of whose evidence no statement has previously been served.

Except with the leave of the tribunal (which shall only be given in special circumstances) no witness may be called at the hearing unless a written statement of his evidence has been provided in accordance with the preceding sub-paragraphs and no evidence in chief may be adduced by a witness to any fact which has not been included in the written statement of that witness.
By [date] the Claimants shall serve a written statement of their submissions.
By [date] the Respondents shall serve a written statement of their submissions.
By [date] each party may serve a written response to the other party's submissions.
Note: The date to be inserted in sub-paragraph 9 should be at least six weeks before the start of the oral hearing.

11 The evaluation of technical expertise and the decision making process

Max W Abrahamson

Synopsis

This paper examines the position of the expert *vis-à-vis* the legal process in general, and the workings of arbitration in particular. It considers the interface between the practical non-lawyer expert, the lawyers and the arbitrator, and examines the problems which can arise. The paper looks at the position of the arbitrator himself and the process of arriving at a decision on the issues.

Introduction

In 1899[1] bricks were one of the few staple building materials. The more successful a bricklayer was in bricklaying the less time he had for the inevitable disputes about bricks, although he might sometimes dispute that a wall was crooked. It was not practicable permanently to support two whole-time versions of the same trade – "laying" brickies, and what may be called "judicial" or "disputes" brickies. Lawyers offered to supply that second version as and when needed.

Members of the judicial branch naturally improved at their job, so far as (not having to lay bricks) they did "direct . . . differently" what they had.[2] The laying branch "sorted" and handled, and as a result got the "feel" of, bricks. The disputes branch "sorted" and handled and got the feel of the concept of bricks (without which abstraction, of course, not

1 The year of the first modern Arbitration Act, and only eight years after the first edition of *Hudson's Building and Engineering Contracts*. By the fourth edition in 1914 a second volume of reports had been added – of a meagre 59 cases over 29 years.

2 The relevant consideration according to Dr. Johnson, who continued – "Had Sir Isaac Newton applied his mind to poetry, he would have made a fine epick poet. I could as easily have applied my mind to law as to tragick poetry": Boswell's *Life of Johnson*, ed. Hill and Powell, 2nd ed. (1964) vol.V p.34.

much could be built with the real things).[3] The branch was largely impotent in look-sniff-feel disputes, and other issues without or beyond words, and most powerful in words about words about bricks. The duty to decide disputes one way or another, made the branch most expert when not much was known about bricks, but not so that it should build walls.

Thus, contrary to popular opinion, there are two different jobs: not one only with two classes of competitor for it, or one surrounded by parasites or critics. Neither branch alone knows everything relevant to brick disputes, and each needs to mind its own business best.

Demarcation disputes between the branches will have to be considered later. The point of this introduction is that, unfortunately for simplicity, times change, so that even specialist construction lawyers cannot live by bricks alone when constructors do not. Legal as much as physical disasters are caused by overlooking changes in scale (as from bricks to modern tunnelling near methane). The risks are compounded if one branch has too much valuable business from the growing complexity of the other to spare time to do that other justice.

Rules for expert witnesses

Attachment A summarises the simple rules on expert evidence. Practice is complicated, particularly because of the oversimplification that almost every issue within almost every dispute under a contract is decided by the same system using the same processes, all chosen before the issues are known. The choices are more or less random.

For example, if the contract happens to be in a UK standard form, by which the President of the Institution of Civil Engineers or of the Royal Institute of British Architects is the appointer, a technical expert is likely to be the sole arbitrator on every issue. With a FIDIC International engineering form and its ICC arbitration clause, probably a lawyer will be either the sole arbitrator, or chairman with one or more parties nominating a lawyer to act with him.

When civil law "inquisitorial" procedure applies, lawyer- arbitrators usually appoint their own experts, who effectively decide technical and trade issues. Typical common lawyer arbitrators inquire into less but decide everything, after hearing only experts chosen and examined by the parties. Despite admitting untidy evidence and procedures not allowed past common law doors, "civil" oral hearings are up to 20 times shorter than ours in similar cases.

Construction risks

An examination of construction risks illustrates the variety which exists in actual decisions by different tribunals on similar issues.

3 British Standard 5628 on Structural use of Masonry now runs to 188 closely packed pages, mostly words.

After a waterworks exploded, the trial judge held three defendants liable for not protecting the public against the known limits of expert knowledge – the known risk that not much was known about an "insidious and deadly" underground gas.[4]. A majority in the Court of Appeal changed his interpretation of some of the expert evidence, which he had heard but not read and they had read but not heard, so as to exonerate the Water Authority.[5]. By reorientating the evidence in law and construction practice, the majority also exonerated the Contractors, and held the design Consultants one hundred percent liable. The dissenting Appeal Judge applied his "robust and sensible . . . instinct or feeling" that no one was liable, because by law, fact and policy combined, the specific risk of the particular kind of methane leaking into the tunnel at the particular time from the particular place was not reasonably forseeable.

The ICE and FIDIC standard contracts compensate contractors for conditions and obstructions that could not "reasonably have been foreseen by an experienced Contractor". In arbitration on claims to compensation for gas entering a tunnel drive, arguments accepted by arbitrators in *Abbeystead* would hardly be worth putting to those engineer-arbitrators who prefer what they see as natural underground, and prefer tendering realities to mere contract words.

No definite information is available on how the varieties of Alternative Disputes Resolution and of disputes are matched to each other in practice. By a sometimes arbitrary division many differences between experts, particularly when they are decided before the harm is done, are not subject to anything like any dispute resolution procedure.[6]

Issue resolution[7]

> "The life of law . . . has been experience."[8]
>
> "Procedural principles are much more difficult to convey. True enough, there are rulebooks, but we all know that the experienced practitioner's stock in trade consists of a feel for underlying principles which often are not written down, and which indeed may be scarcely susceptible of formulation."[9]

4 *Eckersley* v. *Binnie & Partners, Edmund Nuttall Ltd. & North West Water Authority*. The judgments, interpreted very broadly in the text above, were delivered in the High Court (90 pages) in 1987, and in the Court of Appeal (150 pages) in 1988. Methane in the air exploded when the pumps of the completed Abbeystead water scheme were switched on during a demonstration for visitors. It appeared most likely that the methane was not the transient kind tested for during construction, but came from a reservoir some distance away. Although in court not arbitration, the case is used for specific illustrations below.

5 Apparently the transcript of evidence was not ready until the appeal, presumably because of the long trial. The majority of the Court of Appeal held that the trial judge "had not borne all the relevant answers in mind".

6 See for examples, Abrahamson in *The Ombudsman*, ed. Rowat (1965).

7 The term "issue" as used here is not limited to an ultimate claim or counter-claim. Every claim is made of many issues of fact or law, each made up of many sub-issues, and so on ad infinitem.

8 Oliver Wendell Holmes, *The Common Law*, 1.

9 Lord Justice Mustill, "Contemporary problems in international commercial arbitration: a response" [1989] 17 IBL 154 at 164.

> "If the aeons have taught man anything, it is that phenomena lying outside the range of his everyday experience may contain fundamental surprises . . ."[10]

Having profited from the experience of appearing opposite, between, and on the same side as several kinds and combinations of common and civil lawyers and other experts, realisation has eventually dawned on me that we need not hang our customers by rules of thumb (financially speaking or by way of character assassination) in resolving complex disputes. We might instead sort out from issue to issue exactly what each expert is and should be doing, in what system, and for what purpose. Given reasonable versatility, an expert could then do his best on each issue.

That possibility hardly deserves the new name given to it here. "Issue resolution" would be no rarer than fitting crimes with more punishments than hanging, were it fully accepted in practice even that a dispute can include some issues best dealt with in speech, others in writing, and few in both.

Many lawyers still complain that someone keeps making arbitration worse than the worst litigation,[11] although standard arbitration rules already allow procedural options. As the problem in practice seems to be that old presumptions naturally continue to rule internally, rudimentary lists are attached to help this paper jog our memories on the answer to all the important questions - that it all depends, precisely because what it depends on is complex. The important questions are those that arbitrators and their teachers, selectors, regulators and helpers, have to answer by what they do, whether or not they ask them in advance. Some may find that a type of "sorting" is useful.

Sorting the issues

Delivery of a variety of items without loss or damage in a legal, as in a postal, neighbourhood, requires flexible use of limited resources to scrutinise physically and conceptually every scrap of reality which the sorting system is designed to represent, and every clue to the right place of each item in the system.[12]

A complex dispute whether about design or placement needs to be split into manageable issues, so that each round of sorting can be performed on each issue using the most appropriate Systems in list 1, Institutional and Personal Processes in lists 2 and 3, and Expert Classes and Species in lists 4 and 5.

10 Joseph Ford, in *The New Physics*, ed. Paul Davies (1989), 353.

11 For the best of litigation, see "Practice today in the Official Referees' Courts", by His Honour Judge James Fox-Andrews in (1989) 5 Const LJ 246.

12 Clues for all kinds of "sorting" are found in the most unexpected places - hence some of the references in the text. No disrespect is intended to either arbitration or jurisprudence by the comparison with "sorting" – but contrast Dworkin, Hart *et al.* As it is unfortunately not practicable to cite all the valuable jurisprudential (where it deigns to notice the peculiarities of arbitration), arbitral and other literature relevant to this paper, footnotes have been kept to a minimum.

Terms are included in the lists mostly in alphabetical order, because their precedence is such a personal choice. Some are illustrated below. It is of course harder to apply them in practice than on paper. But to concentrate the mind on the need to try, change places with a consumer for whom a single Dispute Resolution procedure that is right for 70% of the issues may turn out to be 100% fatally wrong.

Suppose you are a Resident Engineer who stops a tunnel drive for fear of a gas explosion. The Contractor claims compensation. Score each possible dispute resolution System in list 1, on a scale from 10 for your confidence when returning underground after a decision against you, to 0 for cold feet. Consider particularly if your scoring would be affected by the following (a score card is included as the last table, below).

Complexity

> "I . . . regard with . . . indifference verging on contempt . . . the ignorant clamour . . . that judges should . . . undergo some specialised training in . . . say psychology, sociology, . . . or even mechanical engineering or accounting". . . . The capacity of being a judge is acquired in the course of practising the law."[13]
>
> . . . some kinds of dispute where matters are factually so complex that the classic confrontational adversarial battle becomes so time consuming and expensive that I doubt that justice can ever properly be done . . . Large civil engineering disputes can fall into this category."[14]
>
> "Words are the lawyer's tools of trade . . . vehicle of thought [not] symbols or numbers."[15]

Confusion in the "ignorant clamour" of the first quotation heading this section, is relevant to the second. Mechanical engineers do not pride themselves on having general expertise in the sorting process although, like the other "brilliantly successful physical sciences",[16] they claim to make judgments in their own subject that are too complex for lawyers' words. But the psychologists and others in list 4 do now claim expertise relevant to "sorting" words in disputes of all kinds, not only their own, like accountants on "sorting" construction and other assets.

Despite having had to be psychologists before there were any (as with the hearsay rules), and experts on information processing and disinformation (mainly on behalf of others) before there were so many, the disputes branch seems to have somewhat arrested its own development. It does not fully co-operate or compete with or "sort" the efforts of its rivals beyond the sophistication of bricklaying days.[17] We may have lost

13 Lord Hailsham, *Hamlyn Revisited* (1983) 50–51.

14 Saville J, "Reconciling speed with justice in the decision making process", Chartered Institute of Arbitrators, *Bernstein Lectures* (1989), 179.

15 Lord Denning, *The Discipline of Law* (1979), 5.

16 FA Hayek, *New Studies*, (1978), 30.

17 Two illustrations by Lord Chancellors happen to be quoted in this paper. (Consider the insistence in examining witnesses on detailed recall of matters years passed, with a recent example when recollection was tested in arbitration. It is not breaking confidence to refer to a case where ten or more lawyers were agreed that a document had not been handed in at a hearing in their presence a few months before (with which recollection the Leading Counsel who had intended to hand in the document eventually agreed). It was later found that the document had been handed in after all.)

heart because so much expert information on offer only confirms what we already know – how much easier it is to use the "lawyer's [non-exclusive] tools of trade" to dissipate than recreate reality.[18]

Of course, we are each free to make our own choice of terms from the lists to describe the continued use of our tools to hang a percentage of our customers, and our own guess at what the percentage is. At the same time, we all know it is possible to jump to worse versions of the shortcomings we want to escape – in alternative disputes resolution as in alternative medicine and other alternative sciences. Behind our problems there are the real differences between the type of complexity handled by the physical sciences, and the more difficult kinds which we individually and collectively create for the social and behavioural, including disputes, "sciences" that so far have proved too much for them.

We have to admit that some of the difference between the success of the physical and those other sciences persist because we can tell beyond argument whether waterworks are working or killing. But the separate development of the disputes "branch" has made some progress in telling the difference between effective and dangerous disputes resolution procedures, and in constructing a framework useful at least as a starting point. As will appear later on, there are good reasons why much disputes "sorting" was put in the hands of a separate "legal" branch in the first place, why there have been so many attempts to remove it, and why some keeps returning.

The move from general to particular, as even the simplest sorting must, leads now to a consideration of specific issues, with some suggestions for resolving them collected at the end.

The presumption of advocacy

> "I [the Chairman of the Bar Council] am in the most competitive profession there is . . . Every time I do a case I am on show. My performance is being reviewed not only by the solicitor who has instructed me but also by the other solicitors in the Court".[19]
>
> "The trial is not a search for the 'truth'.
>
> It is an arena in which different versions of reality compete. Legal truth is not a discoverable entity existing outside the trial process: it is a product of the trial process itself."[20]
>
> "In the present case, the curial system could not match the investigation which a highly qualified scientific mind of independent spirit was able to

18 ". . . subjects' recall of the speed at which cars were travelling towards each other in a filmed car crash depended upon whether they were asked how fast the cars were going when they smashed (40.8mph), collided (39.3mph), bumped (38.1mph), or contacted (31.8mph) each other": *The skilful mind, an introduction to cognitive psychology*, ed. Angus Gellatly, 96.

19 Chairman of the Bar Council, as reported in *The Times*. See also Greville Janner, "Lawyer, present yourself", (1989) 139 NLJ, 1271, on the "essentials of presentation skills, for professionals many of whom are actors manqués, but . . . must write and declaim their own scripts".

20 Michael McColville, "Silence in Court", (1987) 137 NLJ, 1169–70.

apply in the field to the resolution of what was wrong, if anything, with the computer".[21]

If the procedures for our tunnel dispute were traditional common law at its very worst, for which the show business analogy in the first quotation is apt, expert evidence will have reached the decision maker through a performance produced, directed, mainly acted and partly scripted by advocates. While a Micawber advocate soliloquised to a large audience, hoping for something to turn up, direct intervention by an expert would have seemed as embarrassing as from a drunk in the gallery.

The second quotation above suggests that such a convincing play in words is better than reality, as though the effects of a legal performance end when the curtain falls. Admittedly, the symptom of the occupational illness diagnosed below, shows itself more often in efforts to justify freeing the guilty than punishing or blowing up the innocent. Certainly, even in commercial arbitration it usually does matter to someone or other (whether a party or executive or witness, and whether in terms of money, reputation or pride) as much as it matters to our Resident Engineer, that the right "sorting" is not only seen, or seems to be, but actually is, done.

The Champion-Advocate

Where expert advice goes directly to arbitrators in one way or another, it is usually absorbed into a somewhat similar overall production, with at least two lawyer-advocates acting as writing or speaking masters of ceremonies. However, the presumption of advocacy appears most difficult to rebut in legal systems where the parties expect (or are led to expect) most control of the resolution of their own disputes, or at least a good view of the spectacle. That may be a relic of trial by battle, hardly intended to be influential when commercial arbitration was developed. In any case, since the original champions died for the litigants and not vice versa, the referee must have had little more to do than enforce elementary rules of fair play, and hold up the hand of the only survivor, as obvious winner.

It would be odd that an arbitrator now trusted to do so much more at the end, is still trusted to do so little during the contest, if so many other relics of simpler times were not preserved.

Whatever its cause, reliance on control of disputes resolution by champion-advocates is risky, since only externals can be controlled, not the internal Personal Processes in list 5. The last and crucial round of "sorting", in which scientific, commercial and other facts are combined with law while keeping an eye on policy, is performed in private by the

21 *Chloride Batteries Australia Ltd.* v. *Glendale Chemical Products PTY Ltd.* (1985) Supreme Court of New South Wales, 19, *per* Cole J.

arbitrator, who may overule whatever provisional "sorting" others have done already.[22]

Even the judges in *Abbeystead* applied their own "sorting" principles[23] flexibly, to discount some expert evidence: there was "no evidence", "no satisfactory evidence", "no evidence from a qualified source", or the "evidence simply [could not] be described as overwhelming"; and, with a double negative, "no single piece of evidence was conclusive, but conversely no expert positively asserted that methane was not entering the tunnel".

It is possible that, as he is submerged in chaos[24] and bewilderment, an arbitrator may grasp at ever smaller straws. His judgment of all the evidence may be determined by a single one of those "facts" that so often by relative simplicity and repetition become bench marks during a hearing, or by his appreciation of the performance of one witness as a witness (credibility will be returned to later). Unknown to others or himself, the last round may even have been decided by "prejudice . . . personal burdens of proof" at the first round, so that all the effort in-between has been wasted (and see the section on the "Semi-conscious arbitrator", below). Of course, incompetence is inherently chaotic, with no limit to the kind of error it can cause.

The internal permutations available multiply vastly when three arbitrators, perhaps of different nationalities and professions as well as temperaments, will be involved in finally choosing which issues are critical (after private discussion without the advocates).

Issue Sorting

Living in terror of all those risks, which he knows only too well, any competent advocate will take the view that not even a first round of "issue sorting" should be allowed until the issues relied on in the last round are made known, which is usually in the award when it is too late. He will resist any "sorting" that discounts or segregates the lightest make-weight, which in the light of all the evidence and the arbitrator's internal processes revealed by the end of the day, he could conceivably by skill or chance add in such a way as to tip the final balance in his client's favour.

Alternatively, his client may want the best value for money spent to buy the greatest possible confusion or spell-binding, to which he hopes

22 See Attachment A on the rule that an expert witness may not be asked the very question that has to be decided. The latest decision is *Re S & B minors, The Independent*, 1 June 1990 where it was held that a psychiatric social worker's view that a witness's accounts of events were credible, were admissible to support her opinion about the witness's psychiatric state. But, although the boundary was fine, any direct expression of opinion that the witness was telling the truth was not admissible, because "the assessment of a witness's credibility is a matter for the Court and not for professionals in other fields".

23 See Attachment A, and the burden of proof below, (see text).

24 See notes 47 and 48 of this paper.

the arbitrator will succumb generously, and which may depend on mixing all available ingredients.

Consequently, one side or the other is likely to resist every effort to separate issues, even efforts to give those issues that are genuinely in dispute for good reasons the time, money and above all concentrated attention they need, and waste as little as possible on the rest. While advocates on both sides may be doing their duty by such opposition, it is as necessary to have effective procedure for resolving obstruction of the resolution process jointly for the parties' different reasons, as for resolving their disagreements – if arbitrators do have rights.

Without first defining what is the purpose of (oral or written) advocacy, it is surely not possible to decide what advocacy is needed and when, on any particular issue or on the issues altogether. Most of that definition is well beyond the reach of this paper, with too many kinds of advocacy even to list. A "sorting" system must be designed for no higher than the general run of "sorters", to us here who do most of the work. What is relevant here is that their advocacy, particularly cross-examination, is invaluable and irreplaceable on some issues, or at least seems so. On others it does not earn its keep. On yet others, by positively dissipating reality, it achieves the opposite of the "sorting" required (how confident might one be to enter a tunnel when a distinguished expert's opinion that it was dangerous had been discredited by one of the famous cross-examinations of Lord Birkett or Sir Edward Marshal Hall?).

In trying to give effect to those divisions, the difference between control by the relevant party and control by advocates has to be taken into account. It is hard for a party to enter the arena in order to combat his own champion, even on issues where that champion's advocacy is wasteful, or even dangerous. Arbitration rules can only do so much by general regulation to get the best and avoid the worst of advocacy. So the remedy has to include more effective discrimination closer to hand.

Where reality has to be reduced to words, it might at least be expected that in accordance with good "sorting" mechanics they would be preserved and communicated as directly, quickly and conveniently as possible amongst the "sorters", all of whom nowadays read roughly three times faster than they speak.

The day in Court

The more important the "day in court", the more important it must be to plan how exactly to spend it. Should it be spent listening, specially to what is already recorded and easily accessible or requires detailed study? The parties are used to being informed by reading and writing in the rest of their business (as indeed are the public and those who report to it, although the public information element is usually missing altogether in arbitration)

The amount we "hear" of all that is said in our presence may be affected by Processes in list 5, from "after lunch" to "personal presumptions", and the difference between sympathetic and suspicious listening. The right to be heard is not guaranteed by the fact that a party is in the presence of the decider, particularly when everything possible is done to put as much distance and as many intermediaries as possible between them (see below).

The invention of writing, being most noticed procedurally as it is engulfed by another word processing revolution, is still so often implemented by duplicating the old oral with the new written presentation. The Bar does seems to believe the worst of even its own most select members – that they lose their great ability to "make up" written briefs, become listeners and not readers, as they ascend to the Bench. Particularly in view of recent developments, I look forward to the class action for the innuendo that judges (and *a fortiori* less select arbitrators) are incapable of retraining, or if they do digest the papers before a hearing, forget their basic training on the distinction between learning about a dispute and deciding it.

Part of the speaking specialist's motivation is that the spoken word may cast its spell by added appeal to the more impulsive Institutional and Personal Processes in lists 2 and 3. The more unusual and/or changeable the client's case, the more flexibility is required. The advocate is naturally anxious that no working space needed on his side is filled by harsh reality in the shape of "hard" facts, sharp words, and fine bright lines, symbols or calculations, in which the best experts prefer to deal, and which are fixed from the start.

The above considerations shift the burden of proving himself separately on each issue on to the advocate, particularly the orator.

Investigation

Days spent on speculative advocacy about (for example) the proper size of an inlet in a process plant that could still physically be changed and tested, keep alive the hope that investigation will eventually be as important as words in dispute resolution and, (and this is the hardest part), will not be defeated by words. All the books emphasise that even successful cross-examination, the jewel of advocacy, depends on the available ammunition. Yet in practice, investigation and real (as opposed to paper) preparation are downgraded.

It would be out of place in this paper to discuss little local difficulties, however topical. But the personal experience already referred to leave no doubt about one result of the organization of our legal professions, and the experience has been unavoidable because there can be no doubt about it. The disadvantage of the present division between solicitors and barristers that far outweighs all others and all advantages, is the amount of relevant information that falls between the two.

The argument that presentation and investigation of a case should be divorced from each other, sustains itself only by that divorce. It could not survive if counsel will recall how often they have blamed instructing solicitors for failing to pass on useful ammunition, and solicitors will publicise how often they have blamed counsel for not using or for misusing ammunition supplied.

Reference to "presentation of a case" as a separate activity begs the questions - which case? Whose case? The case available for presentation must depend on who investigated the facts, and how well. That is, unless the illusion is perpetuated that words are more important than reality, and it does not matter to a presenter whether or not he is presenting his client's best case. It is also relevant that the final "sorter" is far less able to investigate for himself, than to be his own devil's advocate.

In any case, it is not clear where or how the boundaries between investigation, preparation and presentation are to be drawn, so that the legendary High Street solicitor not capable, independant or trustworthy enough to do the last, is fully qualified to do the other two. A safety curtain which enables performers in front to act on instructions from dependant, untrustworthy preparers behind without losing their moral superiority, has obvious advantages. But, again unless we are satisfied with stage illusions, efforts would better be directed to having all those qualities in all the "sorters", from first to last. Those efforts, and the best use of valuable resources, could be helped by the very similar professional abilities required for good investigation, and the substance of advocacy.

The choice from the many ways available to bridge the gaps, has to take several factors into account. They include the different reasons for success or neglect in different systems, the universal virtues and vices of lawyers. Above all there is the problem that in order to perform their duties the lawyers for each party, (and now many forensic experts in breach of theirs), investigate with ulterior motives from the start.

Experts and others

> "Whenever there is a simple error that most laymen fall for, there is always a more sophisticated version . . . that experts fall for."[25]
>
> "It is often . . . the really spontaneous answer [of a witness] which affords the most reliable guide to the truth".[26]
>
> "Good God, people don't do such things".[27]

It is essential that experts are expertly valued so that it becomes a matter of prestige, not fear or disdain, for the very best to help in legal proceeding. But there is some evidence that if a long-haired employee of the Swiss Patent Office had testified in 1904 that time was relative to the observer on a contractor's delay and disruption claim, he would have been successfully cross-examined, and disbelieved. From 1906 his evidence even that the standard Schedules of Plant Hire charges are sensible would have been impregnable.

25 Amos Tversky, "Extensional v. Intuitive Reasoning", *Psychological Review* 90:293–315.

26 Note of Dissent by R J Parker QC, David Hirst QC, and Godfrey Morley to the Law Reform Committee 17th Report (Evidence of Opinion and Expert Evidence), para. 15. This dissent, predicting dire consequences from exchange of expert reports, proved to be of the sky-is-falling school of jurisprudence.

27 Said by Judge Brack, just after Ibsen's Hedda Gabler has done it.

On appeal in *Abbeystead* it was emphasised that the trial judge alone "had the inestimable advantage of seeing and hearing the witnesses both as to fact and as to expert opinion", that "none of the experts heard all the evidence", and that "the Judge had to make up his mind which experts he preferred". In that last process, there was movement between valuing the evidence of various expert witnesses, and valuing their general professional ability and/or personal character: "articulate and lucid witness whose evidence . . . was fascinating"; "robust views . . . were compelling"; "euphemistic to describe the offering [in a professorial report] as a calculation . . . if one of [his] pupils had produced it, he would have received high marks for ingenuity but none at all for likely reliability."; "an enthusiastic scientist [whose enthusiasm] more than once . . . got the better of him ."; "A miner . . . [who] gave every appearance of being an honest and straightforward witness."[28]

Paradoxically, on this issue lawyers seem to employ an alternative science, now itself fashionably derided as much as formerly they were derided for not accepting it. They seem to share the Freudian confidence in untested ability to "express the manifold existence" of a witness in "a few shining phrases" after a short acquaintance, and then to work backwards to find detailed facts. Alternatively, the school report may be the source of these snap judgments. The acquaintance made in court is shorter than that of the schoolteacher (shortest when examination-in-chief is in writing), more isolated from any "history" or background information, and in an odder place to get to know someone than even the analyst's couch.[29] It is also shorter and shallower than the intimate acquaintance with judges that some advocates advertise as their special stock-in-trade.

Given that the mix of valuations of information and informants is a basis for our decisions of all sorts, it may be necessary to settle for less than the ideal that credibility is deduced and recriminations between the parties are untangled from the facts, not the reverse. But there is additionally the special risk in arbitration that the award may be based on an issue of credibility on which there has been no full, fair trial.

Valuation of an expert is itself affected by the valuer's degree of acquaintance not only with him but with what he is talking about, and the extent to which it passes through intermediaries. Potential for contamination is not always as obvious as in a recent example where solicitors wrote ". . . when we have decided what the experts have agreed at their meeting, it will be put before the arbitrator".

28 From the *Abbeystead* judgments, note 1, above.

29 "To do justice to a patient not previously known to him, the consultant probably requires at least one hour . . . thus permitting an assessment of the uniqueness of his personality and the development of his illness", modestly proclaims a Royal College of Psychiatrists memorandum . . . biographers, historians, even theologians, would be interested to learn of the techniques that enable some amongst us to assess the uniqueness of a personality . . . so adeptly." David Abrahamson, "Procedure Re-examined" (1974) *The Lancet*, 1153. Of course, it is of the essence of cross-examination that it aims to do two things at once – obtain specific information, and with sufficient time reveal the real character of the witness from which inferences may be drawn on other matters. The two functions have to be separated in deciding the procedure for any system of dispute resolution, as well as in the mind of the decision-maker (see below).

At least it may be possible to separate one from the other – valuation of a witness from valuation of his evidence – and to check the criteria being applied to the balance between them. Specifically, it is necessary to know when evidence is being valued by reference to nothing better than the ability of a witness to give evidence, or (to quote a notorious judgment) a "fragrance" (of either the witness or an advocate with whom he is identified) which is particularly irrelevant to specialised ability and knowledge. Perhaps expert arbitrators pay less attention to general credibility than lawyers, because it is often deduced by lawyers from the presence or absence of purely lawyerly qualities.

Another issue lies in balancing the distance that lends enchantment against the familiarity that brings knowledge, with or without the accompanying contempt. It seems that if the arbitrator wants to know as much as possible about the witness, he must take some risk of the witness, and advocates, getting to know him. It is conceivable nowadays that awe puts pressure to tell the truth only on the impressionable witness who may be inhibited by it, and particularly not on those with enough self-confidence to ignore the oath.

If that is so, the awe felt by some of the awesome for their awe-inspiring expedients is proportionate to the harm they do in practice. The differences in this context – because of closer physical proximity and eye contact in arbitration than court, the greater possibility of professional contacts, and the practice of going into arbitration battle without what some class as ceremonial dress and others protective clothing – have not been fully explored. Clearly, the right level of formality or informality must (to repeat the point of issue resolution yet again) depend on the particular issue, and persons (this is now accepted for children's evidence) but cannot solely be a matter of age and places involved.

The decision whether or not to call a witness whose expertise has been gained only by experience can be particularly hard, without evidence that putting a laying bricky into a production of the other branch is more likely to improve his memory than cause him to say whatever first comes into his head to get away.

The possibility that, unless special precautions are taken, the sooner opposing experts are required to meet the sooner expert war breaks out, or is made to break out, has obviously wide significance. Generally, few experts of the classes in list 4 do the "sorting" essential to their work with the help of oral cross-examination by an outsider, and the best of them are not necessarily best at articulating the most striking generalisations in the most simplistic terms. Those experts in a position to contribute most to solving disputes tend to prefer working in their own way, in the surroundings and language to which they are used, and for purposes with which they are in sympathy. So do advocates. If experts and advocates cannot both be accommodated, there is a danger that only the latter will remain.

Distinguishing advocates and experts

An advocate does not mention his own opinion; does not ask arbitrators to take on trust what he says because he says it; does not swear to pass on the truth - so cannot professionally commit perjury. An expert witness does and can. What use to an arbitrator is an advocate pretending to be an expert, examining an expert trying to be an advocate?

By jogging memory on the differences between the many classes and species of expertise, the attached lists may help to identify in time the scientific discoveries that mysteriously disappear after being aired confidently by advocates disguised as experts. Although the task can be so hard, occasionally internal disposal can take place almost as soon as the witness arranges his papers confidently with the air of one hired champion preparing to cross swords with another, then on every troublesome question demands to reread all documents, patently for time to hide instead of find the true answer. Sometimes the witness lingers on physically, because an advocate is too modest to trust himself with an elementary textbook in his own preparation time, preferring to get help during the hearing from a witness he is purporting to examine.

According to the high judicial authority that "the state of a man's mind is as much a state of fact as the state of his digestion",[30] this minority of experts has not yet been released formally from the oath. So direct and specific enquiry is perfectly permissible. An advocate, or the arbitrator if necessary, may enquire at least into the roles others played in writing the expert's report; what role he thinks he is playing now; and the whole truth about his opinions, including what they might be next week if he were on the other side. In any case, alarm bells that ring whenever an expert witness says "assume" or any of its many equivalents or guesses to more than two decimal places, must be part of an arbitrator's internal processes.

Separating lawyers from other experts

> ". . . the weakest link in the chain is the lawyer . . . Art or techniques have to be taught. Is it worth making specialists of pedestrian passers-by? . . . do not involve [lawyers] in debates on the imperfect generation of illogical gears . . . Days could be saved by denying them such treats".[31]
>
> "The difference between even a very roughly sketched flow net and an accurate one is commonly small compared to the difference between the flow pattern in the real soil and that indicated by the accurate flow net . . . Indeed, the two flow nets may have no resemblance whatsoever".[32]
>
> ". . . my nature is subdued
> To what it works in, like the dyer's hand,
> Pity me then, and wish I were renewed."

The issue is who should sort what cannot be solved just by name calling. Every class of experts applies double standards as between itself and other classes, in recognising or imagining diseases of specialisation and professional interests. That is the root of the controversy about who should devise and control "sorting" methods, particularly who should make the last all-important decision in law, fact and policy together, as

30 *Edgington* v. *Fitzmaurice* (1885) 29 ChD. 459 at 483, *per* Bowen L J.
31 Cedric Barclay, *Arbitration*.
32 Terzaghi and Peck, *Soil Mechanics* 2nd ed (1968), 163.

already discussed. It is widely acknowledged that lawyers have the most job-specific training and experience to decide what the law is. But if "law" is a genuine speciality, then prima facie lawyers have special qualification for nothing more, nor less. Members of the construction industry complain bitterly that issues of law, facts, language and policy are mixed-up when liability is imposed on them by lawyers, as in *Abbeystead* above. They say design philosophy and tendering art are too subtle for outsiders. Lawyers, specially if they have had the occasional fright when learning the internal thoughts of a non-lawyer arbitrator on law, are inclined to reply in kind. They complain about the short and long term results of arbitration by some engineers and other experts - as in the ground condition claims referred to above.

Yet, ask for a report from a geologist and you will sometimes get legal advice in reply. Surveyors who complain that lawyers make measurement of life too complicated, devote pages of legalese in Methods of Measurement to cast-iron drains. Lawyers' "sorting" ability, even with regard to pure fact, is valued and even emulated in an ambivalent way.

Perhaps that may be partly because the "trained legal mind" is trained by mental and verbal gymnastics that could be considered excessive, even absurd, if practised on material not so revered and, at least financially, rewarding as law. There is theological evidence of the wide value of such vigorous exercise on fully sacred texts. There is also evidence of the price sometimes paid for over-exertion: of minds snapping in the isolation of words, so that the "sorting" exercise becomes more an end in itself than a means of delivery.[33]

'Sorting' at Common Law

The common law "sorting" process known as "distinguishing" provides a striking illustration. It appears that "distinguishing" is useful training for judging even some scientific evidence, because scientific method (whatever exactly that is)[34] has been found to have something in common

33 For the secular benefits and dangers of training in "argument for the sake of heaven", see from Dean Swift, *Tale of a Tub*, to Rabbi Jonathan Sacks (1989) JLQ Vol.36 No. 2, p.30.

34 Most scientists receive no tuition in scientific method, but those who have been instructed perform no better as scientists than those who have not . . . Bacon is best described as an advocate of the . . . belief that natural knowledge was to be acquired not from authority . . . nor by syllogistic exercises . . . but by paying attention to the evidence of the senses . . . [however an] "experiment" today is not something that merely enlarges our sensory experience. It is a critical operation . . . gives a specific direction to the flow of thought" (Medawar, *Pluto's Republic* (1958) 78, 335, and see further below on Lord Chancellor Bacon).
But there and elsewhere the author and others consider it necessary to grapple with the complexities of these issues, not side-step them (see note 39). Contrast even the unusual admission of judicial method by Lord Diplock in *Home Office* v. *Dorset Yacht Co. Ltd.* [1970] 2 All ER 294, 326, 327) – as a first stage that is "analytical and inductive" followed by "the second stage" which is deductive and analytical" ending in a "choice . . . exercised by making a policy decision". Consider the similarity nevertheless between disasters in negligence in and out of court due to over- or under-distinguishing in concepts compared to reality, text above and below.

with it. At the same time, the practice supplies warnings. Those who have sharpened the skill recognise that unintentionally as well as intentionally they may "sort" judges' words more precisely than they "sort" reality. Conversely, a precedent is corrected because some refinement of fact in law was overlooked, and in considering an expert's report or evidence the difficulty for lawyers is not so much in finding any positive mistakes in it, but in appreciating that real refinements have been overlooked.

Obviously, the background sketched above goes some way to explain why lawyers are accused both of over-discriminating with their "hair splitting tools" (to quote a venerable Engineer arbitrator), and of making indiscriminate decisions on the applied sciences. By doing the former to words, we may do the latter in reality.

The background explains also the frequent but unsuccessful efforts by businessmen to return to a lost alleged paradise, where disputes were settled in a "businesslike" way. The belief seems to be that the "reality" felt directly by those working in business or science is lost beneath words which with skilful use can prove everything and nothing. Engineers say they harness the great forces of nature, which lawyers convert into words for play. Geologists claim that they experience rocks directly and naturally whereas some lawyers learn and dissect words about them from a distance.

But it is part of reality that by operating in words more than actions a lawyer can manage a great variety of "sorting". The old style family solicitor was consulted not because he knew more about the particular family than its members but because he had sorted out many families, and more strife in a week than most people have to deal with in their lifetimes.[35] Inexact words due to inexact thoughts that cause many physical disasters are also part of reality, and so it seems is logic.

Expert's Expertise

Experts in a particular list 4 class of expertise are not necessarily the best choice to deal with disputes about it. As most classes include some of the species of knowledge in list 5, it is necessary to distinguish what experts, do, think or say they do, prefer not to, admit they do not, and do not although others do – know. Lawyers are prepared to admit the ignorance of others by applying the valuable burden of proof, that legal equivalent to the "dead letter" "sorting" slot, according to which others do not know at all what they do not know to be more probable than its opposite.

Any science fiction in the contractor's money claim in our test case, would not have been best investigated by those who specialise in it. The opinions of an architect might have been useful if there was an issue of design art, but not on safety from gas. Whether he was motivated by

35 Which is not what Lord Gardner was reported as saying when Lord Chancellor – "Of course, by the time a barrister has been into a hundred divorces, he knows a great deal more about family life than the ordinary person does".

kindness or confusion a decision by a Robin Hood or Solomon obviously would have been particularly dangerous on the ability of methane to travel. An amateur or all-rounder using possibly educated commonsense or a guess might have had a higher chance – at least as high as a tossed coin – than an expert made systematically wrong by an occupational disease or by his investment as a dedicated supporter of one out of several schools of expert thought. However long a cross-examination takes to extract it, evidence of what is possible is irrelevant when the issue is what is probable. A decision from inside the construction industry might not have been satisfactory to the project owner outside it if the issues involved public money and policy.

Binding precedent is neither pragmatism nor necessarily survival of the fittest. The presumption of many expert-arbitrators that law is irrational has to be allowed for by advocates appearing before them, whether or not it is justified.

Generally, different Institutional and Personal Processes are necessary to value and distinguish the following: tested compared to untested or untestable data; hindsight on the past, speculation about the future, and measuring what is present; academic and "muddy boots", street or site wisdom; state of the art and experiments; computer runs, precedent, tradition and fact. Dogma of one system is no more proof than faith in another. Many expert mechanisms only work with the help of nudges, kicks or winks from experienced operators. Special precautions have to be taken when artistry is modestly claimed for science, since no artistic scientist can know more than another about what is not yet known – as in the state of the art.

Generally, comprehension may not be enough. It is possible that a lawyer applies a simple rule of law only when he does not have a sufficient overview of the case to do justice to its peculiarities and patterns by working on it internally. Can he do so much for other specialties, or they for law? The quick making-up of the brief is a recipe for superficiality all round.

The whole purpose of this section is to suggest that helpful criteria in choosing arbitrators may be obtained by comparing the proportion of their training and experience that particular practitioners of each of the classes listed are likely to have spent on relevant kinds of "sorting". I imagine that a nuclear physicist spends a high proportion on "pure" conceptual "sorting", and consequently not enough on the personal behaviour of other nuclear scientists to be best qualified to judge that. A consulting engineer's training and experience may have been largely devoted to specific facts and practical activities on a relatively few projects, for the purpose of avoiding conflict and disaster. But as a result the concrete (the only word) realities of construction will be enhanced immeasurably for him. In three ways already quoted, the importance of actuality over words has been judicially acknowledged.[36] So an engineer may be worst qualified to "sort" some issues arising from construction disasters, physical or financial, and, of course, most qualified to decide others.

36 In the dissenting judgment on remoteness in the *Abbeystead* appeal; the importance attributed to seeing witnesses in *Abbeystead*; and note 6.

On this occasion it is particularly relevant to mention the importance of these criteria for inter-disciplinary teaching. From the side of a lawyer teaching non-lawyers, my problem (no doubt for obvious reasons) has always been to transmit not vices but virtues. The virtue of concentrating on principles may even reduce the need to consult lawyers, and makes legalism no more attractive to non-lawyers than it is to lawyers. The pleasures of constant physical, mental, and verbal movement between construction actuality and our conceptions of it, allows flexibility to us (and sleight of hand to others) in solving legal and technical issues.

The loudest complaint about lawyers, that they create adversarial relations and not merely safeguard adversarial interests, is dealt with later on.

Sorting ourselves – the semi-conscious arbitrator

> "Impartiality does not consist in not having prejudices . . . we all have them. The art consists in the ability to discard prejudices [which] largely depends on a sufficient measure of self-awareness to be conscious of this defect of character, in so far as it is a defect, and to learn to recognise it when the devil comes and tempts one. My advice is: be aware of your prejudices, and hang them upon the peg with your raincoat before you come into court. I would also prescribe..a decent regard for the received wisdom of reported cases."[37]
>
> "The reasonable man is to be expected not to hold an irrational belief . . . the exclusion of the irrational is usually an easy and comparatively unimportant process."[38]
>
> ". . . the automatic selection of ideas, even where very complex information processing is required, is a dominant feature of human thought . . . there is a price to be paid for this enormous processing power. Sometimes important details will be selected out, irrelevant details selected in."[39]

One of the many injustices that make an advocate's lot unhappy, is that he is criticised for being able to set aside his personal views and feelings to represent all-comers, but not praised for the beneficial vacuity in which he is trained so that he can value evidence objectively.

A benefit of changing position from time to time in the practice of law, is the opportunity to appreciate the full extent of judicial conscientiousness: the extent to which the moment of decision concentrates the mind on the evidence. Yet I find it hard to forget what reputedly lives down where my "gut feelings" come from. I fear that threatened feelings – even nothing more sinister, or less powerful, than lifelong pessimism to optimism – may simply go deeper and try harder by creating a feeling of unease unless a particular decision is made. Do I always know for sure how or when I decide – always on the evidence piece by

37 "Of Judges and Judging", Speech delivered to magistrates by the then Lord Chancellor, Lord Hailsham (June 1984).

38 Lord Devlin, *The Enforcement of Morals*, (1965) viii. See also Cohen, "Can human irrationality be experimentally demonstrated", *The Behavioural and Brain Sciences* (1981) 4, 317, 378.

39 Jonathan St B T Evans in *Thinking and Reasoning* (1988) ed. Jonathan Baron, 136. Hence, *e.g.* the "halo effect" by which we may be systematically biased in favour of the good even in respect of matters on which they are bad.

piece, rational step by rational step, or, if instead I decide the case as a whole, how reliable is the sudden vision?[40] Occasionally, I mentally reverse the names of the parties, deliberately, to help isolate what has actually been proved by specific evidence from vaguer impressions in, or even from outside, the proceedings. Still I hope that some such impressions result from experiences that cannot be measured only because they were so immediate. On the other hand, I know we can fill gaps in evidence only on the assumption that others behave as rationally as we hope we do – applying *omnia praesumuntur rite esse acta* writ large while knowing it is the most irrational presumption of all.

Overall, the conviction persists that a system of checks and balances is helpful, using what may be called the arbitral stream of semi-consciousness. The name is intended to steer between the extremes in literature, psychology and law. In law on the one hand there is the belief quoted above, that the irrational even when it is believed to be rational can and should be rationally discarded like an old coat. On the other hand, there is the old justification for arbitration awards without reasons – that arbitrators (like juries) are wrong so far as they are conscious of their reasons. Fortunately, there is support from several classes of expert set out in list 4 for the suggestion that the truth is neither quite so hard nor easy: that re-enforcing the relatively simple habit of checking internal processes in a structured way, may do more for decision-making than either deep self-analysis[41] or easy infallibility.

The rough checklists to jog the mind are attached, but a sample stream might include background material – am I doing the opposite of what I think; making precise calculations from imprecise data; up to my old tricks; if what I am thinking is wrong can I find out in time privately; who is doing what for (to, against) me; do the advocates understand me too little or too well; is anybody playing the three card trick on me – shuffling between reality, computer or other models and words, so I can no longer tell which is which?

Most important, what system are we in (*e.g.* as we do want construction law to be about the system of construction not about the system of construction law, I will not interpret a specification as if it were an imperfect part of a legal system); what tolerances are safe in the system; what tolerances am I applying, and by the end will they cancel out or be cumulative? The dangers of mentally adding one tolerance to another as one (theoretically) provisional conclusion has to be added to another to keep pace with the evidence and argument, are no less than the dangers of adding together physical tolerances in construction. It is alleged that different systems can accommodate different overall tolerances – that in commercial cases the precisely right result may not be crucial. Enough has already been mentioned about the danger that a

40 See note 46.

41 On which see notably the works of Jerome Frank and Julius Stone. Consider in the light of the references in note 34 the simplicity of Stone's suggestion that "although lawyers would do well, to be sure, to learn scientific logic from the expositors of scientific method, it is far more important that they catch the spirit of the creative scientist . . ." (*Law and the Modern Mind*, 98).

small tolerance may make the decision wholly wrong, and every system must have limits on what it can tolerate.

Arbitrators' rights

> "The Arbitrator shall proceed within as short a time as possible to establish the facts of the case by all appropriate means" (ICC Rule 14.1).

That duty prevents a supine inclination by an ICC Arbitrator, even under the weight of common law practice. It seems also to give him rights – to avoid drowning in words; to get whatever information he needs to make the best decision he can; and to preserve the integrity of the system for the benefit of its future customers.

Failure to find the facts, as when both sides fail to carry out some test for fear it will prove too much, can hardly be "appropriate means" of establishing the facts. Scores of hearing days are rarely "as short a time as possible".

When Bacon's *Essay on Judicature* is so often quoted to support the common law presumption against the inquisitor, what follows after his advice that "an over speaking judge is no well-tuned cymbal" is not always included – "The parts of a judge in hearing are four: to direct the evidence; to moderate the length, repetition, or impertinency of speech; to recapitulate, select and collate the material points of that which has been said; and to give the rule, or sentence".

Not only was that written some time before the ICC Rules were conceived, and when an arbitrator had only to adjudicate on the simpler sciences that Bacon investigated, but the weapons used by advocates against each other and jointly or severally against arbitrators were simpler too. The issue of Gentlemen v. Players in law is a difficult one – some of the newer "tactics" may only do in a professional way what was previously done amateurishly.

It will be seen that the problems that have been discussed so far are all interrelated, and their solutions closely related to what is here (partly to avoid propaganda overtones by now attached to other names) called "interactive" procedure. Advance documentation tends to mongrelise procedure towards a desirable blend of adversarial and inquisitorial, particularly by bestowing the confidence without which a wise arbitrator will do little more during the hearing than look wise, or an unwise one ask what a gasket is 50 days into a hearing on a technical engineering dispute. Of course, it is only better for an arbitrator to hide ignorance that he immediately removes privately before full confusion sets in.

The "undoubted advantage of a dialogue between Bench and Bar in detecting, refining and resolving the crucial point or points"[42] must apply to facts as well as law – advocates will not run bad points of fact any more than law when they know the case will not be decided on them. The actual practice is one example of the extent to which the common law system acknowledges the lesser education of lawyers in fact finding

42 Court of Appeal, Civil Division, Review of the Legal Year 1985–86.

than in law (should it increase?) by shielding our mistakes from correction. See generally the restraint in considering trial judges decisions of fact, as explained in the *Abbeystead* appeal, and of course those of lawyer-arbitrators.

Obstinate intervention may also be necessary to ensure effective exercise of the powers which exist to rationalise expert evidence, but which are opposed for reasons discussed above. That is only part of the greater task which interactive procedure has to perform because of the peculiarity that some of the helpers with "sorting" are engaged to produce late delivery, non-delivery, or misdelivery. An unavoidable consequence of the just system that there is no winner or loser until each party has discharged all his evidential ammunition, is that weapons (including advocacy) necessary and legitimate to help the just cause to prevail are available to the unjust during that enforced suspension of disbelief. It is necessary to minimise the resulting conflict between control by advocates and performance of an arbitrator's duties.

On top of that, there are places where fine bright procedural lines simply cannot be drawn. To take a trivial example: because an advocate cannot be required to be positively repellent, he must be allowed to follow the textbook advice that "Having concentrated attention upon himself, [he] should seek to create a friendly and sympathetic link between the tribunal and himself and to use that link for the purpose of inspiring a favourable attitude towards his client" [43] even by laughing too much at an arbitrator's jokes. But an arbitrator does not have to allow himself to be fooled for long.

It must follow that neither the privileges of, nor the opportunities to abuse, the adversarial system are granted for their own sake, still less for the sake of advocates. It further follows that there is good reason why an arbitrator should "strain every nerve and sinew" as much as advocates do[44] even before he writes his award, in order to refine the system for each particular issue, provided he does not defeat the whole system. If spells are being cast, they should be broken as quickly as possible, even when (to change back to the authorised metaphor) that is as daunting as stopping Hamlet in mid soliloquy. (It helps to remember that performers are rarely allowed to decide the length of their own auditions, and even the referee of champions no doubt had to intervene occasionally at the risk of injury to himself.) In addition, the privileges of advocacy exist only within the system, and outside the system (as in public relations exercises intended to permeate to the arbitrator) they must be removed. No general rules can exercise all that control in advance, and only the arbitrator is in a position to do it effectively from tactical and procedural issue to issue.

For example, in normal circumstance the last place where an arbitrator should interfere is in cross-examination. But when an advocate uses his acting skill on the passing pejorative, whether spoken or pantomimed,[45] there are various ways in which an arbitrator may in turn mime his

43 Mazengarb, *Advocacy in our Time* (1964), 141.

44 The quotation is from another Chairman of the Bar Council – Lord Alexander of Weedon.

45 Rumpole's "raised eyebrow or two" is restrained stage business compared to some.

presumption that improper comment is being preferred to privileged questioning because the evidence of the witness is invincible. Obviously, that is most necessary when the opposing advocate fears by intervention to show concern with his opponent's tactics, or lack of confidence in the witness.

In these respects, arbitrators may place greater temptation and danger in the path of advocates than most confident judges. Unlike judges, their alleged eccentricities may not be known in advance – whether more inclined to see ducks, rabbits or stranger species.[46] Deafening silence due to self- restraint, incredulous fascination, fear to spoil the sport or undue deference, encourages (sometimes compels, as already described) irrelevant submissions, and may even lead to tactics no lawyer would dare try-on in court.

The problems go round in several circles. Each advocate has to try both to exploit and protect from his opponent every blind spot and Achilles heel the arbitrator might conceivably have from time to time. Only the arbitrator may know definitely what they are. The less the advocate knows confidently about the arbitrator the less safe he feels in not taking, repeatedly, all the bad points of law or fact. The more he learns, the more he may be tempted to take particular ones.

Parties need to observe that the arbitrator can be trusted when he says he is only probing. They need confidence that he will climb down even from some beloved but wrong "judges point" despite its approval in flattering terms by one side, and can exit gracefully from the arena with his mind more open than it was when he entered, despite being bruised in an argument he started.

Turning to the most difficult case of control of tactics, to separate legitimate strategy from tactics – with their listed alphabetical progression from delay through schoolboy pranks to suicidal (for clients) – a balance is once again necessary between the general institutional rules and the personal processes of the arbitrator that can take account of the specific circumstances of the moment. If procedural rules try to cover all possibilities in advance, less time may be saved by using the powers they give than is wasted in arguing word by word about what they do or do not allow.

An arbitrator can take pride in frustrating only those tactics not too clever for him to detect. But given how different manoeuvres look from the arbitrator's viewpoint and that of their perpetrators, and how eager non-lawyer arbitrators seem to be to have their expectations of lawyers' tricks confirmed, it does seem that many will be caught out without too much waste of time provided the rules are robust enough.

Even the choice of "sorting" processes may raise a tactical issue of demarcation or self-promotion between "sorters". I fear that our particular professional arrangements encourage a few of the more ferocious members of my "lower" branch to squabble with their opposite numbers over the only scraps of reality that (unless they take care) are left to

46 See Wittgenstein's famous optical illusion, in *Philosophical Investigations* (II.ii). Imagery may be more important than words, despite the authority quoted at note 12 above.

them in proceedings, not because the scraps are important but because they are not.

Scoring issue resolution

> "Chaos umpire sits,
> and by decision more embroils the fray
> By which he reigns: next him high arbiter.
> Chance governs all. Into this wild abyss,
> The womb of Nature, and perhaps her grave. . . ."[47]

> "Chaos sets ultimate limits on what science can predict. There is more to chaos than meets the eye . . . It often has deeper structure, a hidden order or surprising simplicity . . . In chaotic systems, predictions are foiled by small errors which creep into measurements, and create unexpectedly huge mistakes later on...by amplifying what we don't know . . . [but] the great promise of chaos lies in the hope that randomness might become predictable'"[48]

Views on scoring our tunneling test case are implicit in what has already been discussed. Attachment "B" adds a Disputes Resolution Index, because until the index returns to the base figure of the very first decision – quick, omnipotent, and at no material expense – a choice of the exact relation between depth (and safety) of decision and cost has to be made. The equation would be simpler if the depth of decision achieved increased in proportion to any resources expended above the cost of the first System in list 1.

It is believed that parties do generally want more depth of decision than coin-tossing despite more cost, and that this paper is right in claiming that the pick of all systems can be matched to each issue. If so, it is helpful to collect together broadly (in no particular order) ways in which the various listed Systems are or could be designed to improve the balance of the Index:

- The parties do more for themselves than in "full" arbitration. At the highest, they decide their own priorities – who they want to do what for them and how in deciding their disputes. At the lowest, they do as much as possible of the administrative and clerical work, copying and bundling etc., that is no more mysterious than the similar work they manage to do in their own businesses, using technology they are used to. They may even do para-legal work in interviewing witnesses etc., particularly in industries such as construction which are well experienced in disputes.
- The parties usually do less for themselves than in full arbitration, in the sense that they forego some of the usual activities of their own champions, and the resources they may deploy are limited, particularly by time-limits on hearings. That is probably the only way to compel each party and his advisers to concentrate on his best points, which they are usually in the best position to judge.

47 Milton, *Paradise Lost*, Book II.
48 Newspaper report, summarising Glick "Chaos" (1988).

That is, presuming their cases exist objectively, and not only in the mind of the decision-maker. In any event, if he disagrees internally with the priorities chosen by the parties, after he has learnt as much as possible from and about them, he can say so and if necessary allow extra time.

- Preparation and planning proceed as soon as possible, and decisions are made as late as possible. The process does not simply begin at the beginning and run without pause or deviation to the end. It may proceed from stage to stage, with gaps to enable more information to be obtained, positions reviewed, issues "sorted" or "re-sorted" and possibly procedure changed. Different parts may even proceed concurrently.
- Of course, the procedure aims to be most user friendly - robust, flexible, informal, without becoming indisciplined or a free for all. Efficiency and the rules of natural justice (not in that order) are what count. The unfriendly user is the most difficult problem, with which a poacher turned gamekeeper may be best able to deal.
- Full use is made of the speciality of investigation/advocacy for specialised work that needs it. The decision maker (if any) generally is more active in master-minding the proceedings, and as master of ceremonies. But he may decide less than an arbitrator. Some or all facts or law may not be determined at all: instead each party may decide them for himself, in the process of deciding what he will unilaterally offer, or will agree in structured or unstructured negotiation. Generally, the decider or conciliator is presumed not to need spoon feeding or to be led by the hand (to the side of the road where he does or does not want to go), but should he prove a danger to himself and the parties the alternative procedure may make it easier to dispose of him.
- When it is part of the system that the dispute decider gives the fullest possible help, at meetings or hearings held wholly or partly for that purpose, his intervention is less easily mistaken for an uncontrollable prejudgment.
- So far as possible the raw data and expert advice are used as directly as possible, minimising intermediate handling by which they may inadvertently be contaminated or dispersed. As always, the aim must be accurately to combine actuality and its interpretation.
- The disputes tax is avoided – the penal processes by which the costs of proceedings are an appropriate percentage of the turnover involved. In construction contracts the turnover may be reckoned to include the whole costs of the works, which consequently are subjected to a total post-mortem however small the part in issue.
- The rules on costs are more flexible. The dispute decider may have power to award separately costs spent "sorting" any issue, and generally have a discretion that goes much further than is normally allowed to an arbitrator.
- Every decision-maker needs the most help he can get from the helpers representing the parties; and the helpers need as much help as possible from the decision-maker to avoid the temptations to abuse the system. It is not improper for the decider to try to

increase the constructive input already made by such helpers – a destructive input is not of the essence even of the adversarial system. For example, helpers may be required to say as soon as possible what proof they offer on each issue, and what method of resolution would be most effective for it, and (if necessary) to defend their offers.

- Special effort is made to make full use of all available resources. A very large issue, which it is not possible to deal with here, is how best to use the expertise of a three-man arbitration tribunal – instead of having a total of, say, nine distinguished lawyers involved in a major case in separated groups. It might also be possible to avoid the embarrassment for an advocate of appearing to flatter an arbitrator to his face – so often it is necessary to answer the reprimands of an opponent for not calling expert evidence, by explaining that the arbitrator was chosen because he is an expert.
- Full advantage is taken of elementary "sorting" mechanics. The written or electronic record is presumed to be the basic source of information and the starting point; the minimum narrative joins the recorded pieces of evidence, only supplementing and completing, correcting and contradicting (as necessary); to avoid duplication, the narrative cross-refers to the record by an agreed system of references and marking-up; reports of cases relied on are similarly marked-up; a code for physical marking on documents and chronologies does much of the work performed by the repetition necessary in oral advocacy for emphasis and in case the arbitrator forgets; practical details, such as putting cross-references used in the working bundle on each copy of every document, apart of course from minimising the number of copies, are agreed or imposed at the start.

Incidentally, the horror of unilateral marking can be overcome by having colour codes for the parties and consolidating marking on a single document as soon as possible (now with the help at least of colour copying machines).

But even with such mechanical matters, of course, nothing is easy – why should it be in complex disputes. A small example is the use of television cameras in Official Referee's Courts, so that all those in attendance can see the details of drawings to which a witness is referring. Even such a beneficial approach has one adverse side-effect. In the past, the huddle over drawings tended to exclude completely those lawyers who would otherwise slow down the proceedings with their charming disclaimers of any knowledge of the subject with which they were dealing.

Conclusion

Having reached such practicalities, the precise implementation of issue resolution has to be left to another day – which it is hoped will arrive at least partly with the New Style Contract of the Institution of Civil

Engineers. But a partial (in both senses) score sheet follows here, at the very end.

In the meantime, we know from other listed subjects how important "testability"[49] and "falsibility" are, and that feedback is necessary if we are not eventually to have as much of the new systems of Alternative Disputes Resolution without knowing how and when it works, as we have of the methods it seeks to replace. But at least the thesis of this paper is accepted as well as rejected in this respect, as we carefully select the issues to which we apply the overwhelming evidence that – "feedback seems to be of very little use in helping to correct and improve performances. It sees that in areas we think we know something about, we persist in thinking we have personal insights that will take our performance beyond the average".[50]

Attachment A – rules relating to experts

English law is tolerant in granting expert status. Expertise gained by practice and experience without formal qualification is sufficient. (*Testis lupinaris sufficit ad factum in lupinari* – an occupant is a qualified witness on events in a bordello). The courts have heard expert evidence since at least the 16th century.

But "If the subject under investigation does not require specialist knowledge, expert evidence will generally be excluded, although a specialist witness may be both an expert witness and a witness of fact."

A court does not have to act in accordance with an expert's approach to a subject, and the weight to be attached to expert evidence is a matter for the court: *R* v. *Rivett* (1950) 34 Cr App Rep 87, CCA. The Court of Appeal in *Abbeystead* (see text and note 1) said that:

> ". . . the Court will not support the dismissal of a witness's evidence where this rests on what is shown to be a misunderstanding or a wrong impression. In resolving conflicts of expert evidence the judge remains the judge; he is not obliged to accept evidence simply because it comes from an illustrious source; he can take account of demonstrated partisanship and lack of objectivity. But, save where an expert is guilty of a deliberate attempt to mislead (as happens only very rarely), a coherent reasoned opinion expressed by a suitably qualified expert should be the subject of a coherent reasoned rebuttal, unless it can be discounted for other good reason."

An expert may refresh his memory by reference to works on the subject of his skill.

There is much law on the restriction that an expert cannot be asked the very question which is to be decided, "unless the issue is substantially one of science or skill merely [and] the expert . . . has himself observed the facts."(Phipson, *Manual of Evidence*, 3rd ed.118):

49 Refer to *Conjectures and Refutations* and other works of Karl Popper, and discussions provoked by them – note 34, above.

50 David Healy, *The Suspended Revolution* (1990).

"I venture to assert that . . . at least 9/10th [of the shorthand notes of patent actions] is devoted to questions which either openly or under more or less skillful disguise are directed to eliciting the opinion of the witnesses upon one or other of the issues in the case, or the construction of documents . . . The amount of time wasted by this irregular method . . . must in the aggregate be fabulous . . . But the waste of time is not the whole of the mischief, for the admission of the opinion of eminent experts upon the issue leads to the balancing of opinions and tends to shift responsibility from the Bench or the jury to the witness box . . . It is rare to find any substantial difference of opinion between eminent experts upon matters of science whenever it is possible to disassociate the question from a mediate connection with the issues in the action . . . whereas on the question of the meaning of documents a contest between counsel and expert witnesses will often be maintained for hours, and not infrequently for days together" (*Crosfield* v. *Techno-Chemical Laboratories* (1913) TLR 378 *per* Mr Justice Neville).

As to procedural developments on expert evidence generally:

". . . there emerged . . . a fundamental misunderstanding between the parties as to the nature of the defendants' case . . . By the stage this trial has now reached I am . . . much better acquainted with the ramifications of the matter than I was when the question of expert evidence was first considered . . . This confirms my original preliminary view that this is the sort of case where the views of experts will be of the greatest value if given in the light of all the available factual material, particularly that shed by the examination and cross-examination . . . I . . . now direct that the expert evidence should be heard after all the oral factual evidence has been given . . . [Counsel] submitted that I have no power to make an order of this kind. He submits that it is a rule of law of fundamental importance that in our adversarial system counsel for each party has the right to call what witnesses he chooses and in the order which he considers best serves the interest of his clients . . . This, in my view, is something which the High Court has power to do under the inherent jurisdiction it possesses as part of the unwritten constitution of this country. Accordingly, if and to the extent that it can be said that this practice purports to override what was previously regarded as the position, the answer is simply that in the Commercial Court at least, the High Court has decided to change the way in which it previously chose to regulate one of its own procedures."

The limits on an arbitrator's right to use his own knowledge are dealt with very fully by Professor John Uff QC, in "Making effective use of the expertise of arbitrators", Chartered Institute of Arbitrators, *Bernstein Lectures* (1989), 26, at 42–50.

Attachment B – Disputed Resolution Index

The Resolution Index for each issue is the Value in dispute (as a rough measure of complexity) multiplied by the Depth of Judgment reached, divided by the full Cost (including costs of time and of any adverse side-effects):

$$RI = \frac{V \times D}{C}$$

List 1 – Systems

1. Tossed coin.
2. Court.
3. A single lawyer arbitrator.
4. An expert in the same business as one or both of the parties, or in a different business, as sole arbitrator.
5. Tribunal of two experts and a lawyer. Either the Lawyer or an expert is chairman or umpire.
6. Two lawyers with an expert-lawyer/expert chairman or umpire.
7. Each of above combinations, with inquisitorial procedure and/or adversarial procedure, and party and/or tribunal experts.
8. Lawyer arbitrator with technical assessor, or vice-versa.
9. Mini-arbitration.
10. Flip-flop arbitration.
11. Conciliation or mediation.
12. Old case stated or limited appeal to Court of First Instance and Appeal Court[s].
13. Referee procedure.
14. Contract Review Boards.
15. Decision by the Engineer or Architect named in a construction contract.
16. Public enquiry of one or the many kinds.
17. Technical investigation and report, without any "judicial" procedure.
18. Agreed settlement.

List 2 – Institutional Processes

Accident (including adjournments, after lunch, weekends).
Administration, filing, "dating service", messenger service.
Admission, confession and avoidance.
Admissibility, credibility, hearsay, relevance.
Adversarial, hypher-adversarial, analytical, enquiring, free for all, inquisitorial, interactive, mongrelised, user friendly, for unfriendly users.
Advocacy, cross-examination, chat, public relations, salesmanship.
Appeals, second and successive thoughts.
Awe, distance, eye contact, entering the arena, familiarity, humanity, (in)formality, (in)discipline, ceremonial and protective clothing.
Burdens of proof, control, hearsay, judicial notice, Judges point, policy, presumptions, relevance, time-limits.
Communications, dialogue, meta-communications.
Cross-fertilisation.
Destabilising, division, fixing what is unbroken, rocking the boat, shallowness, stability.
Doubt (real, lurking, no reasonable), balance of probabilities, possibilities, whitewash.
Fees (amount, instalment system, double bookings).
Gentlemen v. players.
Hearing (day in "court", fair, unfair, hasty, time-(un)limited, leisurely, urgent).
Hidden agenda.
Investigating, "making-up", managing, preparing, playacting, producing, rehearsing.

Kick, nod, wink.
Pleadings, particulars, discovery of documents, interrogatories, marshalling, marking-up.
Strategy and tactics (delay, cost, Micawberism, manning levels, money, page-turning, Rotteweiler, schoolboy, silence, suicidal, surprise, try-on, taking a line), win at all costs.
Tools and tricks of, and stock in, trade, privilege.
Training, re-training.

List 3 – Personal Processes

Achilles heel, bewilderment, blind spot, concentration, confusion,(in)competence, judgment, mistake, obstinacy, self-deception, semi-conscious, spellbound, wisdom (street, site, and other), unconscious, youthful impetuosity.
Bias, empathy, hostility ("halo" effect etc. etc.), (im)partiality, (in)dependance, memory, obsession, optimism, pessisimism, prejudice, professional or psychological investment, naivety, obstinacy, personal burdens of proof and (ir)rebuttable) presumptions, rationalisation, realism, sympathetic listening, suspicious listening, (in)tolerance, tolerances.
Complacency, credulity, desire for advancement or popularity, dryness, inertia, integrity, charity, instinct, feeling mercy, scepticism, sky-is-falling, self-satisfaction, sin (original or deadly).
Communication (with clarity, eloquence, jargon).
Comprehending, descending into the arena, deciding, gut feeling, intuition, learning and learning curve, selecting, "sorting", overview.
Mind (closed, decisive, empty, judicial, open).
Moment[s] of decision.
Personal experience, knowledge, practice, skill (disclosed or not).
Silence, intervention, interaction, self-revelation.

List 4 – Classes of Experts

Amateur, bogus, professional.
Art, commerce, craft, industry.
Commonsense, conventional wisdom, forklore, tradition.
Ethics, ends v. means, philosophy, public and private policy.
Finance, valuation (high-stakes).
Information processing (including advocacy, computer codology, management, recording).
Language (aphoristic, businesslike, euphemistic, jargon, legal, legalistic, literal, sharp-edged, technical, words about words), graphics.
Law, justice (natural, palm tree, of Robin Hood, Solomon), and alternatives (amiable composition, fairness, hard case bad law, bad law hard case).
Logic (deduction, induction, legal, strict, tautology).
Mathematics and statistics (accounting, higher, number crunching, quantity surveying).
Science (alternative, fiction, forensic, applied physical, behaviourial, biological, social, pure).
Technology (high, low, floodgate control).

List 5 – Species of Experts

Abstract, academic, theory (bottom up or top down).
Assumed, calculated, estimated, factual, guesstimated, guessed, knowledgeable, measured, plausible, presumed, skilful, state of the art.
Certain, chaotic, defined (fine bright line), random, rule of thumb, grey area.
Complex, crude, deep, primitive, (ir)rational, simple, simplistic, sophisticated, superficial.
Custom, precedent.
Dogma, faith, fiction, ideology, illusion, stranger than fiction.
Empirical, (selectively) pragmatic, practical, muddy boots.
General, specific, job-specific, occupation disease.
In good faith, bad faith, careful, negligent.
Justiciable, non-justiciable.
Present, hindsight of the past, future.
Recorded, by writing or electronics, doctored, unrecorded.
True, tested (in the field, in the laboratory, by time, survival of the fittest, with ulterior motive, by cross-examination, by feedback), time-honoured, self-fulfilling, untestable.

KEY: [+] = Productive
[−] = Wasteful
. . . [AD] = All depends

TUNNEL GAS – SAFETY AND MONEY DISPUTE
PARTIAL SCORE CARD

(1) ISSUES/SUB-ISSUES/SUB-SUB-ISSUES	(2) COSTS TIME/MONEY/SIDE-EFFECTS	(3) DEPTH
ENDS:		SAFETY : TOLERANCES VALUATION: TOLERANCES [+]
A FAULTY TESTING FOR GAS DURING DRIVE [−] 1 FAULTY EQUIPMENT 2 FAULTY RECORDING AND RECOLLECTION.	A1&2 INVESTIGATION [+] LEGAL LANGUAGE [−] EXPERIENCE: [+] A1 ORAL ADVOCACY [−] A2 CROSS-EXAMINATION [+] (but see D) ORAL ADVOCACY and DIALOGUE [AD]	
B SOLE OR CONCURRENT DELAY TO DRIVE BY GAS?	B INFORMATION PROCESSING [+] COMPUTER CODOLOGY [−] COMMON SENSE [+] SOLOMON [−]	
C VALUATION OF DELAY COSTS	C SITE WISDOM [+] MATHEMATICS [+] NUMBER CRUNCHING [−]	
D CREDIBILITY OF MR X 1 AN EXPERT 2 UNSKILLED WORKER 3 MISTAKEN 4 LYING	D1&4 CROSS-EXAMINATION [+] DISTANCE [+] D2&3 CROSS-EXAMINATION [−] CHAT [+] AWE and DISTANCE [−] D1to4 OVERVIEW [+]	
MEANS: CONSECUTIVE OR CONCURRENT DECISION OF ISSUES HEARING TIME	A&C CONCURRENT [+] TIME-LIMITS [+] But B1&4 UNLIMITED [+]	

12 Getting the best from ICC arbitration

Martin Harman

Synopsis

In this paper a practising English solicitor gives a view on the ways in which the ICC Rules of Arbitration may be utilised to best advantage in terms of economy, speed and achieving an appropriate procedure for each particular case. The position under the ICC Rules is contrasted to the English approach of applying the Supreme Court's Rules by analogy.

Introduction

Arbitrations of any sort are to be avoided. If an arbitration is inevitable, the lawyer must take every opportunity to put his client in a position in which he can either negotiate an advantageous settlement or, if that is not possible, secure the most advantageous award. This is what is meant by getting the best from the arbitration, and the rules and procedures must recognise these practical and commercial requirements.

Getting the best from any arbitration is largely dependent upon making proper provision for the procedure under which it is to be conducted, and thereafter utilising that procedure to the best strategic advantage. Although enormous progress has been made recently, UK arbitrations, particularly those in the construction field, still leave much to be desired. All too often they are allowed to assume a life of their own and what is already financially and emotionally taxing for a client, becomes a positive nightmare. Arbitration grew out of the need of persons of commerce to have a commercially viable dispute resolution procedure which could cope with disputes which the courts were singularly unsuited for. Regrettably, over the years, the arbitration process has been hijacked by lawyers. Now all too often it has become a pale imitation of High Court procedure, to which it is supposed to offer an alternative. What is more, this pale imitation does not possess the sanctions available in the High Court. As a consequence most lay persons with practical experience of an arbitration are usually badly affected by that experience and

Claimants and Defendants alike, who have embarked upon an arbitration emerge sadder, wiser and poorer people.

Lawyers must regrettably take a large measure of blame for this state of affairs. When faced with a commercial framework for which procedural rules are to be adopted, they tend to apply rules with which they are familiar, namely the rules of court. This has in the past created a situation in which it has been said:[1]

> "Where lawyers, having no other procedure to apply, are employed, they can only use their traditional expertise and training. Hence construction arbitrations have become a thing of wonder, even to the legal profession. Their cost and length place them in the Guinness Book of Records and their means is as thoroughly unsatisfactory as their end."

It is my view, and indeed my experience, that properly administered, an ICC arbitration can overcome a great number of the problems which have beset traditional UK arbitrations. One reason for this is the ICC's commitment to a speedy and efficient dispute resolution procedure, a philosophy which finds expression in Article 18 of the Rules of Arbitration which obliges the arbitrator to render an award within six months of the signing of the Terms and Reference. In this paper I shall endeavour to examine the ICC Rules in order to consider:

- how the best use may be made of the ICC Rules, once selected.
- how the adoption of the ICC procedure compares with an arbitration under High Court procedure (which is the almost inevitable result of making no express provision).

Choice of procedural rules

Where there is an agreement for ICC arbitration, Article 11 of the ICC Rules provides that:

> "The rules governing the proceedings before the arbitrator shall be those resulting from these Rules and, where these Rules are silent, any rules which the Parties (or, failing them, the arbitrator) may settle, and whether or not reference is thereby made to a municipal procedural law to be applied to the arbitration."

The Rules themselves thus acknowledge that they do not address all possible questions and envisage that additional rules may be slected by the parties or the arbitrator; indeed one of the more significant features of the Rules is their flexibility and adaptability. The question is whether the parties should, prior to the commencement of the arbitration, make express provision for matters not dealt with. If so, how should they go about this task?

The parties should think hard before declining to take advantage of the opportunity to provide themselves with a set of procedural rules, which may match the dispute between them. There are a number of available options:

- to adopt the procedural rules of a municipal legal system, whether that of the place of arbitration or any other;

1 *New Civil Engineer* 12 March 1981, 13.

- to incorporate a non-municipal set of procedural rules such as the UNCITRAL rules or the Supplementary Rules governing the Presentation and Reception of Evidence in International Commercial Arbitration promulgated by the International Bar Association;
- to construct their own scheme either by invoking rules drawn from any of the above systems or by their own design;
- to do nothing, in which case matters of procedure will be determined by the arbitrator (this is not entirely accurate since under article 11, the arbitrator will be found to accept any decision by the parties on the procedure to be followed even after the arbitration has begun. In practice, however, the chances of the parties reaching agreement so as to limit the arbitrator's discretion is small).

This is a valuable opportunity for the parties to get the best of all worlds. With that possibility in mind, it is my view that parties should avoid opting automatically for the procedural law of the seat of arbitration or of the arbitrator's place of residence. Indeed, Craig, Park and Paulsson (*International Chamber of Commerce Arbitration*) would hazard a guess that parties or arbitrators specifically choose an applicable national procedural law in only a small percentage of ICC cases.

Three points should be borne in mind before any additions to the ICC Rules are attempted. First, any choice made by the arbitrator would be governed by Article 26 which states:

> "In all matters not expressly provided for in these Rules, the Court of Arbitration and the arbitrator shall act in the spirit of these Rules and shall make every effort to make sure that the award is enforceable at law."

Although this discretion is mandatory only so far as the Court and the arbitrator are concerned, it should be regarded by the parties themselves as sound advice.

What is the spirit of the Rules? The most important feature of the Rules which I identify is the facility which they provide for the swift and efficient resolution of a dispute. The time limit provision is referred to further below. For the present it suffices to note that any additional provisions which the parties do choose to adopt should not be cumbersome nor tend to lengthen the proceedings unnecessarily. On the contrary, the steps which I recommend are intended to increase the ability of the parties to achieve speed and efficiency under the rules. The parties will also want to ensure that any rules which they select will not be such as to render any award subject to attack as being unacceptable under the law of the place of arbitration. Equally, regard must be had to the place, if different, in which it is intended to enforce the award. In England, for instance, it should be remembered that, although the courts accept in principle that parties should be free to determine the procedure to be adopted, the more a procedure departs from the rules of natural justice, the less likely the court will be to accept that it was intended by the parties.[2]

The second point to consider before adding to the Rules is that the ICC Court may refuse to accept a fundamental derogation from the Rules. One

2 See Wallace, "Judicial control of arbitration under English law" (Paper 21).

example might be if the parties were to provide that the award did not have to be submitted to the Court of Arbitration prior to its being signed by the arbitrator, contrary to Article 21. The third point to consider is the danger of specifying procedures with which compliance may later become impossible. This is particularly so if serious consequences may follow from non-compliance, for example, if its effect is to put an end to the arbitrator's jurisdiction. This might be the case with a mandatory time limit for delivery of the award.

Particular considerations

The aim in selecting an appropriate procedure should be to steer a middle course. It is suggested that the areas which the parties should address include the following matters:

- the place of arbitration
- witnesses
- discovery and documentary evidence
- timing

The place of arbitration. As is to be expected, the place of arbitration is not stated in the Rules. This should be a matter for the parties. However, in default, the court will select a forum[3] and that often means Paris. Apart from the question of convenience, the choice of location may have important repercussions on procedural matters. Differing attitudes of national courts to rules selected by the parties has already been mentioned.

Where the place of arbitration is London, the following may be regarded as the basic procedural rules to be applied in such circumstances:[4]

- First, the procedure must be of an adversarial nature. That is to say, the function of the arbitrator is not to exercise his own initiative by carrying out an enquiry into the factual and legal issues, but instead to act as the passive recipient of evidence and argument presented by the parties, and to arrive at his decision by choosing between them.
- Second, the arbitrator is not required to follow minutely the procedures of a High Court Action, but can exercise a broad discretion, so long as he adopts a procedure which complies with the essential features of the English adversarial procedure The most important of these are as follows:
- there must be a hearing at which the parties or their representatives have an opportunity to adduce evidence and address argument.
- the arbitrator must not receive evidence or argument from one party in the absence of the other.
- the arbitrator must act only upon evidence which would be admissible in a court of law.

3 Art. 12.
4 Mustill and Boyd, *Commercial Arbitration*, 2nd ed., 288–89.

- where there is more than one arbitrator, they must all act judicially throughout; they must not assume the roles of arbitrator-advocate, or representatives of the parties.
- the arbitrator should not carry out his own investigations into the issues without the prior consent of the parties. If he obtains such consent, he must disclose the results of his investigation and give the parties an opportunity to comment, and to adduce their own evidence upon the issues.
- he must, if called upon to do so, exercise a judicial discretion on whether to order discovery of documents, although it does not necessarily follow that he need order full discovery, or any discovery at all.

The result of these limitations, coupled with the likelihood that English arbitrators and advocates will turn to the rules with which they are most familiar to fill out the procedure to be adopted, is that arbitrations in England will, in default, generally be conducted under a procedure based on that of the High Court. That procedure may be deficient in a number of respects.

The merits of the ICC procedure

The great merit of the ICC Rules is their flexibility. In one sense, therefore, it is not sensible to speak of ICC procedure. It is what the parties and the arbitrators make of it. I propose therefore to suggest how this flexibility may best be used to the parties' advantage and how the resulting scheme compares with an arbitration under a High Court-type procedure.

Preparation for the hearing

If High Court procedure is followed, there is likely to be extensive discovery and the production of bundles of documents for the arbitration, which will range far beyond the matters likely to be raised at the hearing. The ICC Rules conversely contain no express power for the arbitrator to order the production of documents. Insofar as Article 14.1 requires the arbitrator to study, *inter alia*, all documents relied upon, he must at least have an implied power to order that they be produced, albeit without express sanction in the event of non-compliance. The implied sanction is that he may infer that evidence being withheld is unfavourable to the withholding party.

There is in ICC procedure no presumption that there will be discovery. Rather, the reverse is the case: there should be no discovery except to the extent that it is actually necessary for the decision. Although an in-depth inquiry into the facts of a case may be appropriate in some circumstances, it is not so in all cases. Accordingly the Rules require the parties to serve, along with their initial Request and Answer, all documents relevant to establish the circumstances of the case. This gives rise to another beneficial aspect of the ICC Rules, namely that by the time of the hearing, the arbitrator will already have considered the parties' arguments (in written form) together with supporting documentary evidence.

The Terms of Reference for an arbitration are not drawn up until the close of pleadings. The drafting of the Terms of Reference as an exercise to which the greatest care should be devoted if a party is to get the most of an ICC arbitration. The Terms of Reference are to be prepared by the arbitrator(s) and have to contain the following particulars:

(a) the full names and description of the parties;
(b) the addresses of the parties to which notifications or communications arising the the course of the arbitration may validly be made;
(c) a summary of the parties respective claims;
(d) definition of the issues to be determined;
(e) the arbitrator's full name, description and address;
(f) the place of arbitration;
(g) particulars of the applicable procedural rules, and if such is the case, reference to the power conferred upon the arbitrator to act as amiable compositeur;
(h) such other particulars as may be required to make the arbitral award enforceable in law or may be regarded as helpful by the Court of Arbitration or by the arbitrator.[5]

Of paramount importance are items (c) and (d) above. My experience is that it is preferable to require the Tribunal to prepare the first draft of the Terms of Reference, particularly with regard to items (c) and (d). This requires the Tribunal to read and understand the parties' submissions and to concentrate their minds upon the issues in dispute. In so doing, points requiring clarification will undoubtedly emerge, and the parties should encourage the arbitrators to address their minds to the issues to achieve sufficient clarification. If this is done at the relatively early stage of Terms of Reference, it will remove the necessity for this time consuming exercise to be completed orally at the hearing. The parties and the arbitrator will, therefore, be able to approach the arbitration hearing with a greater degree of knowledge and understanding of what each party's case is about, and of the issues separating the parties, than is often the case in a traditional UK arbitration. As a consequence of the analysis of issues at close of pleadings, issues almost inevitably become narrowed, increasing the prospects of settlement. This is particularly so where, as in so many cases, the parties are drawn from different legal jurisdictions where the disciplines of an arbitration may not be familiar.

As a consequence of the early identification of issues and the greater role of the Tribunal in that process, the presence of the parties and their representatives is not required until it becomes indispensable, namely, when examination of witnesses is to occur or the arbitrator requires amplification or clarification of particular issues. This represents a saving not only in the fees payable to the parties' advisers, but also in the extent to which management resources are diverted from the running of the parties' businesses. Further, since the assumption is that the arbitrator comes to the hearing prepared and having read the documents, rather than with no prior knowledge of the case, time will not be spent in the parties' having to explain their contentions in detail and in the reading of documents to the arbitrator.

5 Art. 13.

Both of these time-comsuming activities are features of High Court litigation and arbitrations which follow High Court procedure.

Presenting the parties' cases

This more efficient approach to presenting the parties' cases is made possible by the terms of Article 14.1. which provides that:

> "The arbitrator shall proceed within as short a time as possible to establish the facts of the case by all appropriate means. After study of the written submissions of the parties and of all documents relied upon, the arbitrator shall hear the parties . . . together *if one of them so requests*: and failing such a request he may of his own motion decide to hear them" (emphasis added).

Thus, the primary emphasis is on the documents in the case. In line, with the general aims of ICC arbitrations of speed and efficiency, parties should keep the direct involvement of themselves and their representatives to a minimum. As a natural consequence, proceedings before an ICC Tribunal outside the United Kingdom become more inquisitorial than adversarial, with the Tribunal taking a far more active and positive role.

Presenting the evidence: witnesses

The approach of the ICC Rules to presentation of the cases, and in particular of evidence, is based largely on the civil law inquisitorial trial. As Article 14.1 makes clear, the task of discovering the facts is allocated to the arbitrator himself. The relevant part of this article reads: "In addition, the arbitrator may decide to hear any other person . . . provided they have been duly summoned".

So far as witnesses are concerned the effect of this is that:

(a) which witnesses are required (if any) is a matter for the arbitrator rather than for the parties;
(b) consequently, if the arbitrator considers their appearance unnecessary, they will not be heard. (The parties have no overriding right to call witnesses.)
(c) if witnesses are called, they will be examined primarily by the arbitrator. (This serves to eliminate the unnecessarily extensive questioning to which advocates may be prone.)
(d) at the same time, the parties' representative may, if appropriate and at the discretion of the arbitrator, be allowed an opportunity to examine witnesses. (A further valuable feature of this discretionary approach is that such examination may be limited by the arbitrator, for instance in terms of the time available for this activity.)
(e) if appropriate, witnesses may give their evidence in written form. (The statements may then be considered by the arbitrator in advance of the hearing.)

The cost benefits of reducing the emphassis on direct oral evidence and, indeed, on the hearing itself, and placing such matters in the discretion of the arbitrator, are self-evident. However, in many cases, the receipt by the Tribunal of oral testimony is of paramount importance. In such cases rules for the submission of evidence such as those established by the International Bar Association should be adopted at time that the Terms of Reference are agreed. It is not unusual for the parties to agree to certain time limits being set for the presentation of evidence-in-chief and for cross-examination. This will streamline the whole oral proceedings, prevent unnecessary "fishing expeditions" and require the marshalling of the evidence and questions in the advocate's mind in advance of the hearing. The procedure for the exchange of written proofs of evidence before the hearing does assist this process enormously.

Presenting the evidence: documents

The limited form of discovery required by the ICC Rules and the advantages to be found in keeping documentary evidence to a minimum have already been referred to. A further provision in this area which parties do well to take advantage of is Article 14.3 which allows the arbitrator to decide the case on the relevant documents alone if the parties so request or agree. It is the use of this sort of facility for speed and efficiency that will enable the parties to reap the greatest benefit from an ICC arbitration.

Timing

Article 18.1 directs that the arbitrator shall make his award within six months of the date of signing the Terms of Reference. There are exceptions to this rule, but none gives to the parties themselves the right to any longer period. In fact, the average duration of an ICC arbitration has been estimated as 18 months.[6] But even if that is so, it is an admirable achievement. The mere existence of the time limit undoubtedly serves to discourage the parties from conducting the arbitration in a way which will lengthen proceedings unnecessarily. Furthermore, the six month time limit will be very much in the mind of the arbitrator as he decides, for instance, whether to hear witnesses and whether to allow examination or cross-examination by the parties. Indirectly, therefore, it supports the idea that ICC arbitrations should be an efficient means of resolving disputes.

Adapting procedure to suit the dispute

The importance of keeping costs and the amount of direct involvement of the parties to a minimum has been stressed above. Emphasis has been placed on the flexible nature of the ICC Rules. As the ICC Rules do not deal with every detail of the procedure to be adopted, to the extent that the parties do not provide for such matters, they will be decied by the arbitrator. There is no guarantee that his decisions will accord with the parties' perceptions of

6 Craig, Park and Paulsson, *ICC Arbitration* 2nd ed. (1990).

what is in their best interests. For example, he may wish to enter into a detailed and precise enquiry into events. The parties, on the other hand, may be seeking a rapid determination of a limited range of issues in a fairly broad manner. Alternatively, the arbitrator may take refuge in the Rules of the Supreme Court, which may be exactly what the parties had hoped to avoid by opting for an ICC arbitration.

The best approach to these problems is for the parties to make some specific provision in their arbitration agreement and/or in the arbitrator's terms of reference as to evidence, as to the timetable to be followed and to other matters, so as to ensure that effect is given to their intentions. Whether such matters should be dealt with in the abitration agreement itself, or are best left to be raised through representations to the arbitrator and the terms of reference, is a difficult question. On the one hand, it may not be possible at the time of the arbitration agreement (if made when the contract is entered into) to foresee the type of hearing best suited to a dispute which has not yet arisen. On the other hand, once a dispute has arisen, it may well be that the parties are unable to agree upon anything, least of all how that dispute should be resolved. On balance, leaving such questions until the Terms of Reference are prepared is probably the better option. The possibility of disagreement may not be too great, as it may not be apparent that a particular rule will serve one party better than the other.

Costs

ICC arbitrations have been criticised in the past for being too costly from the point of view of administration, and undoubtedly some of the criticism is valid. The costs are calculated by reference to a sliding scale which is dependent upon the amount at issue. One consequence of this is to discourage claims which are exorbitant or inflated, and this factor should be borne in mind when preparing papers for an ICC arbitration. Also to be borne in mind is that the ICC administrative machinery is there to assist the parties and since the parties are paying substantial sums for this service it ought to be utilised where ever possible. The parties also ought to bear in mind that the most usual cost convention for ICC arbitrations conducted outside the United Kingdom is for parties to bear their own costs, irrespective of the result. This is an incentive to maintain the legal costs at an acceptable level. Since the period of oral presentation of the parties' cases is usually the most costly, the ICC's greater reliance upon written submission thereby leading to a shortening of the oral presentation, does have substantial cost advantages.

Conclusion

Arbitration under the ICC Rules provides an opportunity for parties to secure the resolution of their disputes quickly. There are undoubtedly advantages over an arbitration which broadly follows English High Court procedure. If nothing else, an agreement for ICC arbitration makes clear the intention of the parties that the High Court approach is not to be followed without question. The result should be that procedural rules will only be adopted if their use is justifiable in the dispute which has in fact arisen. To ensure that the parties' intentions are not frustrated by an over-conservative arbitrator, they should try, to as great an extent as is possible, to specify their chosen procedure more precisely than is set out in the ICC Rules.

Part IV

Particular Issues in International Arbitration

Bonds and Guarantees: Their various types and problems

13

Phillip Capper

Synopsis

This paper reviews the differences between bonds and guarantees and the case law relating thereto and offers some interesting analogies with, *inter alia*, the law on letters of credit, reservation of title and the enforceability of so-called penalty clauses in contracts. The following paper examines the ICC draft Uniform Rules and the remedies and powers of a tribunal with regard thereto.

Introduction

The goal of this paper is not to seek to describe comprehensively either the practice and usage surrounding bonds or all the law thereon. Rather the opportunity will be taken to focus on a number of legal problems surrounding the use of bonds in the context of construction contracts.

Legal obligations in bonds

The term "bond" is a loose generic. The actual forms of legal instrument labelled "bond" in this context are very varied. Inspection of the terms of any particular bond may reveal that it comprises in substance one (or more) of the following:

- a guarantee (in the strict legal sense);
- an indemnity;
- an undertaking to make a payment in certain defined circumstances.

Guarantees in the strict sense are secondary obligations obliging the guarantor in the event of default by the principal debtor. An indemnity is a primary obligation. Such guarantees and indemnities are the subject of paper 14. I shall therefore concern myself with those forms of "bonds" which comprise undertakings, typically by banks or insurance companies, to make payments upon the terms stated in the bond. The purpose of such bonds in general is to offer some assurance of payment or compensation from a substantial and solvent paymaster in the event of certain defaults by a contractor during the tendering or construction process.

A typical instance might be this. An international construction contract would require the contractor to procure the issue of the specified bonds. The client employer as beneficiary of the bonds will probably want them issued by a bank in his own jurisdiction. The contractor will want to make application to a bank, local and known to the contractor. The contractor's bank will therefore request the bank in the client employer's jurisdiction to issue the required bond. Apart from any other terms, as to payment etc, the issuing bank will require an indemnity from the contractor's bank. The contractor's bank in turn will require a counter indemnity from the contractor. This contractual framework is in effect a mirror image of that which is typical in the case of letters of credit.

Bonds and letters of credit

The law on bonds owes much to that on letters of credit. However, compared with letters of credit, the law and practice on bonds is in its relative infancy. The law on letters of credit is highly developed and well established. In English law, many of the principles of law applicable to letters of credit have been stated by the judges to be applicable also to performance bonds. One of the main purposes of this paper is to draw out some of the differences between bonds and letters of credit. We may then see whether bonds therefore demand different responses from the law.

Particular kinds of bonds

I shall refer in this paper for most purposes to the generic notion of a "performance bond". The utility of interposing the independent obligation of a bank or similar financial institution as an assurance of means of payment in construction contracts is obvious. Thus, bonds and letters of credit may be used in a myriad of different ways where some assurance or security as to payment, repayment or performance, or some protection against default, is required (whether by the client employer or by the contractor). The typical practice may be illustrated by referring to three common forms of more specific kind of bond in addition to the generic performance bond. The more specific typical kinds are:

- bid (or tender) bonds
- advance payment bonds
- retention money bonds

Even from these descriptions the practical function of such bonds becomes relatively self-evident. The bid (or tender) bond will accompany the contractor's tender. It will give some assurance to the potential employer of the contractor's earnest to enter into the construction contract if the tender is accepted. It will also provide a ready mechanism for the payment of compensation if the contract has to be re-awarded to someone else because the contractor refuses to contract after it is proposed that his tender be accepted.

The advance payment bond safeguards the client employer in regard to re-payment of disproportionately large sums advanced early in the construction process. Retention money bonds are typically given as a substitute for the actual holding of retention monies pursuant to the construction contract.

Of course in all these cases the critical first question for determination is: upon what terms may the bond be called by the beneficiary client employer? We shall see that these terms may vary from relatively "weak" usage (so far as the client is concerned, but prudent usage so far as the contractor is concerned) where calling of the bond depends upon actual proof of the relevant default. The opposite extreme is the ability for the beneficiary to call the bond upon simple demand with no conditions whatsoever; this "strong" usage (from the client's point of view) has obvious risks for the contractor who will have in the end to reimburse the bank(s).

The particular form of bond called "performance bond" may not be tied to any particular purpose or default within the range of the contractor's obligations. Rather it may be required simply to cover *e.g.* 10% of the construction contract tender total, throughout the period of construction and without regard to the increasing value of performance received by the client. It is an incentive to performance without particular regard to the nature and extent of any particular default. The practical and functional use and operation of these bonds (and other such bonds in the construction context) is described in books on trade financing and banking practice.

Legal distinctions and issues

The three specific types of bond listed above all have significantly different legal characteristics.

Bid (or tender) bonds may exist without any underlying contract between the client beneficiary and the contractor. Of course, the submission of a tender may give rise to some form of contractual relationship between tenderer and prospective client: see *e.g.* the Canadian case of *Northern Construction* v. *Gloge*.[1] If there is no contract between the client beneficiary and the contractor then manifestly the bond is not to secure performance of any contractual obligation. The legal ramifications of an allegedly abusive call on a bid (or tender) bond should therefore be viewed very differently from other cases of bonds where the proceeds of the bond can be viewed as some form of compensation for a breach of contract by the contractor.

Advance payment bonds are clearly more likely to have as their purpose the provision of redress to a client upon contractual default by the contractor.

Retention money bonds can be seen as different again. Typically the construction contract will provide for the withholding of, say, 5% of sums certified during the progress of the works as a retention money fund. The bond will be given in consideration of the client agreeing to waive his right

1 [1986] 2 WWR 649

of retention of the actual sums and to substitute for that right a right instead to call upon the independent obligation of the bank under the retention money bond. Difficult questions will, therefore, arise as to the ability to call on the retention money bond. Is it intended to be a means whereby the client may unilaterally at any stage in effect revert to withholding of retention by calling back the whole fund via the bank? Or, is the purpose to provide only a "draw-down" of such sums up to the 5% maximum as reflect any particular actual default by the contractor?

Ease of callability: "first-demand" or conditional?

From a legal point of view the major legal distinction between types of bond is not as to their functional purpose but as to the degree of ease with which the beneficiary can call for payment. Much of the law on bonds is concerned with abusive calling of the bonds, applications for injunctions and allegations of fraud. These problems arise because of the preference (for different reasons) of both beneficiaries and banks for bonds written in "first demand" form.

The bank's undertaking on an first demand form of bond is to pay on demand without proof or conditions. As between the bank and the beneficiary such a bond is tantamount to cash in the hand of the beneficiary.

The more prudent form of bond from the contractor's point of view is the conditional bond. Here the bank's obligation to pay will be conditional upon proof by the beneficiary of the requisite default. Obviously such an instrument is less attractive to the banking community. It draws the bank into complex contractual disputes between the client employer and the contractor. Nevertheless, the bond still offers valuable utility. For, upon proof of default, the client is assured of a solvent paymaster for the sums by way of compensation found to be payable.

The extremes of a first demand form, on the one hand, and the conditional form of bond, on the other, both have serious advantages and disadvantages.

The middle course: the documentary bond

There is a middle course. This comprises what may be called a "documentary bond". The bank's obligation upon a documentary bond is still an obligation to pay on demand. But the demand must include a specified document or documents. These are a means of certifying that there are grounds for calling the bond. The document might comprise a certified report of an independent expert or a certified arbitral award. The documentary bond draws the law and practice of performance bonds even closer to that of letters of credit.

Letters of credit are typically issued as undertakings to pay upon presentation of specified documents. The law governing the form and sufficiency of such documents is highly developed through a great deal of case law. However, it must be recognised that the banks in such circumstances (in the absence of narrow exceptions discussed below) are entitled to act upon the face of such documents as submitted and are not required to go behind the documents to enquire into the underlying contract itself.

Problems arising on the calling of bonds

The term "performance bonds" will be used as a generic for all the contexts discussed above. It will also be assumed that the bond is written in first demand unconditional form. Some of the problems that can arise from abusive or unjustified calling upon such bonds will now be examined together with questions about the legal significance even of justified calls upon the bond. How are the proceeds of the call, whether justified or not, to be treated in subsequent disputes and claims as between the client employer beneficiary and the contractor?

The legal problems arising from performance bonds have two principal sources:

- the independence of the bond from the underlying contract
- the refusal of courts in all major jurisdictions to interfere with that independent obligation of the bank to pay (save in the very narrow exceptional cases of established fraud, illegality, and, perhaps, unusual ancillary circumstances such as allegations by the bank of misrepresentation by the beneficiary or rights of set-off against the beneficiary).

The two principles: independence of the bank's obligation, and freedom from judicial interference

The legal authorities for these twin principles of (i) independence of the bond from the construction contract, and (ii) the courts' universal refusal to interfere with the banks' independent obligation to pay, are expressed in or derived from the law on letters of credit. Indeed, for example, under English law the courts have referred interchangeably to cases on letters of credit and on performance bonds in order to articulate the independence principle and the limiting of injunctions to cases of established fraud.

It appears, however, that there may be good reason for the law to develop a more refined appreciation of the essential differences between performance bonds and letters of credit.

Differences between bonds and letters of credit

The archetypal use of a letter of credit is as a means of payment of the purchase price in an international sale of goods to be shipped by sea. The similarity of the overall contractual framework and the particular independence of the bank's obligation in regard to letters of credit on the one hand and bonds on the other is potentially misleading. The similarity arises through focus upon the nature of the obligation of the bank to the beneficiary. This paper rather questions the effect of a call having been made under a bond upon claims and disputes between the client beneficiary and the contractor. Notice the critical differences between the letter of credit context and that of bonds.

The typical purpose of the letter of credit is actually to perform the principal payment obligation under a contract of sale. Hence this dovetails into the well established principles of law governing the obligations of the buyer with regard to payment of the price and with regard to assessment of damages upon default of payment. The letter of credit works within the context of the underlying contract as part of the actual mechanism of performance.

The second major difference between letters of credit and bonds is that the bank's independent obligation to pay on a letter of credit normally arises upon presentation of documents giving security in the goods themselves. Even if the banks do not in practice look to the value of the pledge of the goods represented by their documents of title, the requirement for a clean bill of lading and appropriate certificates of performance gives substantial protection against abusive calls in practically all cases except those of fraud.

The third and final major difference between the context of letters of credit and bonds is that the law and practice on letters of credit operates by near universal adoption of the ICC's Uniform Customs Practice for Documentary Credits. For bonds, the ICC has of course issued in 1978 its Uniform Rules for Contract Guarantees[2] and its Model Forms for issuing Contract Guarantees.[3] These latter documents have not achieved equivalent universal adoption by any means.

The surprising result of the twin principles

For those not familiar with this area of the law, the absolute and independent nature of a bank's obligation to pay on its undertaking in a letter of credit or first demand bond is no doubt surprising. That said, the law on the subject has become so settled that most of its instances are now relatively trite.[4] Similarly, the narrowness of the "established fraud" exception is well settled in all major jurisdictions, as is evidenced in case after case of unsuccessful attempts by construction contractors or buyers of goods seeking to gain injunctions to prevent payment by the bank under a bond or letter of credit respectively[5]. Slight suggestions of a relaxation of the fraud exception in the English decision in the case of *United Trading Corp SA* v. *Allied Arab Bank Ltd.*[6] was not so much a sign of indulgence as precisely a desire to achieve comity between the major trading jurisdictions in adopting a uniform approach. A less discussed but important qualification upon the bank's obligation to pay is the "illegality" exception articulated and illustrated in *The American Accord*.

2 ICC No. 325, new text in preparation.
3 ICC No. 406.
4 See *e.g. Edward Owen Engineering* v. *Barclays Bank International* [1978] QB 159 and *United City Merchants* v. *Royal Bank of Canada (the American Accord)* (1983) 1 AC 168.
5 See again *e.g. The American Accord* as the recent statement of the House of Lords in England.
6 [1985] 2 Lloyd's Rep. 554.

Wider protection in bond cases?

The English courts have begun to show some limited recognition, still fully to be explored, that some legal protection can be given against abusive calling upon performance bonds in wider contexts than just the limited and established exceptions of fraud and illegality. A way must be found around the fundamental and trite proposition that the promises of banks are the life blood of international commerce and that legal systems must not interfere with them or undermine confidence in them.

The technique for our attention, therefore, is to focus on some route other than injunctions against the bank. Of course the bank's obligation under the bond is independent and absolute and must be seen to be freely enforceable. Rather the focus of attention must move to injuncting the "abusing" beneficiary either from calling upon the bond in the first place or from being able improperly to deal with the proceeds once the call has taken place.

The Bhoja Trader and Potton Homes cases

The clues to this different approach arise from two English decisions: *The Bhoja Trader*[7] and *Potton Homes Ltd.* v. *Coleman Contractors (Overseas) Ltd.*[8]

The Bhoja Trader recognises that so long as the actual payment by the bank to the beneficiary is not interfered with, then even in the absence of fraud a Mareva injunction may be granted to prevent the proceeds of the bond in the hands of the beneficiary being removed from the jurisdiction.

The significance of the *Potton Homes* case arises from *dicta* of Lord Justice Eveleigh:

> "As between buyer and seller the underlying contract cannot be disregarded so readily. If the seller has lawfully avoided the contract prima facie it seems to me he should be entitled to restrain the buyer from making use of the performance bond. Moreover, in principle I do not think it possible to say that in no circumstances whatsoever, apart from fraud, will the court restrain the buyer. The facts of each case must be considered."

Lord Justice Eveleigh went on to point out that the *Edward Owen* case was not concerned with the position as between the buyer and the seller.

Grounds for injunctions against the beneficiary

If it can be accepted that injuncting the beneficiary from calling upon the bond does not strike at the heart of banking confidence in this field, then there is provoked a range of interesting questions as to the possible grounds upon which such injunctions must be sought. The most obvious will of course be cases where the bond require a Form of Demand and that Form of Demand declares default by the contractor. If there is (*e.g.* in an Order

7 *Intraco Ltd.* v. *Notis Shipping Corp.* (*The Bhoja Trader*) [1981] 2 Lloyd's Rep. 256.
8 28 BLR 19.

14 sense) no arguable case of default that can be shown against the contractor then why should a call *e.g.* on a retention money bond not be restrained? The whole value of the bond has not been subverted in such circumstances. There had been and there remains the value to the beneficiary of the assurance of a solvent reputable paymaster for cases of genuine calls upon the bond. It is not necessary to see the sole value of a retention bond as being the ability to call upon it by mere documentary declaration.

However, such an approach as this, combining the principles of the *Potton Homes* case and the *Bhoja Trader* case, raises more fundamental possibilities. Here we have to return to our analysis of the different types of bonds – bid (or tender) bonds, advanced payment bonds, retention money bonds, and performance bonds properly so called.

In so doing, we confront the unfortunate consequence that English law has differentiated doctrines dealing with the related functional concepts of minimum payment termination terms, deposits, penalties, and relief against forfeiture.

The obvious attraction of considering the possibility of relief against forfeiture is misplaced in view of recent court decisions on that topic. Payment under a bond does not relate to a proprietary interest to enable the principles of relief to be called in aid.

What are the purposes of the bonds under the construction contract?

So far as a bid (or tender) bond is concerned the absence of an underlying contract between the prospective client and the prospective contractor seems to require that as between client and contractor the bond must be regarded as an agreed price for the privilege of being permitted to tender. The proceeds of a call cannot it seems be challenged as excessive. Nor are those proceeds to be in any way taken into account in any other computation since no grounds for the award of damages would exist.

An advanced payment bond could be classified like a performance bond (below) but it might alternatively be regarded as a form of minimum payment clause (drawing the analogy from the context of consumer credit and hire purchase cases). In this sense, rather like the bid (or tender) bond the sum is agreed between the parties as a "price" for the privilege of permitted termination and thus is not subject to relief either for forfeiture or as a penalty. Furthermore since the sum is an agreed payment for a privilege and not payment on account of damages, the proceeds of the advance payment bond could not be taken into account in diminution of a later assessment of damages upon a claim by the client against the contractor.

Another way of viewing bid (or tender) bonds, advanced payment bonds and performance bonds would be as having the equivalent nature and purpose to the payment of a deposit pending performance of obligations. As a deposit they would attract an implied condition of forfeiture upon non performance without any advantage of the rules of relief or the rules on penalties.

We have already seen that retention bonds may be viewed differently again. Depending upon how they are worded, their function may simply be as substitutes for the provisions under the construction contract relating to the withholding of retention monies. Thus a call upon a retention money bond may have to be treated as an operation of the withholding provisions under the construction contract with the usual later entitlement of the contractor to release at the appropriate time.

A final and perhaps in many instances more realistic way of viewing many bonds in the construction context is to see them as means of payment on account of damages for one contractual default. This would have two important consequences.

First, the English courts have recently recognised that the rule against penalties may render unenforceable contractual stipulations other than the actual payment of money (as in a traditional penalty clause). Thus if injunctions against a beneficiary calling upon a bond could be grounded on any lawful objection to the underlying construction contract then it might be possible to argue that as between the beneficiary and the contractor the right to the proceeds of the bond is unenforceable as a penalty. Such a conclusion need not be inconsistent with the freedom of the bank to pay on the call. The second consequence of viewing the purpose of bonds in the construction context as sums payable on account of damages for contractual default is that in any subsequent claim or dispute the proceeds of the call would have to be taken into account in diminution of the loss claimed by way of damages.

It will thus be seen that as between the client beneficiary and the contractor there might well be arguments justifying the re-payment to the contractor of (some of) the proceeds of a call under a bond even in the absence of fraud. This is relevant not only to a court or arbitration assessing an award of damages after such a call. The right to re-payment if the proceeds were to be paid over may of itself be arguably sufficient to justify injunctive relief to prevent disposal of the proceeds in the hands of the beneficiary, once the bank has paid.

Bonds and arbitral awards

A note by way of postscript arises with regard to the role of arbitral tribunals in relation to bonds in another way. We noted above that prudent practice is for bonds to be "documentary". That is, the bank's obligation to pay shall arise only upon tender of a certified arbitral award. This gives the contractor some measure of protection against abusive calls by enabling the question of default first to be determined. This device may also provide a further means of securing the contractor against any potential over-payment to the client beneficiary when the whole project comes to be reviewed at a later stage.

Much of the discussion in the English case law on letters of credit and on bonds turns on the assumed direct analogy between the proceeds of a bond and "cash in hand" for the beneficiary. We may here be able to draw analogies with the innovative development of the law upon *Romalpa* clauses in the context of reservation of title. Though much hedged about by restrictions, these cases recognise that the interest of a supplier of goods may be traced into the proceeds of sub-sales by his purchaser. Why then may not the "cash in hand" proceeds of a bond be impressed with the continuing interest of the contractor if circumstances so demand? The concept of such abstract thinking is not entirely alien to the area of bonds and letters of credit.

Consider, for example, how the seller of goods is burdened with the pledge interest of the paying bank under a letter of credit if the buyer of the goods should reject the shipping documents and revest title in the goods in the seller. Thus, it might be that the certified award would declare a sum due for release under a bond but in so declaring would attach a reservation as to the contractor's right of repayment in divine circumstances. Could not the independent but absolute undertaking of the bank under the bond still be honoured by actual payment even though the fund comprising the proceeds were impressed by the reserved interest of the contractor?

Conclusion

It can be seen from even the brief examination of the topic given in this paper that the legal position of bonds in general and so-called on demand bonds in particular, continues and is likely to continue to exercise the English courts for some time. The problem is of course the fundamental one of whether in the absence of fraud an on-demand bond can ever be called unfairly. Is good faith a necessary part of the process at all? The courts are likely to be obliged to concentrate their efforts more on litigation arising out of domestic contracts in the short to medium term where bonds in general are not common, but the problem of on-demand bonds on risky foreign contracts is not likely to go away entirely.

Bonds and Guarantees: Powers of the Tribunal 14

David Marks

Synopsis

This paper examines the ICC draft Uniform Rules and the remedies and powers of a tribunal with regard thereto. It also deals with unfair calling of bonds, reviewing English case law and suggesting possible ways of avoiding the unfair call and its results.

Introduction

I shall begin with a short review of the suggested reforms to the Uniform Rules for Contract Guarantees. The present position is governed by the 1978 edition of these Rules, but there are now new draft Uniform Rules dated 1989[1] which seek to cancel the earlier version. They have been drawn up by an ICC Joint Working Party of members representing the Commissions on International Commercial Practices and on Banking Technique and Practice and are expressed to apply to the worldwide use of guarantees.

The ICC Draft Rules

The overall intention of the new draft Rules is to attempt to "recognise the different interests of the parties involved in a guarantee transaction". These are fairly self-evident though the introduction to the draft Rules deals first with the wish of a beneficiary to be secured against the risk of the principal not fulfilling his obligations towards the beneficiary in respect of the underlying transaction. Secondly, it covers with the legitimate expectation of the principal "on the grounds of equity and good faith" to be informed in writing of the alleged breach and the grounds thereof. Finally, the guarantor is regarded as being able to see clearly whether the beneficiary

1 See Part VI – Appendices.

and principal have or have not fulfilled their obligations under their underlying transaction since the guarantee is expressed as being "wholly independent of it".

The encouragement given by the ICC is laudable, particularly by its novel introduction of a major clause (expressed to be "favourable to beneficiaries") in that claimants no longer have necessarily to present an arbitration award or other independent documentary evidence in support of a claim to trigger the liability of the guarantor. The introductory remarks indicate a certain degree of confusion about the terminology which is alluded to by Phillip Capper in his paper, but it is clear that the Rules in their draft form address themselves to guarantees or bonds "payable on first demand" stressing the independent or autonomous character of the document. The ICC, however, clearly regards simple demand guarantees as embodying an undesirable commercial practice but then rather wistfully assumes that every claim will be "made in good faith as to its reasons and as to the amount".

It remains to be seen how the Rules emerge in final form and how they will be adopted in practice. The probability at the moment is that they will throw up as many problems as they seek to solve.

Remedies and powers of a tribunal

I turn now to deal with various matters which commonly have to be addressed by a tribunal adjudicating upon a bond, and not simply a tribunal regulated by ICC procedure. The first particular problem concerns the existence of an overriding requirement for notice of default to be given by owner to guarantor. Ultimately the matter is a question of construction, but there seems no reason in principle why there should be such a requirement. Article 20 of the draft Rules addresses itself to the need for a guarantee to provide for a claim against a guarantor not only to be in writing but also to be supported by suitable written confirmation as to breach. Much turns upon the ingenuity of the particular bondsman, no doubt encouraged by the lasting effect of the House of Lords decision in *Clydebank and District Water Trustees* v. *Fidelity Deposit Co. of Maryland.*[2] Here the wording of the bond provided that the surety was to be notified in writing of:

> "any non-performance or non-observance on the part of the contractor of any of the stipulations or conditions contained in the contract . . . which may involve the loss for which the surety is responsible within one month after such non-performance or non-observance shall have come to the knowledge of the employer . . . ."

Doubts as to the true facts of the situation placed the owner in a quandary as to whether an extension of time might or might not be due. The Scottish Court of Session held that there was a duty to notify the bondsman of potential late completion coupled with a possible claim for liquidated damages. Despite a trenchant dissenting judgment by Lord

2 [1915] SC 36: [1916] SC 69 (HL).

Strathclyde in the Court of Session, the House of Lords in a short speech delivered by Lord Buckmaster affirmed the lower court's decision despite two convincing arguments to the contrary.

The first was that it would not be until the contract was completed or at least until completion date had passed that there could be any certainty even of a claim for liquidated damages, and secondly it was held that the notice requirement under the bond had to relate to the claim made against the bondsman whilst the present claim was for the abandonment of the contract by the contractor of which prompt notice was given and not for delay in the preceding year which formed the basis of the claim against the bondsman.

The result is that an owner is driven by virtue of wording such as the passage quoted above to examine minutely the conduct of the parties to the contract to see whether there may be some default which would trigger the liability of the surety, failing which the latter could claim to be released from his obligations. Despite this unfortunate situation, the decision must be taken to represent the law.

The *Clydebank* case shows the difficulty which can be created by ambiguous wording where the court might have to enter into an analysis of whether wording contains an implied right of release in addition to any consideration of whether a particular default or defaults are sufficiently serious to fall within the terms of such provision. There has been much Commonwealth judicial activity on this score, particularly in Canada, where a rather more practical and robust approach is taken.

The nature of the guarantor's liability

The next area which often causes concern is the true nature of the guarantor's liability. It seems reasonably clear from Lord Atkin's famous speech in *Trade Indemnity Co.* v. *Workington Harbour and Dock Board*[3] (a case which repays continued study) that a bondsman is not an insurer. It follows that there will be no duty of disclosure upon an owner although there is at least one English decision, namely *Stiff* v. *Eastbourne Local Board*[4] which throws some doubt on that proposition. Again much will turn upon the wording of the provisions in the bond and in a given case it may well be that extreme circumstances might be found by a court to be properly the subject of warning to the surety by the owner. The *Trade Indemnity* case contains a robust rejection of any suggestion that there should be a duty to disclose. This is based on the simple proposition that the guarantor looks no further than the skill and experience of the contractor to guard against risk of unknown difficulties in the performance of a complex matter such as a building contract.

Lord Atkin explained that guarantors in such a case are "primarily concerned with the financing ability of the contractors to complete [their] contract, whether it results in a loss or not." It seems, therefore, to come down to custom of the trade and whether in present day conditions a

3 [1937] AC 1 at 17.
4 [1869] 20 LT 339.

bondsman is still bound to know, in effect, of the peculiarities (particularly inherent in the world of building contracts) such as to dispense with any need to warn him of any peculiarities in that respect. In North America where there is a widespread practice of active sureties taking over the contract, there is even less scope for a doctrine of disclosure.

The wording of a bond

It really all comes down to the wording. There is no doubt that if it can in any way escape the trappings of the old archaic forms the modern bond should include a number of basic provisions in clear and concise language. First there should be some form of requirement that the general contractor in a complex building arrangement be the judge of whether and to what extent a sub-contractor has been in serious default. Secondly, questions of release should be clearly addressed and an ideal clause would be one in which release is triggered not only upon due performance but also upon completion and the issuance of any appropriate certificates or even after payment of premiums in respect of the bondsman remaining further at risk. Thirdly, there seems every reason for imposing express monetary limits. These are no more than suggested general improvements and happily are often met with in practice, in part at least.

Defences to calls

The question of on demand bonds has been dealt with by Phillip Capper in his paper, but I should like to say a few words about possible defences and related matters. It is perhaps a misnomer to talk of defences since only what has been called "established fraud" on the part of the beneficiary known to the issuing bank in a typical unconditional bond scenario will be regarded as sufficient, at least in English law, to justify refusal of payment by the guarantor. The leading case sets out the relevant principles in very firm tones, particularly in the speech of Lord Diplock in *United City Merchants (Investments) Ltd.* v. *Royal Bank of Canada*.[5] The approach in the American cases is perhaps rather more flexible since there are some authorities suggesting that "fraud of a transaction" will be sufficiently made out in cases where there is a clear demonstrable breach of contract by the beneficiary followed by a demand made on apparently no justifiable basis.[6] The basic problem remains however: fraud is difficult to establish even at the best of times and there is the added reluctance to make a finding in the absence of the beneficiary. There may, however, be a case for intervention by the courts if the issuance of the bond itself was perpetrated by fraud or misrepresentation: this would no doubt in a suitable case justify refusal of payment by the issuing bank.

5 [1983] AC 168.

6 See *e.g. Harris Corporation* v. *National Iranian Radio* (1982) 619 F 2d 1344 (11th Circuit Court of Appeals).

There seems no reason in principle, at least in the case where English law is the proper law, why an issuing bank cannot claim set-off in respect of a beneficiary's claim when the bank has a liquidated cross-claim against such beneficiary. No doubt the general principles of set-off will apply, *i.e.* that the claims be mutual and made in the same right, but the difficulty in practice will be that the proper law may well not be English causing the prospects of a satisfactory resolution of such a contest to be questionable. Again illegality would no doubt in a proper case be a bar to a beneficiary calling on the bond, but it would need to be an illegality under the proper law of the bond such as to justify an injunction. Some illustration as to the principles involved is offered by *Power-Curber International* v. *National Bank of Kuwait.*[7]

Philip Capper in his paper discusses the significance of the *Potton Homes* case and in particular the *dicta* of Eveleigh LJ.[8] The approach is highly commendable but it is to be doubted whether it will not be in only the most exceptional cases that the approach of the learned Lord Justice will be pursued. In one way the approach attacks the very *raison d'être* of the on demand bond, namely that the furnishing of it is itself designed to circumvent any possible argument as to whether the underlying contract has been infringed or not.

The learned Lord Justice suggests that failure of consideration should not be sufficient to entitle a claimant to an injunction to restrain a beneficiary from making a demand. It may well be that he was addressing himself to the wrong contract, since the only relevant contract for this purpose is the contract between the beneficiary and the contractor or supplier under the principal contract.

One solution presents itself and that is that the parties to a bond can specify arbitration in the event of default. There are no doubt many difficulties in the way of this course not the least of which being the conceptual one that the guarantee is not meant to spawn any more litigation than is absolutely necessary. There seems no reason in principle why a bond should not provide that, on objecting to a clear default, the contractor may demand a speedy arbitration on the sole issue of default.

Finally, it seems surprising that there has been no resolution, at least in any reported judicial case, of the position of the bank, – *i.e.* the guarantor of the bond – consequent upon payment of monies under the bond. If the bond provides that the guaranteed sum "shall be paid . . . without objection or contestation whatever on our part or any other party" the bank will have no rights in the bond monies since the sum is paid with the express intention that the bank will not object or contest the payment. The result of this will be that the bond monies properly become monies belonging to the employer. So much seems established since in the words of Donaldson J. in *The Bhoja Trader*:[9]

> "It is the natural corollary of the proposition that a letter of credit or bank guarantee is to be treated as cash but that when the bank pays and cash is received by the beneficiary, it should be subject to the same restraints as any other of his cash assets."

7 [1981] 1 WLR 1233.
8 (1984) 128 SJ 282, 28 BLR 19.
9 [1981] 1 Lloyd's Rep. 256.

A contractor should therefore have no right in the bond monies since they will be the bank's or the guarantor's which each of those parties will have paid to an employer pursuant to a specific contractual obligation. Nor should the existence of any counter indemnity between bank or guarantee on the one hand and the contractor on the other affect the position. The only remedy available to a claimant contractor will be any which it might possess under the underlying contract.

It will be remembered that in the *Harbottle*[10] case Kerr J. characterised first demand guarantees as in effect representing "a discount in favour of the buyers." This view of the discount was echoed by Lord Denning in the *Edward Owen*[11] case in similar terms. Nor will there be any question of subrogation and even if there were a duty to account to a guarantor or to a bank in a situation where a performance bond were called, it would need to be shown that it was limited to liquidated damages at most. Put shortly, therefore, the bond monies simply pass into the general assets of an employer in a case where payment has been made and a possible surplus arises. There remain, however, strong reasons for objecting to such a result since in effect it represents a windfall which was never or could never have been envisaged at the outset. Furthermore it could be said that all the authorities which bear upon the subject concern the grant or discharge of injunctions and therefore any references to discounts does not in any way mean there can be no account for the bond monies between the parties to the principal transaction, whether buyer and seller, or contractor and building owner.

It is true that none of the English authorities deal with the possibility that there might be some contractual obligation to bring the bond monies into account. The dicta which appear on one view to address themselves to this question are no more than reflections of extreme consequences which can follow where an on demand bond is given and called. Such authorities as do exist, for example the *Edward Owen*[12] decision, do contemplate that when an on demand bond is called, for example, by a buyer and paid by a bank the seller will have some rights against the buyer. If the contention that no account is required is correct it would mean that in the event of delay in completing a building, carefully thought out provisions for liquidated damages subject to limits would in effect be pointless.[13]

Conclusion

As in all the topics covered by this paper much will turn upon the wording not only of the particular bond but also the overall conditions of contract between the principal parties as to whether or not in an arbitration to determine the final rights and liabilities of the parties before the tribunal an employer or seller should not bring the monies paid under bonds into account.

10 *Harbottle (Mercantile) Ltd.* v *National Westminster Bank Ltd.* [1978] QB 146.
11 *Edward Owen Engineering Ltd.* v. *Barclays Bank International Ltd.* [1978] QB 159.
12 *Ibid.*
13 See Paper 2.

International arbitration under public works contracts 15

Jeremy Winter

Synopsis

This paper contains an examination of the enforceability of arbitration clauses in international public works contracts (*i.e.* where the client is a foreign government or governmental body) with particular reference to the problems encountered in civil law based jurisdictions. It contains a review of relevant cases and examines concepts such as the administrative contract in civil law jurisdictions.

Introduction

The hazards of doing business across national borders whether in developed or undeveloped countries and in whatever kind of business are often underestimated. The businessman with a lifetime's experience and advice in his own country decides that his product or service can be marketed in another country. If his own countrymen buy it, why should not everyone else? With a good product this should be the case. It is, however, impossible to be certain of this without extensive information from many sources which in his own country the businessman would think it unnecessary to obtain because his own experience provides him with the answers. Finding answers to all the questions (particularly when one does not even know what the questions are) is expensive, and the cost of doing so may make the businessman uncompetitive against local competition or his (albeit less well prepared) fellow countrymen.

Certain familiar features may lull the outsider into a false sense of security. In the construction industry for example, rock to be excavated may look the same as material found at home. The documents may be familiar: in the construction industry, the contract may be in the FIDIC form, familiar in itself and rooted firmly in British tradition. There is a feeling that if a straight path can be steered through the contract clauses, all will be well (even if a foreign law governs the contract).

Unfortunately the sense of security this induced is all too often a false one. The rock has not undergone the same weathering process as the local material and is very difficult to excavate. The context within which the contract is to be carried out is wholly different from that anticipated. The governing law may be rooted in a wholly different tradition to the British one and have a quite unexpected impact on the contract.[1]

The influence of civil code systems of law

The particular problem with which this paper is concerned is one which occurs in systems of law which have French law as their root. It relates to the ability to have disputes resolved by arbitration. It therefore pre-supposes that the contract has run into difficulties already and therefore the foreign businessman is already beginning to feel that his overseas venture may not have been worth the trouble.

The problem concerns the arbitrability of disputes under contracts with governments, or government departments, or contracts for public works. Examples of the problem are contained in the following provisions:

- Article 2060 of the French Civil Procedure Code contains a general prohibition of arbitration of matters in which the interests of public organisations are involved;
- Article 1676 of the Belgian Code Judiciaire provides that:

> "With the exception of public law legal entities, whoever has legal capacity or power to compromise can enter into an arbitration agreement. The State may enter such an agreement when a treaty allows it to resort to arbitration;"

- Article 315(2) of the Ethiopian Code of Civil Procedure prohibits arbitration of disputes under administrative contracts, and Article 3132 of the Civil Code defines an administrative contract, inter alia, as a contract which contains "one or more provisions which could only have been inspired by urgent considerations of general interest extraneous to relations between private individuals".

It might be thought that where government bodies have entered into contracts containing arbitration clauses, the point might not later be taken that arbitration was prohibited. This would be an unwise assumption, even in the case of the more developed countries such as France and Belgium. Decisions on the topic continue to emanate from the Cour de Cassation in France, although by 1964 the position was reasonably clear (and some of these cases will be discussed later in this paper). The Belgian State has done so as recently as 1984 (again in a case which will be discussed), as have government bodies in Ethiopia. There is, therefore, a real prospect that if a dispute arises under a contract with a governmental body whose system of law emanates from French law, attempts will be made to block the arbitration. This will no doubt be done on two fronts – in the arbitration which the overseas claimant attempts to begin, the defendant government

1 This has been discussed in detail in the article by Max Abrahamson "Checklist for foreign laws – FIDIC forms in context", *International Construction Law Review* (1988).

body will submit that the arbitrators have no power to proceed, and probably also in the local court of the defendant government body, that body will bring its own proceedings for declaratory relief.

Possible solutions

What then is the solution? It is an over-simplification to say that any businessman planning to do business in a foreign country should check that any arbitration clause inserted in his contract will be unchallengeable because, as already stated, this is only one of a myriad of problems that the businessman will face. It might also be said that if he had seriously thought at the outset that his venture was likely to result in arbitration proceedings, he would not do business in a foreign country in the first place. In the construction industry this may not be true, firstly because disputes are referred to arbitration with relative frequency and secondly the presence of an arbitration clause tends to encourage resolution of disputes before they reach an unmanageable state. A discussion of the approach taken by some of the courts and arbitrators to this problem may help to indicate some of the solutions.

Fortunately for the lawyer advising a client who faces a situation where arbitration is being blocked by the proposed defendant by reference to a regulation of the kind set out above, (but perhaps unfortunately for his client), there is quite a considerable amount of written material available on this topic.[2]

It is fortunate for the lawyer because he does not have to do all the ground work himself, but perhaps unfortunate for his client (who is paying the lawyer's fees) in that the topic is such an interesting one and raises so many varied questions of international law that the lawyer may have to read a considerable amount before satisfying himself that he has covered the ground.

The foreign businessman has, through most eyes, "right on his side". In the following typical example, it is not hard to see where the sympathies of unbiased arbitrators or judges would lie:

> Foreign contractor and national government body enter into contract for the execution of civil engineering works. The contract is in FIDIC form, containing the standard Clause 67 arbitration clause. A dispute arises under the contract in which the contractor is claimant. The claimant seeks to refer the dispute to ICC arbitration in, say, Paris. The defendant government body tries to block the arbitration by challenging the jurisdiction of the arbitrators, and begins its own proceedings in its domestic court seeking a declaration that the arbitrators have no power to act.

The history of the decisions on this point demonstrate the inherent sympathy that the foreign contractor is likely to receive from the duly appointed arbitrator(s) under the contract. Arbitrators and judges alike have

2 As an example in English, see Schwebel, *International Arbitration: Three Salient Problems*, Grotius Publications (1987).

traditionally looked for solutions which will allow the arbitration to proceed; some of these methods have been less logically justifiable than others.

The first (and crucial) requirement if the foreign contractor is to avoid being totally blocked by this approach is for the arbitrators appointed under the arbitration clause to have power to determine their own jurisdiction. Of course the ICC Rules of Arbitration contain such power in Article 8, the relevant parts of which read as follows:

> "3. Should one of the parties raise one or more pleas concerning the existence or validity of the agreement to arbitrate, and should the court be satisfied of the prima facie existence of such an agreement, the court may, without prejudice to the admissibility or merits of the plea or pleas, decide that the arbitration shall proceed. In such a case any decision as to the arbitrator's jurisdiction shall be taken by the arbitrator himself."

If such a provision is absent, (and particularly in the context of an applicable procedural law which does not give the power to an arbitrator to determine his own jurisdiction), the foreign contractor will be left with the uncertain prospect of the issue being decided by the local court of the defendant governmental body. The question of the ability of arbitrators to decide on their own jurisdiction (*Kompetenz Kompetenz*) is a quite separate issue in itself which has greatly interested commentators on the subject.

If a power on the part of the arbitrators to decide their own jurisdiction is successfully incorporated (as in the ICC Rules), the foreign contractor would be well advised to try to ensure that there is at least one francophone academic lawyer on the panel of arbitrators, because of his likely familiarity with some or all of the following cases.

The landmark case under French law is *Trésor Public* c. *Galakis*.[3] The contract in question was a charterparty under which a French governmental body (Mission des Transports Maritimes) chartered a vessel from the owner, Galakis, to transport goods. The charterparty contained a stipulation that any disagreement arising from the contract would be submitted to arbitration in London. Galakis referred a dispute to arbitration in London. The French Government refused to participate in the proceedings in London, whereupon an award was made against it in Galakis' favour. Galakis tried to enforce the arbitral award through the courts in France. The lower court declared the arbitration clause void and refused to give effect to the arbitral decision, because of Articles 83 and 1004 of the Code of Civil Procedure (the predecessors of Article 2060 referred to above). The Paris Court of Appeal reversed this judgment, and the Cour de Cassation agreed with the Court of Appeal stating (in translation) as follows:

> "That the invalidity required by Articles 83 and 1004 of the Code of Civil Procedure does not raise any question of capacity within the meaning of Article 3 of the Civil Code; that the primary duty of the Court of Appeal was to decide whether the Rule, enacted for internal contracts, should be applied as well to international contracts made to suit the needs of, and under conditions conforming to the usages of, maritime commerce; that the judgment under attack decides justly that the rule denying validity does not apply to such a contract."

In other words, the Court recognised a distinction between domestic and international contracts and then held that a prohibition against a state or

3 Judgment of the Cour de Cassation on 2 May 1966, on Lexis.

state entities agreeing to arbitration is applicable only to domestic matters. Since the relevant provisions of the Code of Civil Procedure do not make this distinction, there is clearly a certain amount of judicial creativity involved in this decision.

The *Galakis* case came shortly after the case of *Office National Interprofessionel des Crales-c-Capitaine du San Carlo*,[4] another shipping case, in which the Cour de Cassation held that:

> "Since the invalidity arising from Articles 83 and 1004 of the Code of Civil Procedure is a matter of internal law, it is not a matter of international law, and does not prevent a government owned enterprise from submitting, as could any other contracting party, the private law agreement which it makes to a foreign law that recognises the validity of the arbitration clause, when the contract is of an international nature."

In other words, the Court treated the governing law of the contract as the crucial factor, allowing arbitration providing the proper law of the contract allows arbitration (the governing law in the *San Carlo* case was Italian law). This decision too was the result of some creative thinking; one commentator has said of both the *Galakis* and *San Carlo* decisions:

> "The commercial and political rationale for the decisions here under discussion is quite clear; the more difficult task is justifying the result juridically."[5]

The difficulty with the *San Carlo* approach is that the prohibition of arbitration is the product of the system of law under which the relevant governmental body operates, and it is not possible to escape the effects of that law merely by providing that the contract is to be governed by another system of law. The approach in the *San Carlo* case has however been followed see *e.g.* the 22 March 1976 decision of the Tribunal of Tunis.[6] The weight of academic criticism of this approach is such that it might not be the safest argument on which to rely.[7]

Theories regarding the status of international arbitration

From the principle established in the *Galakis* case (of the difference between international and internal public order) has arisen the concept, developed primarily by francophone academic lawyers, that international arbitration has its own existence and status independent of domestic law. One of the most ardent advocates of this theory is Professor Goldman, whose writings are referred to above. In his article in *Revue de L'arbitrage*, 1980, he discusses the *Galakis* and other cases and in relation to the decision in *Galakis* states:

4 Judgment of 14 April 1964.
5 H Batiffol "Arbitration Clauses concluded between French Government owned enterprises and foreign private parties", 7 *Columbia Journal of Trans National Law* (1968), 32 at 35.
6 Extracts in III *Yearbook Commercial Arbitration* 283 (1978).
7 See for example the comment of Professor Goldman in *Repertoire Dalloz de Droit International*, V. Arbitrage No. 78–80.

"The simple respect for honesty in contracts and the self interest of the state, which is to benefit from the credibility of its signature, particularly in its international economic relations, imposes this solution."

In his note to the judgment in *SPP* v *EGOTH*[8] (the *Pyramids* case), Professor Goldman says:

"There is in fact no doubt that the acceptance by the state of an arbitration clause manifestly and necessarily implies waiver of immunity from jurisdiction, in any event in arbitration proceedings."

In a preliminary decision in ICC Case No. 5542 of 1987, a case concerning a FIDIC contract governed by Ethiopian law, the Tribunal (which included Professor Goldman as chairman) made the following comment:

"In addition the Tribunal deems fit to observe that the contract at stake in the present arbitration is an international contract in that the parties' seats are in two different states and it concerns international economic activity. This arbitration itself is equally international, since it deals with an international contract and the parties have referred in Article VIII of the Principal Agreement and in the arbitration clauses of the other contract documents to the ICC Rules. Under the circumstances, by virtue of a general principle of international arbitration, a state may not refuse the application of arbitration clauses it has agreed to, by invoking its domestic legislation."

Professor Goldman is certainly not alone in this. The well known Swiss commentator, P Lalive, states that restrictions on a state's power to arbitrate cannot be used as a defence against foreign individuals acting in good faith.[9] In a considerable number of arbitrations, the arbitrators have taken the same positive approach (see for example the award of the arbitrators in the *SPP* v *EGOTH* case,[10] even though this decision was overruled by the Paris Court of Appeal), and ICC Case Nos 1526 of 1968 and 2521 of 1975.

The principle has also been applied in some of the courts where an overseas contractor might have some doubts as to the independence of the forum concerned. For example, in the case of *Ethio Marketing Ltd.* v *Ministry of Information,*[11] the Ethiopian Supreme Court, interpreting the provisions of the Civil Code and Civil Procedure Code referred to at the beginning of this paper decided:

"A contract concluded pursuant to the provisions of the Civil Code is law between the two parties. The appellant and the respondent having, on the basis of the Civil Code, agreed to resolve the dispute between them by arbitration, the Civil Procedure Code should not prevent the enforcement of this contractual agreement."

"Administrative" contracts

At the outset reference was made to the definition in the Ethiopian Civil Code of an administrative contract, being one that contains "provisions

8 Decision of the Paris Court of Appeal 12/7/84.
9 In Uni Droit 1977.
10 ICC Arbitral Award No. 3493 of 16 February 1983.
11 Decision of 29 March 1975.

which could only have been inspired by urgent considerations of general interest extraneous to relationships between private individuals". This too emanates from French law where there is a concept of "clauses exorbitantes du droit commun", which are the features which distinguish an administrative contract from an ordinary commercial agreement. As was noted in the *Texaco Calasiatic* case (Section 56)[12] one of the principal characteristics of an administrative contract is its fundamentally and essentially unequal nature. In an administrative contract under a French based system of law, the administrative authorities will often have the power unilaterally to impose on the person contracting with them modifications to the contract.[13]

The way to deal with the contention that a contract is an administrative contract and therefore not susceptible to arbitration will be to look at the contract itself. An ICC arbitration of a construction dispute will usually result from a contract under the FIDIC form. The FIDIC form does not fit into the concept of an administrative contract. The clearest example is the provision that any amendments to the contract document shall not be valid unless made in writing by mutual consent. Also, the very fact that the FIDIC form of contract is designed for international use and is widely accepted by all those in the construction industry militates against it being interpreted as an administrative contract.

Pacta sunt servanda

Intermingled with the theory of the independence of international arbitration is the overwhelming desire of judicial bodies to see that the parties are bound to the obligations they agree to (the principle of *pacta sunt servanda*). This principle is applied not only in cases bearing on the subject of this paper, but in any situation where a government body is seeking to avoid being bound by a contract which it has entered into. The principle is helpful in cases where it is contended that, no matter what the intentions of the government body when entering into the contract, it was simply prohibited from doing so by its domestic law. The argument continues that its intentions are therefore irrelevant, just as the intentions of a minor would be in entering into a contract under English law. The distinction is made that the incapacitated person may not voluntarily waive the protection that exists for his own protection, whereas a government or government body being the creator of the law can also be the breaker of it. The principle has been put forcefully by an often quoted English arbitrator in the case of *Solel Boneh* v. *Uganda*.[14]

> "I must admit that I have found some difficulties to follow a line of reasoning that a state, just because of its supreme position and qualities, should be unable to give a binding promise. The principle of Pacta Sunt Servanda is generally acknowledged in international law and it is difficult to see any reason why it should not apply here. A sovereign state must be sovereign enough to make a binding promise both under international law and municipal law."

12 Translated in 53 *International Law Reports* 389.
13 See *e.g.* Art. 3179 of the Ethiopian Civil Code.
14 *Year Book Commercial Arbitration 1975*, 133–35.

The Theory of Severability

Another principle which assists arbitrators in determining their own jurisdiction is the theory of severability of an arbitration clause - that is, that an arbitration agreement, apart from exceptional circumstances, always assumes full legal autonomy. It therefore remains valid notwithstanding any contrary provisions of the law of the state of one of the parties - this was determined in *Meniucci-c-Mahieux.*[15] and the *Gosset* and *Hecht* cases which preceded it.[16] The theory has been used by arbitrators see the decision of the sole arbitrator in *Texaco Calasiatic* v. *The Government of Libya.*[17]

The fact that all these so-called principles are in fact devices or techniques developed by adjudicators to avoid the strict wording of domestic law and ensure that parties are kept to their obligations was noted by the arbitrators in the 1984 case of *Benteler* v. *Belgian State.*[18] In that case the arbitrators frankly describe the principles as "techniques". This case is interesting in that it demonstrates that even a sophisticated country like Belgium was as recently as 1984 still contending that it is prevented from submitting to arbitration, notwithstanding a clear obligation to do so in a contract that it has entered into. It did so in the face of the European Convention on International Commercial Arbitration of 21 April 1961 to which Belgium is a party. This Convention specifically empowers public law legal entities to enter legitimately into arbitration agreements.

The Belgian Government argued that the Convention did not apply, because the dispute was not one of international trade as defined under the Convention; it also argued that the *Galakis* principle did not apply, because the relevant provision of the Belgian Civil Procedure Code post-dated the Galakis decision and did not make the *Galakis* distinction, notwithstanding submissions by Belgian academics, before it was passed, that it should do so. The arbitrators found that the dispute did fall within the terms of the European Convention, and did not therefore need to make a ruling on the *Galakis* point.[19]

Unfortunately, the Geneva Convention is not of great assistance in resolving the present problem, because it has been ratified by only a limited number of states, principally in Western and Eastern Europe (one of the main purposes of the Convention was to establish an arbitration system for relationships with Eastern Bloc countries).

It is interesting to note that the problem of arbitrability of public works contracts does not arise under German law, and therefore presumably under systems of law which have their roots in German law. German law does distinguish between private contracts and public contracts, the former being governed by the provisions of the Civil Code and the latter by the Code of

15 Judgment of the Paris Court of Appeal on 13 December 1985, and the *Gosset* and *Hecht* cases which preceded it.

16 *Etablissements Raymond Cosset* c. *Soc Carapelli*. Semaine Juridique 20/11/63. *Hecht* c. *Buismans*. Rev. de l'Arbitrage February 1972.

17 *Ibid.*

18 Reported in *Journal of Arbitration* (1984), 184.

19 For further commentary on this decision, see J Paulsson "May a State invoke its internal law to repudiate consent to International Commercial Arbitration?" (1986) 2 *Arbitration International*, 90.

Administrative Procedure. To establish whether a contract is private or public, one looks at the content of the contract. If it relates to a subject matter that is normally regulated by public law then it will be a public contract. The distinction is a fine one and construction contracts could fall either side of the line. Where public entities conclude private contracts in order to fulfil public tasks they are bound to observe general principles of public law, but are not precluded from agreeing to an arbitration clause and conducting arbitration in accordance with the Code of Civil Procedure.

Where public entities conclude public contracts, they are permitted to use arbitration clauses to resolve all disputes as long as the parties are legally competent to dispose of the subject matter of the contract. The test as to whether the parties are legally competent to dispose of the subject matter of the contract is whether the parties can lawfully conclude a public contract. Whenever the parties can lawfully conclude such a contract, they can also agree on arbitration clauses.

Conclusion

In conclusion, therefore, a foreign contractor, faced with a submission by the government body with which he has contracted that his dispute is not susceptible to arbitration, is likely to prevail by virtue of the application of one or more of the principles or techniques outlined above, and providing he has rules of arbitration which empower the arbitrators to decide on their own jurisdiction, and those arbitrators are robust and preferably French trained, will be able to do so within the context of the arbitration itself, and not by reference to any domestic court. He must however expect that the process will be a lengthy, expensive and frustrating one which will prevent him for a considerable period from reaching the point where the arbitrators can actually decide on the merits of his claim.[20]

20 With thanks for assistance received from Prashant Popat (London), Horst Eidenmller (London/Frankfurt) and Eric Lasry (Paris).

16 Choice of disputes machinery in international arbitration

Anthony A Edwards

Synopsis

This paper examines the origin and processing of disputes which inevitably arise in international commercial contracts particularly in the construction field. Suggestions are given as to the material matters which need to be considered in the choice of appropriate means of dispute resolution.

Introduction

The choice of machinery for resolving construction disputes must have regard to the nature of the construction process and the types of dispute that tend to arise. Such disputes generally involve issues both of fact and law, either or both of which may be complex. The issues of fact may involve matters of design and use of materials, and these issues may involve the principles of physics and chemistry, as well as engineering. The disputes machinery must therefore allow sufficient flexibility to deal adequately with this type of issue, as well as related issues of law.

The factual issues may also involve questions about delay and extensions of time. These issues are likely to involve examination of detailed events on site, perhaps throughout the entire period of the contract works. The evidence will be detailed, and may well be conflicting, as witnesses try to recall the minutiae of daily events of perhaps a decade ago.

In construction disputes, the financial stakes are often substantial. Claims may run into tens of millions of pounds sterling, and it is therefore unlikely that the parties will, at least initially, be reluctant to commit themselves to the substantial levels of fees necessary to investigate and contest such cases fully. However, the parties will expect, particularly having regard to the level of financial commitment, that the disputes machinery will be sufficiently robust to permit proper handling of all aspects of the dispute and to produce a fair result (even accepting that a decision in favour of one side is necessarily against the other). These are the matters which place a heavy burden on the machinery for resolving major construction disputes, and which make the choice of the particular machinery a matter of some importance.

Incidence of Disputes

In the United Kingdom, the majority of construction operations fall into one of two broad categories: building construction or civil engineering. The first category has given rise to a significantly greater number of reported legal decisions, and there are undoubtedly larger numbers of these disputes. The building contractor tends to operate more within the commercial sector, that is, working for clients involved in development operations, or perhaps companies intending to relocate their own operations by new building or refurbishment. In the civil engineering field, operations tend to concentrate much more in the public sector, involving projects such as major roads, bridges, tunnels, and other public utility works. The greater incidence of disputes in the building sector may reflect simply the additional numbers of projects and contracts. It may also indicate a greater willingness by the parties involved to undertake the risks inherent in pursuing claims.

Standard forms of contract

Both in building and in civil engineering, standard forms of contract have been in use for many years. For civil engineering works, the principal standard form used within the United Kingdom is the ICE Conditions of Contract. Under this form, the appointed Engineer is given a pre-eminent role with wide discretionary powers, seemingly with little limitation. The widest power is that contained in Clause 13(1), where the contractor is required to carry out the works "in strict accordance with the contract, to the satisfaction of the Engineer and (to) comply with and adhere strictly to the Engineer's instructions and directions on any matter connected therewith (whether mentioned in the contract or not)". The international FIDIC form of contract contains a similar obligation in Clause 13.1 to "comply with and adhere strictly to the Engineer's instructions on any matter, whether mentioned in the contract or not, touching or concerning the works". The hallmark of these forms is that the Engineer is given very wide powers over the works and their execution.

The equivalent standard form in the building sector, for work within the United Kingdom, is that issued by the Joint Contracts Tribunal (JCT). This form has an appointed Architect who fulfils the same essential function as the Engineer, but generally possessing much more restricted and limited powers. There is no international version of the JCT form, and international building projects often use the FIDIC form adapted to suit the particular circumstances, often with an Architect appointed with the same sweeping powers as the Engineer.

The decision making process

There are many common features between the roles of the Engineer and Architect (now referred to as the Supervisor) under both UK domestic and international forms. Thus, the Supervisor is invariably empowered to vary the contract works, by addition or omission. In such a case, the decision is being made in the interest of one party to the contract only, *i.e.*, the Employer. In other cases, the Supervisor is required to act as an adjudicator between the two parties, as to their respective rights and obligations. In many cases the position of the Supervisor mirrors the disputes that may arise later under the contract. For example, the Supervisor may have to decide whether work or materials are in accordance with the contract or should be rejected. In other cases, the Supervisor has to decide whether delay and inefficiency in the work, involving additional cost, are the responsibility of the contractor or the employer. In such a case, a finding in favour of the contractor will involve financial consequences adverse to the employer, through relieving the contractor of the obligation to pay damages and possibly giving the contractor a right to financial compensation. It is well settled that in approaching these questions, the Supervisor must hold the balance fairly between the parties, and his decisions are usually capable of being challenged later by arbitration. But it is nevertheless the case that these contracts have the potential for dispute built into them; and those disputes which eventually appear in formal arbitration usually have their origin in issues which arise and call for settlement during the course of the works.

While construction contracts must necessarily provide this initial machinery for settlement of disputes between the parties, it is appropriate to consider why it is that a general right of challenge is then provided by arbitration. There is no reason in principle why parties should not agree to abide by the initial decision of the Supervisor. Architects and Engineers are professionals who would strongly assert their ability to act impartially when necessary, even though they are employed and paid by one of the parties. The subsequent stage of arbitrating decisions of the Supervisor usually involve bringing in other persons who may be architects, engineers or lawyers to adjudicate, in effect, by replacing the decision of the original Supervisor by that of the arbitral tribunal. It is appropriate to ask whether this is necessarily an efficient procedure, and why parties deem it necessary to retain a right of challenge to the original Supervisor. The objection to his decision is unlikely to be on the grounds that he does not know about the facts; and if the objection is to his judgement, there could be a system for bringing in another, more acceptable supervisor, to make the initial decision rather than going to arbitration. Thus, the initial question in regard to choice of disputes machinery should be whether formal arbitration is the necessary and indeed, the only, way in which disputes can be properly processed.

Arbitration and the courts

Virtually all common form construction contracts, including those already mentioned, provide for disputes which arise, either during the course of or after completion of the project, to be referred to arbitration with machinery provided for the appointment of an appropriate tribunal. The FIDIC form incorporates and binds the parties to the ICC Rules, under which the ICC Court has the power to approve or confirm the arbitrators, and if necessary to appoint a chairman. Under the FIDIC form (and the ICE form) provision is made for a further decision by the Engineer on the dispute in question before it may be referred to arbitration. If not challenged within the stated time limits, the Engineer's decision may become binding, and under English law such a provision will be upheld by the courts.[1]

In the United Kingdom prior to 1984, it was common for disputes arising in construction to be referred to the courts for decision, notwithstanding the existence of an arbitration clause. The view of practitioners and of the courts, without there being any definitive decision on the point, was that the courts had an inherent jurisdiction to exercise at least all those powers expressly given to the arbitrator under the contract, and that any provision to the contrary would be void as an ouster of the court's jurisdiction. This view was definitively reversed by a decision of the Court of Appeal given in February 1984 in the case of *Northern Regional Health Authority* v. *Derek Crouch Construction Ltd.*[2] The Master of the Rolls, in his judgment, stated that the courts would not interfere if commercial men chose to designate arbitrators, and not judges, as the people to hear and resolve their disputes. The initial effect of this decision was that many cases then in progress through the courts found themselves in the position that the court was stripped of jurisdiction to decide the issues. Parties and their legal advisers have had to come to terms with this new situation and there has inevitably been a material increase in the volume of arbitration (it should perhaps also be observed that, owing to the general increase in the volume of construction disputes, there has been no corresponding decrease in the amount of litigation).

The cornerstone of the *Crouch* decision, which related specifically to the JCT form of contract, was the provision empowering the arbitrator to "open up, review and revise" decisions of the Supervisor. A parallel power is to be found in the ICE form of contract. The *Crouch* decision drew on a passage in the judgment of Lord Wilberforce in *Kay* v. *Hosier and Dickinson*,[3] in which he said:

> "The contract confers very wide powers on arbitrators to open up and review certificates which a court would not have. . . ."

The effect of the *Crouch* decision as interpreted in subsequent cases[4] is that decisions of the Supervisor or other third party adjudicator are capable of challenge only within the express provisions of the contract. Thus, it becomes essential in drafting disputes machinery to operate under English law that express provision is made for challenge of those matters intended to be open to review. A contract that contains no disputes machinery at all will no longer be interpreted as empowering the courts to open up all decisions, indeed the reverse is likely to be the case. Consequently, it

1 *Kaye* v. *Hosier and Dickinson Ltd.* [1972] 1 WLR 146.
2 [1984] QB 644.
3 [1972] 1 WLR 146.
4 See particularly *Finnegan* v. *Sheffield CBC* (1988) 43 BLR 124.

follows that if arbitration is not the chosen system for dispute resolution, provision needs to be made for the court to be empowered to challenge particular decisions.

As stated in the *Crouch* case, the court will always retain power to interpret the contract, including power to decide whether one party is in breach. Thus, a substantial range of disputes may still be brought before the English courts. But if they involve challenging third party decisions, power to open up such decisions must be found in the contract. One alternative available under the English Arbitration Act 1950 is to appoint an Official Referee (a specialist judge dealing with construction disputes) as arbitrator. Section 11 of the Act provides as follows:

> "Reference to Official Referee. Where an arbitration agreement provides that a reference shall be to an Official Referee, any Official Referee to whom application is made shall, subject to any Order of the High Court or Judge thereof as to transfer or otherwise, hear and determine the matters to be referred."

An agreement to refer to an Official Referee may be entered into at any time, and may be made after the dispute has arisen. It is doubtful, however, whether by these or other means, the parties can create a right to challenge decisions which would not otherwise be capable of challenge under the contract at all.

One of the major limiting factors in arbitration, particularly in the construction field, is in the inability to create effective multi-party procedures. Such procedures are desirable where alternative claims exist against, for example, contractors and sub-contractors, or contractors and designers. Before the *Crouch* decision, the solution frequently adopted was to abrogate the arbitration clauses and take all such disputes to court, relying on the court's powers of joinder and third party procedure.[5] Since the *Crouch* decision, this is often impossible, because part of the court's jurisdiction will be lacking. The result has been that disputes have had to be referred to separate arbitrations, unless the parties have been prepared to agree to rules giving arbitrators power to determine different disputes together. This poses considerable problems in arbitration, both at domestic and *a fortiori* at international level, and there is no ready solution.

Arbitration under ICC Rules

The detailed rules are examined in other papers. It is proposed here to consider some particular points which may be relevant to the choice of these rules as an appropriate means of dispute settlement. One particular problem which legal practitioners must be aware of is the time bar provided by Clause 67 of FIDIC and the effects of incorporation of the ICC Rules. Clause 67 of the Third Edition of FIDIC provides that the Engineer's decision becomes binding on the parties if no claim to arbitration has been communicated to him within 90 days from receipt of his notice of decision.

5 RSC Ord. 15, 16.

The clause goes on to provide that the party dissatisfied with the Engineer's decision must:

> "Within 90 days after receiving notice of such decision . . . require that the matter or matters in dispute be referred to arbitration as hereinafter provided. All disputes or differences in respect of which the decision, if any, of the Engineer has not become final and binding as aforesaid shall be finally settled under the rules of conciliation and arbitration of the ICC. . . ."

It is possible to argue and there appears to be no definitive decision on the point, that the "claim to arbitration" necessary to prevent the Engineer's decision from becoming binding is a request for arbitration in accordance with the ICC Rules.[6] This is, primarily, a function of the FIDIC contract rather than the ICC Rules, and the point appears to have been clarified in the Fourth Edition of FIDIC which requires only that one party should notify the other "of his intention to commence arbitration as hereinafter provided as to the matter in dispute".

The broader question of whether disputes machinery should contain a time bar of this type is a matter which should properly be considered by the parties when entering into the contract. The Third Edition of FIDIC provided a period of 90 days to challenge the Engineer's decision, while the Fourth Edition provides 70 days, and the ICE Conditions three months. Against the time bar is the fact that it may, by inadvertence, rule out proper claims, and may create considerable procedural difficulties where what has been ruled out is part of a larger claim, for example, an extension of time claim, where the contractor still intends to pursue a claim for additional payment. The converse argument is that neither party is obliged to submit its disputes to the Engineer at any particular time, and the time bar has the effect of discouraging the early submission of disputes, arguably undesirable when early disputes may be overtaken by later events in the contract.

Particular features

Discovery of documents represents one of the major points of difference between continental, code-based systems and common law procedure. While there may be an express or implied choice of forum and therefore procedural law in the contract, the position is often that the parties have different intentions and expectations as to this fundamental question, which is bound to have a strong influence on the course of the dispute. One practical problem is that in the international context, the arbitrators may have no effective sanction or means of enforcing the production of documents. One compromise available to the arbitrators is to require mutual production of documents, linked with a stated declaration that adverse inference may be drawn against a party who fails to produce relevant documents without good cause.

Expedition is generally regarded as desirable, in that all parties in arbitration wish to achieve a speedy result. The ICC rules provide expressly by Article 14.1 for the arbitrators to:

6 Wallace, *Construction Contracts, Principles and Policies*, Chap. 18.

"proceed within as short a time as possible to establish the facts of the case by all appropriate means".

The concept of a "short" time may have difference meanings. In continental terms, this may mean weeks rather than months, as opposed to the common law interpretation, which would be months rather than years. The ICC Rules in fact specify a time limit of six months to render the award, although it is well known that extensions to this period may be granted. In practice, the degree of expedition possible in a case is heavily dependent on the preparation needed, particularly in regard to discovery. It should also be noted that the period of 6 months under the ICC Rules[7] runs from the signing of the terms of reference, before which each party must have made a full statement of its case, including the production of documents and statements. In an equivalent common law case, this stage would be equivalent to a point after the close of pleadings and well into the preparation for the hearing.

There are a number of other matters under the ICC Rules that may influence the parties' choice as to the appropriate machinery to adopt. Thus, by Article 9, payment of the advance on costs is required before the arbitration can effectively proceed. However, since January 1988 the ICC's administrative expenses are fixed at a maximum of US$50,500.[8] The arbitrator's fees are based on a percentage of the "sum in dispute": and although the fees paid are in the discretion of the court, they are not primarily linked to the time expended.

Parties using the ICC Rules, particularly from a common law background, should always be aware of the potential limitations on amendment to claims. Article 16 provides that a party may make a new claim or counter-claim on condition that these remain within the limits fixed by the Terms of Reference or that they are specified in a rider. The latter appears to require agreement of both parties, which is unlikely to be forthcoming in the case of an increase in the claim of one party.[9] It should also be noted that Article 24 of the ICC Rules contains a deemed waiver of appeal, which has been held binding for the purposes of the English Arbitration Act 1979.[10]

Arbitration Rules in the United Kingdom

The London Court of International Arbitration has its own set of arbitration rules,[11] which have a number of similarities to the ICC Rules in their detail. However, the LCIA Rules are based on common law procedure in that the parties are to submit only a brief statement of the nature of the case, sufficient for the choice of arbitrators. Thereafter, statements in the nature of pleadings are exchanged. There is no requirement to draw up Terms of Reference, and the issues emerge in the conventional common law manner, during the preparation and conduct of the arbitration. The LCIA Rules

7 Art. 18.1.
8 ICC Rules, App. III, para. 5.
9 But see Paper 3, Stephen Bond.
10 *Marine Contractors* v. *Shell Petroleum Nigeria* [1984] 2 Lloyd's Rep. 77.
11 See Paper 24, B. Vigrass.

create a degree of flexibility at least as great as that under the ICC Rules, and the role of the court itself is significantly less prominent than that of the ICC Court.

The LCIA Rules, by Article 5 encourages the parties themselves to agree on the arbitral procedure. In the absence of agreement the tribunal is to have:

> "the widest discretion allowed under such law as may be applicable to ensure the just, expeditious, economical and final determination of the dispute"

There is no time limit for conclusion of the arbitration. Article 6 lays down a timetable for the exchange of written statements subject, however, to rules established by the parties or the arbitrators. In distinction to the ICC Rules, which are silent on the matter, Article 11 of the LCIA Rules makes provision for oral testimony, including written statements of evidence. Article 13 provides a substantial number of additional powers, which may not necessarily be available under English procedural law. One power which would be available under English law, but not necessarily under the ICC Rules, is the express power to allow a party to amend claims or counter-claims.[12] The arbitrators are given express power under this Article to order production of documents, a power available under English law, but not necessarily elsewhere.

There are a number of other forms of UK arbitration rules. In the field of construction disputes, there are available rules specially drafted for civil engineering and building contracts, being respectively the ICE arbitration procedure (1983) and the JCT arbitration rules (1988). Each of these sets of rules contains particular procedures intended to govern particular types of dispute, for example, disputes primarily of a technical nature[13] and for smaller disputes.[14] These features are notably absent in international rules but are within the overall wide discretion given to the arbitrators, for example, under the ICC Rules, Article 11 or the LCIA Rules, Articles 5 and 13.

Conclusion

The particular choice of dispute machinery needs to have regard to the needs and interests of the parties, the nature of the project and the particular dispute involved. In regard to the latter, this is not known *ex hypothesi*, until after the contract has been made. It could be argued that this is the appropriate time to make an arbitration agreement and to settle the appropriate procedure. However, experience indicates that an agreement about procedure is unlikely to be forthcoming at the time that the parties are in dispute.

Consequently, the parties and their advisers must endeavour to cover foreseeable eventualities by providing a procedure which is sufficiently flexible to accommodate a wide variety of potential disputes, including those

12 Art. 13.1(d).
13 See ICC Procedure Part G: Special procedure for experts.
14 ICE Procedure Part F; JCT Rules, Rule 5.

of a technical and legal nature, having a wide variety of financial values and complexity. While some procedures contain much useful detail, it is evident that the parties and the arbitrators need to be given considerable discretion in settling the detailed procedure. For this purpose, the parties and the arbitrators are likely to be assisted by reference to other existing procedures, particularly where experience is available as to their use.

The drafting of disputes clauses 17

Elizabeth Jones

Synopsis

This paper deals with the problems of drafting effective arbitration clauses, reviews the authorities and offers some good and bad examples of clauses used in international commercial agreements.

Introduction

The technique of drafting disputes clauses is much like that of drafting contract clauses in general – the end must be held in view constantly, the wording must be as clear and unambiguous as possible and the structure adopted by the parties for (in this case) the settlement of their disputes must be workable in practice. Unfortunately this is not always the case –

> "There is an astonishing contrast between the degree of sophistication reflected in the substance of some voluminous international contracts prepared by highly competent and resourceful personnel and the primitiveness of the errors to be found in the arbitration clause. Since the binding nature of the agreement and in a real sense its entire legal premise is to be determined by the forum one has apparently attempted to select in the last article of the contract the perfection of the first fifty articles is all too often for nought".[1]

As a lawyer who spent a number of years drafting and negotiating large-scale international contracts for a major contractor, I can say that we were concerned with the forum and governing law – including the procedural law of the potential arbitration – such that it should be workable and as little cumbersome as possible. Our aim was to achieve a set of contract terms which were themselves so unambiguous as to the rights and duties of the parties that they would, it was hoped, not consider it worthwhile undertaking the expense and commitment of an arbitration but rather settle any dispute which might arise.

1 Quoted in Craig, Park and Paulsson, *International Chamber of Commerce Arbitration* 89.

That being said, the following clauses quoted by Craig Park and Paulsson[2] in a chapter entitled 'Pathological Elements' are clearly beyond the pale, if only for their sloppy wording:–

> "All disputes arising in connection with the present agreement should be resolved by negotiation and friendly settlement. If this method of resolution should be impracticable the disputed questions shall be decided in accordance with the Rules of Arbitration of the ICC in Paris. In the event the proceedings were not able to decide the question for any reason whatsoever the judicial courts of the injured party shall decide the dispute on a legal basis".
>
> "All disputes arising in connection with the present agreement shall be submitted in the first instance to arbitration. The arbitrator shall be a well-known chamber of commerce (like the International Chamber of Commerce) designated by mutual agreement between buyer and seller".
>
> "Disputes hereunder shall be referred to arbitration to be carried out by arbitrators viewed by the International Chamber of Commerce in Geneva In accordance with the arbitration procedure set forth in the Civil Code of Venezuela or the Civil Code of France with due regard for the law of the place of arbitration".

Basic elements

Section 32 of the Arbitration Act 1950 defines an arbitration agreement as "a written agreement to submit present or future differences to arbitration whether an arbitrator is named therein or not". The basic elements of an effective arbitration clause can therefore be said to be the following:–

a clear commitment by both (or all) parties to refer any dispute to arbitration;
a clear procedure for triggering the start of the arbitration process;
a clear forum for the arbitration;
a clear choice of law governing the procedure of the arbitration;
a clear method of appointing the arbitrator;
clear procedural rules governing the conduct of the arbitration (if not covered in (d)).

Part of the problem is, of course, that, in negotiated contracts in particular, the lawyers on each side may have their own strong views on the optimum disputes clause. Disagreement on whose form of clause is to be employed is unlikely to appeal to the commercial client as a deal-breaker when his prime interest is in the price he can get and the technical difficulty of the work. The practical chaos of the final stages of negotiations – a combination of tiredness, frustration and pressure of time – may also have something to do with the rather strange clauses quoted above. The psychology of negotiation is not however a topic for this conference.

Mustill and Boyd[3] divide an arbitration agreement into

> "two distinct obligations which the Courts will enforce:

2 See *ante*.

3 *Commercial Arbitration*, Butterworths (1989), 2nd ed.

1. One party (B) promises to the other party (A) that if a valid award is made in favour of A in relation to a dispute which falls within the scope of the agreement B will perform the award.
2. B promises to A that if B has a claim which falls within the scope of the agreement B will enforce that claim only by means of a reference to arbitration.

These undertakings by B are matched by similar promises on the part of A."

Legal meanings of words

The authors go on to give an instructive review of the legal meanings of words commonly used in arbitration clauses. References for example to "claims" "differences" or "disputes" have the widest possible scope[4] although they have to be construed by reference to the subject matter of the contract in which they are included. The term "disputes" was defined in *Re Hohenzollern* to mean "all disputes that may arise between the parties in consequence of this contract having been entered into".

The words "in connection with" and "in relation to" have been held[5] "wide enough to cover claims for notification and damages for innocent misrepresentation inducing the contract". Generally however they have been given a restricted meaning, viz: they do not cover claims for damages based on fraudulent inducement[6] claims for payment on a *quantum meruit*[7] or a claim for breach of an implied contract not to impede building works[8]. The words "relating thereto" and "relative to" have been held to cover allegations of termination through failure of a condition or non-disclosure.[7]

"In respect of" and "with regard to" have been stated[9] to cover disputes about whether there has been a breach by one side or the other or whether circumstances have arisen which have discharged one or both parties from future performance. "Arising out of" has been held[10] to cover every dispute except a dispute as to whether there was ever a contract at all. It covers disputes between the parties as to contingent rights following operation of the contingency;[11] It embraces frustration,[12] non-disclosure,[13] a dispute as to whether the contract has been varied or replaced by a fresh contract[14] and a claim for damages for breach of the arbitration agreement itself.[15]

4 *Woolf* v. *Collis Removal Service* [1948] 1 KB 11. *Re Hohenzollern Act for Locomotivebahn and the City of London Contract Corporation* [1886] 54 LT 596. *F & G Sykes (Wessex)* v. *Fine Fare Ltd.* [1967] 1 Lloyd's Rep 53.
5 *Ashville Investments Ltd.* v. *Elmer Contractors Ltd.* [1988] 2 Lloyd's Rep 73.
6 *Monro* v. *Bognor UDC* [1915] 3 KB 167.
7 *De la Garde* v. *Worsnop & Co.* [1928] Ch 17.
8 *Lawson* v. *Wallasey Local Board* [1883] 2 QBD 229.
9 *Per* Viscount Simon LC in *Heyman* v. *Daiwins Ltd.* [1942] AC 356.
10 *Per* Pilcher J in *AE Daniel Ltd.* v. *Carmel Exporters & Importers Ltd.* [1953] 2 Lloyd's Rep 103.
11 *Per* Viscount Dilhorne in *The Evje* [1974] 2 Lloyd's Rep 57.
12 *Kruse* v. *Questier & Co.* [1953] 1 Lloyd's Rep 310.
13 *Stebbing* v. *Liverpool & London & Globe Insurance Co. Ltd.* [1917] 2 KB 433.
14 *Faghirzadeh* v. *Rudolf Woolf SA [& Pty] Ltd.* [1977] 1 Lloyd's Rep 630.
15 *Mantovani* v. *Carapell SpA* [1980] 1 Lloyd's Rep 375.

Reference to disputes arising "under" a contract may be subject to a more narrow interpretation than disputes arising "out of" the contract.[16] Issues of non disclosure and supervening illegality[17] are, however, included. The words "during the execution of" refer to the performance or purported performance of the contract and take in claims in tort as long as there is a sufficiently close connection with the performance of the contract.

Clauses referring to the "meaning and intention of the contract" – see *post* the clause for a contract for the construction of a university in the Middle East where *ex aequo et bono* is also used – entrust the arbitrators with jurisdiction over liability but not over the amount of the claim.[18]

The above factors will, of course, only be relevant where English law or a common law based governing law is adopted. In such a case Mustill and Boyd[19] take the view that "the existence of an arbitration agreement" does not afford a defence to an action brought in breach of it nor does it deprive the court of jurisdiction over the dispute. "The court retains a residual jurisdiction superior to that of an arbitrator which it may either assert or relinquish depending on the circumstances". The point about a defence to an action is of course subject to the existence of a *Scott* v. *Avery* clause,[20] where the award of an arbitrator is expressed to be a condition predecent to the enforcement of any rights under the contract.

Practical considerations

Obviously in international contracts resort to the English courts may be neither possible or appropriate – problems of enforcement have always been a factor which commercial lawyers have to take into account in advising their clients and which may have a greater influence on the terms of a disputes clause and the venue of that dispute hearing than almost anything else. The client is not, unfortunately, going to be particularly interested in winning if he cannot collect on the award, and where some third world projects are concerned, it may be easier to obtain compliance with a decision obtained locally, (if such a thing is possible), than with a decision given in Europe or America. In Saudi Arabia and some at least of the Gulf States, for instance, most of the work done during the oil money boom of the late seventies and early eighties was done on the basis of Sharia law, *i.e.* the provisions of the Koran as applied by local courts. As the Employers of the day were usually the Governments of the various countries it was Hobson's choice for the contractor. Either he took the contract, disputes provisions and all, or the Koreans probably would.

Where slightly more scope was allowed – and not wishing to spread too much gloom and despondency amongst the aficionados of ICC arbitration – other devices were tried (although not by me personally). It was thought for example that perhaps an *ex aequo et bono* provision would serve as well

16 *Per* Sellers J in *Government of Gibralter* v. *Keeney* [1956] 2 QB 410 but not that this distinction was doubted in *The Evje* at 66 and 67.
17 *Mackender Hill & White* v. *Feldia AG* [1966] 2 Lloyd's Rep 449.
18 *Richards* v. *John Payne & Co.* [1917] 86 LJ KB 937.
19 See *ante*.
20 [1856] 5 HL Cas 811.

if not better in some cases than an attempt to graft a complex set of procedural rules on to what was in essence an agreement to carry out specified work on specified terms for specified payment. An example used in a contract for a university in a Middle Eastern country where the State was the Employer is set out below:

> "1. If any dispute or difference shall arise between and relating to the Agreement which cannot be settled amicably between the parties it shall be finally settled under the Rules of Conciliation and Arbitration of the International Chamber of Commerce by one or three arbitrators appointed in accordance with those rules. The venue of the arbitration shall be Geneva. The arbitrator shall have regard to the terms and conditions of this Agreement and if such terms and conditions do not resolve the dispute or difference then the arbitrator will apply the principles "ex aequo et bono". So far as practicable performance of this Agreement will continue notwithstanding any arbitration proceedings.
> 2. This Agreement is drawn up in the English language according to which it shall be construed and interpreted and in two original copies duly executed by and in accordance with their respective constitutions, one such copy being delivered to and held by each party."

It can be seen that the clause in point does opt for ICC Arbitration in Geneva but with "the terms and conditions of the Agreement" as the criteria in lieu of a governing law, failing which the principles *ex aequo et bono* were to be applied. In view of the problems encountered in Swiss arbitrations in past years one would not with hindsight have chosen Switzerland as the venue although the new Swiss Law on International Arbitration[21] which came into effect on 1 January this year is, I understand, intended to alleviate many of those problems. Equally the relevant part of the ICC rules (which provided that the seat of arbitration automatically decided the law governing the procedure unless the parties agreed otherwise) has been changed.

"Equity" clauses

There are conflicting views on so-called "equity" clauses of which *ex aequo et bono* is one form. Other examples are:

> "The Arbitrator shall be entitled to decide according to equity and good conscience and shall not be obliged to follow the strict rules of law"
> or simply
> "The arbitrator shall be entitled to act as amiable compositeur"

Mustill and Boyd take the view that the whole thing is really rather foreign and not likely to be accepted by the English courts in the forseeable future. Problems have already been encountered on the rare occasions when our courts have been asked to consider a concept so foreign to the common law, and some conflicting views have already been advanced (see *post*). Mustill and Boyd suggest that the following:

> "are amongst the interpretations which will have to be considered:
> – The clause empowers the arbitrator to adjust the bargain in the light of changed circumstances. This power may be exercised as regards future

21 Chap. 12 of the Swiss Act on Private International Law of 1 December 1987.

obligations in addition to those which are the object of dispute. The powers extend to a revision of the express terms of the contract as well as those which are imposed or implied by law.
- Once the arbitrator is seized of a dispute as to obligations existing or said to have existed in the past the clause frees him from any duty to respect the rules of law when deciding upon the merits of the dispute.
- The clause has the same effect as set out in 2 above except that the arbitrator is obliged to give effect to rules of public policy.
- The clause has the same effect as set out in 2 or 3 above except that the arbitrator cannot depart from the express terms of the contract.
- The clause empowers (and indeed requires) the arbitrator to apply a system of law but not a system which is that of any individual state.
- The clause enables the arbitrator to ignore technicalities and strict conditions.
- The purpose of the clause is only to ensure that the arbitrator need not conform with ordinary legal procedures when conducting the reference".

When it comes to point 5 the possible systems of law are considered and rejected namely "international law", "international arbitration law" and *lex mercatoria*. Indeed Mustill and Boyd question "whether a contract which contains both an arbitration clause and an equity clause can be regarded as an 'arbitration agreement' for the purposes of the Acts".

Other members of the common law tradition take a rather more positive view. According to the Hon Justice Andrew Rogers of the Supreme Court of New South Wales[22] "There is a recent but developing tendency of common law courts to accept that instead of decisions strictly in accordance with law the parties should be left to choose either the system of law that most appeals to them or indeed have the matter determined in accordance with 'equity'".

He quotes several cases where the matter was considered by English courts; a treaty of reinsurance for example[23] which included a provision that:

> "The Arbitrator and Umpire shall not be bound by the strict rules of law but shall settle any difference referred to them according to an equitable rather than a strictly legal interpretation of the provisions of this Agreement."

In that case Denning MR rejected the view that the clause was invalid as being contrary to public policy saying: "It only ousts technicalities and strict conditions. That is what equity did in the old days and it is what arbitrators do today under such a clause as this."

The Hon Justice Rogers goes on to quote another case, before the Privy Council this time[24] where the clause provided for reference to an amiable compositeur and where it was stated that:

> "Their lordships would no doubt hesitate much before they held that to entitle arbitrators named as amiables compositeurs to disregard all law and to be arbitrary in their dealings with the parties; but the distinction must have some reasonable effect given to it and the least effect which can reasonably be given to the words is that they dispense with the strict observance of those rules of law the non-observance of which as applied to awards results in no more than irregularity".

22 See *International Business Lawyer*, April 1989.

23 *Eagle Star Insurance Co. Ltd.* v. *Yuval Insurance Co. Ltd.* [1978] Lloyd's Rep 357.

24 *Roland* v. *Cassidy* [1888] 13 App Cas 770.

The supporters of total flexibility of procedure and forum and of the existence of concepts such as *lex mercatoria* are to be found principally in France where it has been held[25] that arbitrators are entitled to avoid the strict application not only of provisions of law but also of contractual clauses as long as they did not infringe the rules of *ordre publique*.

In Australia it appears that the uniform arbitration laws there permit the parties to agree that the arbitrator may depart from the strict law and act as amiable compositeur.

In general it appears that the common law (principally English) opponents to the idea of *lex mercatoria* and "floating" or transnational arbitration[26] are antagonistic as much to the threat to the strict rules of procedure with which English law governs the conduct of a dispute, whether referred to arbitration or to the courts, as to the apparent challenge to the supremacy of English legal principles which the adoption by the parties of lex mercatoria or ex aequo et bono represent. In an article,[27] as much as in his magnum opus on commercial arbitration,[28] Sir Michael Mustill having recited the *dicta* in the *Amin Rasheed*[29] case about legal *vacua* says that "international arbitration cannot effectively exist without at least some background of external procedural law" . . . nor "without an internal procedural law". He finds "objectionable" the absence of "any method of enforcing whatever internal procedural norms may exist" and takes the view, perhaps not without justification, that "the businessman may be attracted in the abstract by freedom from meddling by the court but will take a different view when confronted with a demand to honour an award arrived at by demonstrably unfair means".

This criticism of the lack of structure of a "floating" arbitration governed by *lex mercatoria* or some other non-national legal principles speaks of a certain naivety as to the position in which companies and others doing business across national frontiers and possibly with national governments find themselves, particularly if one of the contracting parties is a so called developing country.

Western – and these are essentially Western systems of law and disputes resolution – are essentially suspect. If they do not smack of neo-colonialism, they may be caught by political (*i.e.* capitalist/communist) or religious prejudices. The problems of enforcing judgments under the New York Convention, even in countries which subscribe to the "Western" philosophy of legal systems, are well known. The difficulties of persuading foreign, third world governments with perhaps, in our eyes, under-developed legal systems, to arbitrate outside their own boundaries must surely be apparent.

If it is accepted that disputes resolution of some kind to which both parties submit voluntarily is the way forward in international commerce, as distinct from the force majeure approach of sending in a gunboat, freezing

25 *Sociétés Intrafor Color et Subtec Middle East Co.*, MM Gagnant Guilbert et al *Revue de l'Arbitrage* [1985] No. 2 300.

26 For a detailed discussion of this latter topic see Paulson "Delocalisation of International Commercial Arbitration: when and why it matters" ICLQ vol.32, 53 and "Arbitration unbound: Award detached from the law of its country of origin" ICLQ, vol.30, 358.

27 "Transnational arbitration in English law", *Current Legal Problems* (1984) 133.

28 Mustill and Boyd, *Commercial Arbitration*.

29 See note 26 above.

assets in third countries' banks, or cutting off oil supplies and declaring a holy war, then *ex aequo et bono* and transnational arbitration may be the essential, the lowest common denominator of acceptable "legal" principles on which international business is to be done.

Martin Hunter[30] commenting on the decision in *Deutsche Schatbau*[31] quotes Baxter[32] as saying:

> "A new direction is needed in the legal systems of the world's major commercial centres – to depart from the choice of legal system techniques and to develop rules within the forum legal system that are specially designed for situations of modern transnational business and for the practice and expectations of the parties involved. Although their business activities have long been consigned to history, the Romans and the medieval architects of the law merchant pointed the way".

Professor Schmittoff, a lawyer trained in a more liberal tradition, quotes himself[33] saying in 1957 that:

> "We are beginning to rediscover the international character of commercial law and the circle now completes itself: the general trend of commercial law everywhere is to move away from the restrictions of national law to a universal international conception of the law of international trade".

He goes on to make observations about the nature of what he calls "the modern law of international trade":

> "It is not a branch of international law: it is applied in national jurisdictions by tolerance of the national sovereign whose public policy may override or qualify a particular rules of that law.
>
> "It is not 'of haphazard and casual provenance' but consists of normal practices or usages expressed in a number of authoritative texts.
>
> "It is practically the same in all countries of the world 'its similarity transcends the division of the world into countries of free-market economy and centrally planned economy and of common law or Roman tradition'."

He says that this is because two fundamental principles of the law of contract are recognised – the principle of autonomy of the parties' will and the principle of *pacta sunt servanda*. If this is so, and it would appear to be a reasonable hypothesis, is the English dislike of such concepts really rooted in the dangers to the parties of a lack of procedure for appeal, or is it rather the traditional xenophobia of the English and the distrust of all things foreign showing itself in yet another form?

The ICC clause

Turning to the ICC itself its recommended clause is extremely simple

> "All disputes arising in connection with the present contract shall be finally settled under the Rules of Conciliation and Arbitration of the International

30 (1987) LMCQ, 277.

31 *Deutsche Schatbau und Tiefbohrgesellschaft mbh* v. *The R'As Al Kharmah National Oil Co. and Shell International Petroleum Co.Ltd.*, *The Times*, 27 April 1987.

32 34 ICLQ 538.

33 (1968) JBL 105.

Chamber of Commerce by one or more arbitrators appointed in accordance with the said Rules".

The ICC, according to Schmitthof,[34] "is the most important institution for the arbitral settlement of international trade disputes. It is widely used and enjoys the confidence and respect of businessmen all over the world and is also frequently resorted to in East West Trade". Craig Park and Paulsson[35] suggest that the addition of the following elements in an arbitration clause should be mandatory:

- Number nationality and qualification of arbitrators.
- Place of arbitration – preferably not on the grounds which they cite in one instance of "the convenience of airline connections". (The popularity of Paris as a venue may one suspects be influenced by factors other than its position as the seat of the ICC however.)
- Language of arbitration – references to the ruling language of the contract will be found in the examples of disputes clauses in the Appendix to this paper.
- Law applicable to the merits of the dispute – one hopes in fact that most contracts will already automatically state a governing law although the FIDIC forms do not do so as a matter of course in the main body of the document and it normally has to be put in the so called "Special Conditions" in Part II.

Other factors which in their view should be considered for inclusion are the following:

- Negotiation conciliation or mediation as a pre-condition – this again can be seen in some of the clauses in the Appendix particularly for Joint Venture and Consortium agreements.
- Rules or law of procedure – the comments as to the minefield which Swiss law proved to be in this area have already been referred to and this is an extremely important aspect of effective arbitration.
- The law governing the arbitration agreement – on the basis that this has a separate legal existence to the remainder of the contract.
- The rules of conflict of laws – where a substantive law cannot be agreed.
- The inclusion of powers of "amiable composition" – apparently more often carried out by US than French arbitrators.
- Powers to adapt the contract – in the sense of filling gaps and also automatically modifying the terms of the document. (The ICC offers conciliation, technical expertise or reference to a Standing Committee on the Regulation of Contractual Relations.)
- Powers and procedures for provisional relief – *i.e.* interim orders.
- Procedural rulings.
- Use of discovery.
- Apportionment of costs.
- Entry of judgment stipulations – very important in practice.
- Waiver of appeal.

34 *Export Trade*, 8th ed. at 599.
35 See *ante*.

- Waiver of sovereign immunity – vital where a foreign government or government agency is the employer.
- Accommodation for multi-party disputes.

A great number of the clauses for one-off contracts with which the author had some connection or knowledge (some of which are set out in the Appendix to this paper) contain a reference to ICC rules, although there is frequently a reference to initial conciliation and sometimes to a governing "law" which if not English was at least not that of the host country, who was also usually the Employer.

Practical difficulties of contracting overseas

The difficulties of contracting overseas in the less accessible parts of the world will be well-known to some readers. For those who are not familiar with them and are perhaps too ready to insist after the event that more care should have been taken with this or that clause – in this forum the disputes clause – let me enumerate them:

- Could they pay?
- Would they pay?
- If so in what currency and could it be got out of the relevant country without withholding tax?
- Could the materials and equipment be got there:–
  (a) at all? and (b) to programme?
  If so how and at what cost?
- Would the expats be safe – where was the nearest war?
- Was there an upset target price? (otherwise sometimes called a guaranteed maximum price).
- What were the legal liabilities, particularly design (including that of others) – were they absolute, i.e. did the project manager get jailed if there was an error?
- What were the technical difficulties – was the design buildable?
- Could the contractor terminate if he didn't get paid?
- What were the tax and local law complications?
- Where was the labour going to come from – at what cost?

This of course is merely a selection. You will notice that none of these risks – and engineers are very prone to inform their legal advisers that "Contracting is a risk business" – include any consideration whatever of the legal disputes procedure. This may be partly because in a number of cases it was well known that if everything really went wrong, as it did in Iran for example – one would be lucky to get out at the point of a gun and claim ECGD insurance. ICC arbitration would be considered a distinctly luxury item in such a scenario.

Nonetheless, the world is a great deal more civilised now and much of the large-scale construction work has moved to the United Kingdom and Europe. Bodies like UNCITRAL with its Model Law, ORGALIME, and the UN Economic Commission for Europe have been busy trying to ensure that everyone adopts a sensible disputes procedure for international dealings of every sort, including joint ventures and some include model clauses.

Conclusion

In conclusion it should be borne in mind that none of the contracts or joint ventures with which I was involved ever resulted in arbitration proceedings, something which may perhaps be due more to luck than good judgement but which also says much for the pragmatism of large construction companies and those with whom they do business.

Appendix

Specimen Arbitration Clauses

All the Clauses set out below were used in one-off international agreements in recent years. For those unfamiliar with the terms, a vertical joint venture is one where each party has separate functions and responsibilities in respect of the project to be carried out; and a horizontal joint venture is one where the parties share the provision of men and materials in agreed proportions but do not split the responsibility for carrying out the work.

They are not intended as "model clauses" but merely as examples of good and bad practice internationally. Any use made of the contents of this Appendix by the reader is entirely at his own risk.

1. Vertical Joint Venture Agreement between a UK Contractor and a UK Manufacturing Company

"Any dispute or differences relating to the Venture or arising under the Contract or the provisions of this Agreement which may arise between the Joint Venturers shall be referred initially to *the persons referred to in Clause 9(5) hereof*. In the event of failure so to resolve any dispute or other difference such dispute or difference shall be finally settled under the Rules of the London Court of Arbitration. Judgment upon the award rendered may be entered in any court having jurisdiction or application may be made to such court for a judicial acceptance of the award and an order of enforcement as the case may be." (Clause 9(5) provides for amicable resolution between the Chairman of one and the Managing Director of the other)

2. Road Contract Guyana: EDF Conditions

"Chapter III

Settlement of Disputes

Article 56

Amicable settlement of disputes

No dispute arising either between the Contracting Authority and a tenderer in connection with the procedure for the placing of a contract or between the Contracting Authority and the Contractor resulting from the interpretation or performance of a contract shall be referred to arbitration unless an attempt has first been made to settle the dispute amicably.

Where the complainant is the Contractor or a tenderer, the attempt to reach an amicable settlement shall be conducted before the various administrative authorities responsible if the national law applicable makes provisions for the possibility of review by non-contentious administrative procedure. If national law does not provide for such possibility, the attempt to reach an amicable settlement shall be initiated by notification of the complaints to the Engineer in the case of a dispute concerning the interpretation or performance of a contract, or to the Contracting Authority in the case of a dispute concerning the procedure for the award of a contract.

Where the complainant is the Contracting Authority, the attempt to reach an amicable settlement shall in all cases involve a procedure under which complaints are notified to the opposing party (the contractor or tenderer).

The amicable settlement stage shall be deemed to be at an end if no definitive decision has been taken within a period of four months from the date of the application for a review or of the notification of the complaints.

Article 57

Arbitration

If the procedures laid down in Article 56 have been exhausted and the attempt to reach an amicable settlement has failed, the dispute shall be settled by arbitration in accordance with the rules of conciliation and arbitration of the International Chamber of Commerce by one or more arbitrators appointed in accordance with those rules.

Article 58

Request for settlement

The request for settlement of a dispute before the arbitrating authority must be submitted, on pain of being time-barred, within 90 days from receipt of the decision which terminates the phase of amicable settlement provided for in Article 56, or within 90 days from expiry of a term of four months provided for in the last sub-paragraph of Article 56."

3. *Joint Venture for Work In the Gulf: 3 UK Contractors*

"This Agreement shall in all respects be construed and interpreted in accordance with the laws of England provided always that under no circumstances shall failure by the parties to agree upon the terms of the Further Agreement or the Tender be a matter for submission to Arbitration or other legal process."

4. *Standard Preliminary Agreement to form a Joint Venture*

"(a) All disputes arising in connection with this Agreement which cannot be settled to the mutual satisfaction of the parties concerned will be referred to the President for the time being of the I.C.C. who shall appoint an Arbitrator whose decision shall be final and binding

"(b) Performance of this Agreement will continue notwithstanding any arbitration proceedings

"(c) The formal Joint Venture Agreement shall in all respects be construed and interpreted in accordance with the Laws of England"

5. *Vertical Consortium Agreement – Rumania: 6 parties*

"(a) All disputes arising in connection with this Agreement which cannot be settled to the mutual satisfaction of the concerned parties will be referred to the President for the time being of the Institute of Arbitrators who shall appoint an Arbitrator mutually acceptable whose decision shall be final and binding on the concerned parties

(b) Performance of this Agreement will continue notwithstanding any arbitration proceedings."

(English Law Governed).

6. *Technical Advice Agreement Outline: Construction of Middle Eastern University*

"Arbitration – under Rules of Conciliation and Arbitration of International Chamber of Commerce. Provision first for amicable settlement of disputes and differences

(a) at senior management level and

(b) at highest management level, eg Chancellor of University and Managing Director of Technical Advisers

Award of arbitrators final and binding"

7. *Joint Company UAE – Heads of Agreement: UK Contractor and UAE nationals*

"(a) In the event of a dispute between the parties concerning this agreement or other corporate documents settlement shall be in accordance with the arbitration procedures of the International Chamber of Commerce, Paris.

(b) This agreement shall be interpreted and construed in accordance with the Laws of England, which shall have jurisdiction over the subject matter of the Agreement (providing that they are not in conflict with the legislation of UMM-AL-QUAIN)

(c) This agreement shall be interpreted and construed in accordance with the Laws of England, which shall have jurisdiction over the subject matter of the Agreement (providing that they are not in conflict with the legislation of UMM-AL-QUAIN)"

8. *Construction of University: Middle Eastern Government Employer*

"Settlement of Disputes – Arbitration

If any dispute or difference of any kind whatsoever shall arise between the Employer and the Contractor with or arising out of the Contract or the carrying out of the Works (whether during the progress of the Works or after their completion and whether before or after the termination abandonment or breach of the Contract) it shall in the first place be referred to and settled by the Engineer who shall give notice of his decision to the Employer and the Contractor. Such decision in respect of every matter so referred shall be final and binding upon the Employer and the Contractor until the completion of the Works and shall forthwith be given effect to by the Contractor who shall proceed with the Works with all due diligence whether notice of dissatisfaction is given by him or by the Employer as hereinafter provided or not. If the Employer or the Contractor be dissatisfied then with any such decision and In any such case either the Employer or the Contractor may within 30 days after receiving notice of such decision require that the matter be referred to a Committee of Arbitration to be formed in the following manner.

The Employer and the Contractor shall each appoint one member to the Committee and the two members thus appointed shall agree upon a third member to act as a Chairman of the Committee. If agreement on the appointment of a Chairman cannot be reached within 14 days from the last date of their appointment then the Employer or the Contractor shall each have the right to ask a competent court to appoint the third member in accordance with proceedings provided in the Code of Civil Procedures or in accordance with proceedings provided in a special law of arbitration

The Committee of Arbitration shall have full power to open up review and revise any decision opinion direction or certificate of the Engineer the award of the Arbitration Committee shall be binding unless one of the parties postulate its avoidance in accordance with the provisions provided in the Code of Civil Procedures.

The reference to arbitration shall not enter until after the completion or alleged completion of the Works unless with the written consent of the Employer and the Contractor. Provided always that postponing the determination of the dispute shall not cause damage to any of the parties or obstruct the progress of the work. All fees and other costs shall be paid to arbitrators by the party requiring arbitration provided that such fees and costs shall be payable by the party against whom the award has been pronounced.

9. *Heads of Agreement : UK Contractor and Middle Eastern Government*

"(a) Any dispute or difference relating to the Joint-Venture or the provisions of the said formal Agreement (except as herein provided to the contrary) which may arise between the parties during the life of this Agreement shall be finally settled under the Rules of Conciliation of the International Chamber of Commerce by a single arbitrator appointed in accordance with the Rules. Judgement upon the award rendered may be entered in any court having jurisdiction or application may be made to such court for a judicial acceptance of the award and an order of enforcement as the case may be.

(b) The said formal Agreement shall be interpreted and construed in accordance with its wording.

(c) The ruling language of the said formal Agreement shall be English."

10. *Contract for Construction of Airport: Pakistan*

"ARBITRATION

All disputes arising out of this agreement whether during the continuance of this agreement or otherwise shall be settled by Arbitration. Each party shall nominate one arbitrator and the said arbitrators shall, before entering upon the reference, appoint an umpire. The provisions of the Arbitration Act 1940 shall apply to any such reference and the venue of Arbitration shall be at Karachi.

JURISDICTION

This contract shall be deemed to be subject to and shall be construed according to the laws of Pakistan and the parties hereby submit to the jurisdiction of the High Court of West Pakistan, Karachi Bench."

11. *Letter of Intent for Hospitals Contract: Iran*

"Any dispute or difference arising out of this Letter Agreement which cannot be settled amicably shall be settled definitively in accordance with the Rules of Conciliation and Arbitration under the International Chamber of Commerce by a panel of three arbitrators. Each party shall nominate one arbitrator and the third to be nominated by the Director General of the World Health Organization. Arbitration shall take place in Geneva and Iranian Law shall govern all aspects of this Letter Agreement."

Experience from non-construction arbitration 18

Peter Rowland

Synopsis

This paper contains a review of "non-construction" forms of arbitration. It concentrates particularly on maritime and commodity arbitration which appear to be both more certain in their procedures and more efficient in their workings than those often met with in the context of construction contracts.

Introduction

In this paper I shall mention the salient features of a few types of arbitration which differ materially from construction disputes which are resolved under ICC rules. First, however, I will deal with the question of the composition of an arbitration panel and the number of arbitrators who should, and do, sit.

Numbers of arbitrators

In ICC arbitrations the number is normally three though a single arbitrator may be appointed where the amount in issue is small. By way of contrast, in the United Kingdom most arbitrations have only one arbitrator and this in fact is what the parties are deemed to have agreed unless the arbitration agreement indicates to the contrary.[1] Less common than the single arbitrator is the case where each party nominates an arbitrator and the latter appoint an umpire should they disagree. It has advantages and disadvantages. There is the obvious disadvantage that the original arbitrators cannot determine whether they are likely to disagree without an initial discussion on the merits which may involve prejudging the case without the benefit of either

1 See Arbitration Act 1950, s.6 and compare ICC Art. 2.5 and Art. 5 of the UNCITRAL Rules, Rule 3 of the ICSID Rules and Art. 10 of the Model Law.

evidence or argument. Accordingly, they often take the precaution of making a formal appointment and asking the umpire to sit in during most of the hearing. This avoids having to begin all over again if a disagreement arises but wastes money if it does not. [I point out in passing that some time and expense may be saved if, when it appears that disagreement will be inevitable, the arbitrators make an interim award covering the issues on which they do agree before their disagreement is formally announced.]

The idea behind the appointment of an umpire in the manner indicated is that it involves determination by a single person of matters of controversy in accordance with general practice in this country. This in itself, however, may be accounted a disadvantage on the Continent, where the preferred number of arbitrators is generally three. Why this should be so may be worth a moment's discussion. Is it because our courts have accustomed us to rely on the views of a single judge at first instance? Is it perhaps because the English arbitrator tends to be a practical person with some legal or arbitral experience, whilst on the Continent he is very often an academic?

In concluding consideration of this question I should add that a very common alternative to the appointment by the original arbitrators of an umpire is for them to appoint a third arbitrator. That is normal Continental practice and its main disadvantage is the additional time and expense which it inevitably entails. This may, however, be outweighed by the satisfaction it may give to the parties that each of them has a member of the tribunal who at least understands his point of view.

English maritime arbitration

With regard to other types of arbitration I propose to begin with the English maritime arbitration which some might assert is the "creme de la creme" of arbitrations. Such a claim would be mainly based on the efficiency of the procedure evolved by a compact and very experienced group of practitioners and embodied in the London Maritime Arbitrators' Association Terms, 1987.

Some of its distinctive features are as follows:

- Strict rules minimise delays arising from the lack of availability of an arbitrator. A sole arbitrator who is unable to offer a hearing date within a "reasonable" time of the date of estimated readiness must offer to stand down. For a hearing estimated to last up to two days, four months is considered reasonable; if the estimate is three to five days, five months; if six to ten days, ten months; if more, the tribunal decides what is reasonable. Where there is more than one arbitrator the hearing must normally be fixed at the earliest date any one of then can manage unless all can offer a matching date within the same time scale; any arbitrator(s) finding he cannot attend must retire having given six weeks notice. It should be noted that (a) the parties may jointly elect to waive this requirement, and (b) the President of the Association will nominate if there is a difficulty in regcrd to a substitute.
- Once a date has been fixed it will only be vacated in exceptional circumstances and these do not include the convenience of either counsel or expert witnesses, or both.

- On the other hand, the frustrations to arbitrators of adjournments and cancellations, whether by reason of settlement or otherwise are also reccgnised. When a date is fixed a booking fee of £150 per person per day is payable and detailed rules cover various contingencies such as when a further fee becomes payable.
- An attempt has been made to tackle the knotty problem of consolidation. Where the same tribunal has been appointed to more than one arbitration with related facts it is given power to hear the cases concurrently and to make such procedural directions as economy and expedition require. Further, on the application of a party to a reference the tribunal may join any other party or parties willing to be joined. In addition, the tribunal has power to determine any later dispute which arises out of the same subject-matter if it considers this desirable.
- Unless the parties otherwise agree, the tribunal does not have jurisdiction to determine either a claim for rectification or as to whether the basic agreement was binding.
- It is customary for the parties' representatives to agree amongst themselves most of the matters which are usually discussed and determined at the preliminary meeting with the arbitrator; a check list is to be found in the Fourth Schedule to the Terms. In fact, particularly if the case is likely to last more than five days, progress is often reviewed at a preliminary meeting without troubling the tribunal. In due course, the tribunal may meet to confirm matters provisionally agreed and to clear up any points of dispute.
- As it is seldom necessary to have a tribunal of three to determine interlocutory matters, the appointment of a third arbitrator (or umpire) is usually deferred until that stage is passed.
- If the original arbitrators disagree, they may act as the advocates of the respective parties who appointed them, if asked to do so.
- Among the specific sanctions given to the tribunal is the power to find in favour of a claim without a hearing if no defence is submitted within the time specified in a peremptory order. Again, the tribunal may stay the proceedings until a claimant complies with an interim order to provide security for the other side's costs.
- Where, as sometimes happens, more than two views are tenable the views of the third arbitrator are to prevail.
- An award is normally to be available within six weeks but should be ready substantially earlier if it is urgent. The tribunal need not meet to sign it.
- Unless a reasoned award is requested, the Terms provide that reasons should normally be supplied separately, and in confidence.
- The Terms also deal with the questions of possible publication of the awards in summary form with names omitted provided the parties consent, and with the disposal of documents three months after publication of the final award.

Flip-flop arbitrations

In a "flip-flop" arbitration proper, the arbitrator must make his award in a figure which coincides with that which either the claimant or the respondent claims is correct. In these circumstances, each party will clearly have an incentive to approximate his claim to what he judges the tribunal is likely to award on pain of losing the case and perhaps paying the costs of both sides.

There is accordingly much to commend flip-flop arbitrations in suitable cases, that is to say, where the issue is one of valuation or otherwise of figures, such as in rent review cases or wages disputes, or as to the quantum of damages suffered. Not only is it an excellent antidote to exaggerated claims but it frustrates those arbitrators, hopefully increasingly uncommon, who make a practice of awarding a figure roughly halfway between competing claims.

An attempt to gild this particular lily is sometimes made by providing that the arbitrator, having made his own evaluation, is to award a sum halfway between his own figure and that of the party who is the closer to it.

Commodity arbitrations

Commodity arbitrations vary in form from so-called "look/sniff" physical examinations as to quality or condition to more formal "technical" arbitrations.

The former are usually decided without pleadings by two independent experts, one appointed by each side, with recourse to a third expert in the case of disagreement. A common procedure is for the complaining party to despatch a sample together with a copy of the relevant dccuments to the trade association, which acts as administrating authority. The arbitrator/experts very often examine the sample without the parties being present – one party at least may live very far away indeed. They will consider condition as well as quality (or instead) if condition at discharge is warranted by the seller, (*i.e.* it is a Rye Terms contract). The normal form of their award is a declaration as to what diminution, if any, is to be made in the contract price.

What are known as "technical" arbitrations seem in fact to the outsider to be rather less technical consisting as they do mainly of claims for breach of contract – failure to deliver the goods at the stipulated time, (or at all), incorrect packaging or shipment, demurrage, faulty documentation, or damage resulting from negligence or other causes. Any such arbitrations are likely to be dealt with under special rules promulgated by the relevant trade association itself.

Some idea of the number and vitality of these trade association may be gauged from the Arbitration (Commodity Contracts) Order 1979. It will be remembered that under Section 4 of the 1979 Act, except in the case of a contract governed by foreign law, an exclusion agreement entered into before an arbitration has commenced has no effect if it relates to a "commodity contract", that is to say, a contract for the sale of goods regularly dealt in on a market to be specified by Order. The 1979 Order specifies nine such markets and then goes on to include contrasts for the sale of goods which are subject to the arbitration rules of the London Metal Exchange or of any of 17 Associations listed in Part II of the Schedule to the Order whether or not there is physically a market where commodities are bought and sold.

Common features

There are naturally many differences between the rules of the different Associations but the following features are either characteristic or commonly found. First, standard forms of contract are prescribed which usually provide, inter alia, that English law applies. Secondly, there is generally a desire to settle all disputes "in house" so far as may be, the contract usually contains a *Scott* v. *Avery* clause[2]; other common features are the following:

(a) The employment of lawyers is discouraged, *e.g.*, by requiring the governing body of the Association to give prior consent.
(b) Where the parties are members of the Association they may both be automatically bound by a provision that the governing body, or its board of appeal on appeal, has power to determine whether a contract has been entered into. This avoids jurisdictional problems for the arbitrator(s).
(c) The usual methods of enforcing awards may be supplemented by publicising defaulters and/or taking disciplinary action within the Association.
(d) In the case of some Associations disputes are referred to a number of persons on its panel of arbitrators, perhaps five or even more of them, who make their award either on documents or after a hearing.
(e) In the case of other Associations the dispute is referred first to a tribunal of three, alternatively to two with an umpire if there is disagreement. They reach a preliminary conclusion but their award is subject to appeal to other members of the Association's panel of arbitrators, perhaps five of them, when the proceedings tend to be more formal. The appellant may be required to deposit with the Association monies equal to those already awarded.

String arbitrations

The rules of some Associations provide that where the dispute is as to quality or condition and the goods have passed through a number of hands on terms which only differ as to price and date the arbitration may be between the first and last in the "string" notwithstanding that there is no contract between them. The parties in between will then be bound and may rely on the award provided they have consented and have produced a copy of the purchase contract showing that they form part of the string.

There is no reason in theory why such a procedure should not be adopted in certain construction cases where the same issues arise in successive

2 The effect of a *Scott* v. *Avery* clause is that no action will lie for breach of the contract until the matters in dispute have been submitted to arbitration unless the condition has been waived by the party relying on the clause or if the neglect or default has prevented the other party from obtaining an award.

disputes, for instance, as to the quality of a particular building material which has passed through several hands. However, differences between the different contracts are likely to render this almost impossible to achieve in practice.

Conclusion

The experience to be gained from non-construction arbitrations therefore is that they are often quicker, cheaper and more flexible, and tend to be conducted by laymen rather than lawyers. This latter fact may of course be significant in achieving the former state. Construction contracts and disputes tend by their nature to be highly complex, more so than a simple contract for the sale and purchase of goods for instance, and it is therefore to be expected that the systems developed for dealing with disputes arising from such contracts should also be longer and more complex. The current trend towards and interest in however more informal methods of disputes resolution would seem to indicate that the pendulum has swung too far and needs to be brought back again.

19 Choice of applicable law in international construction contracts

Michael Davis

Synopsis

This paper examines the choice of applicable law in international construction contracts. It deals with the rules for determining the applicable law and the presumptions applied where the parties fail to make an express choice, and with the significance of the chosen of seat of arbitration, referring to relevant English case law.

Introduction

In considering the laws applicable to international construction contracts, it is necessary to consider not only the law applicable to the contract, but also the law applicable to the arbitration. As a rule parties from different countries, negotiating an international contract for the construction of a particular project, and faced with the necessity to consider a dispute resolution procedure for inclusion in the contract, would normally prefer to refer disputes to the courts of their respective countries with which they are each familiar.

As each party is likely to refuse submission to the other's national courts, both are, as an alternative, normally prepared to agree to a form of international arbitration.

Basic questions

Merely to agree to refer disputes to a form of international arbitration does not represent a complete solution. There remain a number of questions which must be resolved before an effective dispute resolution procedure is in place. Many of these involve decisions on precisely those same issues which may originally have caused the parties to refuse submission to the other's national courts. These are:

- the nature and identity of the tribunal which will decide the dispute between the parties;
- the manner in which that tribunal is to be appointed;
- the geographical location in which the tribunal will sit for purposes of determining the dispute;
- the law to be applied for the purposes of resolving the dispute.

Types of arbitration

Administered

Some of these questions can often be dealt with by negotiation in a non-contentious fashion by adopting a standard form of construction contract like the FIDIC conditions and adopting the standard dispute resolution procedure of arbitration as found in clause 67 of that Contract. Clause 67 provides for disputes to be finally settled under the Rules of Conciliation and Arbitration of the International Chamber of Commerce (ICC). By submitting to an institution such as the ICC or the London Court of International Arbitration (the LCIA) such a clause provides for what is known as an administered arbitration, incorporating into the arbitration clause a standard framework of rules and procedures according to which the arbitration is implemented.

Under the Rules of the ICC,[1] the ICC International Court of Arbitration may appoint the arbitrators to form the tribunal (Art 2). The ICC Rules will govern the proceedings (Art. 11) and the ICC Court may fix the place of arbitration (Art. 12). In the absence of any indication by the parties of the law to be applied to the merits of the dispute, the arbitrator shall determine the proper law (Art. 13(3)).

The rules of most arbitral institutions allow considerable freedom to the parties to choose the form of the arbitration. The ICC Rules provide, for example, for the parties to nominate arbitrators (Art. 2), for the parties to choose rules governing the proceedings insofar as the ICC Rules are silent (Art. 11) and for the parties to choose the place of arbitration (Art. 12). Article 13(3) also provides that:

> "The parties shall be free to determine the law to be applied by the arbitrator to the merits of the dispute".

Ad hoc

An alternative to an administered arbitration is a form of ad hoc arbitration. In this case, arbitration takes place outside the established arbitral institutions such as the ICC with its corpus of rules, so that it is necessary for the parties to provide their own rules within the arbitration clause. This permits the parties to exercise complete freedom to provide a code in the contract for the type of tribunal, its appointment, procedure, the location or seat of the arbitration and governing law.

1 See Part VI, App. II.

Applicable Law

Whichever basic form of arbitration has been decided upon, whether administered or ad hoc, it is of particular importance to consider the law which is to be applied to the various aspects of the arbitration.

Fundamental premise

In approaching the question of applicable law, it must be appreciated that different laws may be applied to different aspects of the overall contractual relationship between the parties. When a dispute is referred to arbitration not one, but two, contractual agreements are in operation, each of which may, in theory at least, have its own applicable law. Furthermore, the procedural aspects of an arbitration may result in bringing into effect a third applicable legal system, that of the procedural law.

The first contractual agreement within the overall contractual relationship is, of course, the underlying contract and the law applicable to this will govern the substantive rights and obligations of the parties with regard to the purpose for which the contract was concluded, for example the construction of the project. The second contractual agreement is formed by the arbitration agreement itself as expressed in the arbitration clause. An arbitration clause is an agreement between the parties to refer any disputes which arise from the underlying contract to arbitration. Such a clause, while being part of the underlying contract, is nevertheless a distinct agreement. As Dicey and Morris[2] write:

> "an arbitration clause in a contract constitutes a self-contained contract collateral or ancillary to the main contract of which it forms a part".

Accordingly, an arbitration clause continues to exist notwithstanding, for example, that the underlying contract may have been repudiated or frustrated or is illegal. This is, of course, necessarily so, since if the arbitration agreement were to terminate on the purported termination of the underlying contract for whatever reason, then the whole purpose of the arbitration clause would be frustrated: the arbitration clause exists precisely for the purpose of determining the rights and obligations of the parties in respect of the underlying contract.[3]

To meet the final aspect of the overall contractual relationship, consideration must be given to the manner in which the arbitration is to be conducted and the law governing it: that is, the procedure of the arbitration.

2 Dicey and Morris, *The Conflict of Laws*, 11th ed., ed. LA Collins, London, Stevens & Sons Ltd., (1987), 536.

3 See *Black Clawson International Ltd.* v. *PapierwerkeWaldhof-Aschaffenburg AG* [1981] 2 Lloyd's Rep 446. An additional contractual agreement may arise from the proposition that a distinct and separate contract comes into existence as soon as the parties invoke the arbitration agreement to resolve a particular dispute. The subject matter of this distinct contract is the particular reference to arbitration of a particular dispute referred by the parties for resolution pursuant to the arbitration clause. This distinct contract of the particular reference to arbitration has been described as an "individual agreement" in contrast to the "continuous agreement" of the arbitration clause which survives for as long as disputes continue in respect of the underlying contract.

It is essential to distinguish between these three aspects as a different law may apply to each. It is only by carrying out this analysis that it is possible to identify the law to be applied to any particular issue arising within the overall contractual relationship and therefore the legal principles according to which that issue will be decided. It is, therefore, necessary to examine the different laws which may be applicable to the contractual relationship and the issues which each governs.

Effect of applicable laws

First, the proper law of the underlying contract will determine the substantive rights and obligations of the parties contained in that contract: for example, issues such as whether an alteration to the construction project amounts to a variation as defined by the contract and if so, the amount recoverable by a contractor as a consequence, whether a contractor is entitled to an extension of time for completion of the Project, quantification of damages for breach of contract and so on.

Secondly, the proper law of the arbitration agreement will determine the validity of the arbitration agreement itself, the jurisdiction of the arbitrators to decide the dispute, including whether or not a dispute falls within the arbitration agreement, the right of the arbitrator to decide that issue, the formal validity of the award and whether the parties remain bound to their obligation to submit disputes to arbitration.

Thirdly, the procedural (or curial) law will usually regulate the appointment of arbitrators, the extent to which an arbitrator's authority can be revoked, the procedural rules for the arbitration relating to the obligation to hear oral evidence, discovery of documents, joinder of causes of action, the availability of an application for security of costs, payment of interest and the availability of judicial remedies to challenge an award and the extent to which such remedies may be excluded. An important aspect of the procedural law is that where the parties have not expressed a choice of proper law of the underlying contract, the procedural law will probably also determine the proper law of the underlying contract, so that where the procedural law is English, determination of the proper law of the underlying contract will be decided in accordance with English private international law.

Illustrations

The distinct nature of these three applicable laws is well illustrated by case law. An example of the distinct nature of the proper law of the arbitration agreement is provided by *Hamlyn and Co.* v. *Talisker Distillery*.[4] In that case a dispute arising under a construction contract between Scottish and English companies signed in London and providing for arbitration in London, required the House of Lords on appeal from the Scottish Court of Session to decide whether an arbitration agreement was valid. The Scottish company argued that this was a matter of procedure governed by Scots law. The House of

4 *Hamlyn and Co.* v. *Talisker Distillery and others* [1894] AC.

Lords rejected this argument, stating that the issue related to the validity of the arbitration agreement, and distinguished the proper law of the underlying contract from that of the arbitration agreement. Lord Herschell referred to the arbitration clause saying:

> ". . . it seems to me that they [the parties] have indicated that that particular stipulation, which is a part of the contract between them, shall be interpreted according to and governed by the law not of Scotland, but of England."[5]

Similarly, the distinction between the proper law of the underlying contract and the procedural law has been highlighted in the House of Lords case of *Compagnie Tunisienne de Navigation SA* v *Compagnie d'Armement Maritime SA*[6] in which Lord Diplock said that it was:

> ". . . not now open to question that if the parties to a commercial contract have agreed expressly upon the system of law of one country as the proper law of their contract and have selected a different curial [procedural] law by providing expressly that disputes under the contract shall be submitted to arbitration in another country, the arbitrators must apply as the proper law of the contract that system of law upon which the parties have expressly agreed".[7]

The Court of Appeal case, *Bank Mellat* v. *Helliniki Techniki SA*[8] further illustrates the point. Helliniki and a Danish company embarked on a construction project for development of land near Tehran. The parties stated that the contract was to be governed by the laws of Iran and that disputes arising under it should be settled by arbitration in London under the ICC Rules. Helliniki commenced an arbitration in England and Bank Mellat applied to the English court for security for costs against Helliniki. It was held that, notwithstanding that the proper law of the underlying contract was Iranian, the question of whether the court could make such an order was determined by the procedural law governing the arbitration. As the parties had provided for arbitration in London, English law was the procedural law of the arbitration and therefore the English court did have a discretion to order security for costs.

It is not uncommon in the context of international disputes to find that the procedural law of the arbitration is different from the proper law of the underlying contract and there may be many reasons for this. It may be because the parties wish to avoid a particular procedural law because the courts of the system of law of that country apply mandatory rules to the arbitration irrespective of the parties' choice; conversely, the parties may choose a particular procedural law for the arbitration precisely because they wish to adopt these mandatory rules. It may also be that the parties wish to take advantage of the high reputation of a particular country as a forum for the resolution of disputes. Again, in *Compagnie Tunisienne* Lord Diplock said:

> ". . . it is possible for parties to a contract to choose one system of law as the proper law of their contract and a different system of law as the curial [procedural] law. Although they may want their mutual rights and obligations under the contract

5 *Ibid.*, at 208.

6 *Compagnie Tunisienne de Navigation SA* v *Compagnie d'Armement Maritime SA* [1970] 2 Lloyd's Rep. 99.

7 *Ibid.*, at 117.

8 *Bank Mellat* v. *Helliniki Techniki SA* [1984] IQB 291.

> to be ascertained by reference to the system of law of a country with which the transaction has some close and real connection, they may none the less consider that the arbitral procedure adopted in some other country, or the high reputation and commercial expertise of arbitrators available there, make the curial [procedural] law of that country preferable to the curial [procedural] law of the country whose system of law they have chosen as the proper law".[9]

The choice of applicable law governing the various aspects of a contractual relationship is of such importance that the choice of law in relation to each aspect should be made expressly by the parties.If, notwithstanding the importance of making an express choice, the parties fail so to express their intention, then it is necessary to determine the law applicable to each of the three distinct aspects of the overall contractual relationship and to consider the rules that will be applied for this purpose.

Proper law of underlying contract

Turning first to the rules for determining the proper law of the underlying contract: as has been mentioned, in the absence of express choice, this question will probably be determined by the procedural law. It is assumed for the purposes of this paper that the procedural law is English, so that English conflict of law rules are applicable for the purposes of expressing rules for determination of the proper law of the underlying contract. If the arbitration clause provides in express terms for a choice of proper law of the arbitration agreement then it is likely that the proper law of the underlying contract will be the same as the proper law of the arbitration agreement.

If the parties do not expressly choose the proper law of the arbitration agreement but do provide for a venue for the arbitration then there is a presumption that the proper law of the contract, in the absence of express choice will be the law of the country in which the arbitration takes place. In other words, where for instance, an arbitration clause identifies the seat of the arbitration by providing for arbitration in London, there is an inference that the proper law of the underlying contract is English. This inference will be particularly strong where the parties to the contract are of different nationality and the arbitration clause provides for arbitration in a third country.

This presumption is illustrated in *Norske Atlas Insurance Company Ltd.* v. *London General Insurance Company Ltd*[10] where Mr Justice Mackinnon said:

> "When there is a question as to whether the law of England or the law of a foreign country is to be applied to a contract, that question always depends ultimately upon the consideration, what was the law which the parties intended should apply? In many cases they are careful to say expressly in the contract . . . if they do not do so expressly it may be necessary to find their intention from implied stipulations or from the whole tenor of the document [T]here is, in my judgment, the clearest indication in this contract, in Clause 9 – providing for arbitration in Norway by Norwegian or Danish arbitrators, and that the arbitrators are to meet at Christiania, and that any omission in their body is to be supplied by the chief officer of the

9 *Op. cit.* at 117.

10 *Norske Atlas Insurance* v. *London General Insurance Company Ltd.* [1927] 28 Lloyd's Rep 104 at 107.

> Maritime Court of Christiania, and so forth – that the parties mutually agreed and intended that the law of Norway should apply to this contract".[11]

The present law is that there is a strong but not irrebuttable presumption that where choice of scat operates as an implied choice of procedural law, it may also operate as an implied choice of the proper law of the contract.

In *Compagnie Tunisienne* Lord Diplock said:

> "where the only express choice of law in a contract is that of curial [procedural] law, resulting from the inclusion in the contract of a provision for arbitration in a particular country, an intention of the parties to exercise their right also to choose a proper law of the contract and, if so, the proper law which they have chosen, can only be deduced by implication from what they have expressly agreed and the circumstances in and in relation to which their agreement was made. The fact that they have expressly chosen to submit their disputes under the contract to a particular arbitral forum of itself gives rise to a strong inference that they intended that their mutual rights and obligations under the contract should be determined by reference to the domestic law of the country in which the arbitration takes place, since this is the law with which arbitrators sitting there may be supposed to be most familiar.[12]

Proper law of arbitration agreement

Turning next to the proper law of the arbitration agreement, as has been made clear the parties may exercise their choice of applicable law either in express terms or, impliedly, by selection of a venue. However, in the absence of any such choice it is generally presumed that the proper law of the arbitration agreement will follow the proper law of the underlying contract. In *Black Clawson International Ltd.* v. *Papierwerke waldhof-Aschaffenburg AG* Mr Justice Mustill (as he then was) said:

> "In the great majority of cases the same law governs all aspects of the matter. Where the laws diverge at all, one will find in most instances that the law governing the continuous agreement [*i.e.* the arbitration agreement] is the same as the substantive law of the contract in which it is embodied[13]

Procedural law governing the arbitration

Finally, in determining the procedural law governing the arbitration, in the absence of express choice, there is, as already discussed, a presumption that the parties intended the procedural law to be the law of the country in which the arbitration takes place, that is the seat of the arbitration, because it is the country most closely connected with the proceedings. This principle was established in *Whitworth Street Estates (Manchester) Ltd.* v. *James Miller & Partners Ltd.*[14]

11 *Ibid.*, at 107.
12 *Op. cit.* at 117.
13 *Op. cit.* at 455.
14 [1970] AC 583.

In that case a Scottish construction company undertook work on behalf of an English company to a factory in Scotland. The contract did not provide for an express choice of proper law for the underlying contract or for the agreement to arbitrate or provide a venue for the seat of the arbitration, but did provide that any dispute should be referred to an arbitrator to be appointed by the President of the RIBA. The President of the RIBA appointed a Scottish architect as arbitrator, practising in Scotland, and the arbitration took place in Scotland. The House of Lords held that the proper law of the underlying contract and the agreement to arbitrate was English as a standard English RIBA form of contract had been used.

Nevertheless, on the facts, the conduct of the parties after the appointment of the arbitrator sufficiently showed an agreement or acceptance on the part of the English company that the arbitration proceedings should be governed by the laws of Scotland. This case not only demonstrates that the procedural law can be different from the proper law of the contract, but also that, where the parties have not expressly chosen an applicable procedural law to govern the arbitration proceedings, those proceedings will be deemed to be governed by the law of the place where the arbitration is held.

In *Compagnie Tunisienne* Lord Diplock said:

> "An express choice of forum by the parties to a contract necessarily implies an intention that their dispute shall be settled in accordance with the procedural law of the selected forum and operate as if it were also an express choice of the curial [procedural] law of the contract. . ."[15]

This principle established in *Whitworth Street Estates* was followed in *Bank Mellat* where Lord Justice Kerr expressed the view:

> "The fundamental principle . . . is that under our rules of private international law, in the absence of any contractual provision to the contrary, the procedural (or curial) law governing arbitrations is that of the forum of the arbitration, whether this be England, Scotland or some foreign country, since this is the system of law with which the agreement to arbitrate in the particular forum will have its closest connections."[16]

Choice of seat of arbitration

And, just as there is a presumption that the procedural law will follow the law of the seat of arbitration, so is there a presumption that the choice of seat may be inferred from the choice of procedural law. This point was made clear in a recent Court of Appeal case, *Naviera Amazonica Peruana SA* v. *Compania Internacional de Seguros del Peru*[17] in which Lord Justice Kerr said:

> "In the absence of some express and clear provision to the contrary, it must follow that an agreement that the curial or procedural law of an arbitration is to be the law of X has the consequence that X is also to be the "seat" of the arbitration"[18]

15 *Op. cit.* at 117.
16 *Op. cit.* at 301.
17 [1988] 1 Lloyd's Rep. 116.
18 *Ibid.*, at 119.

In that case the arbitration clause provided for "arbitration under the conditions and laws of London" and accordingly it was not disputed that the agreement to arbitrate was governed by English law. But the parties had not expressly chosen the venue for the arbitration and this fell to be decided by the Court. (The question of what was the proper law of the underlying contract was discussed but was not significant in this case). The parties were Peruvian, the contract was in Spanish, and it had been concluded in Lima. It was held that reasonable businessmen were very unlikely to have intended the arbitration to have its seat in Lima and to be subject to the supervisory powers of the Lima Courts whilst being subject to English procedure; and accordingly, it was decided that in this case the seat was to be London.

Chain of presumptions

Taken together these presumptions establish a chain, whereby choice of seat of the arbitration may determine the law applicable to all three aspects of the overall contractual relationship. The presumption is that the proper law of the underlying contract will be the law of the country in which the arbitration takes place. There is a further presumption that the law of the arbitration agreement follows the proper law of the underlying contract and that the procedural law will also follow the law of the country in which the arbitration takes place.

Where this chain of presumption applies it results in one applicable law governing all three aspects of the overall contractual relationship with the consequence that the seat of the arbitration may assume crucial importance. However, it must be emphasised that the chain is merely a matter of inference, so that while an agreement to refer disputes to arbitration in a particular country may carry with it an implication that the parties have further agreed that the law governing the underlying contract is to be the law of that country, it is not an irresistable inference.

Exception

One circumstance in which this inference cannot operate is where the seat of the arbitration was not specified in the contract or where it is chosen by some third party, be it either by one of the arbitral institutions such as the ICC or LCIA or by the arbitrators.[19] In such a situation the seat of the arbitration may be chosen for reasons, such as neutrality and convenience, which have no connection with the parties, the contract or the place of performance. In these circumstances, it would be perverse to contend that the law of the seat of the arbitration should be a determining factor in deciding the proper law of the underlying contract.

19 The parties' intention is determined at the time the contract is made so that the proper law of the contract cannot be decided by reference to some future uncertain event. The conduct of the parties after the contract is made cannot be referred to for the purposes of deciding the proper law of the contract.

Rebutting the presumptions

Any of the presumptions to which reference has been made, whether arising from choice of seat or from other presumptions in the chain, may be rebutted by implications to the contrary where other express provisions of the contract or relevant surrounding circumstances are so compelling as to lead to the identification of another system of law which the parties must have intended to be the proper law of the underlying contract.

Therefore, it is important to consider, in further detail, the circumstances in which this somewhat simplistic chain of inferences may be rebutted and in particular, the means for determining the law applicable to the contract where no clear presumptions can operate.

Determining the proper law of the contract

In determining the applicable law relevant to a contractual relationship the English courts will establish the proper law of the underlying contract by seeking to determine whether the parties intended to exercise a choice of law by contract, and if so to determine the law chosen. The courts will determine this by applying the ordinary rules of English law in construing contracts. If, having construed the contract, the courts fail to determine the law, either because the courts conclude that the parties did not intend to exercise any choice of proper law, or because the choice made cannot be identified, then the courts will apply the English rules of conflict of laws relating to determination of the proper law of the underlying contract. According to these rules, the proper law of the underlying contract will be that system of law with which the transaction has its closest and most real connection.

This process of determination of the proper law of the contract can be seen clearly in *JMJ Contractors Ltd.* v. *Marples Ridgeway Ltd.*,[20] a case relating to a contract for land reclamation works in Iraq. In that case the court had to determine, as a preliminary issue, the proper law of a sub-contract which was signed in the standard FCEC "blue" form intended for use with the ICE Conditions of Contract but which contained no express choice of law clause. The main contract was subject to Iraqi law and was based on conditions of the FIDIC Standard Form (Second Edition). Mervyn Davies J first sought to establish what intention with regard to choice of law applicable to the sub-contract could be inferred from the terms and nature of the contract and from the general circumstances of the case. He said:

> ". . . my judgment is that the proper law of the sub-contract is Iraqi law. There are pointers towards English law, such as the hope that the litigation would be in England, that the parties were British, that the sub-contract is English in form and drafting, etc. But the overriding consideration is, to my mind, that one plainly has to operate the sub-contract in conjunction with the main contract and the main contract is governed by Iraqi law . . . One is virtually obliged to impute an intent that the sub-contract is to be governed by Iraqi law."[21]

20 *JMJ Contractors Ltd.* v. *Marples Ridgeway Ltd.* (1985) 31 BLR 100.
21 *Ibid.*, at 115.

However, he went on to consider what the situation would be if no such intention could be inferred, stating that it would be necessary to decide with what system of law the contract has its closest and most real relationship. He said:

> "If I am in error in imputing an intention to the parties, I would still hold that Iraqi law applies by answering in favour of Iraq . . . the question as to the 'system of law with which the transaction has its closest and most real connection'. The sub-contract has its closest and most real connection with Iraqi law because the sub-contract is expressly linked with the main contract and the main contract is governed by Iraqi law".[22]

Accordingly, on the facts, it was held that the proper law of the sub-contract was the law of Iraq. (This is not to say that it is not permissible, at least under English law, to have a sub-contract governed by a different system of law from the main contract but the commercial desirability of such an arrangement must be highly questionable.)

Many factors will contribute to a determination of which legal system is applicable, notably the place where the contract is to be performed, the place where the contract was made, the nationality of the parties and the language of the contract. In *Compagnie Tunisienne* there arose a dispute as to whether the proper law of the underlying charter party contract was English or French and the action centred on two relevant clauses as follows:

Clause 13 provided, *inter alia*:

> "This contract shall be governed by the laws of the flag of the vessel carrying the goods . . ."

Clause 18 provided, *inter alia*:

> "Any dispute arising during execution of this charter party shall be settled in London . . ."

The arbitrators found as a matter of fact that the parties contemplated at the time of making the contract that the flag of the vessel carrying the goods would be French. So the question was whether the proper law of the underlying contract was French, the law of the flag referred to in Clause 13, or English, the proper law of the arbitration agreement as implied by the provision for arbitration in London referred to in Clause 18. The problem arose here because it was argued that Clause 13 should be ignored as it appeared on a printed form of contract which had been wrongly used for a different purpose to that for which it was intended. The question went to the House of Lords where three of their Lordships held that Clause 13 was an effective agreement by the parties that the proper law of the underlying contract should be French law. But assuming that Clause 13 failed to operate as an express determination of the proper law of the underlying contract, was the proper law of the arbitration clause, that is English law as provided by Clause 18, decisive in determining the proper law of the underlying contract? All their Lordships were of the view that the arbitration clause would not be decisive in this way. In considering the notion that the proper law of the arbitration clause overrides all other factors in determining the proper law of the underlying contract, Lord Wilberforce said:

22 *Idem.*

"Neither authority, nor commercial reality support the necessity for so rigid a rule. An arbitration clause must be treated as an indication, to be considered together with the rest of the contract and relevant surrounding facts. Always it will be a strong indication; often, especially where there are parties of different nationality or a variety of transactions which may arise under the contract, it will be the only clear indication. But in some cases it must give way where other indications are clear . . . [T]he question is one of estimating competing factors in the light of commercial intention".[23]

Lord Morris said:

"The balance comes down heavily in favour of French law. On the one hand, there are the place where the contract was negotiated and signed, the place of performance, the place where and the currency in which the freight was to be paid, and the place where the parties resided and carried on business: on the other hand, there is only the place where disputes were to be settled by arbitration . . . It would in my view be highly anomalous if our law required the mere fact that arbitration is to take place in England to be decisive as to the proper law of the contract".[24]

Choice of Seat

Despite the fact, however, that the contract must be construed as a whole, together with surrounding circumstances, choice of seat for the arbitration may assume a crucial importance, particularly where the parties have failed to express a choice of the proper law of the underlying contract. As previously mentioned, mere identification of the geographical location for the seat of the arbitration may, in the absence of indications to the contrary, determine the law applicable to the merits of the dispute. However, even if the choice of seat is held not to determine the law applicable to the merits of the dispute in this way, the parties should nevertheless appreciate its significance.

Significance of choice of seat

The seat will carry with it a submission by the parties to the mandatory rules and procedural law of the country in which the arbitration is to take place, although the degree to which this assumes significance will vary from country to country. At the most extreme, these procedural rules may affect the very extent to which the parties are free to exercise their choice of applicable law. For instance, Switzerland has recently introduced a new federal statute on private international law which has brought into effect new rules on the conflict of laws. As already mentioned, it is according to such rules, that the law applicable to the various aspects of the contractual relationship is determined. Article 19 of the new statute gives the arbitrator or judge a wide discretion to substitute another legal system for that which would otherwise be applicable. In particular, it appears to facilitate mandatory substitution for the applicable

23 *Op. cit.* at 114.
24 *Op. cit.* at 103.

law which was chosen by the parties.[25] Awareness of such problems should therefore lead the parties, when making their choice of venue for the arbitration, to consider the extent to which the mandatory legal rules will be applied to the arbitration, the extent of judicial intervention in the course of the arbitration and the nature of the procedural law applicable in the country chosen.

It may be this very enquiry into choice of seat at the time of negotiating the contract which leads the parties, in the event that they disagree, to adopt an administered form of arbitration such as that of the ICC. The ICC Rules provide by Article 12 that the International Court of the ICC will fix the place of arbitration unless agreed upon by the parties. In fixing the place, the ICC endeavour to avoid choosing places where the prevailing local law permits and the local courts tend towards interference in the course of arbitration proceedings taking place in their territory. It will generally seek a venue which is neutral with regard to the respective domiciles of the parties, and geographically and administratively convenient for the parties and the arbitrators. Other factors are also considered by the ICC, such as availability of suitable accommodation for the hearing and modern communications and other infrastructure.[26]

It is partly in recognition of the way in which a body such as the ICC approaches the question of the location of seat that certain commentators, have argued that, just as it is wrong to infer the proper law of the underlying contract from the seat where the seat has been chosen, usually on grounds of neutrality and convenience, by a third party such as the ICC, so it is wrong to impose upon the parties the procedural law prevailing in the country of the seat of the arbitration when that seat may have no connection with the parties or the contract. It is contended that the parties and arbitrators in international arbitrations should be free of any local legal constraints imposed upon the arbitration proceedings. Such a concept is reflected in Article 11 of the ICC Rules, which provides that:

> "The Rules governing the proceedings before the arbitrator shall be those resulting from these Rules and, where these Rules are silent, any Rules which the parties, (or, failing them, the arbitrator) may settle, *and whether or not reference is thereby made to a municipal procedural law to be applied to the arbitration*". [Emphasis added]

However, in England, *Naviera Amazonica* reasserted the principle that, at least insofar as the English courts are concerned, every arbitration must have a seat and a national system of procedural law.[27] (See also *Bank Mellat*.[28]) Provided the seat is established, however, hearings may take place in various locations to suit the convenience of the parties.[29]

It is essential that parties meet the mandatory requirements of local law if they are not to run the risk of obtaining an award which could be set aside

25 See FA Mann, "New dangers of arbitration in Switzerland", *Financial Times*, 24 November 1988.

26 See G Pointon, "The Court of Arbitration of the ICC and Arbitration Proceedings Under the ICC Rules", paper presented at the Institute of International Business Law and Practice, Paris.

27 See FA Mann, "English Procedural Law and Foreign Arbitrations" (1969) 18 ICLQ 997.

28 *Op. cit.* at 301.

29 See *Naviera Amazonica*, *op. cit.* and FA Mann, "Lex Arbitri and Locus Arbitri" (1988) 104 LQR 349.

under local law or refused international recognition or enforcement. In this context it is important to consider what would happen if the parties were to choose a procedural law which were to be different from the seat of the arbitration. There is no English authority for the case where parties have referred disputes to arbitration in England subject to a procedure governed by a foreign law. Although it may be possible to do so by incorporating an express term in the contract to that effect.

In *Naviera Amazonica*, the Court emphasised the practical difficulties that would be encountered in such a situation. The difficulties arise principally from the relationship between the place of arbitration and the supervisory jurisdiction of the local courts: in particular, which courts would have jurisdiction where the parties expressly chose English procedural law for an arbitration taking place in France? Assuming that it is the courts of the procedural law, that is the English courts, rather than those of the seat, how are those courts to enforce their orders in respect of an arbitration taking place outside their territory in France? It is almost inconceivable that an English court would intervene in the procedure of an arbitration taking place in a foreign country where the obvious competent court should be that of the country in whose territory the arbitration is pending.[30]

The seat will therefore almost certainly determine both the identity of the courts of competent jurisdiction and the procedure of the arbitration but subject to compliance with mandatory local rules, the parties and the arbitrators have considerable freedom to agree the type of procedure to be adopted by the arbitral tribunal.

Enforcement of awards

The English courts will only enforce an award if it complies with the procedural law of the seat of the arbitration. If the English courts are to recognise and enforce an award then, if the arbitration takes place in England, it must conform to English law whether the form of the arbitration is administered or ad hoc; if it takes place abroad then it must conform to the foreign procedure of that seat.

It is particularly important that an award should be internationally enforceable as the seat in which the award is made is likely to be a country neutral to the parties, where neither party will be resident nor have a place of business and may have no assets. Accordingly, it is likely that the award will not be able to be enforced in the country of the seat of the arbitration, but must be enforced in another country where assets are available.

New York Convention

The New York Convention on the Recognition and Enforcement of Foreign Arbitral Awards 1958[31] is the most significant international treaty governing

30 See FA Mann (1969), *op. cit.*

31 Convention on the recognition and enforcement of foreign arbitral awards. Done at New York, on 10 June 1958 (1959) United Nations Treaty Series (1959) 330.

the ability of parties to enforce an award in a country different to that of the seat of the arbitration.

In general terms, Article V of the Convention provides that enforcement of an award may be refused where the arbitration agreement is not valid under the law chosen by the parties, or, in the absence of choice, under the law of the country where the award was made, or, where the arbitral procedure was not in accordance with the law of the country where the arbitration took place. The nationality of the award is determined by the procedural law of the seat of the arbitration, so that as a matter of prudence the parties should ensure compliance with the requirements of the law of the seat of the arbitration, both so as to avoid the risk of contravening the New York Convention and the risk of intervention by the local courts, and, as a practical matter the award should be made in the country of the seat.

Conclusion

When negotiations for the construction contract reach the stage of considering a dispute resolution procedure, the parties should apply their minds to the three aspects of the overall contractual relationship and make an express choice of law to govern each. This will avoid the expense, delay and uncertainty arising where it is necessary to search for a law once a dispute has arisen. The procedural law should generally be that of the seat of the arbitration. The venue for the seat of the arbitration is of particular significance, not only because it is a powerful factor in determining the proper law where the parties have failed to express a choice, but because, even where they have expressed a choice, the procedural rules of the seat may have a profound impact on the way and extent to which that choice may be exercised.

The procedural rules of a particular legal system may assume great importance for the outcome of a dispute in the way in which they affect the procedural aspects of the arbitration. They may affect the ability of one of the parties to proceed with the arbitration; for example, had the Court in *Bank Mellat* ordered security for costs that order may well have prejudiced the aggrieved contractors' ability to obtain an award simply through lack of funds. They may determine whether an award, once made, can be set aside on appeal to the courts; this was the risk for instance, in *Whitworth Street Estates* where the House of Lords determined that the Scottish arbitrator was correct in refusing to state his award in a form which would allow it to be reviewed and perhaps set aside by the English High Court. They may determine the validity of an award and hence its enforceability in a foreign country; for example, in *Norske Atlas* an attempt by the defendants to avoid enforcement of a Norwegian award in England was denied when the English Court held, applying English procedural rules, that the proper law of the contract was Norwegian and that therefore, notwithstanding that the contract and therefore the submission to arbitration award would not have been valid under English law, the contract was valid under Norwegian law and hence the award was valid and enforceable in this country. The mandatory procedural rules of the seat must also be considered in the context of the enforceability of the award under the New York Convention.

Part V

UK Attitude to International Arbitration

The attitude of the English courts to ICC arbitration 20

Sir Edward Eveleigh

Synopsis

This paper surveys the evolution of attitudes by the English courts to ICC arbitration. It examines *dicta* in cases like *Bank Mellat* and describes particularly the English attitudes to the scrutinising process carried out by the ICC Court and the extent to which the ICC Rules have, or should have, a persuasive effect on English decisions.

Introduction

The ICC Court of Arbitration was founded as long ago as 1923, yet until about 1980, a speaker asked to say what was the attitude of the English courts to it, would have replied: " They don't have one". Although it is said that in the year before the Arbitration Act 1979, there were some 10,000 arbitrations current in the United Kingdom, and very many were international, they were largely in the maritime and commodity fields.

The pre-1979 position

The power of the courts to stay an action to give effect to an arbitration clause in an international arbitration was discretionary until 1975. Until 1979, the courts could be invited to intervene for the purpose of quashing an award for error of law or of fact upon the face of it. Furthermore, at any stage of the proceedings an arbitrator could be compelled or was able of his own volition to state a case for the opinion of the Court on any question of law arising in the course of the reference. An agreement to exclude this supervisory jurisdiction was void. It is not surprising, therefore, that England was not a natural choice for the ICC to fix as the place of arbitration when Article 24 of its rules provided that the award should be final and that the parties were deemed to have waived their right to any form of appeal "in so far as such waiver can validly be made".

The post-1979 position

The Arbitration Act 1975 gave effect to the New York Convention and the Arbitration Act 1979 abolished the special case procedure, and restricted the right of appeal in all cases and permitted the parties to exclude the right of appeal in non domestic arbitrations by an agreement in writing (subject to limited exceptions). England has thus become acceptable as the place for arbitration and since 1980, there have been a number of significant decisions from which it is possible to give some kind of an answer to the question posed above.

Relevant decisions

In *Janos Paczy* v. *Händler and Natermann GmbH*[1] the plaintiff started an action on a contract which contained a clause providing for arbitration under the ICC Rules. He claimed that as he could not raise the deposit which the rules required the arbitration agreement was "incapable of being performed" within the meaning of section 1 of the 1975 Act and consequently the court was not obliged to stay his action.

The Court referred to the ICC Rules and in particular Article 9, which dealt with the deposit required to cover the costs of the arbitration. Article 9.4 provided:

> "the terms of reference shall only become operative and the arbitrator shall only proceed in respect of those claims for which the deposit has been duly paid to the International Chamber of Commerce."

The Court held that the agreement was not "incapable of being performed", although the plaintiff might be incapable himself of performing it. It refused to read into the 1975 Act words which would have the effect of relieving the plaintiff from his inability to comply with the rules. Buckley LJ said:

> "It is for the arbitration court to decide by whom the deposit shall be paid and if the deposit is to be paid partly by one party and partly by another, to decide in what proportions it is to be paid. It is for the parties to abide by whatever directions that court gives in that respect."

It is clear, therefore, that the Court would not seek to find ways to limit a party's obligations under the rules, at least in so far as the payment of the deposit is concerned and it rejected an assertion that the defendant should be called upon to put up the whole of the deposit although one party was entitled to do so under the rules.

1 [1981] 1 Lloyd's Rep. 302.

In *Bank Mellat* v. *Helliniki Technicki*[2] the provisions in the rules relating to deposits were seen to have relevance in determining whether the court should exercise its power under the Arbitration Act 1950 section 12 to order security for costs and two members of the Court of Appeal placed particular weight upon the fact that the Arbitration was under the rules of the ICC.

Kerr LJ at p.303 said:

> "The particular combination of circumstances in the present care is that the contract provided that the arbitration should take place in the City of London, albeit that the substantive law was to be foreign, that the originating contracting parties and the subject matter of the contract had no connection with this country and that the arbitration was to be conducted under the ICC Rules. It is the latter factor, the parties' agreement to subject themselves to the ICC Rules, that is in my view ultimately the most important one in considering the exercise of the court's discretion in this combination of circumstances, and I therefore now turn to these rules."

He examined the rules and went on to say that the application before the Court was inconsistent with the scheme and spirit of the ICC Rules to an extent which made it inappropriate in principle for the court to exercise its discretion to order security for costs.

Goff LJ, did not attach such weight to the fact that the arbitration was under ICC Rules but regarded it as a factor in considering the closeness of the connection of the arbitration with England.

In *Arab African Energy Corporation Ltd.* v. *Glieprodukten Nederland BV*[3] a telex confirmation of a contract contained the words "English law – arbitration, if any, London according to ICC rules." The Court refused leave to appeal saying that the rules of the ICC provided that the award was final and that the parties "waived their right to any form of appeal" where this was legally permissible and consequently the parties had made an agreement to exclude an appeal. It was later held that the same reasoning applied to an interim award.[4]

Choice of law

When faced with a question of choice of law the English courts applying English principles of conflict of laws have proceeded upon the basis that the proper law must be some recognised system of national law. In so far as arbitration is concerned the case of *DST* v. *Raknoc*[5] may be thought to have opened the way to a different approach in an arbitration held in England under ICC Rules.

Article 13.3 reads:

> "The parties shall be free to determine the law to be applied by the arbitrator to the merits of the dispute. In the absence of any indication by the parties as

2 [1984] QB 291.
3 [1983] 2 Lloyd's Rep 419.
4 See *Marine Contractors Inc.* v. *Shell Petroleum Development Company of Nigeria Ltd.* [1984] 2 Lloyd's Rep 77.
5 [1987] 2 All ER 769.

to the applicable law, the arbitrator shall apply the law designated as the proper law by the rule of conflict which he deems appropriate."

Does this rule allow the choice of rules of law which are not part of a national system?

The above case concerned an arbitration under ICC Rules held in Geneva between a consortium of companies registered in various countries and a government and a state company. The case was decided on the facts but the terms of reference had included the issue, "what body or bodies of substantive law should be applied by the arbitral tribunal? The tribunal answered the question and held that the law was "internationally accepted principles of law governing contractual relations." It was said that with parties involved who were organised under various laws on the one hand and a state company on the other reference to the law of any one of them would be inappropriate and was seen as such by common practice, particularly in the field of oil drilling concessions (which was this case) and especially to arbitrations located in Switzerland.

The matter came before the English Court where, in reliance on section 5(3) of the 1975 Act, it was submitted that it would be contrary to English public policy to enforce an award which holds that the rights and obligations of the parties are to be determined, not on the basis of any particular national law but on some unspecified and possibly ill-defined internationally accepted principles of law.

In the Court of Appeal the case was decided upon the finding of fact, but the Master of the Rolls, having been told that the above submission was a matter of considerable importance in international commerce, expressed his opinion upon it. He said:

> "By choosing to arbitrate under the rules of the ICC and in particular Article 13.3 the parties have left the proper law to be decided by the arbitrators and have not in terms confined the choice to national systems of law".

Therefore, in his opinion, such an award would be enforceable under the New York Convention.

It must be remembered that the court was dealing with an award which was treated as being valid by the law of Switzerland and the Master of the Rolls was only concerned with whether public policy prevented it from being enforced in England. However, his words would seem to be in favour of affording similar recognition to such an award in an arbitration held in England under the rules of the ICC. There is not space to consider how the arguments would run, but the exclusion of a right to appeal if permissible and a consideration of the closeness of the arbitration with England would seem to be very relevant factors.

From the foregoing one might have thought it possible to generalise and say that an ICC arbitration which would give effect to the ICC Rules as being agreed to by the parties and administered by an institution which had earned respect over very many years in operation was readily acceptable to the courts. However, in a careful and skilfully written article by Antoine Kassis[6] entitled "The questionable validity of arbitration and awards under the Rules of the International Chamber of Commerce," the writer, after

6 *Journal of International Arbitration*, Vol. 6 No. 2 at 79.

recognition of the dominant position of the ICC in international commercial arbitration, asserts that:

> ". . . the system instituted under the ICC Rules is not a true arbitration process and awards made in accordance with them are not true arbitral awards enforceable by State Courts with national laws".

He cites the 1986 Edition of the Rules but there is no significant difference in the 1988 Edition. After referring to Article 2.1 of the Rules which begins "The Court of Arbitration does not itself settle disputes," it is then said that despite Article 2.1 some decisions of the Court provided for in the Rules "exceed the organization and administration functions of the arbitral process and are actually and objectively jurisdictional. This means they involve direct and very definite intervention in settling the dispute by the arbitrator as a private judge."

Participation by the ICC Court

Three specific provisions for the intervention by the Court are cited as involving the participation by the Court in the decision that resolves the dispute. The first and most important is Article 21.

> "Before signing an award, whether partial or definitive, the arbitrator shall submit it in draft form to the Court. The Court may lay down modifications as to the form of the award and, without affecting the arbitrator's liberty of decision, may also draw his attention to points of substance. No award shall be signed until it has been approved by the Court as to its form."

The second is Article 2.8. "if the Court, after having considered the arbitrator's observations, decides that the arbitrator is not fulfilling his functions in accordance with the Rules, or within the prescribed time limits, he shall be replaced . . . ."

The third is Article 13.1(h) which requires the Terms of Reference to include:

> "such other particulars as may be required to make the arbitral award enforceable in law or may be regarded as helpful by the Court of Arbitration or the arbitrator."

This is coupled with Art.13.2. which provides that the Court may set a time limit for signature of the terms by a defaulting party on the expiration of which "the arbitration shall proceed and the award shall be made."

It is said that in practice the mandatory power of the Court concerning the form of the award is used to require correction in such cases as contradictory findings in the substance of the award and failure of the reasons given to sustain the award rendered. Further, relying upon Craig, Park, and Paulsson[7], it is said that the mandatory power covers defects in the arbitral process itself so that, for example, the Court returned an award to the arbitrators for deliberation when it appeared that at their first meeting after the hearing the minority arbitrator was faced with a draft award signed by the other two without prior discussion.

7 *International Chamber of Commerce Arbitration 1984.*

The author points out that the difference between form and substance may be difficult to recognise. He quotes Article 26 which requires the Court and the arbitrator to make every effort to "make sure that the award is enforceable at law" and concludes that the Court would point out a serious error of substance, the existence of which would mean that the award was unenforceable and although its suggestions in the matter would not be binding it might refuse to give notice of the award and on the failure of the arbitrator to modify the draft it could set in motion the procedure for replacing the arbitrator under Article 2.8.

In these circumstances it is argued that there could be an interference as suggested. However, the record of the ICC in relation to arbitrations since 1923 has been such as to attract the greatest respect. Consequently such interference seems extremely unlikely. To this Kassis in effect replies that this is not the point because the existence of rules which permit such interference invalidates the arbitral process. Supporters of ICC arbitrations contend that this answer makes a false assumption. Rules should not be interpreted as conferring unlawful powers if a lawful interpretation is possible. The rules should not be interpreted as giving the widest powers (the words used do not compel such an interpretation) but as permitting intervention so far as that is lawful to ensure an award which is widely enforceable. If there were an attempt at unlawful interference by the Court it should be treated like any such attempt by anyone else. The arbitrator should treat it appropriately and report it to the parties. The award should stand or fall according to the facts constituting the alleged interference and not because it might literally be possible to construe the rules as being wide enough to allow such interference. They further argue that the parties have agreed to the rules and that when none of the arbitrators may be familiar with the relevant national rules for the validity of the award it is invaluable to have available the expertise of the Court to draw attention to possible pitfalls.

Examples of the attitude of the English courts

What should be the attitude of the English courts? Some indication is to be found in the case of *Bank Mellat* v. *GAA Development and Construction Company*.[8] In an arbitration under ICC Rules a majority award was made in favour of the GAA Development and Construction Company. The Plaintiffs by an originating motion sought an order under section 23(2) of the Arbitration Act 1950 to set aside the award on the grounds of misconduct of the arbitrators who made the majority award. The ICC Court of Arbitration had referred the draft majority award back for reconsideration of the reasons. The Plaintiff claimed that despite a request by the dissenting arbitrator the majority declined to convene a further meeting of the tribunal and made certain amendments to the reasons in their draft award without reference to the dissenting arbitrator. The validity of Article 21 was not directly in question but, as Steyn J pointed out, the issue to be decided arose in the context of the Court's power of scrutiny of awards. The 1986

8 [1988] 2 Lloyd's Rep 44.

Rules were in fact applicable but again there is no significant difference between them and the current 1988 edition. The judge recited Article 21 and then said:

> "Article 21 should be read with Article 22 of the Internal Rules of the Court of Arbitration (which came into force on March 1 1980). This provision reads as follows:
>
> 22. When it scrutinizes draft arbitral awards in accordance with Article 21 of the ICC Rules of Arbitration, the Court of Arbitration pays particular attention to the respect of the formal requirements laid down by the law applicable to the proceedings and, where relevant, by the mandatory rules of the place of arbitration, notably with regard to the reasons for awards, their signature and the admissibility of dissenting opinions."

Since the Court's power of scrutiny of awards is sometimes misunderstood, I propose to describe briefly the relevant function of the Court. Arbitration under the ICC Rules is a form of institutional arbitration. But it differs from other systems of institutional arbitration. The distinctive feature of ICC arbitration, built into the Rules, is supervision by a permanent body, the ICC Court of Arbitration. Despite its name the Court has no arbitral or adjudicative function. It merely supervises the application of the Rules by the arbitrators. The supervisory function which is germane to the issues in the present case is the Court's power of scrutiny of awards before they are published. That power exists, because the ICC system, the most truly international of all arbitral systems, provides for the conduct of arbitrations in most countries of the world, and the members of a three man tribunal frequently come from different continents, or at least from different countries, with fundamentally different legal systems.

It is regarded as the first imperative of the ICC system that awards rendered under it should be enforceable. It has been pointed out that something like 90% of ICC awards are voluntarily complied with and that ICC awards have a good record of enforcement in national courts.[9] The system of scrutiny of awards by the Court contributes to the enforceability of ICC awards. The Court has a mandatory power "to lay down modifications as to the form of the award." An example of such a matter of form may be a case where the damages awarded under different claims do not add up to the aggregate awarded. The Court also has an advisory power. It may, "without affecting the arbitrators liberty of decision", draw the arbitrators' attention to "points of substance". For example, it may draw the attention of the arbitrators to a possible conflict between a particular ruling and an express provision in the contract. The decision remains that of the arbitrators. The court does not review the evidence or the arguments. The process of scrutiny is directed at the internal coherence and consistency of the award. But it may also sometimes reveal a procedural flaw which can be corrected. Craig, Park and Paulsson, *op. cit.* points out (para. 20.02):

> "In its review of the award submitted to it, or of correspondence concerning the award, the Court may become aware of a procedural defect not revealed on the face of the award. In other words, the process of scrutiny of the award

9 See Craig, Park and Paulsson, *International Chamber of Commerce Arbitration*, 1984, para. 20.01.

may bring to light a defect in the arbitral process itself which may yet be curable.

The issue most often raised before the Court at this stage is an alleged failure in the process of deliberations by the arbitrators. This may occur if one of the arbitrators informs the Court that the draft decision contains elements which were not the subject of a discussion and deliberation among the arbitrators. In one case, the Court returned the award to the arbitrators for deliberation when it appeared that at the first meeting of the arbitrators after the hearing, the minority arbitrator was presented by the chairman with a draft award already signed by the other two arbitrators and prior to discussion of any of the issues."

This is then a general description of the nature of the system of scrutiny of awards which parties accept when they agree on arbitration in accordance with the ICC rules.

After stating the facts relating to discussions between the arbitrators, which led to the submission of the draft majority award and the dissent to the Court, the judge said:

"The Court did not approve the draft majority award. What happened is described in the letter from the ICC Secretariat:

The draft award of the majority was, however, not approved at said session. the arbitral tribunal was rather asked by the Court of Arbitration to provide it with a strengthened motivation of two issues raised in the award. This request concerned a matter of form, not of substance. The Court's request fell within the power conferred on it under Art 21. of its Rules which states that it "may lay down modification as to the form of the award". The Court's request was communicated to all three arbitrators by a letter of March 27. The communication from the ICC court to the arbitrators was not placed before me, and that is perfectly understandable. But it is clear from secondary evidence that it related to the reasoning of the majority in support of their decision on the merits, and the reasoning in support of the award of interest."

He then related the communications which took place between the arbitrators and the refusal of the majority to take part in a further meeting and he said that the amended majority award after being sent to the third arbitrator was placed before the Court for approval. The Court took into account correspondence between the arbitrators and considered the dissenting arbitrator's request for a meeting and it declared itself satisfied that "the revised draft award submitted by the majority had been made by the arbitral tribunal in a proper way."

In contending that the majority committed misconduct in not holding a final meeting counsel submitted that the fact that the ICC Court took the view that there was no procedural irregularity was irrelevant. To this the judge said:

"I accept that the view of the ICC Court cannot in any way be determinative of the issue. But it is in my view unrealistic to describe it as entirely irrelevant. For example, it may be helpful as throwing light on the question whether a further face to face meeting between the arbitrators was necessary. That question cannot entirely be divorced from what is usual in ICC practice".

He then recognised the difficulty of drawing the line between form and substance and said that he would approach the case on the assumption that the amendments made as a result of the communications from the Court were matters of substance. He pointed out that there had been extensive oral deliberations between the arbitrators before the majority drafted its award and said that it had never been suggested that any of the observations of the ICC Court or amendments to the reasons for the award involved anything that had not been canvassed at the hearings and discussed at meeting between the arbitrators. He held that there was no misconduct.

It is of some significance that, with distinguished counsel involved, it was not argued that the ICC Rules themselves and Article 21, in particular, invalidated the arbitral process. The judge himself clearly treated the rules as playing a useful part in an ICC arbitration to assist in ensuring an enforceable award.

Conclusion

It seems safe to say that the attitude of the English courts to ICC arbitration will be a benevolent one. Fully recognising the consensual nature of arbitration the courts will give effect to rules agreed upon by the parties subject to any mandatory requirements of the law, a qualification which makes it clear that the courts will not abandon their final supervisory role however prestigious the institution may be under whose rules the arbitration is conducted. However, many of the powers of the High Court which are contained in the Arbitration Act 1950 are prefaced with the words "where a contrary intention appears" or are declared by saying "the High Court may". Consequently the ICC Rules will often show a contrary intention or their existence and the manner in which the Court of Arbitration exercises its powers will be a very important consideration in the High Court if it is asked to exercise its discretion and intervene.

21 Control by the Courts: a Plea for more, not less

Ian N. Duncan Wallace

Synopsis

In this thought-provoking paper, Professor Wallace reviews in some detail the powers of the English courts to control the conduct and outcome of arbitrations. He comments particularly on the influence of the decision in the *Nema* and goes on to deal as well with issues such as the place of conciliation in international arbitration and the problems created by the procedure in Clause 67 of the FIDIC form of contract.

Introduction

There is currently a wide-spread international movement, supported by civil lawyers perhaps more strongly than by common lawyers, advocating international arbitration even between developed countries and systems of law in the much wider context of commercial disputes generally rather than construction contracts in particular. In some cases an overriding role for an international *lex mercatoria* is also advocated in such situations.

In the narrow context of construction disputes with which this paper is specifically concerned, these tendencies are strongly supported by civil engineers, architects and other technical arbitrators and experts and their institutions, and above all by contractors' organizations in all countries. Both movements appear to be in favour of removing arbitration generally, and international arbitration in particular, as far as possible from the oversight or control of the Courts (usually, of course, those of the *lex arbitrii*). Civil lawyers, in many cases coming from jurisdictions where much less interest or control has been exercised in the past by their own courts in either commercial arbitration or construction law have, as stated, and perhaps for this reason, been in the forefront of this movement. Thus the UNCITRAL Model Law of International Commercial Arbitration appears to permit judicial intervention only in cases of incapacity to contract, invalidity of the agreement, awards in default of service or notice, or excess of jurisdiction. Remarkably, it seems, no attack on an arbitrator's assumption of jurisdiction is permitted until after his award. These various tendencies have, of course, attracted powerful and persuasive criticism in England (notably by Lord Justice Kerr and Dr FA Mann).

Tending in the same direction, Article 24 of the ICC Rules (in the rather more specific context of appeals from awards on the ground of errors of law) provides for a deemed waiver of the right to any form of appeal from its awards to the Courts, insofar as that is permitted by law. That article has, of course, been enforced in England where parties had agreed to an arbitrator giving his reasons for an interim award.[1]

On the other hand, and very understandably, the Cour de Cassation has recently over-ruled an ICC award which purported to give a preferential right of payment, as against other creditors, to a claimant against an insolvent French sub-contractor, in conflict with French bankruptcy law. Without going into the specific reasons, which involve the application of the new French civil procedure code, it is interesting to consider what the response of the English Courts would have been in such a case.[2]

The English position

To an English readership there is little need to over-emphasise the detail of what has occurred through judicial intervention since the 1979 Arbitration Act. Before that Act, arbitrators who stated a case when requested to do so (the vast majority) thereby conferred an effective right to have the point of law involved canvassed before the High Court. Only in the relatively rare case where an arbitrator refused or failed to state a case did the court have a discretion whether or not to order him to do so, and the discretion to refuse such an order was very sparingly exercised (*e.g.* where there had been a specific submission to a lawyer of a point of law, or where no real point of law, or one which would not dispose of the case, was involved).

After the 1979 Act, which on a first reading was welcomed by many as simplifying the Case Stated procedures, and as generally sharpening up arbitrators by encouraging them to give reasons for their awards, it was considered by the courts themselves for at least a year that the right to take a bona fide point of law to the High Court (save of course in the case of the new exclusion agreements) was the same as under the old legislation.[3]

The Nema doctrine

Lord Diplock's *obiter* observations in the *Nema*,[4] rapidly elevated to the status of law binding on the judges of the High Court, and the later decision in the *Antaios*,[5] put paid to that. They brought about possibly the greatest

1 *Marine Contractors* v. *Shell Petroleum Nigeria* [1984] QB 291.
2 *Soc Thinet-c-Labrely as liquidator of Soc SRA*, Cour de Cassation, 8 March 1988, 237.
3 See Mustill and Boyd, (2nd ed.), 588, and see my own CCPP, para. 17–49(e).
4 [1982] AC 724.
5 [1982] AC 191.

revolution in the law of arbitration for more than a century – all the more remarkable, perhaps, for being virtually invisible in the wording of the 1979 Act itself. Given the tendencies of contemporary modern parliamentary draftsmanship, as exemplified by the Unfair Contract Terms and Latent Damage legislation, with their painstaking descent to detail for the guidance of the courts, one might have expected to find detailed lists of the criteria to be applied by the Courts in giving leave, if such indeed was the intention.

On the basis of the *Nema dicta*, the arbitrator's decision in the case of "one-off" contracts must be "obviously wrong on mere perusal of the reasoned award", and in the case of more standard and widely used terms, the appeal must be seen to add to the clarity and certainty of English law, but even then only if there was "a strong prima facie case" that the arbitrator was wrong. All this has to be established on an application for leave lasting from 10 to 15 minutes.[6]

As of today, the reported experience of most practitioners in the construction field appears to be that only in the rarest of cases is it now possible to overcome these obstacles so as to obtain leave to appeal, if the case involves a construction contract.

The Case Stated procedure

Mustill and Boyd give as reasons for the previous liberal regime of Case Stated, as it had grown up over the previous century, that it was first made possible by the legislature because the parties desired it, and later imposed as an obligation in all cases because it was believed to be in the interest of the commercial community that arbitrators should be restrained from binding the parties, whether accidentally or by design, by an award which did not give effect to their true contractual rights.[7]

Their latest and, it is submitted, realistic and fully justified assessment of the *Nema* guidelines is that "It is no longer axiomatic that the Courts should be allowed to protect parties against decisions made contrary to the system of law which they have selected as applicable to their disputes" and that, on the contrary, "the Courts will assume that the parties to an arbitration agreement are content to take the risk that the arbitrator will make mistakes of law."[8]

Additionally, they point out that some judgments indicate that, in the interest of avoiding delay caused by unmeritorious appeals, the court will regard it as acceptable to risk enforcing an award which the individual judge may consider to be wrong.[9] On the other hand, it is said that a consideration which "will take priority over the wishes (sic) of the parties" will be the need to retain arbitration appeals to "provide the raw material for decisions by the Court on matters of general legal import."

6 See the "guidelines" expanded and explained as a philosophy in seminal terms in the new Mustill and Boyd (2nd ed.), 602–608.

7 *Ibid.*, 583.

8 *Ibid.*, 604.

9 Mustill and Boyd themselves do not support this latter view very strongly. See *ibid.* 604, note 9.

Rights of appeal

I have suggested elsewhere, although it is of course a purely personal value judgment, that the so-called desire of litigants, whether "businessmen" or not, for "speed and never mind the justice," and for finality of awards without appeal, has simply no basis in fact, and has been used as a convenient judicial myth to justify government policies which are primarily political and administrative and designed to achieve financial savings in the administration of justice by restricting access to the courts and transferring the expense wherever possible to private tribunals.

Of course, it is very possible that the arbitration "industry" may well have put forward this view about their prospective clients' alleged "desires" in the working parties leading up to the 1979 Act.[10] But this view in any event seems inconsistent with section 3(6) of the 1979 Act, which in domestic arbitrations requires an exclusion agreement to be made after the arbitration commences rather than in the arbitration agreement itself – hardly, one would think a recognition by the legislature itself of any widespread domestic desire for finality of awards without appeal let alone of a legislative desire to work to that end.

Arbitration v. the courts

While, of course, the *Nema* guidelines must unquestionably be followed in England unless and until legislation supervenes, I believe that the view that I have expressed about the wishes of "businessmen" may have the authoritative support of Sir Michael Mustill himself. Thus, writing in the rather different context of businessmen desiring uniformity of international arbitration law, he has very recently written

> "I question whether, in any but a small minority of cases, the businessman contracts to have his disputes resolved by arbitration for reasons which have anything to do with the merits of the arbitral process. By far the majority of arbitrations, both domestic and foreign, take place because the parties have contracted on the basis of standard forms which happen to include an arbitration clause . . . if they can agree on questions which are left open in the standard form, such as price, specification, quantity . . . they are unlikely to spend time and energy in complicating their bargain by varying a standard term relating to the adjudication of a dispute which they probably never even contemplate will occur. . . . The parties have enough on their minds without worrying about disputes. If they think about the subject at all each will no doubt prefer a submission to the courts of his own country. If this proves unacceptable . . . they will simply agree upon arbitration as an easy option to prevent the deal from foundering on an issue which they hope will prove academic."[11]

The nature of construction contracts

What is, I submit, crucially important in the present discussion, concerned as it is with construction contracts, is to recognise the fundamental difference

10 See my *Construction Contracts: Principles and Policies* para. 17–46(f), referred to hereafter as "CCPP."

11 "Contemporary Problems in International Commercial Arbitration", IBL April 1989, Vol. 17, No. 4, 145–192.

between a construction contract and the "commercial" contracts which are at the heart of the Commercial Court's jurisdiction, and which may have had a strong influence in the emergence of the *Nema* guidelines and their philosophy.

A construction contract is not a contract between "businessmen," whatever their supposed desires as to finality and lack of judicial control may be. A construction contract (except in the case of developer-owners, many of whom in any event use "in-house" lawyers or joint venture contractors, or are themselves "developer builders,") is in essence a consumer or end-user or retail contract. Even if some public entity such as a hospital board, or a large company, commissions a building for its needs, it is essentially a customer and not usually in the business of building for profit. The elderly lady having her retirement house built, or the young couple having a conversion done, or the company commissioning a factory, are not "businessmen" in the sense used by the judicial language on this subject. Nor is the government of a third world country commissioning a hospital or power station a "businessman" in this sense.

Construction contracts, (other than those between main and sub-contractors) are not like "string" contracts between buyers and sellers, charter parties, or contracts of insurance or freight or of carriage of goods, which indeed are contracts between "businessmen". If I have understood him aright, Sir Michael Mustill does not consider even that these latter are conscious users of arbitration with a desire to escape the control of their own Courts. But in the examples I have given all the various classes of construction owner to whom I have referred would, I suggest, be seriously disturbed to be told by their legal advisers that, along the lines of the *Nema* as analysed by Mustill and Boyd, they were, by agreeing to arbitration "content to take the risk of the arbitrator making a mistake of law" (for example, in interpreting their contract, or in applying some purported principle of contract law to the facts of the dispute which was incorrect).

They would, I also suggest, be even more disturbed to be told that, in denying them relief, the courts will even be prepared to take the risk of enforcing against them what the individual judge believes to be a wrong decision (for example, an incorrect award for additional payment by the owner to the contractor) in order to discourage delay in making payments to contractors. Owners are, of course, the paymasters (unlike contractors), and will always be, therefore, the party subject to this special judicial presumption that their main motivation in litigating is to secure delay in payment – an intriguing example, it may be suggested, of judicial consumer protection in reverse, perhaps more accurately, a new judicial policy of producer protection.

IFC 84: contracting in

There appears to have been a remarkable straw in the wind, totally opposed to the purported basis of the *Nema* philosophy, which has already taken place within the JCT/RIBA body responsible for the building standard forms. In a new amended Article 5.3 of the "Intermediate" standard form, which I believe is intended for comparatively modest contracts of intermediate size, it is left for stipulation in the Appendix that the new Article should apply. If so, under the terms of the new Article the parties agree and consent in advance that not only appeals on a question of law arising out of any award, but also applications on questions of law arising in the course of any reference, shall be within the jurisdiction of the High Court pursuant to sections 1(3)(a) or 2(1)(b) of the 1979 Act. This constitutes, of course, a deliberate "contracting in" in advance of the rights of appeal under the Act, and is the precise opposite of the exclusion agreements permitted by section 3 of the Act. while the source of or pressures for this provision can only be the subject of speculation, it suggests at least some undercurrent of, almost certainly, owner resistance which finds the *Nema* philosophy of arbitration unacceptable. Furthermore, the *Nema* philosophy, on similarly worded legislation, has not been deemed acceptable on policy grounds in the Australian courts.[12]

Delay

Returning for a moment to the question of delay, there have been fairly frequent assertions by the judiciary that the old Case Stated procedures were abused by debtors in order to secure delay, and it may be that this view was coloured by experience at the commercial bar, on which I am not myself qualified to speak. It has certainly not been my own experience at the construction bar,[13] and it seems that this view is shared by the experienced editors of BLR.[14] In the great majority of cases I would suggest that such delay as may lie at the door of irresponsible appeals pales into insignificance by comparison with the delays inflicted on litigants by the under-staffing and inadequate provision of courts and judges by government.

Indeed, it is these very administrative failures and their attendant very long delays, which lie at the door of government, which provide an undoubted incentive to make irresponsible and hopeless appeals which would otherwise not be present. I have previously suggested in CCPP[15] that the desire of the honest litigant may, no doubt, be for a speedy result, provided it is a correct one, but that the desire for a correct decision greatly outweighs any wish for speed and premature finality, and the rapidly lengthening Official Referee's lists are a testament to the same attitude by the parties in construction cases, as also the recent JCT/RIBA initiative to which I have referred.

If litigants before a judiciary of the quality of the High Court appear to require the resources of the Court of Appeal and of the House of Lords, that is surely overwhelming evidence of the over-riding desire of all litigants, including businessmen, for a correct decision even at the price of delay. The only class of litigant who genuinely desires quick finality will be the speculative claimant aware that his case is doubtful

12 *Qantas Airways* v. *Joseland and Gilling* (1986) 5 ACLR 47, and the *Abignano* and *Thompson* cases cited by David Byrne QC in (1988) 5 ICLR 73.
13 See CCPP para. 17–47(f) at 267.
14 See their recent commentary to *Anglian Water Authority* v. *RDL Contracting* (1988) 43 BLR 98 at 100–101.
15 See note 10.

or exaggerated, and that speed may well advantage him by prejudicing a careful and satisfactory defence. I may perhaps add that it is a strange law which makes appeals on a point of law available as of right from Official Referees (and directly, moreover, to the Court of Appeal) but offers only a minimal prospect of appeal to a single judge from an arbitrator who will be unknown to the parties in the vast majority of cases at the time of contracting and is frequently appointed by a third person and not by the parties themselves.

I have given my view on this subject in considerable detail elsewhere.[16] Broadly speaking, I there suggested that owners' legal advisers would increasingly advise them against arbitration (or arbitration clauses), as the *Nema* consequences became more generally known, and I was able to state of my own knowledge that highly responsible advisers in the international field outside England were advising important and responsible contracting parties to remove London arbitration clauses from their contracts as a direct result of the *Nema*.[17]

I also suggested, from the more parochial view of construction contracts, and for a variety of reasons which I there deployed and which are known to every practitioner (and indeed to contractors), that arbitration was likely to be a much less favourable tribunal for owners than the courts, and that for that reason also owners should remove arbitration clauses from their contracts, only using arbitration by way of specific submission of a particular dispute which might arise if it appeared to warrant it. The device of prior agreement by the parties to a future appeal on a point of law or under the English Act at the time of agreeing such a specific submission is also obviously attractive.

The influence of *Crouch*

There has, of course, been another quite separate judicial development in England having the effect of denying the courts to litigants in the construction field. This arises from the *dicta* of the Court of Appeal in the *Crouch* case, which have not as yet been seriously questioned in the courts.[18]

This case appears to hold that, in the event of the courts being seised of a construction dispute where the arbitration clause confers the traditional "open up, review and revise" power on the arbitrator, the courts will have no power to decide disputes on the merits in the face of any relevant certificates or decisions of the architect.

Thus, as a consequence, contractors are effectively barred from proceeding to summary judgment for money due, if without the support of an architect's certificate, for fear of the owner obtaining leave to defend and

16 In CCPP para. 17-47-48 at 264–66, and also much more shortly in my "Policy for Money" in Centre of Construction Law's recent publication of the papers at their September 1988 seminar, "Construction Contract Policy" at 236.

17 CCPP para. 17-47(f).

18 *North Regional Health Authority* v. *Crouch Construction* [1984] QB 644 analysed and doubted as contrary both to binding authority and principle in CCPP Chap. 17 (reproducing (1986) ConstLJ 13).

then availing himself of the tactical advantage offered by *Crouch* by deliberately not seeking to stay, thus, on the *Crouch* theory, effectively disfranchising the contractor from any claim at all. The Master of the Rolls additionally expressed the hope that if the *Crouch* view was accepted it would reduce the amount of business in the Official Referee's lists and that, if not, legislation providing for compulsory arbitration of construction disputes should be considered.

On that view, arbitration would be forced on parties to such disputes without their consent and with, it now seems, little likelihood of any appeal to the courts by reason of the *Nema* guidelines and practice. Quite apart from being unjust, this seems extremely unwise in view of the public importance of well and economically built buildings, which are not, in my view, in safe hands in a largely secret and industrially influenced system of arbitration.

Removal of arbitrators for misconduct

In common law countries misconduct can afford parties a remedy even though it is of a purely technical kind, but there have been quite a spate of cases reported, for example in the *Australian Construction Law Reporter*, of arbitrators whose misconduct has certainly not been merely technical, and in addition two or three striking examples of arbitrators of surprisingly high status in English arbitration circles whose conduct has rightly had to be similarly reviewed.[19]

It is surely common sense to recognise that the further from outside control any person, whether arbitrator or not, believes himself to be, the greater the likelihood of unjudicial or unfair attitudes or conduct emerging, even if, as is usually the case, they are, subjectively at least, well-intentioned. In the case of arbitrators any such tendencies must be powerfully reinforced by the essential lack of publicity attending arbitration proceedings as well as, in many cases, the lack of legal training or experience of technical arbitrators.

If judges of first instance, with a life-time of experience and training, and under the full glare of publicity, are subject to appellate control and review in this area, there must be a strong if not overwhelming case for arbitrators' institutions, in their own enlightened self-interest, to welcome, and not to seek to exclude, control in this area as well as in the area of mistakes of law.

Particularly those concerned, whether by legislation or otherwise, to promote or create a framework for international arbitration in their own countries should, I would submit, think carefully before deciding to remove or restrict the control of the courts in such cases, in what would, I again believe, be a wholly mistaken belief as to the true wishes of the parties themselves, whether businessmen or not, and whether the arbitration is domestic or international. In any event, of course, the courts themselves may insist on this type of control whatever their attitude may be to

19 See *Turner (East Asia)* v. *Builders Federal* (1988) 42 BLR 122, and *Town & City Properties* v. *Wiltsher Southern Ltd*. (1988) 44 BLR 109, both cases showing in varying degrees an inquisitorial attitude and an excessive desire to control and shorten the interlocutory processes and bring on an early hearing.

redressing mistakes of law in the light of the provisions in Article 24 of the ICC Rules.

Judicial control in international disputes

I am well aware that hitherto this paper has discussed the problem of judicial control almost entirely in its domestic English context. Turning to international disputes, and in particular from the point of view of the ICC Court of Arbitration or other international arbitration institutions, there are obviously different and delicate considerations present.

In the international construction contract field, however, it is even more true that international arbitration can only prosper if international owners as a class and their advisers can be persuaded that it is in their interest to include clauses providing for it in their contracts. The average international owner, certainly in the ICC field, will frequently be a government or government entity of a third world country, sometimes without a Western-style system of law, but in any case without sufficiently experience domestic courts, or experienced legal or technical manpower such as to induce confidence in domestic arbitration.

In other cases, of course, there may well be a very important pricing advantage for a foreign government in whose courts or contract administration international contractors do not feel confidence, if they are offered the improved degree of confidence and enforceability afforded by, for example, an ICC or other international arbitration clause and award.

It is self-evident, however, that an owner of this type in the construction field, who will undoubtedly see himself as a potential future defendant exposed to sophisticated claims by international contractors for additional payment and the merits of which in many cases he may justifiably not understand, will wish to be assured that, where he is contractually in the right, he can at least rely on international arbitrators to construe the contract strictly and send away the powerful international contractor empty-handed.

There is also, of course, a quite different side to the coin. There are undoubtedly irresponsible international owners who interfere with the judgment of any independent engineers or architects they may have engaged, exercise undue interference with their own in-house technical departments, take every possible (or impossible) jurisdictional procedural objection, or who abuse the party appointed arbitrator relationship during the arbitration itself. Some at least, though not of course all, of these obviously wrong attitudes may themselves be a response to the fact that the standard forms of contract which some international owners have been advised to use have failed in the past to give them what they believe to be a proper protection of their reasonable interest, or have exposed them to unexpected and unmeritorious and sometimes legalistic claims, which can easily happen under many of the forms currently in use, as I have endeavoured to explain in my "Policy for Money" paper already referred to.[20]

For example, as I explained in that paper,[21] the "Clause 12" or "changed conditions" clause in its present generalised form in western contracts is

20 See note 16.
21 *Ibid*. at 221.

difficult if not impossible, on analysis, for an adviser to justify to an owner, who will usually prefer either a higher but firm price to cover the contingencies in question, or a more precise definition and pricing of such risks should they eventuate. It is now fairly well known that, prior to the Fifth ICE Edition, the copyright of a completely drafted new ICE contract was "bought in" and then scrapped when it was appreciated by the contracting side of the industry that its distinguished draftsman had effectively dropped the clause. Yet the clause remains a firm part of the FIDIC contract, as also, of course, of the new domestic Fifth Edition ICE contract which replaced the scrapped version, and is a constant source of friction with foreign owners with a relatively simplistic view of contracting obligations, let alone with domestic owners.

So, too, the principle of many measurement claims under the English standard methods, and the wording which permits it, could not possibly be recommended to an owner, particularly in the international field."[22]

Exclusion of such control

My own suggestion is, therefore, that the bodies responsible for international arbitration should not, in principle, automatically reject judicial control, in particular in regard to errors of law, in the interest of the success of international arbitration itself. For this purpose I suggest that international arbitration bodies should encourage the parties to international contracts to choose those systems of law in which they have confidence, and to opt expressly for or against judicial control on questions of law.

This will usually, given the rules of private international law, involve a place of arbitration being stipulated in the arbitration clause. A policy of blanket or overriding exclusion of judicial control such as that in Article 24 of the ICC Rules must, I believe, in the long run lead to the diminished use of that particular form of arbitration by international owners, as they become more enlightened, and as has been seen has already begun to emerge among public owners in England.

I would suggest that the matter is best tested by considering the position of a legal adviser asked to advise an international owner at the pre-contract stage on the drafting of his contract documents and of the arbitration clause in particular (assuming, of course, that, after full discussion, commercial or other considerations have made international arbitration desirable in principle).

The first task of a legal adviser clearly requires that the contract documents should give the required substantive protection of the construction owner's reasonable interest. As to arbitration, the advice I suggest, would be to choose a system of law which could be relied on to interpret and enforce the contract so drafted with precision. A forum for the arbitration should be named where not only experienced and efficient legal services are available, but where (having regard to the built-in disadvantages for owners which all arbitration is likely to involve in any event) experienced judicial control and procedures are also available in the event of the

22 *Ibid.* at 211.

services are available, but where (having regard to the built-in disadvantages for owners which all arbitration is likely to involve in any event) experienced judicial control and procedures are also available in the event of the arbitrator's award either mistaking or disregarding the law chosen by the owner or the terms of the contract he has drafted.

My own advice to a responsible owner, quite independent of any degree of chauvinism, would have been to choose English law as the proper law if an English language construction contract was being used, and, prior to the Nema to name London as the forum. In the light of the Nema it would obviously be sound advice to owners to recommend a provision expressly "contracting in" to the right of appeal in the 1979 Act (though current judicial and government attitudes might possibly seek a means of denying effect to such initiatives), and it would be a major improvement if the Act were itself to be amended so as expressly to permit "contracting in" in advance on the lines of the recent RIBA/JCT initiative.

Conciliation and mediation

There has also been a widespread trend in the field of international construction arbitration suggesting the inclusion of *amiables compositeurs* or conciliation or mediation provisions into construction contracts, or for arbitration to be expressly conducted in accordance with principles of equity and fairness.

In my view no construction owner would be well advised to accept such concepts. In the first place, many of these procedures are of a preliminary nature, prior to full-scale arbitration subsequently taking place should they fail. As such, they amount to little more, from an owner's point of view, than permitting contractors to advance claims for additional payment during the construction period in two stages, with no assurance that an adverse decision at the first stage will prevent or embarrass a later presentation of the same or larger claims.

Moreover, these concepts of conciliation, equity or fairness, let alone of a *lex mercatoria*, seem particularly unsuitable in the context of the complexity of construction contracts with all their variants of type and drafting, and with the differing budgeting needs of different classes of owner. It is of the nature of concepts of "conciliation", "mediation" and "fairness" in the special context of a construction contract that they are likely to be applied in practice so as to permit some additional payment where none is strictly due, rather than to deny payment which is strictly due.

Thus they serve to conceal essentially one-way concepts favouring additional payment of the contractor. Even if that were wrong, the concept of "splitting the difference" in the name of "equity" (in my opinion the greatest danger to owners of arbitration itself) is simply likely to lead to the presentation of increasingly unrealistic and exaggerated initial claims. In true "businessmen's" arbitrations (*i.e.*, with businessmen on both sides) the parties may or may not see advantages in avoiding judicial control and in concepts of "splitting the difference" or of apportionment and compromise.

I do not myself believe that this is so, except in very unusual situations or "quality" arbitrations, but in any event construction owners do not, in my view, fall into this category, nor should government and government entity owners, however producer-orientated they may be in other departments, adopt such attitudes when commissioning construction work on behalf of their public.

Already assailed by standard forms emanating from bodies where owners are not represented or under-represented international owners can be expected, as they become more educated by experience, either to draft their own contracts or (as, for example, FIDIC in fact invites them to do in Part II of the Conditions) to modify the standard forms at any desired points. Third world or other international owners, I believe, may see many advantages in international arbitration which produces objective findings of fact and law reached by specialist experts. They will not find attractive a system of arbitration which is effectively free to misinterpret the third world owner's drafting of his contract or to misapply the system of law which the owner has chosen and in the light of which the contract will have been drafted on his behalf, or to apply allegedly over-riding concepts of *lex mercatoria* or of conciliation so as to defeat his draftsman's intention.

Clarification : Clause 67 of the FIDIC form

There is another reason why in my view a blanket waiver of rights of appeal, unless positively desired by the parties themselves, may disadvantage international arbitration and its sponsoring institutions. This is because a ruling from a court commanding respect, particularly in relation to a system of law chosen by the parties themselves, may be of great value to the arbitration institution itself in clarifying a problem underlying its own arbitration provisions, and perhaps ultimately questions of jurisdiction. Without such assistance, only conflicting decisions of individual arbitration tribunals are likely to occur, between the authority of which it will be impossible if not invidious to distinguish.

A perfect example of this has occurred in the case of the ICC, where an entirely novel point was taken fairly recently on the long-established wording of Clause 67 of the FIDIC Third Edition Conditions, to the effect that its 90-day time limit for arbitration after the Engineer's preliminary decision contemplated the institution of proceedings in the ICC Court by a formal Request for Arbitration within that period, and not a simple written notice requiring arbitration of the disputed matter following the adverse decision. After considering the English authorities I myself expressed the considered view that this argument was not valid,[23] but that is beside the point. There are now a number of awards of arbitrators released for publication by the ICC[24] some of which have effectively deprived contractors who have only given a written notice of arbitration within the period of any means of

23 See (1985) 2 ICLR reproduced in CCPP Chap. 18.

24 Extracts only in the *Journal de Droit International*, and fuller versions in *The Hague Year Book of International Law*. Though these reports are apparently "sanitised" by removing the parties' names, publication without consent of the parties seems inconsistent with the consensual basis of arbitration. Moreover a process of selection appears to be involved, which may be open to criticism in implying ICC approval of published awards and disapproval of an opposing view which has not been published.

advancing their claim at all, and some which, on the contrary, have allowed them to proceed with their claims.

In consequence, no adviser can safely say today to a contractor that he can rely on the point being held to be a bad one before unknown ICC arbitrators, with the result that, to avoid this risk, a series of separate arbitrations, sometimes with different arbitrators, have to come into being arising out of different disputes on one contract and project--truly a very costly procedural nightmare and a fertile source of injustice and procedural objections by opportunistic owners against contractors.[25]

Since FIDIC Third Edition claims are likely to come forward for years to come, these unattractive and impractical procedural technicalities will presumably persist to dog all ICC arbitrations. Since the point is very n[illegible] one depending on the English language, and on historically well-known English wording derived from the English domestic engineering contracts, it is obvious that a decision of an English commercial judge on this clause (different versions of which have been previously ruled on in the English courts in other respects) would be of the greatest value, and enable the ICC to give a clear directive or advice based on the judgment to its own arbitrators.

Does Article 24 of the ICC Rules, however, permit such a point to be taken before an English court, since ICC arbitrators effectively finally rule on all points of law, including questions of their own jurisdiction, when making their awards? I am not certain of the answer, nor how an English Court, in the light of section 3 of the Act and Article 24 of the ICC Rules, would deal with the matter if seised of it. But since a decision in favour of the owner would appear to be a simple question of interpretation of Clause 67, whereby the Engineer's decision will become final and binding in a certain event, and not a true jurisdictional point, it is very difficult to see how it could be presented to the court other than as a point of law on appeal coming within the exclusion ambit of Article 24 of the ICC Rules.

Conclusion

This paper is intended to provoke discussion. It does not seek to offer solutions, let alone comprehensive ones. Its broad message is that all arbitration in the construction field, and in particular international arbitration, must offer greater, not less, precision and safeguards to owners in return for what is very often, in the international field, a conscious surrender of sovereignty by a government or government entity owner.

Owners as a class have not been well served by the standard forms in many developed western countries, while Western governments have shown themselves producer-orientated with little consumerist interest on owners' behalf, even where the owner is also the taxpayer. Equally, international owners have not been well served by the World Bank or UNCITRAL or others in regard to the substantive content of their contracts with international construction contractors.

25 See further particularly for these serious procedural anomalies CCPP para. 18–14.

On the other hand, there are undoubtedly some highly irresponsible international owners. It is a mixed picture. But in my view strict enforcement of contracts in a disciplined environment, with access to competent courts if they are available, is an essential building block to create the necessary confidence between two inevitably strongly opposed commercial interests. Judicial control, in the form of the correction of mistakes of law or interpretation where it is desired and possible, is an aid, not an hindrance, to that end, as the quite extraordinary international success of the English commercial courts of the last century has very clearly shown.

International construction arbitration should not, in my view, seek to hinder or remove this control if that is what owners desire, because, in the last resort, it is only they who have international arbitration in their gift. For obvious reasons it should be conceded, in the international context, that judicial control by the courts of the host country of the project will undermine the original reasons for choosing international arbitration in the first place. Nor do I, of course, for a moment advocate judicial control in the above sense if owners really do not wish it. The essential "end-user" difference between international construction contracts and other contracts in international commerce should be kept firmly in mind at all points when considering this very difficult problem. The end-user owner must ultimately decide if the attractions of arbitration, international or otherwise, including its very great expense, outweigh the alternatives.

Serious "market research" with international owners by all international arbitration institutions is badly needed, and some form of appellate control over mistakes by arbitrators, whether by the courts of the *lex fori* or whether by some special panel of lawyers giving reasons would, in my view, reinforce rather than weaken confidence in international arbitration.

22 English practice in a continental framework

Anthony Thompson

Synopsis

This paper discusses areas in which continental and English practice differ, including the question of discovery. This is a process apparently unknown to continental lawyers and which they regard with, according to the author, "incredulity". He also looks at different practices in timing, venue and procedure.

Introduction

Most English solicitors and barristers tend to look upon arbitration as a slightly inferior but otherwise identical form of procedure to a High Court action. This is probably due to a rightful recognition of the very high calibre of English judges, and a chauvinistic and thoroughly misplaced belief that English practice and procedure are probably the only, and certainly the best available machinery for achieving the just result. Our continental brethren tend to see the position differently.

Continental practice

There can be very few Requests for Arbitration or Defendants' Answers which enter the portals of the ICC in Paris which measure up to the standards of pleading set by the average English junior when drafting a Statement of Claim or Defence. The inclusions of evidence in what is regarded as a pleading, the omissions of particularity and similar heresies would soon have any self-respecting English pleader reaching for his pen, and long before finishing the reading of the document he would have in mind a sizeable request for particulars and possibly a summons to strike out as well. But does it really matter?

English pleadings

The object of pleadings is said to be to identify and to limit the issues in dispute between the parties. It should be possible to do that succinctly, yet even in the Commercial Court where Order 72, rule 7(1) specifically requires that "The pleadings . . . must be as brief as possible" there is often considerable prolixity. I have personally experienced pleadings in that Court, admittedly in a very complex case, which exceeded 100 pages.

Whatever the requirements of pleadings in the English legal system there can be no justification for trying to incorporate them into an international arbitration and foisting them on unwary foreigners.

It is important to bear in mind that the majority of parties who agree to resolving their disputes by arbitration do so with the earnest desire of obtaining a fair and rapid result after an informal hearing in private before a tribunal which is sympathetic to and understanding of their problems and which is neither formalistic in approach nor over concerned with its own dignity.

Terms of Reference

It seems to me that if the Terms of Reference are properly drafted and contain a careful distillation of the issues set out in the Request for Arbitration and the Defendant's Answer and Counterclaim (if any) there can be no need and no justification for any further pleadings other than a Defence to Counterclaim where appropriate. This does involve some effort on the part of the Arbitral Tribunal in making sure that the issues have been appropriately defined. The representatives of the parties will however be present at the signing of the Terms of Reference, and they can usually be relied upon to ensure that every issue which they wish to have resolved has been appropriately listed, with one notable exception, to which I will now come.

Proper law

The one issue for which the parties invariably omit to cater is that of the proper law to be applied. Although the agreement between the parties will have contained an arbitration clause, or the parties will subsequently have agreed upon arbitration in some other way, as for instance by exchange of letters, they all too rarely agree upon the proper law, and even when they do under certain systems of law such an agreement may be *ultra vires*.

There may be no dispute as to the proper law; it may be clear and obvious which system of law should be applied; but if one party is going to rely upon the law of Saudi Arabia and the other on the French Civil Code it is helpful to know that in advance, and to remember that that most arrogant of all English assumptions, namely that foreign law is the same as English law unless the contrary is proved, does not apply to international arbitrations.

Procedure

Continental lawyers never cease to be amazed, or perhaps I should say horrified, at the length of oral hearings in English courts. The Commercial Court judges and the Official Referees have succeeded in making substantial inroads into the time spent in oral hearing by requiring the submission of skeleton arguments in advance and the exchange of witness statements between the parties. As the English legal system requires that justice should be seen to be done, and in the days when all civil actions were tried by jurors not all of whom may have been literate, there may have been some justification for Counsel for the claimant solemnly reading out all the exchange of correspondence and all the documents which have been placed before the court.

In an arbitration, however, where the members of the Tribunal are presumably literate and the hearing is in private anyway there is no reason why the members of the Tribunal should not read in advance all the documentation relied upon, that is to say both the correspondence and the contractual documents, as well as the witness statements. This will greatly reduce the amount of time that needs to be taken up with an oral hearing.

The anxiety which I frequently hear voiced is that although the members of the Arbitral Tribunal can read the documentation in advance, will they? Or can they be relied upon to read it properly?

We have all had experience as advocates of the judge or arbitrator who says "Yes, I have read the documents, what do you want to say about them?" for it to be revealed shortly, or not so shortly, thereafter that he either has not read the documents, or if he has that he has not read them properly or alternatively not appreciated which were the significant ones. This is every advocates' nightmare, but what is to be done about it?

It seems to me that the faults lie in all probability on both sides of the table. Judges or arbitrators who say that they have read the papers when they have not must be rare indeed, but those who say that they have read the papers and who have not comprehended them are not so uncommon. This I think is largely due to the excess amount of paper that is put in the average case or arbitration. The word processor, the telex and the fax machine have led to an explosion in the amount of paper which is exchanged between parties who are negotiating, contracting and arguing with each other. The English rules of discovery which require that all documentation which is or may be relevant to any of the issues in dispute should be disclosed to the other side results in all this volume of paper and much more besides being incorporated into the documentation of the case.

Some hapless youth in the office of the claimant's solicitors is usually then required mindlessly to photocopy this mountain of documentation which is then placed in ring files, paginated and thrown at the head of the court or the arbitrator.

I sometimes think that the photocopier is the invention of the devil. If a rule were made that all documentation to be relied upon had to be hand-copied, preferably by the barrister or solicitor introducing the document in evidence, it would have a dramatic effect in reducing the volume of paper.

In recent years in the Commercial Court and in the Chancery Division and also I believe in the Official Referees Courts a practice has grown up of having a separate folder of key documents in cases which involve a large amount of paper.

Supplying the arbitrator with a small bundle of key documents may be the best way of ensuring that the Tribunal does read the documentation before the hearing, but even that has its pitfalls. A sparse collection of documents and letters may be so disjointed as to be incomprehensible. It is therefore necessary that the parties should supply the Tribunal with a skeleton argument which is sufficiently pithy to retain the attention of the reader and at the same time sufficiently reasoned and cross-referenced to the documentation as to make the case coherent.

It will always be appropriate and necessary to place before the Tribunal the whole of the contractual documents between the parties, no matter how long and tedious, but the skeleton argument or draft submissions should highlight the sections which are germane to the present dispute, refer to the passages in the witness statements which are relevant, and address the arguments which it is hoped the Tribunal will accept.

Remember always that a continental arbitrator will probably expect to complete in three days the hearing of a dispute for which an English court would allow three weeks.

Timing

Ideally arbitration should be swift. There are however a number of practical difficulties, some of which are of the parties own making.

As the arbitrators are themselves often busy professional men or women who have numerous other commitments finding a date convenient for all three can present a problem. Even when this has been done it not infrequently transpires that the date is inconvenient for one of the parties or their legal representatives. Provided more than one month's notice is given of the appointment there should be no reason why the parties or their representatives should not be able to attend and agree and sign the Terms of Reference.

The next stage often witnesses the longest delay of all. The Terms of Reference once approved by the court only become operative and the arbitrators can only proceed when the whole of the advance on costs has been duly paid. This prudent provision of Article 9 of the ICC Rules of Arbitration often has a serious delaying effect. A party which is reluctant to arbitrate, or one which anticipates losing (which may be the same thing) will simply decline to pay its share of the arbitration costs fixed by the court. Eventually the party not in default is invited to pay the defaulter's share of the costs. There is an understandable reluctance on the part of most parties to adopt this position, and there is often some further delay before this is grudgingly complied with. At that stage the arbitrators are permitted to proceed to the hearing.

Article 18 which requires the arbitrator to render his award within six months from the time when the Terms of Reference became operative must surely be a pious hope rather than a practical expectation. Again the major problem is finding a date when the arbitrators, the parties, their representatives and any witnesses whom it is necessary to call can be available to attend the hearing.

Provided the arbitrators themselves can agree upon such a date I see no point in giving more than three months' notice of the hearing. English lawyers accustomed to having 12 months or more notice of a fixed hearing date will throw up their hands in despair. In my experience however the reality of the situation is that if parties are given 15 months notice nothing much will be done until about three months before the hearing is due. Then there will be great activity by way of preparation.

My attitude is to cut out the 12 months respite, and let the minds be concentrated immediately upon the impending hearing.

The greatest impediment to an expedited hearing is usually the reluctance of the parties themselves to get on with the job of preparing the case. As an arbitration is a consensual matter there is little that the Arbitral Tribunal can do about it if the parties state that they can neither of them be ready for a projected hearing in May and would prefer a date in October. Unlike the High Court, arbitrators have no means of putting the screws on the parties, and merely to inform them that if they vacate the hearing date in May they may not get another one until the following May could well be counterproductive as this might be just what the parties (or more exactly their legal representatives) are hoping for. This dilemma admits of no obvious solution.

Venue

Article 12 of the ICC Rules of Arbitration provides that the place of arbitration should be fixed by the court, unless agreed upon by the parties. At first blush that would appear to be the end of the matter. Other considerations however may apply.

If both parties are represented by Swiss lawyers and one of the arbitrators is Swiss it may well make more sense to deal with an interlocutory application, at which only the arbitrators and the lawyers are present, in Switzerland rather than in Paris if that is where the arbitration is due to take place. It is clearly less costly and less time consuming for two people to travel to Switzerland rather than for three, four or even five people to have to travel to Paris. For the avoidance of recrimination it is advisable to make provision for such a contingency in the Terms of Reference.

A much more difficult problem arises when subsequent to the fixing of the place of arbitration in a third world country an outbreak of civil war or a change in the political climate makes attendance there hazardous or even impossible if one or some of the parties or witnesses or arbitrators are no longer able to obtain visas to visit that country. The question then arises as to whether the Arbitral Tribunal can sit elsewhere without invalidating the award.

There is a remarkable dearth of English authority on the point. The question did arise for consideration in 1966 in India in the case of *President of India* v. *Kesar Singh*.[1] That concerned an arbitration relating to the

1 53 All India Reports 1966 2JK 113 at 116.

supply of charpoys in Jammu. For reasons that do not appear in the report of the case, but which I believe concerned an outbreak of civil unrest in the Jammu province, the arbitrator decided to sit in Delhi. An attempt to impeach the award on that ground failed, Bhat J in delivering the judgment of the Court of Jammu and Kashmir said that there was no possible justification for the Court interfering with the exercise by the arbitrator of his discretion to sit in Delhi.

In the ordinary course the hearing of the arbitration will be at the appointed place. The discretion invested in the arbitrators to sit elsewhere must be exercised judicially and, I would suggest, for good cause and not merely for reasons of personal convenience, and above all the alternative location selected must not be prejudicial or unduly inconvenient for either of the parties or their witnesses.

It is important also to bear in mind that the place appointed for the arbitration will determine the supervisory court, and it will be to the courts of that place to which any application to impeach or challenge the decisions of the arbitrators will be made, including any purported exercise of discretion to sit elsewhere.

Discovery

In *Riddick* v. *Thames Board Mills*[2] Lord Denning MR described the discovery of documents as a most valuable aid in the doing of justice. After referring to the requirement to disclose on oath all documents relating to the matters in issue in the action he went on as follows:

> "Many litigants feel that this is unfair. I have often known a party, faced with such an order, saying to his solicitor: 'Need I disclose this document to the other side? It will damage our case greatly if they get to know of it.' The solicitors answer is, and must be: 'Yes, you must disclose it, however much it damages your case.'"

That is very much an Anglo-Saxon attitude.

I sometimes think that the English rules of discovery were invented by English lawyers for the benefit of English lawyers. An enormous amount of effort, energy and time are expended, and consequently fees earned, in compiling lists of documents which are or have been in the possession, custody or power of the parties to an action and which relate to any matter in question between them and which contain information which may either enable a party to advance his own case or to damage that of his adversary or which may fairly lead him to a train of enquiry which may have either of these two consequences. Continental systems have no comparable rule, and continental litigants and lawyers alike regard the English rule with incredulity.

The general rule in civil law systems is that all documents which it is intended to use at trial must be submitted in advance to the other party for examination before being produced in evidence. In practice these days that means supplying photocopies to the other side but with a right of

2 [1977] 3 All ER 677 at 687.

inspection of originals when required. Otherwise in the absence of any special relationship (such as co-ownership) there is no duty to make available to the other side documentary or other tangible evidence that one does not intend to use, *nemo tenetur edere contra seipsum* (nobody is bound to produce documents against himself).

There is neither need nor justification for trying to incorporate the English rules of discovery into an international arbitration. In the first place the ICC Rules contain no provision for discovery, and an Arbitrator who makes an order for discovery is liable to find that his order is written in water. In the English system the sanction for failure to comply with the order for discovery is a liability to have ones claim or defence struck out, or worse still if the omission is deemed contumacious the miscreant is liable to be committed for contempt. Arbitrators have no such ultimate power.

Conclusion

Parties to an arbitration have arrived there by mutual consent. They seek a swift and fair adjudication of the dispute between them without recourse to the full panoply of the law. Each is entitled to say in effect: "I am right for these reasons and these are the documents I intend to rely upon to prove my case." If the other party can show that there are or must have been other documents which have been suppressed then that will shake the faith of the Arbitrator in the credit of the party in default.

If a party, perhaps egged on by his English lawyers, has no faith in the ability of an arbitral tribunal to do justice without a full blown discovery exercise he has a simple remedy in his hands. When he enters into a contract let him exclude the arbitration clause and bestow sole jurisdiction on the High Court of England and Wales.

The future of international arbitration in the United Kingdom 23

John Uff

Synopsis

This paper examines the claims of London as an appropriate centre for international arbitration. This involves the question of recognition of international arbitration under English law. Consideration is given to possible advantages of English law and procedure, and to the relevant professions which service arbitration.

Introduction

The United Kingdom, and London in particular, has in the past enjoyed pre-eminence as a centre for international arbitration. This has been due to its position as the centre of world trade, with UK companies frequently being parties to the relevant transactions; and to the use of UK inspired contracts and other documentation. The parallel development of an advanced system of commercial law led to the frequent choice of English law to govern the contracts; and this tended naturally towards the choice of London as a venue for international arbitration. The volume of work led to the development of high quality legal services, particularly in London. Whether the availability of action through the English courts to ensure the correct application of English law was regarded as an advantage or not, arbitration awards (including a high proportion of international cases) have made a major contribution to the development of English commercial law.

The last three decades have shown a steady decline in several of the factors mentioned, particularly the United Kingdom's dominance of world trade and the selection of English law to govern international contracts. This would inevitably have led to some decline in the attraction of London as a venue for international disputes; but it is impossible to form a reliable judgment because there are so many variables, not the least of which is the commercial decision in each case whether or not to pursue a formal dispute.

Such statistics as are available[1] suggest that while there are more international arbitration disputes, the proportion using London as a venue has declined. This does not mean that there has been any overall decline in the number, size or complexity of international arbitration disputes using London. Indications are that in real terms there is a greater volume of international dispute work in London than ever before. But this is almost certainly true of most other major venues.

While domestic disputes, whether conducted in court or in arbitration, may be seen in economic terms as a drain on commerce which is best avoided, international disputes brought to the United Kingdom represent a valuable export of professional and other services. Consequently, there is a clear incentive to attract international work to the United Kingdom. The question is whether the commercial law industry, including the courts and the law itself, can offer a sufficiently attractive structure to bring a greater proportion of international disputes to this country for resolution.

What is international arbitration?

There is no generally accepted or satisfactory definition of international arbitration.[2] For the purpose of this paper it is relevant to divide international arbitration into the following categories, based on the type of underlying transaction:

(i) transactions in the United Kingdom which have some foreign element (for example, one foreign party);
(ii) transactions which are partly or wholly foreign but have some close connection with the United Kingdom, (for example, one party being an English company);
(iii) transactions having no connection with the United Kingdom.

Arbitrations arising from category (i) will naturally select the United Kingdom; category (ii) may well select the United Kingdom, but if they do not, this may be for a particular reason unconnected with the merits of the venue. It is arbitration arising under category (iii) where the selection of venue will involve serious consideration of the merits of possible alternatives, and where the United Kingdom in general and London in particular will wish to ensure that its qualities are properly considered.

When does the choice of venue occur?

In many commercial transactions, there is an express choice of arbitration venue, so that the relevant decision is made at the date of the contract. This may constitute a direct choice where the parties consider and select an appropriate venue, or the venue may be stated in a standard form.

Alternatively, where institutional arbitration is provided for, such as arbitration under the ICC Rules, the governing rules will usually provide

1 The ICC publish what are probably the most reliable statistics for international arbitrations.
2 Hunter and Redfern *International Arbitration*, 13.

for the administering body to determine the venue in the absence of an express choice.[3] The usual criterion is to select a neutral venue, but this will, in most cases, leave the choice between a large number of potential places for the arbitration. The choice will clearly depend on perceptions both general and particular, about the suitability of any venue being considered. It may be anticipated that such considerations will be made against a background of generally accepted international criteria for multinational arbitration.

Where arbitration is prescribed by the contract but no venue is selected directly or indirectly, either party is in theory free to proceed to appoint arbitrators in accordance with the terms of the contract in any country they may choose. It would then be a matter for the rules of private international law in the particular country to decide how the venue was to be fixed. The arbitrators, when appointed, may have the power to select the venue, either under the contract or under the relevant curial law. A further alternative is that the parties may agree the venue themselves. In the great majority of cases, however, there is likely to be some means of fixing the venue which operates either at the date of the contract or at the date of the submission to arbitration.

The applicable law

Perhaps as a result of the very attraction of the United Kingdom and English law for international disputes, the United Kingdom has not hitherto developed a special law applying to international arbitration. This is in contrast to a number of other countries with highly developed commercial codes. The form of a special law may vary from particular principles[4] to a comprehensive code applied to international arbitration.[5]

In England, the particular status of international arbitration has been recognised in terms of the enforceability of arbitration clauses, by enactment of the New York Convention of 1958.[6] Arguably, this type of recognition goes further than is needed on account of the very wide definition of "non-domestic arbitration".[7] The courts have made a modest contribution, for example, in refusing to order security for costs in respect of a foreign company being party to an arbitration in London.[8] In general, however, the courts continue to apply precisely the same rules to international arbitrations (including those in category (iii) above) as they apply to domestic arbitrations, including questions of granting leave to appeal[9] and challenge

3 See ICC Rules of Arbitration, Art. 12. Part VI, Appendix II.

4 USA has developed particular principles applying to disputes which are not justiciable for domestic purposes but may be referred to international arbitration: see *Mitsubishi* v. *Soler Chrysler* (1985) 105 SC 3345; and Arb.Int. V2, 116 and 178.

5 For example in Switzerland: see Arb. Int. V4, N.1.

6 Arbitration Act 1975, s.1.

7 See s.1(4).

8 *Bank Mellat* v. *Helliniki* [1984] 1 QB 291: see particularly judgment of Goff, LJ. at 314–16.

9 See *Marine Contractors* v. *Shell Nigeria* [1984] 2 Lloyd's Rep 77 at 82.

to the tribunal on the ground of misconduct.[10] The English courts will pay regard to rules adopted in international arbitration in the same way as in domestic cases.

A further and perhaps inevitable feature of the lack of distinction between domestic and international arbitration under English law, is that there can be no general contracting out of English procedural arbitration law.[11] It is theoretically possible to conduct an arbitration in England or elsewhere in the United Kingdom which does not adopt the *lex loci* as the curial law.[12] However, this would not exclude the supervisory jurisdiction of the English courts. Such provisions of English law as do allow contracting out apply equally to international arbitration as to domestic arbitration, for example, in allowing the exclusion of a right of appeal.[13]

The implementation of the UNCITRAL model law on international arbitration, therefore, poses a dilemma for the UK legislature. The course which the United Kingdom will adopt remains to be seen, but its implementation in any form would create the distinction which English law has eschewed for a century, between domestic and international arbitration. The UNCITRAL law[14] has been brought into effect in many countries, including recently Canada and Australia.

Availability of appeals

The introduction of the English Arbitration Act 1979 is generally thought to have been inspired by the supposed desirability of bringing English law more into line with international arbitration practice, with a view to removing any disadvantage which the previously existing appeal system might have created.[15] In keeping with the established English practice, the new law applied both to domestic and international arbitrations, with very minor exceptions.[16] Its effect was apparently to introduce a general right of appeal on questions of law.[17] But the Act was subsequently interpreted by the House of Lords as creating a severe restriction on the availability of appeals, through the requirement of obtaining the leave of the Court.[18] In effect, appeals are available in only a very small minority of cases, where error of law is plainly shown.[19]

The correctness of the House of Lords' interpretation of the new statute is not in practice open to question, but its effect is very properly the subject

10 *Bank Mellat* v. *GAA Development*. judgment Commercial Court of 12 January 1988. See also generally on question of challenge to arbitrators: Tupman, ICLQ v38 p.36.
11 See Dicey and Morris, *Conflict of Laws*, vol. 1, 540.
12 See *Whitworth Street Estates* v. *Miller* [1970] AC 583 at 616.
13 See Arbitration Act 1979 s.3 and *Marine Contractors* v. *Shell*, *ibid*. Note however that in international cases the parties are permitted to exclude the right of appeal before a dispute arises: see s.3(6).
14 See Hermann, Arb.Int. V2, No.1 and V3, 278.
15 Arbitration Act 1950 s.21: the "Case stated" procedure was generally available on demand.
16 See note 13 above.
17 Arbitration Act 1979 s.1.
18 *BTP Tioxide* v. *Pioneer Shipping (The Nema)* [1982] AC 724, HL.
19 For the detail "rules" applying to the grant of leave, see Mustill and Boyd: *Commercial Arbitration* (2nd ed.) 602–608.

of debate.[20] It is entirely appropriate that an open mind should be kept as to the necessary balance between the achievement of finality and the upholding of proper standards. It may be that the balance should itself be capable of adjustment and the English courts have shown some support for this approach.[21]

Summary of position under English law

International arbitration conducted in England has the benefit of the existing, highly developed, system for domesic commercial arbitration. There are very few special rules applying to international arbitration. The question whether English law applied to international arbitration should be modified in the future is properly a subject of debate and mature consideration. Without doubt, the opinions and wishes of the international commercial community and particularly of the international institutions will be considered in any further development.

Particular advantages of English Law

The general applicability of English commercial law in international arbitration means that parties are able to take advantage of particular features of the law.

Discovery

One such feature is the availability of discovery of documents, given statutory effect in arbitration by the Arbitration Act 1950.[22] The power of the courts to order discovery in an arbitration is discretionary. Consequently, it may be anticipated that the courts, in exercising their discretion, will have regard to the degree of connection of the dispute and the parties with England.[23] Further, since the ordering of discovery is initially within the discretion of the arbitrator, it may be anticipated that the particular procedural rules imposed or adopted and the opinion of the arbitrators would be regarded as relevant and material. The parties may agree to dispense with discovery, and such an agreement would undoubtedly be respected in an international arbitration.

Settlement and conciliation

English law recognises, and where appropriate, supports attempts to conciliate and settle disputes. For example, there is a well developed system of

20 See paper of Professor Ian Duncan Wallace.
21 *Antaios Comp. Naviera SA* v. *Salen Rederierna AB (The Antaios)* [1985] AC 191; *Aden Refinery* v. *Ugland Management* [1987] QB 650.
22 Arbitration Act 1950 s.12(1), 12(6)(b).
23 There is no direct authority, but see *Bank Mellat* v. *Helliniki* (*ibid*).

law which renders privileged certain documents written with a view to achieving settlement.[24] A clear distinction is drawn, however, between the formal dispute process and settlement, such that the two are regarded as mutually inconsistent. English arbitration law and practice clearly requires arbitrators to refrain from "entering the fray" or becoming involved in the argument or merits of the case.[25] Separate and well-developed procedures are available for various conciliation processes.[26] A conciliator may subsequently be appointed as arbitrator but this will require express agreement. Whether or not the English view of conciliation is regarded as superior to, for example, the French acceptance of *amiable composition* as part of the arbitration process, the English position is quite clear.

Costs

Under the English Arbitration Acts the High Court may, in theory, be utilised for the purpose of taxation of costs in an international case.[27] However, the more usual practice in international arbitration is for the amount of any costs to be awarded to be determined by the arbitrators.[28] Often the parties agree to bear their own costs of legal representation. In such a case, English law may render such agreement void;[29] but this difficulty may be overcome by a fresh agreement after the dispute has come into existence.

Representation

A most material factor in the choice of venue will be the freedom to be represented as a party may choose. In some countries, statutory or other rules require either representation by members of the local legal profession or admission of the foreign advocate to the local Bar, this being a matter of discretion. No such restrictive practices operate in the United Kingdom. Parties are perfectly free to be represented by members of the English legal profession or by their own foreign legal advisers. Parties may also employ non-legal advocates or they may choose to use in-house representation. Many non-United Kingdom corporations maintain in-house counsel who regularly represent them in arbitrations.

Experts

English law and procedure possesses a number of distinct characteristics regarding the provision of expert evidence. Experts are not required to

24 For example, those marked "Without Prejudice". See *Cutts* v. *Head* [1984] Ch 290; *Calderbank* v. *Calderbank* (1976) Fam 93.
25 Arbitration Act 1950 s.23: See also Mustill and Boyd, *ibid.* at 550.
26 See *e.g.* Proceedings of Conference on New Concepts in the Resolution of Disputes in International Construction Contracts, London, 15–16 June 1989.
27 Arbitration Act 1950 s.18(2).
28 Also contemplated by Arbitration Act 1950 s.18(1); see also ICC Rules of Arbitration, Art. 20.
29 Arbitration Act 1950 s.18(3).

qualify or be admitted as experts[30] and there are no mandatory requirements to be satisfied.[31] The relatively informal procedure for the admission of experts may be considered an advantage, particularly in the context of a relatively unstructured arbitration. English rules of court make detailed provision for the submission of experts' reports.[32] In consequence, UK experts have developed extensive expertise in the techniques of presentation and assessment of expert evidence.

There is available throughout the United Kingdom a large number of comparatively small specialist firms of consultants in all technical fields. Consequently, experienced individual experts are readily available to take on arbitration assignments. Likewise, such experts are available to act as advisers to the arbitration tribunal. The relevant professional bodies[33] enforce appropriate standards of independence and probity. In addition to the primary professional bodies, the British Academy of Experts, aims to lay down uniform and acceptable rules for all types of expert.

Legal services

The United Kingdom and London in particular has available an unrivalled range of legal services, together with a considerable experience in international work. The use of English legal services permits the separate employment of solicitors to undertake advisory preparation and investigatory work. In addition, or alternatively, specialist advocacy services are available from the independent Bar. Where parties in international cases are represented by foreign law firms, members of the Bar may be instructed directly.

Both branches of the English legal profession maintain regular and strong foreign connections, so that advice and other services at the foreign locus of the dispute are readily available.

There is extensive expertise available, particularly in London, in the field of international arbitration, including ICC arbitrations. This expertise includes the particular blending of English procedural rules with the ICC Rules of Arbitration. A particular procedural feature of English arbitration and litigation is the technique of cross-examination. This is rarely practised outside the common law system. One of its supposed disadvantages is the time taken up in oral probing of the opposing case. In a number of ICC cases involving UK practitioners, procedures have been developed by the arbitrators and the parties to produce a satisfactory compromise between the necessarily truncated procedures envisaged by the ICC Rules and full English adversarial procedure. This may take various forms, usually including specifying the time available to each party for advancing the case orally, the time being apportioned as the particular party wishes. This has generally been found to be workable, effective and highly efficient in economic terms, so much so that it is tending to be adopted in domestic arbitrations as well.

30 As in, for example, USA.

31 *James Longley & Co.* v. *SWR Health Authority* (1983) 25 BLR 56.

32 RSC Ord. 38. These provisions apply also to arbitration in England; see Civil Evidence Act 1968, ss.2(4), 5(2), 10(3).

33 The Association of Consulting Engineers, the Institution of Civil Engineers, and many others.

In general, English procedure and the ICC Rules can be combined to form a most effective investigatory procedure.

In an earlier paper discussing the merits of England as a forum for arbitration in international construction disputes,[34] it was suggested that English lawyers showed a tendency to follow High Court civil procedure in international cases, with the result that hearings tended to be protracted. A comparison was drawn (under the heading "A Tale of Two Cities") between an arbitration in London which lasted 70 days, compared to a hearing in Paris which occupied no more than a week, in which only a limited number of documents was produced. That comparison was drawn in 1985. A more up-to-date comparison could be made between an ICC arbitration recently conducted in Paris lasting well over 50 days and an ICC arbitration in London (where part of the arbitral tribunal was English) which, despite adopting reasonably comprehensive discovery of documents, dealt with a substantial number of complex issues in several hearings occupying in all well under half the length of the Paris arbitration.[35]

Thus, UK practitioners have now acquired the particular abilities required to conduct international arbitrations with the degree of expedition demanded by modern commercial pressures without, however, abandoning the techniques of thorough probing for which the common law system is renowned. London bears favourable comparison with the best procedures offered elsewhere. Obviously, if parties choose to conduct arbitrations in London without discovery, even more rapid and summary procedures can be made available.

Arbitration institutions and bodies

London has long and distinguished connections with arbitration in general and international arbitration in particular. The Chartered Institute of Arbitrators was founded in 1915 and has maintained links with the international arbitration field throughout its history. The London Court of International Arbitration is one of the oldest arbitration bodies in the world, having been inaugurated in 1892 as the London Chamber of Arbitration on the initiative of the Corporation of the City of London. The LCIA maintains extensive links through its regional users councils with all major commercial centres in the world.

Both of these bodies maintain harmonious links with the permanent London representation of the ICC, through ICC United Kingdom. The aim of all three bodies is to encourage the flourishing of international arbitration in London, and all have a distinguished record of service to those having recourse to arbitration in London or elsewhere in the United Kingdom.

Through the Chartered Institute of Arbitrators, and through the separate specialist bodies such as the London Maritime Arbitrators Association (LMAA) and the Society of Construction Arbitrators (SCA) there is a strong pool of experienced arbitrators available for international work. In addition,

34 Redfern: ICLR v2, p.3.

35 No detail can be given as, at the date of this paper, neither case is technically completed.

there is a substantial pool of English lawyers who are available for and experienced in sitting as arbitrators.

Conclusions

As the end of the century approaches, and the nations of the world compete for trade rather than empire, the United Kingdom can be seen settling into a well prepared and well suited role as one of the most experienced trading and commercial nations, with a medium sized economy exceptionally well served by the professions and business services. The United Kingdom, unlike most other nations in the world, has a palpable tradition of avoiding sudden and unexpected changes either in political or commercial life. As it has been better said elsewhere, it is a country "where freedom broadens down from precedent to precedent".[36] More specifically, the concept of the acceptable "legal environment" has been suggested as a dominant factor in assessing the suitability of international arbitration venues.[37]

This paper has examined particular aspects of English law and procedure. It should not be supposed that the laws of any country are ideally suited to arbitration. Indeed, one should always bear in mind that, to the practitioner, there is no such thing as "arbitration", there are simply arbitrations. Each arbitration has its own requirements and necessarily some will find the particular features of one country (for example, excluding appeals) more conducive than another. Further, the demands of international commerce are changing at a considerable pace, as witness the enormous growth in the volume of international arbitration work. It is suggested that what any particular country should aim at in terms of attracting international dispute settlement is, first, the achievement of a perceived balance between control and freedom of action; and secondly, provision for adjustment of that balance as is appropriate in the light of developments in international trade generally and arbitration in particular.

It is suggested that the United Kingdom compares favourably with other centres for international dispute settlement in that there is a ready availability of all appropriate services and expertise for the conduct of such disputes, the parties being generally free to bring in their own professional advisers or to use the services available in this country, as they may choose. It would be unjustified to suggest that standards of probity and independence available in the United Kingdom are unique, but the standing of UK professionals throughout the world is such that foreign parties using UK professionals can be confident that these qualities will be brought to bear in the work that is carried out.

Specific reference to arbitration centres within the United Kingdom in this paper have been limited to London. While this is, perhaps, natural having regard to the central and dominant position of London as the administrative capital as well as the centre of the legal profession, there are several other highly important commercial centres within the United Kingdom. Manchester and Birmingham are two such examples within

36 Tennyson (1833): You ask me why.
37 Redfern, *op.cit.*

England, and other parts of the United Kingdom should also be considered as potential centres for international dispute resolution. For example, whilst Scotland retains a distinct legal system, including different domestic arbitration laws, the traditional barriers created by the two legal systems have effectively been breached by the European community rules and proposals are in hand to consolidate the unifying process through new internal rules.[38]

In conclusion, therefore, it is suggested that the United Kingdom presents a strong case as one of the major centres for international arbitration, whether as a "neutral" venue or in disputes having some connection with this country. It is to be anticipated that future developments within the United Kingdom will enhance and consolidate this position.

38 White paper on the Future of the Legal Profession; July 1989, now Courts and Legal Services Act 1990.

The London Court of International Arbitration 24

Bertie W Vigrass

Synopsis

This paper outlines the evolution of the LCIA since its inauguration almost a century ago, concentrating on the special features of its Rules, its procedures, and its world wide "Users" Council structure which is designed to bring together those involved in international commercial dispute settlement – international and multinational industrial, commercial and trading organizations; international lawyers and firms of lawyers; and practising international arbitrators.

Introduction

Based in London, the London Court of International Arbitration (LCIA) provides an international arbitration service available in any venue throughout the world. Its Arbitration Rules are suitable for operation under any system of law and are available in a number of languages. The aim of the LCIA, through its dispute settlement system, is to promote a climate of confidence between companies, firms, state agencies and others involved in international commerce, trade and industry. It is a service arm of the international business community.

History

The LCIA is perhaps the oldest arbitration body in the world today, having been inaugurated in 1892 as the London Chamber of Arbitration on the initiative of the Corporation of the City of London. This name was changed in 1903 to the London Court of Arbitration (LCA) and again in 1981 to London Court of International Arbitration (LCIA). This reflects the present situation as its work is now devoted entirely to international arbitration.

From the outset it operated under the auspices of the Corporation of the City of London and the London Chamber of Commerce and Industry. In 1975 these two bodies were joined by the Chartered Institute of Arbitrators, and the three bodies exercised control through a Joint Committee of Management. In 1986 a major change in organizational structure took place. The LCIA was incorporated as a company limited by guarantee ("LCIA Ltd") and the Board of Directors of this Company took over operational control of the activities of the organization. The involvement of the constituent bodies of the LCIA, to which reference is made above, is maintained through a Joint Consultative Council (the JCC) composed of six representatives from each of the three organizations.

Present structure

The permanent staff of the LCIA is headed by the LCIA Executive Director who is a member of the Board. The staff structure provides for a Registrar (a task at present undertaken by the Executive Director) a Deputy Registrar, and a number of administrative and secretarial staff. The Board exercises general control over the work of the LCIA, but the day-to-day activities and development of the LCIA are a matter for the Chairman of the Board and the Executive Director.

The Board has available to it advice and assistance from the Joint Consultative Council (JCC) and the LCIA Users' Councils which have been formed to cover the major trading areas of the world. There are at present four Councils:

LCIA North American Council covering the United States of America, Canada and adjacent countries;

LCIA European Council covering Europe, including countries of Eastern Europe and also the Mediterranean and Middle Eastern countries;

LCIA Asia-Pacific Council covering countries of South East Asia and around the Pacific rim;

LCIA Pan-African Council covering sub-Saharan African countries.

The key to the effective operation of the international arbitration system which the LCIA seeks to provide is however the LCIA Arbitration Court ("the Court"). This is a truly international body. Its 26 members are carefully selected to provide and maintain a proper balance of leading practitioners in the field of international commercial arbitration, drawn from the major trading areas of the world. Details of membership of the Court appear in Appendix I to this paper.

Evolution of the LCIA Rules

The LCIA (and the LCA before it) has maintained and published Arbitration Rules since it was inaugurated almost a century ago. Prior to 1981 these Rules were based on English Court procedure. In 1981 new Rules were introduced which incorporated an entirely new and radical concept. These

Rules were designed to be as simple and flexible as possible, and to meet the needs of users in all parts of the world. Four years later, in 1985, the LCIA reviewed the operation of the 1981 Rules in the light of changes in legislation, developing trends and the reaction of users. This led to the introduction of the 1985 Rules which apply today. (*See Part VI Appendices.*)

The basic concept remains the same, but a number of new and additional features have been added in the light of modern trends. Under the Rules the parties have maximum possible freedom to agree the manner in which the proceedings are to be conducted. If they fail to agree the arbitral tribunal has the widest possible discretion to conduct the proceedings in a manner which it considers to be most efficient and effective in the particular circumstances of the case. The Rules also provide the LCIA Arbitration Court and the arbitral tribunal, where appropriate, with robust weapons with which to neutralize the dilatory tactics which some parties adopt to undermine the effectiveness of the arbitral process.

The Rules also take advantage of recent national court decisions which acknowledge the right of parties in international contracts to waive the right of appeal against the merits of an award as well as to waive any possibility of applying to national courts for security for costs. When preparing the latest edition of the Rules, the LCIA took into account the deliberations which were taking place regarding the UNCITRAL Model Law on International Commercial Arbitration, as it was felt that these could fairly be taken to represent prevailing contemporary international opinion on various issues of importance in relation to the conduct of arbitrations.

Special features of the Rules

The LCIA, with almost a century of experience in arbitration matters, has designed arbitral rules which are flexible and practical. As such, they permit the parties to focus on the real issues in dispute and can be tailored by the parties and the arbitrator or arbitrators to meet the needs of the parties. This flexibility and practicality also encourages the resolution of disputes between parties who have ongoing commercial relationships.

The LCIA Rules are available in English, French, German and Russian, with Spanish, Portuguese, Arabic and Chinese texts in preparation. They are the basis of the commercially attuned and reliable arbitral system which the LCIA seeks to provide and which has many special and unique advantages such as:

Flexibility

- parties are expressly encouraged to determine for themselves the procedures to be followed (Rule 5.1.) and to agree on as many issues as possible relating to the arbitration;
- where parties are unable to agree, the Tribunal has maximum flexibility to act in the interests of speedy and effective resolution;
- parties may agree to the place and language of the arbitration; failing agreement the Tribunal will decide;

- parties to a dispute may agree to LCIA arbitration even where the contract provides for a different forum or different rules, or where there is no provision for arbitration in the contract;
- LCIA Rules minimise formalities and other restrictions.

Time

- arbitrators are appointed with speed and efficacy;
- prompt disposition of disputes is encouraged;
- issues or challenges relating to the Rules of Appointment are dealt with promptly;
- the LCIA and the Tribunal are provided with effective weapons to neutralise delaying tactics where encountered and where necessary.

Costs

- low registration fee and no initial deposit;
- deposits called for only when payments become due, and all bank interest on the deposits is credited to the parties;
- tight control of costs; all costs are computed on a time basis and not on the amount in dispute;
- preference for sole arbitrators but three may be appointed if the parties so wish.

Finality and enforceability

- no interference by the LCIA with Tribunals or their awards;
- emphasis on enforceability of awards in all jurisdictions.

The LCIA Arbitration Court

The LCIA Arbitration Court was set up in its present form in 1985 as the central body of LCIA. The function of the Court is prescribed by the LCIA Arbitration Rules and by its own Constitution. A copy of the Constitution of the Court appears in Appendix II to this paper.

The Court's main functions under the Rules are: to appoint arbitrators; to deal with challenges to arbitrators; to deal with any other disputes which arise in the course of hearings conducted under the Rules. The Court's functions under its Constitution are to keep the Rules under review; to give directions to the Registrar and Deputy Registrar in relation to pending arbitrations and other matters as necessary; to ensure a fair and proper selection of appointed arbitrators; and to keep its own membership under review to ensure an appropriate regional and national world balance.

When dealing with challenges and other issues which arise during the course of a hearing, the Court operates in Divisions. This is to ensure minimum delay and a quick and final decision on the issue. The procedure in these circumstances is for the President to appoint a Division of three members of the Court consisting of a Vice-President and two other members. The nature of the issue in dispute, together with relevant and geographical factors, are taken into consideration when such a selection is made. It is normal for the Division of the Court, once appointed, to consider the matter and to give a ruling within a matter of days, communicating by telephone, facsimile and letter and perhaps holding a short hearing if appropriate. The ruling of the Division of the Court does not require ratification by the whole Court, as this would only delay matters. This speedy procedure has proved to be entirely satisfactory and acceptable to parties wishing to use its services.

Appointment of arbitrators

Parties are encouraged to agree the number of arbitrators in the Arbitration Clause or when the arbitration takes place. If they fail to agree, the LCIA Arbitration Court, through its President will decide. In the interests of economy and speed, the Court will normally appoint a sole arbitrator unless the parties have agreed otherwise or in view of the circumstances of the case a three member tribunal is appropriate.

The parties may nominate arbitrators, but the Court alone is empowered to appoint arbitrators. Such appointments are made in the name of the Court by the President or one of the Vice-Presidents. This enables the LCIA to act very expeditiously in the appointment of arbitrators. The Court may refuse to appoint nominees of the parties if it determines that they are not suitable, independent, or impartial. Parties may challenge appointments, and these challenges are dealt with speedily by the Court under the procedure outlined above.

Conduct of the Proceedings

Procedure

Parties are encouraged to agree on arbitral procedure (Article 5.1). Where there is no agreement:

> "the tribunal shall have the widest discretion allowed under such law as may be applicable to ensure the just, expeditious, economical, and final determination of the dispute" (Article 5.2.).

Submission of written statements and documents

Article 6 provides for the filing of written statements and documents by each party. Written evidence should also be filed before the hearing. The intent is to reduce the length of the hearings, and in this respect the Rules borrow from the civil law traditions.

Hearings

Any party has the right to be heard before the Tribunal, unless of course the parties have agreed to a "documents only" procedure. This does not however apply to oral witness testimony. Article 11.2. provides that:

> "the Tribunal has discretion to allow, refuse, or limit the appearance of witnesses".

The testimony of witnesses may however be presented in written form (Article 11.2). This is a useful way of limiting the length of hearings. Generally a witness who has given oral testimony will be made available for oral examination if the other party requests it, although again the Tribunal has discretionary powers (Article 11.4).

Discovery

The Rules provide for a compromise in respect of the unpopular matter of discovery of documents. Article 6.6 requires the parties to submit copies of all essential documents on which they rely with their Statement of Case. Article 13.1 (i) gives the tribunal power to order any party to produce copies of all documents or classes of documents which the tribunal determines to be relevant.

Experts

The Rules also provide for a compromise in respect of experts and draw on both common and civil law procedures. Article 12 provides the tribunal with a procedural device which may permit it to shorten the arbitral process in appropriate cases by securing technical assistance which it deems necessary. It is given power to appoint experts to render reports on specific issues.

This borrows from the civil law procedure, but supporters of the common law procedure should be satisfied as the Rules also provide that the parties may question the "expert" and produce party expert testimony on the point at issue.

Recourse to courts of law

A number of Articles in the Rules are specifically intended to prevent premature recourse to the courts of law and also to exclude judicial review, where this is possible, by agreement between the parties.

These Articles include:

Article 3.9 – relating to the appointment of the tribunal;
Article 13.2 – relating to the production and preservation of property and documents;

Article 14 – which gives power to the Tribunal to rule on its own jurisdiction;
Article 15 – which gives the tribunal power to order deposits and security and forbids parties requesting such relief from the courts of law;
Article 16.8 – which constitutes an exclusion agreement.

The award

There is no interference or administrative review by the LCIA Arbitration Court in matters related to the award of the tribunal. As far as the Rules are concerned Article 16 provides that:

- the tribunal shall render a reasoned award, unless the parties agree otherwise;
- if not unanimous, then a majority, of if there is no majority then the chairman decides;
- the award may be rendered in any currency;
- the tribunal may order simple or compound interest at any rate it deems appropriate;
- the tribunal has power to rectify an Award in respect of errors of computation, clerical, typographical and the like.

Costs and deposits

Fees of arbitrators, as well as administrative charges of the LCIA, are computed on the basis of the time spent on the case (Article 18.1 and the Schedule of Costs). This avoids the criticism that charges based on the amount in dispute may result in under or over compensation for arbitrators and the administration. A copy of the Schedule of Costs appears in Appendix III to this paper.

The daily or hourly fees of arbitrators are charged at rates appropriate to the particular circumstances of the case, including its complexity and any special qualifications of the arbitrators. The rates are advised by the Registrar to the parties at the commencement of the proceedings. The LCIA Rules do not provide for payment of an advance on costs as a condition precedent to the commencement of the arbitration and the appointment of the Tribunal.

The issue of deposits is left to the discretion of the Tribunal. In practice the Arbitral Tribunal makes a procedural order providing for funding of clearly anticipated costs when appropriate, reserving the right to increase the deposit if events prove this to be necessary. The setting of deposits in this way avoids the embarrassing situation of a Tribunal, which has performed substantial services without guarantee of payment, having to hold back the award from the parties until fees and costs have been paid.

A separate bank deposit account is opened for each arbitration and all interest accrued is credited to the party making the deposit. In lieu of a deposit, the Tribunal may at its discretion order alternative forms of security such as bank guarantees or irrevocable letters of credit.

The Rules provide for interim payments covering fees and costs. Article 15.1 provides that the Tribunal:

> "may direct the parties, in such proportions as it deems just, and subject to the confirmation of the Court (the LCIA Arbitration Court) that the amounts are in conformity with the Schedule of Costs, to make one or several interim or final payments on account of the costs of the arbitration".

Case administration

Commencement of an arbitration under the LCIA Rules is relatively simple. The party wishing to proceed to arbitration is required to send to the Registrar (in accordance with Article I) a written request for arbitration which shall include or be accompanied by:

(a) the names and addresses of the parties to the arbitration;
(b) copies of the contractual documents in which the arbitration clause is contained or under which the arbitration arises;
(c) a brief statement describing the nature and circumstances of the dispute, and specifying the relief claimed;
(d) a statement of any matters (such as the place or language of arbitration, or the number of arbitrators, or their qualifications or identities) on which the parties have agreed in relation to the conduct of the arbitration, or with respect to which the requesting party wishes to make a proposal;
(e) if the arbitration calls for party nomination of arbitrators, the name and address (and telephone and telex numbers, if known) of the Claimant's nominee;
(f) the fee prescribed in the Schedule of Costs;

Confirmation is required by the Registrar that copies have been served on the other Parties. The procedure to be followed by the Respondent is set out in Article 2 of the Rules.

If the recommended LCIA Arbitration clause has been used (see Appendix IV to this paper) there is usually no delay in proceeding to the appointment of the Arbitral Tribunal. However, if another form of clause has been used, or if the LCIA clause has been modified in such a way as to cast doubts on the jurisdiction of the LCIA, considerable delays may occur. In certain circumstances arbitration may simply not be possible because of the wording of the clause – unless of course the parties make a further agreement. Parties to a contract are therefore strongly advised to use the "Model" clause without modification.

The parties are not required to agree Terms of Reference. The claimant has 30 days from the date of the appointment of the tribunal to send to the Registrar a Statement of Case setting out in sufficient detail the facts and any contentions of law on which it relies, and the relief claimed. The Respondent then has 40 days in which to submit his Statement of Defence and any counterclaims (Article 6 sets out the procedure for these submissions and exchanges). Arbitrators appointed by the LCIA are provided with general guidelines (a copy is in Appendix V to this paper). They are also required to sign a Form of Acceptance, the terms of which are set out in the guidelines.

LCIA arbitrations are of course "institutional" arbitrations. The Registrar (or his Deputy) has a major role to play at the commencement of an arbitration and at the conclusion when the Award is issued. However, he can serve as an important communication link between the parties, the Court, and the Tribunal throughout the arbitration. Sometimes he can even resolve a breakdown in communication between the parties. The Registrar's department is a repository of how the arbitral process may be expedited and about procedural problems which may arise. It also serves to preserve the momentum of the proceedings, particularly when difficulties arise between the parties or with the Tribunal. In some cases, early discussion of problems with the Registrar can lead to early agreements on procedural matters and even sometimes a settlement.

Other arbitration rules

Whilst the LCIA is of the view that its current Rules have a great deal to offer parties in international arbitration, it is aware that there may be circumstances in which other procedural rules may be more attractive to the parties for some reason. Accordingly it is happy to co-operate fully with other arbitral bodies worldwide which provide for institutionalised arbitration. In particular it offers its services in respect of the UNCITRAL Arbitration Rules to act as appointing authority and to provide full administrative support as required.

The view of the LCIA is that the interests of parties to international arbitration are best served where procedural rules are adopted rather than the ad hoc method.

Conciliation

The aim of the LCIA is to provide a comprehensive dispute resolution service for all involved in international commerce, trade and industry. It is aware that from time to time there are circumstances when parties require a means other than arbitration to enable them to settle a dispute.

The LCIA is prepared to offer systems specially tailored to meet the needs of the parties including conciliation, mediation and adjudication. It decided against preparing special LCIA Conciliation Rules to operate alongside its Arbitration Rules as it considers the UNCITRAL Conciliation Rules of particular merit. It therefore offers to appoint conciliators under these Rules and to provide the necessary administration and facilities.

LCIA "Users" Councils

The concept of "User" Councils emerged when the requirements were being considered, and the Councils were introduced into the LCIA structure in

1987. There are now four LCIA Councils covering the major trading areas of the world as mentioned earlier.

Membership of the Councils is by invitation and LCIA defines "users" of its services as corporate lawyers and others from international and multinational industrial, commercial and trading organizations; international lawyers and firms of lawyers; and practising international arbitrators. Companies, law firms and other organizations exercise their membership through nominated representation.

Present membership of the four Councils is over 500 from 40 countries worldwide. Each country has a President, a number of Vice-Presidents, an Executive Committee and a Secretariat. The Secretariats are based in Washington DC, USA; Zurich, Switzerland; Hong Kong and Sydney, Australia. The Secretariat for the Pan-African Council is in the process of being formed.

The aim is to create and maintain a balanced forum for the exchange of information and experience between lawyers and others engaged in the development and widespread application of arbitration as a means of international commercial dispute settlement. An important function of the Councils is to ensure that the services and facilities provided by the LCIA are continually updated to meet the practical needs of Users of all categories worldwide. All Council members receive copies of the LCIA quarterly journal *Arbitration International* and bi-monthly *Briefing Notes*. They also have access to the comprehensive LCIA information service.

LCIA has appointed National Liaison Members to the majority of the 40 countries from which LCIA membership is drawn, and Special Liaison Members to such bodies as the United Nations (UNCITRAL) and the Commission of the European Community. This network, combined with the LCIA Council Secretariats in North America, Europe, the Asia-Pacific region and Sub-Sahara Africa, provide the base for the comprehensive worldwide information service in commercial dispute settlement matters which the LCIA seeks to provide.

Conclusion

The LCIA provides a comprehensive arbitration and dispute resolution service available for use in any other venue throughout the world. It is essential for the ultimate users of this service – members of the international business community – to be kept aware of what is available, and for the LCIA to identify the changing needs of users and potential users and to react to these. The LCIA, by keeping in close touch with its users' attempts to fulfill this difficult role with, it is hoped, some success.

APPENDIX I

THE LONDON COURT OF INTERNATIONAL ARBITRATION LCIA ARBITRATION COURT ("the Court")

President	
The Rt Hon Sir Michael Kerr	United Kingdom
Vice-Presidents	
Gerald Aksen	United States of America
Jan Paulsson	France
Dr Werner Melis	Austria
Other Members	
Avv Professor Giorgio Bernini	Italy
Clifford A L Clark	United Kingdom
Dr Bernardo M Cremades	Spain
Jean-Louis Delvolve	France
Dr Ottoarndt Glossner	Federal Republic of Germany
Dr Gerold Herrmann	Federal Republic of Germany
J Martin Hunter	United Kingdom
Professor Kazuo Iwastoki	Japan
Dr Fathi Kemicha	France
Professor Pierre Lalive	Switzerland
Professor Sergej N Lebedev	USSR
Dr Horacio A Grigera Naon	Argentina
Fali S Nariman	India
Mrs Tinuade Oyekunle	Nigeria
The Hon Sir Laurence Street	Australia
Professor Jan Rarnberg	Sweden
Kenneth Rokison QC	United Kingdom
Norman A Royce	United Kingdom
Professor Pieter Sanders	Netherlands
Tang Houzhi	Peoples Republic of China
Dr Albert Jan van den Berg	Netherlands
VV Veeder QC	United Kingdom
Registrar	
B W Vigrass	
Deputy Registrar	
Miss J Cubitt-Smith	

APPENDIX II

THE LONDON COURT OF INTERNATIONAL ARBITRATION ARBITRATION COURT ("the Court") CONSTITUTION (effective from 1 January 1990)

A. COMPOSITION

1. The Arbitration Court ("the Court") shall consist of up to twenty-six members appointed by the Board of Directors of LCIA ("the Board") on the recommendation of the Court, of whom up to six shall be from the United Kingdom and the remainder from other countries.
2. The members of the Court shall serve for a period of up to three years and be eligible for reappointment.
3. The Court shall make recommendations to the Board to fill appointments arising from retirements or casual vacancies and on other issues relating to the composition of the Court from time to time as appropriate.

B. OFFICERS OF THE COURT

1. The Officers of the Court shall consist of:
   (a) A President from the United Kingdom appointed by the Board on the recommendation of the Court
   (b) Three Vice-Presidents appointed by the Court. Due regard shall be given to a balanced international representation, and whenever possible the Vice-Presidents shall be from different countries.
2. Presidents and Vice-Presidents may serve for a period of up to three years and shall be eligible for re-appointment.
3. At the request of the President, or if he is not available of the Registrar or Deputy Registrar, any Vice-President shall be entitled to exercise any of the functions and powers of the President.

C. REGISTRAR AND DEPUTY REGISTRAR

There shall be a Registrar and Deputy Registrar appointed by the Board.

D. FUNCTIONS OF THE COURT

1. The Court shall have power to do anything which it may consider appropriate for the proper performance of its functions and shall in particular:
   (a) act as appointing authority under the LCIA Rules, the UNCITRAL Rules, and in any other case where an arbitration agreement provides for appointments by the LCIA;
   (b) perform the functions conferred on it by any applicable rules of arbitration, whether the LCIA Rules, the UNCITRAL Arbitration Rules or any other arbitration rules;
   (c) keep the LCIA Rules under review;
   (d) make recommendations to the Board as appropriate concerning the introduction of new general or specialist rules;

(e) set keep and maintain lists and records (which shall not be published) of potential arbitrators for appointment to arbitrations conducted under the auspices of the LCIA;

(f) promote the objectives of the LCIA and of international commercial arbitration generally.

2. The functions of the Court under 1 (a) and (b) above shall be performed in the name of the Court by the President or a Vice-President, or by divisions of 3 or 5 members of the Court appointed by the President and chaired by him or a Vice-President, or in the case of administrative functions, by the Registrar or Deputy Registrar pursutant to G (i) below.
3. For the purpose of performing specific tasks in relation to the functions of the Court under 1 (c) to (f) above, the President may set up ad hoc sub-committees of the Court chaired by any members appointed by him which shall report back to the Court.
4. In the performance of its functions under this Constitution the Court, its Officers and members shall at all times act independently of the Board.
5. No member of the Court who has any interest in or connection with an arbitration in relation to which the LCIA exercises any functions of any kind may participate in or influence any decision relating to such arbitration.

E. MEETINGS OF THE COURT

1. The Court shall meet as often as required and at least once a year, in London or wherever may be convenient.
2. Meetings shall be chaired by the President or a Vice-President and a quorum shall be nine. The Chairman of the meeting shall have a casting vote.

F. APPOINTMENT OF ARBITRATORS

1. All appointments of arbitrators in the name of the Court pursuant to D1 (a) shall be made by the President or by a Vice-President on his behalf pursuant to B4 above.
2. All members of the Court shall be eligible for appointment as arbitrators, However, the President and Vice-Presidents shall only be eligible if the parties agree to nominate any of them as sole arbitrator or as Chairman, in which event the person nominated shall take no part in the appointment of the Tribunal nor in any other function of the Court relating to the arbitration in question.
3. Appointments shall in all cases be made with due regard for the suitability of the person or persons appointed for the dispute in question. Appointments may be made of persons outside the lists referred to in D1(e) above.

G. FUNCTIONS OF THE REGISTRAR AND DEPUTY REGISTRAR

The Registrar and his Deputy shall

(i) carry out in the name of the Court such day to day operations of the Court and administrative functions under any applicable arbitration rules as may by authorised by the President from time to time;

(ii) service the Court and any division or sub-committee set up under D2 or D3 above.

H. AMENDMENTS

The provisions of this Constitution may only be amended with the mutual consent of the Court and the Board.

APPENDIX III

Schedule of Costs

(effective 1 January 1990)

Administrative Costs

(a) Registration (payable in advance with Request for arbitration – non refundable	£500
(b) Time spent by the Secretariat of the LCIA in the administration of the arbitration (payable with award or on interim invoice)	Per hour £100
(c) Specific expenses such as postage, telephone, facsimile, travel, etc. incurred by the Secretariat of the LCIA in connection with the arbitration (payable with award or on interim invoice)	at cost
(d) Additional arbitration support services, whether provided by the Secretariat of the LCIA from its own resources or otherwise (payable with award or on interim invoice)	as appropriate

Costs of the Tribunal

(e) The Tribunal's Fees will be calculated by reference to work done by its members in connection with the arbitration and will be charged at rates appropriate to the particular circumstances of the case, including its complexity and any special qualifications of the arbitrators. These rates will be advised by the Registrar of the Court to the parties at the time of the appointment of the Tribunal but may be reviewed annually if the duration of the arbitration requires. (By way of guidance, the rates for arbitrators' fees as at 1 January 1990 fell, in most cases, within the following range:	
Time for meetings or hearings	£600–£1500 per day
Other time spent on the arbitration	£100–£300 per hour

However, in exceptional cases the
rates may be higher or lower)

(f) Members of the Tribunal may charge at the full rate or such lesser rate as they consider appropriate for time spent travelling or time wasted by late postponement or cancellation.

(g) Where the Tribunal takes over the administration of the proceedings by arrangement with the Court, time spent by the Tribunal on administration thereafter will be charged at its hourly rate.

(h) Specific expenses incurred by the Tribunal in connection with the arbitration will be charged at cost.

(i) The Tribunal may require interim payments by the parties in respect of its costs, having regard to the duration or anticipated duration of the arbitration.

Notes

(a) Parties are jointly and severally liable to the LCIA for all costs of the arbitration until all such costs have been paid in full, but if any party pays any amount of such costs which the Tribunal directs should be paid by another party, the party paying shall be entitled to recover that amount from that other party.

(b) Value Added Tax may be added as appropriate.

(c) Fees will be invoiced in sterling but may be paid in other convertible currrencies at rates prevailing at the time of payment.

(d) The rates quoted in this Schedule may be reviewed from time to time.

(e) Any dispute regarding administration costs or costs of the Tribunal shall be determined by the Court.

APPENDIX IV

LONDON COURT OF INTERNATIONAL ARBITRATION RULES RECOMMENDED CLAUSES

FUTURE DISPUTES

Parties to an international contract who wish to have any disputes referred to arbitration under the LCIA Rules are recommended to insert in the contract an arbitration clause in the following form:

> "Any dispute arising out of or in connection with this contract, including any question regarding its existence, validity or termination, shall be referred to and finally resolved by arbitration under the Rules of the London Court of International Arbitration, which Rules are deemed to be incorporated by reference into this clause"

Parties are also reminded that difficulties and expense may be avoided if they expressly specify the law governing their contract. The parties may if they wish also specify the number of arbitrators, and the place and language of the arbitration. The following provisions may be suitable.

> "The governing law of this contract shall be the substantive law of . . .
>
> "The tribunal shall consist of . . . (a sole or three arbitrator(s))".
>
> In the case of a three member tribunal, the following words may be added:
>
> "two of them shall be nominated (by the respective parties)"
> "The venue of the arbitration shall be (city)"
> "The language of the arbitration shall be . . ."

EXISTING DISPUTES:

If a dispute has arisen when the contract or agreement does not contain an arbitration clause, or when the parties wish to change a clause to provide for LCIA arbitration, the following form of agreement is recommended:

> "A dispute having arisen between the parties concerning . . . the parties hereby agree that the matter shall be referrred to and finally be resolved by arbitration under the Rules of the London Court of International Arbitration"

Additional provisions as suggested above relating to the governing law, number of arbitrators, venue and language, may be appropriate in certain circumstances.

APPENDIX V

DECEMBER 1988
GENERAL GUIDELINES
for arbitrators appointed by
THE LONDON COURT OF INTERNATIONAL ARBITRATION ("LCIA")

ACCEPTANCE OF APPOINTMENT

1. The current rules applicable to LCIA Arbitrations are the LCIA Rules 1985 Edition. Arbitrators appointed by the LCIA will be required to sign a Form of Acceptance which will state:
   1. I ACCEPT the above appointment.
   2. I UNDERTAKE to act in accordance with the LCIA Rules applicable to this arbitration.
   3. I DECLARE that there are no circumstances liable to give rise to justifiable doubts as to my impartiality or independence and that I will forthwith disclose any such circumstances to the LCIA Arbitration Court and to the parties if they should arise after the date of my acceptance of this appointment and before the arbitration is concluded."

CASE ADMINISTRATION

2. Arbitrators unfamiliar with the LCIA Rules should particularly note the following:
   (i) Arbitrations are usually administered by the Registrar who liaises with the Tribunal and keeps the Tribunal informed as to the progress of the case.
   (ii) All communications between the Tribunal and the parties are to be made through the Registrar (Article 4.1).
   (iii) If the Court determines that it would be appropriate for the Tribunal to take over the day-to-day administration of the arbitration and directs that communication shall take place directly between the Tribunal and the parties, the Tribunal shall ensure that simultaneous copies of all communications, orders or directions are sent to the Registrar, in order that the LCIA is kept fully informed as to the progress of the case.
   (iv) If, following a direction by the Court, the Tribunal takes over the administration of the arbitration, the Tribunal shall take active steps to ensure that the arbitration proceeds expeditiously. The Tribunal should not intervene only on the application of one or other party. Thus the Tribunal should contact the parties when, for example, time limits (whether set out in the Rules, agreed by the parties or directed by the Tribunal) are not complied with, and also when no application for directions is made following the submission of all statements referred to in Article 6. This assists in progressing the case and also ensures that the Tribunal (and the LCIA) is informed of any agreements reached by the parties, e.g. to adjourn the matter generally.

ADMINISTRATIVE COSTS AND FEES

3. Guidelines in respect of procedures related to administrative costs and fees: Background

(i) A party wishing to commence an arbitration under the LCIA Rules is required under Article 1 to pay a fee as prescribed in the Schedule of Costs. This covers the initial administrative costs up to and including the appointment of the Tribunal by the Court.
(ii) All other deposits, payments and fees require the authority of the Tribunal under Article 15.1.
(iii) The daily and hourly fee rates for members of the Tribunal are established at the time of the appointment, but may be reviewed) annually if the duration of the arbitration makes this appropriate.
(iv) Guidelines relating to fee rates for the Tribunal are provided in the 'Schedule of Costs'. The Tribunal may wish to consider making provision for the payment of cancellation fees.

Stage Deposits

(v) When appointed, the Tribunal with the Registrar should assess the likely cost of the proceedings up to and including the preliminary meeting stage. The Tribunal should then order the parties to deposit with the LCIA an amount of money sufficient to cover these costs.
(vi) If there are a number of preliminary meetings or if the Tribunal is required to spend a substantial amount of time considering interlocutory matters or applications, the same procedure should apply in each case.
(vii) When arrangements for the main hearing have been agreed, an order should be made by the Tribunal to cover the likely cost of the hearing in respect of the Tribunal's fees and expenses and the LCIA administrative costs.
(viii) The hearing should not be commenced if the amount ordered has not been deposited by a specified date. The time limit for deposits will have to vary with the circumstances. The Tribunal, for example, may wish to specify cancellation payments to take effect in the event of cancellation. In these circumstances, deposits would have to have been made to cover these payments prior to a date to be specified.

Interest on Deposits

(ix) Monies deposited with the LCIA are to be placed in a deposit account and the interest accruing is to remain with the account and credited to the amount deposited by the parties.

Stage Payments

(x) When stage payments are required to cover the LCIA administrative costs or the Tribunals travel and other costs, the Tribunal should issue the appropriate order to the Registrar to withdraw money from the deposit account and to make the required payments.

Liability for the Tribunal's Fees and Costs

(xi) The LCIA will accept responsibility for the Tribunal's fees and expenses only up to the amount secured from the parties in respect of these items as ordered by the Tribunal.

Part VI: APPENDICES

Appendix I—Specimen Arbitration Documents

Appendix II—ICC Rules

Appendix III—ICC Draft Uniform Rules for Guarantees (June 1989)

Appendix IV—ICC Draft Uniform Rules for Guarantees (September 1989)

Appendix V—LCIA Rules

Appendix VI—FIDIC Clause 67 (3rd and 4th edition)

APPENDIX I

SPECIMEN ARBITRATION DOCUMENTS

The following documents comprise part of a demonstration arbitration conducted according to the ICC Rules. The purpose is to illustrate the procedure in a particular case, which is typical of a substantial volume of disputes in the construction field. The documents are illustrative only: this is not a real arbitration, nor does it bear any relation to any actual case, past or present.

The documentation is not complete, but is intended to illustrate the course of an arbitration from its inception up to the first substantive meeting at which the arbitral tribunal is asked to resolve one of the issues. The documentation concludes with a specimen award. These documents form the basis of a demonstration arbitration during the conference at King's College London on 22nd September 1989, and the specimen award is the award actually prepared by three arbitrators after hearing the oral argument of counsel for the parties.

Index of Documents

TO THE SECRETARIAT OF THE ICC COURT

COMPAGNIE INTERNATIONAL DE TEXAS EN PLASTIQUE SA — CLAIMANT

and

GENERAL ARAB TRADING CORP. INC. — DEFENDANT

REQUEST FOR ARBITRATION

The Claimant hereby requests the Arbitral Tribunal to grant the relief and awards requested on the undernoted grounds

The following are the particulars in accordance with Article 3 of the ICC Rules of Conciliation and Arbitration.

A. THE PARTIES

1. The Claimant, Compagnie International de Texas en Plastique is a company incorporated under the laws of France whose address is:

Maison Houston
25 Avenue Montaigne
Beauvais, France
The Claimant is represented by:
Messrs. Goldman and Higgins
6943 Franklin Avenue
Houston
Texas, U.S.A.

2. The Defendant, General Arab Trading Corp. Inc. is a corporation incorporated under the laws of the Republic of South Yeravani, whose address is:

Progress House,
Avenue Abdullah IV
Yeravani City,
South Yeravani
The Defendant is represented by:
Messrs. Linkfields & Co.,
21 Coptic Street,
London WC1

B. STATEMENT OF CLAIMANT'S CASE

1. The Claimant made a contract (Annex I) with the Defendant for the construction of a chemical plant at Abdullah City, South Veravani, for the manufacture of plastic airframe components in accordance with certain licences (Annex II) negotiated by the Defendant's Agents with the Claimant's associated company, Texas Plastics Inc., for the fixed sums of US$5,785,000 and Yeravani Dinar 256,000 (the contract price).
2. The contract between the parties required the Claimant to deliver the chemical plant complete in accordance with the specifications and performance requirements (Annex III) and for the Defendant to certify handover in accordance with the protocol contained in the said contract (Article 29.7).
3. The Defendant certified provisional handover on 1 February 1988 and final handover on 1 April 1988 (Annex IV) and duly took possession and operated the chemical plant. The said contract required payment of 80% of the contract

price 28 days after provisional handover and the balance 28 days after the certificate of final handover (Article 30.10.7).

4. The Defendant has paid all sums due in Yeravani Dinars but wrongfully and in breach of contract has paid only US$3,285,000 leaving outstanding a balance of US$2,500,000.
5. Despite requests to pay the said balance the Defendant refuses, falsely claiming that the Claimant has agreed to allow a reduction of this sum from the contract price.

WHEREFORE the Claimant claims an award of US2,500,000 together with interest and costs

C. AGREEMENTS AND DOCUMENTS

1. The Contract (Annex I) wherein the claimant was referred to as CITEX and the Defendant as GAT, was made on 25 February 1986 and provided, *inter alia*, as follows:

   Article 2.1.2 : CITEX shall procure, manufacture, erect, commission, complete, set to work and deliver the plant all in accordance with the specifications hereunto annexed and conforming to the licensing agreements also hereunto annexed (Annexes II and III).

   Article 29.7.2 : GAT shall upon delivery in accordance with Article 2.1.2 certify in writing provisional handover of the plant.

   Article 29.7.3 : Upon CITEX providing all proper certificates of compliance with performance requirements contained in the specifications in the contract and upon the plant being put to work for an uninterrupted period of 72 hours GAT shall certify in writing final handover of the plant.

   Article 30.10.7 : On delivery of the certificate of provisional handover there shall become due within 28 days thereof 80% of the contract price and the balance of the contract price shall be due 28 days after the certificate of final handover.

   Article 32.2 : This contract shall be deemed to comprise the whole agreement between the parties hereto, and shall be interpreted solely in accordance with the written terms hereof. No variation hereto shall be valid unless signed by authorised signatories of both parties and witnessed by a Notary Public.

   Article 32.3.2 : Payment under this contract shall not be held up and any dispute between the parties shall be promptly referred for resolution in accordance with Article 35 hereof
   Article 32.5 : This Contract shall be governed and interpreted in accordance with the laws of France.

2. The Agreement to arbitrate is contained in the following Article of the contract:

   35.1 Any dispute or difference arising shall first be referred to the President of GAT and only in the event of this producing no resolution shall the matter be settled in accordance with the Rules of Conciliation and Arbitration of the International Chamber of Commerce by three arbitrators each party having the right to nominate one arbitrator

3. The documents which establish the Claimant's case are the following:

   Annex I: the Contract
   Annex II: the Licensing Agreements
   Annex III: Specifications
   Annex IV: Handover certificates

Annex V: Testimony of John B. Kornhash
Annex VI: Testimony of William C. Goldman
Annex VII: File of relevant correspondence

D PARTICULARS OF ARBITRATORS

The contract (Article 35.1) provides for three arbitrators and for each party to nominate one such arbitrator. The Claimant hereby nominates as its arbitrator the undernoted person:

Dr. Julius Gillis Wetter, Solicitor-Royal, of Royal Palace 11130 Stockholm, Sweden

DATED this lst December 1988

Goldman and Higgins
6943 Franklin Avenue
Houston
Texas, U.S.A.

ANNEX V

TESTIMONY OF JOHN B. KORNHASH

1. I am the Chief Engineer of the claimant company (CITEX). I was seconded for the GAT project from Texas Plastics Inc where I have been a Senior Project Engineer for the past 15 years. My assistant on the site was Engineer Jean-Paul du Luc.
2. The construction of this plant was a comparatively routine operation. I have been responsible for upward of 20 such plants throughout the world and there was nothing special about this one. The plant was designed to manufacture a range of plastic components for the aircraft industry including seats, interior panels and containers for holding in-flight meals.
3. I was not aware at the commencement of the contract where the raw materials and fuel were to be procured from. The contract included the construction of various hoppers, bunkers and fuel tanks, but the materials themselves did not arrive until comparatively late on and there were certain problems in utilising the supplies which were of suspect quality. I reported all these matters direct to head office in Houston, and I was given to understand that these problems were to be sorted out by higher management and the site team were to continue and to do the best that they could.
4. On completion, we tuned the plant to its optimum performance and handover certificates were duly delivered. I had no further involvement with the plant and I am now working on the construction of a synthetic rubber plant in Iceland.

Sgd ....
JOHN B. KORNHASH

ANNEX VI

TESTIMONY OF WILLIAM C. GOLDMAN

1. I am an attorney registered in the State of Texas and resident counsel on behalf of Texas Plastics Inc. I acted on behalf of CITEX in negotiating the contract with GAT for the South Yeravani plastics plant and I was also responsible for negotiating with the agents of GAT the appropriate licensing agreements for use of the necessary know-how and construction and operation of the plant.
2. Towards the end of the project, in late 1987, it was brought to my attention that there were major discrepancies between the input parameters to the plant and the minimal requirements of the contract documentation to the effect that the only viable solution was going to be optimisation and this was duly communicated to GAT. My understanding is that the Defendant duly accepted the shortcomings and that until these were the subject of rectification procedures, the plant had to be taken by the client for what it could produce. Following upon certain discussions in early 1988, instructions were relayed to the site to tune the plant to its optimum performance given the input parameters. The handover certificates were duly given GAT signed by their authorised representative, Mr. A. Burani.
3. I am able to verify that the final instalment of US$2.5M remains unpaid and I believe there is no reason in fact or law why this is so. The Claimant has completed its obligations and is now entitled to payment of the balance due.

Signed ....

W.C. GOLDMAN

IN THE INTERNATIONAL CHAMBER OF COMMERCE AND IN THE MATTER OF AN INTERNATIONAL ARBITRATION

BETWEEN

COMPAGNIE INTERNATIONAL DE TEXAS EN PLASTIQUE SA
CLAIMANT

and

GENERAL ARAB TRADING CORP INC.
DEFENDANT

DEFENDANT'S ANSWER AND COUNTERCLAIM IN ACCORDANCE WITH ARTICLES 4 AND 5 OF THE ICC RULES OF CONCILIATION AND ARBITRATION

Part I

1. The Defendant denies that the Claimant is entitled to the sum claimed or to any sum and further or alternatively claims the sums set forth in the counterclaim herein.
2. The Defendant admits the contract and documents referred to in paragraphs B(1) and (2) of the Claimant's Request. The taking over certificates referred to in paragraph B(3) and Annex IV are invalid and of no effect as the plant is not and never has been complete nor has it been set to work in accoordance with the contract or the specifications.
3. In particular, the plant has never achieved more than 95% of the rated daily throughput and the consumption of raw materials and fuel further exceeds what is stated in the contract. Full particulars are set out in Annex A hereto.
4. The matters set out in Annex A were acknowledged by the Claimant at a meeting in Houston, Texas, on 5th January 1988 when the parties agreed that the contract should be varied by the Defendant accepting the plant as it was and the Claimant accepting a reduction in the contract price (Annex B).
5. Pursuant to the agreement aforesaid ("the Houston Agreement") and not otherwise, the Defendant issued the documents in the Claimant's Annex IV and took the plant over and the Claimant accepted a reduction in the contract price.
6. Further or alternatively the Claimant has committed breaches of the said agreement as set forth in Annex A and the Defendant is entitled to counterclaim damages in respect of the anticipated cost of remedial work, loss of production and loss of profit in the sum of US$10,958,255. Full details of such counterclaims and damages are set out in Annex C.

Part II

1. The Defendant acknowledges the provisions of Article 35.1 of the contract as set out in the Claimant's Request.
2. The Defendant says that the Claimant's claim has not been referred to the President of GAT and accordingly the arbitral tribunal had no jurisdiction over the claim.
3. Conversely, the counterclaim referred to in Part I, Paragraph 6 hereof, was referred to the President of GAT on 5 January 1988 and in consequence the arbitral tribunal had jurisdiction over the said counterclaim.
4. Without prejudice to Paragraph 2 above, the Defendant hereby nominates as its arbitrator:

Mr. Anthony Thompson, QC of 1 Essex Court, Temple, London EC4, England.

DATED the 31st December 1988
Linkfields & Co.,
21 Coptic Street,
London WC1

STATEMENT of Professor Sidi Handani

1. I am the President of General Arab Trading Corporation, a company incorporated under the laws of the Republic of South Yeravani. I was appointed President on the formation of the company, which was set up for the express purpose of the creation of a modern plastics industry in the Republic.
2. I am also a professional attorney in practice in Yeravani City. I am a Notary Public and Barrister-at-Law, having been admitted to the Bar at Lincoln's Inn in 1947. I am also Professor of Law at the University of Yeravani.
3. The contract for construction of the new plastics plant at Abdullah City proceeded without problems until the late 1987, when I was informed by Mr. John Kornhash, the engineer in charge, that they were experiencing problems with comissioning the plant. He attributed these to the feedstock supplied by ourselves, but I made it clear to Mr. Kornhash that CITEX had always been aware of the quality of materials and fuel which were to be provided, and I believe that samples were taken and tested before the contract was signed.
4. It was agreed that these problems should be discussed at a high level meeting and I attended with my colleage Mr. Ali Burani at the CITEX headquarters in Houston on 5 January 1988.
5. At this meeting, I first made it perfectly plain that unless something was done, GAT intended to call the performance bond to the value of US$2.5M, and that this had to be regarded as the minimum level of compensation unless CITEX could guarantee the plant would work in accordance with the specification. This they refused to do and I was accordingly left with the choice of having a plant working below specification or having no plant at all.
6. CITEX agreed to make certain modifications to improve performance at the plant and I agreed that upon this being done, GAT would accept the plant, but only on condition we were to be compensated for the lack of performance. I am quite clear that it was understood and agreed that the sum of US$2.5M was to represent the minimum level of compensation. We would like to have negotiated a higher figure, but realised that the value of the bond was a limiting factor. Accordingly, the result of the meeting was that the contract price was to be reduced by US$2.5M unless CITEX were able to bring the plant up to specification.
7. I refer to Annex C attached and confirm that GAT have suffered considerable losses of production and loss of profit through the inability of the plant to meet the specification. These sums, together with the anticipated costs of remedial work which GAT are advised may be necessary, total well over US$10M.

(Sgd) ....

S. HANDANI

To the Secretariat of the ICC Court

COMPAGNIE INTERNATIONAL DE TEXAS EN PLASTIQUE SA
CLAIMANT

and

GENERAL ARAB TRADING CORP INC.
DEFENDANT

CLAIMANT'S REPLY AND DEFENCE TO COUNTERCLAIM

1. In response to the Defendant's Defence, the Claimant freely admits that the plant has never achieved more than 98% (not 95%) of the rated daily throughput and that the consumption of raw materials and fuel have, on occasions, exceeded the figures stated in the contract.
2. The reason for this, as is well known to the Defendant and has never been denied by them, is that the raw materials and fuel provided for the plant do not comply with the requirements of the licensing agreements and consequently do not comply with the requirements of the contract. Full details of these matters are set forth in Annex VIII.
3. The Claimant further freely admits that a meeting took place on 5 January 1988 at the Houston office of Texas Plastics Inc., such meeting being attended by Dr Nabil Hagami, Ingenieur Jean-Paul du Luc and attorney WC Goldman on behalf of CITEX and Mr. Ali Burani and Professor Sidi Handani (the President) on behalf of GAT. It was conducted part in Arabic and part in French and the matters there agreed were rendered into a Minute (in English) signed by Mr. Goldman and Professor Handani (Annex IX).
4. It is denied that any variation to the contract was agreed at the said meeting, and particularly denied that the Claimant agreed to any reduction of the contract price. The effect of the meeting was that the Defendant acknowledged that it was unable to comply with the requirements of the specification as to raw materials and fuel and consequently the Claimant could not be held to the performance requirements.
5. The Claimant also relies on Article 32.2 of the contract and denies that any purported variation to the contract complies with the requirements of that Article. The Claimant further relies on Article 32.3.2 as precluding the Defendant from withholding payment on the alleged or any ground.
6. The claimant serves herewith the following further documents:
   Annex VIII: Particulars of discrepancies in the Defendant's supply of raw materials and fuel for the plant
   Annex IX: Minutes of meeting of 5 January 1988.
   Annex X: Testimony of Dr N Hagami
7. The Claimant denies that the arbitral tribunal will lack jurisdiction as alleged. The Claimant contends:
   (a) on a proper construction of Article 35.1 reference to the President of GAT is not a condition precedent to arbitration; alternatively
   (b) the claim herein was referred to the President of GAT at the meeting in Houston on 5 January 1988; alternatively
   (c) the Defendant has waived the right to rely on any such reference by seeking an/or asserting the existence of a compromise regarding the sum outstanding to the Claimant, and further by bringing the counterclaim herein.

DATED the 15th February 1989

Goldman & Higgins,
6943 Franklin Avenue,
Houston,
Texas, USA.

ANNEX IX

MINUTES of Meeting 5 January 1989
at Texas Plastics Inc. Houston, Texas

PRESENT: WC Goldman Attorney
JP du Luc Engineer
Dr N Hagami
Mr A Burani
Professor S Handani

This is an agreed record of the points of agreement.

1. GAT would not accept the plant until CITEX had at their own expense made necessary modifications to improve performance. If performance was not improved, GAT would call the Bond for US$2.5M.
2. CITEX agreed to make the necessary modifications but stated that the plant was unlikely to reach spec standard because of feeder supply problems.
3. CITEX and GAT agreed that if the plant did not reach spec standard they would mutually consider the question of compensation up to the value of the Bond.
4. In return for this assurance GAT undertook that they would not call the Bond at this point and would accept the plant when the modifications had been carried out.
5. GAT emphasised that the level of compensation must be equivalent to the Bond, otherwise they would proceed to exercise their rights.

Sgd ....
WC GOLDMAN for CITEX

Sgd ....
S HANDANI for GAT

ANNEX X

TESTIMONY OF DR NABIL HAGAMI

1. I am qualified as an attorney-at-law in Kuwait and France. In 1986 I was appointed as resident agent in South Yeravani for CITEX and have acted in that capacity in the course of the contract for the new plastics plant.
2. In late 1987 I was consulted about certain discrepancies which had been found in the plant's feedstock and I understood the effect of this would be to preclude CITEX from meeting the spec. At this time it was common knowledge in Yeravani City that owing to a downturn in the plastics industry, consideration was being given to abandoning the contract and calling the performance bond. I therefore feared that GAT might use the feedstock discrepancy as an excuse to bring about this situation.
3. I was able to persuade Professor Sidi Handani, who is an old acquaintance, that it would be preferable to hold a meeting in Houston, Texas, to discuss what was to be done. I attended this meeting and it was evident that Professor Handani was fully aware of the true reason why the plant would not operate up to spec, but nevertheless felt obliged to threaten calling of the bond. On behalf of CITEX I also felt obliged to seek to agree a form of words which would satisfy GAT but not otherwise prejudice the situation. I refer to Annex IX which is a minute of the meeting. I believe this does nothing more than state that the parties were going to negotiate. I further believe that it was evident both to Mr Burani and to Professor Handani that they had no moral alternative but to allow the plant to be completed and to pay the price.
4. The meeting was conducted in a variety of languages, including French and Arabic, and there was therefore considerable scope for misunderstanding. However, I believe the outcome of the meeting was perfectly clear, namely, that the parties had left open the possibility of negotiation, but neither party had bound itself to anything.

Sgd. ....
N HAGAMI

INTERNATIONAL CHAMBER OF COMMERCE
CHAMBRE DE COMMERCE INTERNATIONALE

21.05.1989
9511/MB
Compagnie International de Texas en Plastique
SA (France) -v- General Arab Trading Corp Inc.
(S. Yeravani)

Counsel in charge of the file: Mr. Marcel Brown

Sir Edward Eveleigh,
c/o Royal Courts of Justice,
Strand,
London WC2,
UK

Dr J Gillis Wetter,
Solicitor Royal,
Royal Palace,
11130 Stockholm,
Sweden

Mr Anthony Thompson, QC,
1 Essex Court,
Temple,
London EC4,
UK

Dear Sirs,

I. Constitution of the arbitral Tribunal

1. At its last session of May 15th 1989, the Court appointed as Chairman of the arbitral tribunal:
Sir Edward Eveleigh,
Royal Courts of Justice,
Strand,
London, WC2,
UK.
2. The Court at its session of February 20th 1989 confirmed as member of the arbitral tribunal the person proposed by the Claimant:
Dr J Gillis Wetter,
Solicitor Royal,
Royal Palace,
11130 Stockholm,
Sweden.
3. The Court at its session of February 20th 1989 confirmed as member of the arbitral tribunal the person proposed by the Defendant:
Mr Anthony Thompson, QC,
1 Essex Court,
Temple,
London EC4,
UK.

II. Documentation for the arbitral tribunal

1. In accordance with the provisions of Article 10 the Rules of Arbitration I now enclose the file in this case which consists of the following documents:
   (a) submitted by the Claimant:
      Request for Arbitration dated lst December 1988 with Exhibits.
   (b) submitted by the Defendant:
      Defence and Counterclaim dated 31st December 1988 with Exhibits
   (c) submitted by the Claimant:
      Reply dated 15th February 1989 with Exhibits.

2. Amount in dispute

The sum currently claimed by parties amount to:
By the Claimant US$2,500,000
By the Defendant US$10,958,255

3. Place of the arbitration

The Court has determined that the place of the arbitration shall be London.

III. Addresses of the parties and their Counsel

Claimant:
Compagnie International de Texas en Plastique
Maison Houston
25 Avenue Montaigne
Beauvais, France

Represented by:
Goldman & Higgins,
6943 Franklin Avenue,
Houston,
Texas, USA.

Defendant:
General Arab Trading Corp Inc.,
Progress House,
Avenue Abdullah,
Yeravani City,
South Yeravani

Presented by:
Messrs Linkfields & Co.,
21 Coptic Street,
London WC1.

IV. Advance on costs

The arbitrators are requested to transmit to the Court the original of the Terms of Reference in accordance with Article 13, when the Court will verify whether the requests for the advance on costs has been complied with by the parties.

V. Reimbursement of expenses and payment of fees

Please find enclosed a note to the tribunal dealing with expenses. The Court will determine the cost of arbitration including the fees of the arbitrators in accordance with Article 20. upon approval of the draft of the Final Award.

VI. Miscellaneous

The parties are invited to correspond henceforth exclusively with the arbitrators, while forwarding copies of the relevant correspondence to the Secretariat for information.

Yours very truly,

MARCEL BROWN
Secretariat of the ICC
Court of Arbitration

1. Compagnie International de Texas en Plastique, Claimant party
2. General Arab Trading Corp Inc., Defendant party.

ICC Case No. 9511/MB

MINUTES OF MEETING held on 1 August 1989

1. The parties assembled at the Great Eastern Hotel, Fenchurch Street, for the purpose of drawing up and signing the terms of reference. There were the following persons present on behalf of the parties:

   For the Claimant:
   William C. Goldman (Attorney)
   Jean-Claude du Luc (Engineer)
   Miss J Williams (Assistant)
   Mr Vivian Ramsey (Counsel)

   For the Defendant;
   Mr Nicholas Padfield-Jones (solicitor)
   Dr N Hagami (attorney)
   Mr Paul Darling (Counsel)
2. The meeting commenced at 10 a.m. and commenced by the Chairman inviting each party to outline its observations on the draft terms of reference previously circulated.
3. After extensive discussion, Terms of Reference, consisting of a typed draft with manuscript amendments were agreed and signed on behalf of both parties and by the Tribunal by 3.15 p.m. Messrs. Linkfields undertook to prepare and circulate typed copies. The Chairman took possession of the original copy for transmission to the ICC Court.
4. Counsel for the Claimant, Mr. Vivian Ramsay stated that the Claimant wished to make application to the Tribunal to determine certain preliminary issues and/or make a partial award in favour of the Claimant. Counsel for the Defendant, Mr. Paul Darling, stated that the Defendant also wished to invite the Tribunal to make certain preliminary rulings relating to jurisdiction on the claim.
5. The Tribunal determined that there should be a further oral hearing on 22 September 1989 and gave directions accordingly.
6. Consideration was also given as to whether the Tribunal should appoint an expert pursuant to Article 14.2 of the ICC Rules. The tribunal determined that this matter would be held over and considered further at the oral hearing.
7. The meeting concluded at 4.45 p.m., the Chairman expressing the gratitude of the Tribunal to those who attended.

E Eveleigh (Chairman)

ICC Case No. 9511/MB

ORDER FOR DIRECTIONS

Upon hearing the Claimant by its Counsel, Mr Vivian Ramsay and the Defendant by its Counsel, Mr Paul Darling, at the Great Eastern Hotel, Fenchurch Street, EC1 on 1 August 1989, the Tribunal hereby gives the following directions:

1. There shall be an oral hearing on Friday 22 September 1989 for the purpose of considering and ruling on certain preliminary issues namely:
   (a) whether the Tribunal has jurisdiction over the Claimant's claim;
   (b) subject to (a) whether the Claimant is entitled to a partial Award in respect of the claim or some part of it.
2. The Claimant and the Defendant shall each serve written submissions by 1 September 1989.
3. The oral hearing shall be conducted at a venue to be agreed by the parties and notified to the arbitrators accordingly.
4. At the conclusion of the oral hearing the Tribunal will give consideration to whether they should appoint an expert pursuant to Article 14.2 of the ICC Rules for the purpose of investigating the performance of the plant, the alleged defects therein, and the alleged deficiencies in the fuel and raw materials supplied. The Tribunal will consider the oral addresses of the parties before giving a decision.
5. The Tribunal reserves all further directions to the meeting on 22 September 1989.

On behalf of the Tribunal

E EVELEIGH (Chairman)

ICC CASE NO. 9511/MB

TERMS OF REFERENCE

In accordance with Article 13 of the ICC rules of
conciliation and arbitration

The particulars required by Article 13 of the ICC rules are the following:

A. Names and Descriptions of the parties

The Claimant is Compagnie International de Texas en Plastique SA, a company incorporated under the laws of France.

The Defendant is General Arab Trading Corporation Inc, a company incorporated under the laws of the Republic of South Yeravani.

B. Addresses of the Parties

The Claimant's address is:
Maison Houston
25 Avenue Montaigne
Beauvais, France

The Claimant is represented by its attorney :
William C Goldman,
Messrs Goldman & Higgins,
6943 Franklin Avenue,
Houston,
Texas, USA

The Claimant is also represented by counsel, Mr Vivan Ramsay, Barrister.

The Defendant's address is:
Progress House,
Avenue Abdullah
Yeravani City
South Yeravani

The Defendant is represented by:
Mr Nicholas Padfield-Jones, solicitor,
Messrs Linkfields & Co.,
21 Coptic Street,
London, WC1

The Defendant is also represented by counsel, Mr. Paul Darling, Barrister.

Communication shall be deemed validly served, in the case of the Claimant, on its attorney, and in the case of the Defendant, on its solicitor

Summary of parties' respective claims

1. The Claimant claims payment in accordance with a contract dated 25.2.86 for the construction of a chemical plant for the Defendant. The Claimant claims the unpaid balance of the contract price, namely US$2.5M together with interest thereon

2. The Defendant admits non-payment of this sum but contends that the plant does not operate in accordance with the requirements of the contract. The Defendant asserts an agreement to reduce the contract price by the amount of US$2.5M on account of certain defects alleged to exist.

3. Alternatively the Defendant counterclaims loss and damage in the amount of US$10,958,255 representing the anticipated cost of necessary remedial work, loss of production and loss of profits, together with interest on these sums.

4. The Defendant also asserts that the Claimant's claim has not been referred as required by the arbitration clause which is as follows:

> "Any dispute or difference arising shall first be referred to the President of GAT and only in the event of this producing no resolution shall the matter be settled in accordance with the Rules of Conciliation and Arbitration of the International Chamber of commerce by three arbitrators each party having the right to nominate one arbitrator"

5. Accordingly, the Defendant asserts that there is no jurisdiction to entertain the claim.

6. The Claimant contends by way of reply that the raw materials and fuel to be provided by the Defendant pursuant to the said contract were not in accordance with the specification and that this is a condition precedent to the obligation of the Claimant to comply with the contract.

7. The Claimant denies that any agreement was made varying the terms of the contract or affecting the right of the Claimant to be paid. The Claimant relies on Articles 32.2 and 32.3.2 of the contract which are as follows:

Article 32.2: This contract shall be deemed to comprise the whole agreement betweem the parties hereto, and shall be interpreted solely in accordance with the written terms hereof. No variation hereto shall be valid unless signed by authorised signatories of both parties and witnessed by a Notary Public.

Article 32.3.2. Payment under this contract shall not be held up and any dispute between the parties shall be promptly referred for resolution in accordance with Article 35 hereof.

8. The Claimant asserts that the Tribunal does have jurisdiction over the claim because:
(a) reference to the President of GAT is not a condition precedent;
(b) the claim has been referred to the President of GAT;
(c) the Defendant has waived its right to insist on such reference.

D. Definition of the issues to be determined

The issues to be determined by the arbitral tribunal are the following:
(i) Does the tribunal have jurisdiction to determine the claim?
(ii) Was a compromise effective in law made on 5th January 1988, and if so what were the terms of such compromise?
(iii) If such a compromise was made, did it affect the right of the Claimant to be paid the outstanding balance of the contract price?

(iv) If such a compromise was made, did it affect the right of the Defendant to bring the counterlcaim?
(v) To what degree was the performance of the plant not in accordance with the requirements of the contract?
(vi) Did the provision of raw materials and/or fuel by the Defendant accord with the requirements of the contract?
(vii) If the answer to question (vi) is no, was the provision of raw materials and/or fuel in accordance with the contract a condition precedent to the Claimant's obligation to comply with the specification?
(viii) If the answer to question (vi) is yes or if the answer to question (vii) is no, subject to question (iv), in what respects was the Claimant in breach of the contract and what damages flow from any such breaches?
(ix) If the answer to question (vii) is yes, and subject to questions (i), (ii) and (iii), does the failure of the plant to accord with the requirements of the contract affect the Claimant's right to be paid?

E. The Arbitrators' full names and particulars

Arbitrator appointed by the Claimant:
Dr Julius Gillis Wetter,
Solicitor Royal,
Royal Palace,
11130 Stockholm,
Sweden.

Arbitrator appointed by the Defendant:
Mr Anthony Thompson, QC
1 Essex Court,
Temple,
London EC4.

Chairman:
The Rt Hon Sir Edward Eveleigh,
c/o The Royal Courts of Justice,
Strand,
London WC2.

F. Place of Arbitration

The place of arbitration shall be London, England

G. Particulars of applicable procedural rules

The rules governing the proceedings in this arbitration shall be those resulting from the Rules of Arbitration of the ICC and, where those Rules are silent, any rules which the parties (or failing them the Arbitrators) may settle.

The Arbitrators shall not without the written consent of the Parties, act as amiables compositeurs.

H. Further Particulars

(i) The language of the proceedings shall be English.

(ii) A party intending to rely on a document not in English shall furnish an appropriate translation thereof.

(iii) The substantive law to be applied by the tribunal shall be the laws of France.

(iv) The arbitral tribunal shall be empowered to sit whether for the purposes of hearings or otherwise, in any country or place they may decide and the proceedings shall nevertheless be deemed valid.

(v) The arbitral tribunal shall be empowered to make a partial award, which may include:

   (a) final decision on any issue or part of an issue deemed by the arbitrators appropriate to a partial award.

   (b) the award of any sum of money which the tribunal is satisfied is due to either party after taking account of any cross-claim.

SIGNED by the members of the Tribunal and on behalf of the parties:

Sir Edward Eveleigh
Dr J Gillis Wetter
Mr Anthony Thompson QC

Goldman & Higgins
Attorneys for Claimant

Linkfields & Co.,
Solicitors for Defendant

DATED in London this First August 1989

CASE 9511/MB

IN THE COURT OF ARBITRATION OF THE INTERNATIONAL CHAMBER OF COMMERCE AND IN THE MATTER OF AN ARBITRATION

BETWEEN:

COMPAGNIE INTERNATIONAL DE TEXAS EN PLASTIQUE SA

Claimant

- and -

GENERAL ARAB TRADING CORPORATION INC

Defendant

CLAIMANT's SUBMISSIONS FOR ORAL HEARING ON 22 SEPTEMBER 1989

1.0 The Matters to be determined

1.1 At the hearing the Arbitral Tribunal should determine:

(1) Whether the Claimant's claim
  (a) is required to be referred to the President of GAT as a condition precedent to arbitration;
  (b) has been referred to the President of GAT;
  (c) is not required to be referred to the President of GAT because the Defendant has waived its right to insist on such reference

(2) Whether the Claimant is entitled to a partial Award in respect of the claim or some part of it

(3) Whether the Tribunal should appoint an expert pursuant to Article 14.2 of the ICC Rules for the purpose of investigating the performance of the plant, the alleged defects therein, and the alleged deficiencies in the fuel and raw materials supplied.

2.0. Jurisdiction

2.1. The Defendant seeks to deprive the Claimant of its right to have the dispute determined by the Arbitral Tribunal by reliance upon a narrow and highly technical point with which it has not itself complied in respect of its counterclaims

2.2. Consideration of Article 35.1 of the Contract shows that the Defendant's reliance on that Article is ill-founded.

2.3 Article 35.1 provides that "Any dispute or difference arising shall first be referred to the President of GAT and only in the event of this producing no resolution shall the matter be settled in accordance with the [ICC Rules.]"

2.4 In order for reference to the President of GAT to be a condition precedent to arbitration there must be clear language to give that effect. Article 35.1 provides the only remedy is that of settlement in accordance with the ICC Rules. There is no alternative or prior remedy.

2.5 Article 35.1. contemplates that the dispute will be referred to the President of GAT who might produce a resolution. It does not prevent the matter being referred to Arbitration in accordance with the ICC Rules. The ultimate settlement or award will necessarily occur after the Defendant, GAT, has failed to resolve the dispute or difference.

2.6 The dispute is therefore properly referred to the Tribunal who will settle it when necessarily no resolution has been produced by GAT. Accordingly Article 35.1 does not contain a condition precedent to arbitration but rather the expression of a hope, with which the claimant concurs, that the President of GAT can produce a resolution of the dispute.

2.7 In any event Article 35.1 does not contain any express machinery for reference to the President of GAT. The dispute was referred to the President, Professor Sidi Handani, as appears from his statement and the minutes of the meeting on 5th January 1988: see paragraphs 3 and 4 of the statement of Prof. S. Handani (Annex B to Defendant's answer).

2.8 The Defendant has put forward in its Answer a Counterclaim based upon the matters which are the subject matter of the claim. The Defendant has thereby waived its ability to rely on reference to the President of GAT. Alternatively the Terms of Reference include, within their limit, the matters which are the subject of the claim and the Claimant can assert its claim under Article 16 of the ICC Rules. Further the Defendant asserts the existence of a compromise of the dispute and therefore has waived its right to rely on a reference to the President of GAT.

3.0 Partial Award

3.1 As Mr Goldman states in his statement (Annex VI to Request) the handover certificates were duly given by GAT, signed by their authorised representative, Mr. A. Birani. This point is unchallenged.

3.2 Under Article 30.10.7 the Claimant is entitled to US$2.5 million. Article 32.3.2 prevents the Defendant from holding up payment. Accordingly there can be no dispute that the Claimant is entitled to US$2.5 million.

3.3 The Counterclaim can be determined in due course, if the Defendant decides to continue to pursue it.

4.0 Expert

4.1 The Claimant would welcome an expert appointed in accordance with Article 14.2 but believes that the precise scope of the matters to be determined by that expert should await an exchange of expert reports by the parties.

4.2 In principle the procedure suggested by the Claimant would be:

(1) Exchange of experts' reports by the parties.

(2) Definition of technical issues to be agreed by the parties or, in default, stated by each party by letter to the Tribunal.
(3) Terms of reference of expert to be drawn up by the Tribunal.
(4) Report to be produced to the Tribunal and the parties.
(5) Parties to have an opportunity to comment upon the expert's report and ask questions of that expert.
(6) Tribunal to determine the issues on the basis of all the evidence.

Served this lst day of September 1989
Goldman and Higgins
6943 Franklin Avenue
Houston
Texas, USA.

IN THE COURT OF ARBITRATION OF THE INTERNATIONAL CHAMBER OF COMMERCE
AND IN THE MATTER OF AN ARBITRATION BETWEEN

COMPAGNIE INTERNATIONALE DE TEXAS EN PLASTIQUE SA

Claimant

and

GENERAL ARAB TRADING CORP INC

Respondent

RESPONDENT'S SUBMISSIONS

1. Jurisdiction

1.1 On the true construction of Clause 35.1, a valid reference to Arbitration requires
(a) that there must be a dispute or difference between the parties
AND
(b) the dispute or difference must first be referred to the President of GAT
AND
(c) the reference to the President of GAT must have failed to produce a resolution.

This is clear from the wording of Clause 35.1.

1.2 GAT therefore submit that before there can be a valid reference to Arbitration, the three above-mentioned steps must be satisfied. The steps in effect amount to a condition precedent.

1.3 The Clause itself is clear and unambiguous. The words used with regard to ICC Arbitration are in fact those used in standard ICC Arbitration Clauses. This demonstrates that the parties intended to make the reference to the President of GAT a condition precedent. GAT submit that to do so is not unusual in International Commercial Contracts. The policy of the provision is clear - to encourage resolution by negotiation rather than by expensive and time consuming legal proceedings.

1.4 The clause clearly predicates that some disputes will be resolved by agreement as a result of a reference to the President of GAT. It is axiomatic that once there has been a resolution after a reference to the President of GAT, there is nothing to Arbitrate about and/or the Arbitration Clause is inoperable.

2. GAT submit

2.1 There never has been a dispute or difference between the parties about the sum of $2.5 million now claimed. The facts of this matter and the minutes of the meeting of 5 January 1988 clearly show that the parties were *ad idem* as to the following matters
(A) the plant had not and could not reach its specification and/or performance requirements;
(B) $2.5 million represented the minimum level of compensation payable to GAT
(C) Provisional and Final Handover Certificates would be issued on the basis of this agreement.

Such a compromise is, GAT submit, common in international contracts of this size and type.

2.2 Alternatively if there was a dispute or difference, there has never been a reference to the President of GAT of any of the matters in issue upon the Claimant's claim. A reference is a formal matter and must formally request the intervention of the President of GAT to resolve a pre-existing dispute.

2.3 The meeting of 5th January 1988 did not constitute a reference to the President of GAT, the meeting being both informal and preliminary.

2.4 If it did, then it led to a binding contract resolving the dispute, it led to "points of agreement", [according to the title of the allegedly agreed record (Annex IX)] thereby rendering the Arbitration Clause inoperable. The circumstances of this meeting clearly demonstrate that there is and can be no dispute or difference between the parties, any such dispute or difference having been resolved. GAT will submit that the principles of French Law and/or Lex Mercatoria support such contention.

2.5 If in fact there is any dispute between the parties, it is in reality about the subject matter, content and effect of the settlement and/or agreement of 5th January 1988. It is not contended on behalf of the Claimant that such a dispute has been referred to the President of GAT. It has not. Accordingly there can have been no valid reference to Arbitration.

3. The Claimants are not entitled to rely upon waiver

3.1 The issue is one of jurisdiction. Jurisdiction that does not exist can not be established by waiver.

3.2 There has in fact been no waiver

(a) it is the contract of compromise that precludes jurisdiction; it can not at the same time establish it.

(b) the counterclaim is a separate claim and precedurally separate. There can be no question that the service of a counterclaim was itself waiver because the Jurisdictional point is clearly taken in the pleading.

4. Application for an Interim Award

4.1 GAT requests the arbitrators to ascertain whether the Claimant has complied with ICC Rules as to the deposit.

4.2 A partial award should only be made if the tribunal is satisfied that the sum is due to the Claimants.

4.3 The circumstances of this case do not permit the Arbitrators to be so satisfied. On the contrary money is due from the claimants to GAT.

4.4 GAT rely upon the agreement reached at the meeting on 5 January 1988, whether to be regarded as a binding contract of compromise or merely a consensus, as preventing the Arbitrators from being satisfied that any sum is due to the Claimant.

4.5 Certificates of provisional and final handover do not assist the Claimants. Both of them post date the meeting on 5 January 1988 and the contractual effect which they would otherwise have (if any) is subject to and qualified by the agreement and/or meeting.

4.6 Clause 32.3.2 does not require the Arbitrators to disregard GAT's Defence.

4.6.1. The words used do not have the effect of entitling the Claimant to payment pending resolution of a dispute. Nor do they preclude rights to set-off. Clear words would be necessary to achieve that result. On the contrary they clearly predicate the withholding of sums pending rapid arbitration.

4.6.2. There is to put it at its lowest a dispute as to whether any payment is due under the contract. There is therefore a dispute as to whether there is anything to be held up.

5. Tribunal Expert

5.1 GAT submit that before deciding what type of expert evidence is necessary, the Arbitral Tribunal should first identify the issues to which such evidence would be relevant. GAT submit that expert evidence is not necessary and/or admissible in relation to the Claimant's claim, it relating purely to issues of contractual construction.

5.2 GAT contends that there ought only to be a Tribunal Expert in the event that the parties are not permitted to call expert evidence of their own. If there is a tribunal expert as well as party experts, then there will be a duplication and waste of costs.
5.3 GAT prefers that there should be party experts. The Arbitrators will therefore be presented with opposing evidence between which the Arbitrators having had the benefit of cross examination can then decide.
5.4 If there is a tribunal expert, he will effectively decide the technical issues. The parties have referred their dispute to Arbitrators, not to an as yet unnamed expert.

Served the lst September 1989

Linkfields & Co.,
21 Coptic Street,
London WC1

THE INTERNATIONAL CHAMBER OF COMMERCE CASE NO. 9551

Between

COMPAGNIE INTERNATIONAL DE TEXAS EN PLASTIQUE SA
Claimant

and

GENERAL ARAB TRADING CORPORATION INC
Defendant

Before
Sir Edward Eveleigh (Chairman)
Dr Julius Gillis Wetter
Mr Anthony Thompson QC

PARTIAL AWARD

1. Preambles

1.1 By a written contract, signed by both parties, the Claimant undertook to construct for the Defendant a chemical plant at Abdullah City, South Yeravani, for the fixed sum of US$5,785.00 and Yeravani Dinars 256,000.

1.2 The contract contained the following Article:

"35.1 Any dispute or difference arising shall first be referred to the President of GAT and only in the event of this producing no resolution shall the matter be settled in accordance with the Rules of Conciliation and Arbitration of the International Chamber of Commerce by three arbitrators each party having the right to nominate one arbitrator."

1.3 The Claimant submitted a Request for Arbitration with exhibits dated lst December 1988 to the International Chamber of Commerce whose Secretariat sent a copy thereof to the Defendant for his answer. In the said Request the claimant claimed an award of US$2,500,000 together with interest and costs alleging that that sum was due as the balance of the contract price.

1.4 The Defendant submitted an Answer and Counterclaim with exhibits dated 31st December 1988 and the Claimant further submitted a Reply with exhibits dated 15th February 1989. In the said Answer and Counterclaim the Defendant pleaded that the Tribunal did not have jurisdiction to decide the claim, it denied that the Claimant was entitled to any sum, and further or alternatively it counterclaimed US$10,958,255 damages for alleged breach of the contract on the grounds that the plant was defective.

1.5 On 1 August 1989 at a meeting in London the parties and the arbitrators drew up and signed Terms of Reference herein in accordance with Article 13 of the ICC Rules. Further at the request of Counsel for the parties the Tribunal determined that there should be an oral hearing on 22 September 1989 for the purpose of:-

1.5.1 considering and ruling on the following preliminary issues:
(a) whether the tribunal has jurisdiction on the Claimant's claim
(b) Subject to (a) whether the Claimant is entitled to a Partial Award in respect of the claim or some part of it.

1.5.2 considering whether or not an expert should be appointed to investigate the condition of the plant.

1.6 Written submissions of the Parties were served on 1 September 1989, as ordered by the Tribunal.

1.7 An oral hearing was held on 22 September 1989 in London. The Tribunal was addressed by Counsel as follows:
(i) For the Claimant, Mr Vivian Ramsey, Barrister
(ii) For the Defendant, Mr Paul Darling, Barrister.

Counsel elaborated upon their written submissions and invited the Tribunal's attention to documents already submitted with the pleadings including written statements of witnesses. No additional evidence was tendered.

2. Summary of the Relevant Facts as found by the Tribunal

2.1 The contract between the Parties required the Claimant to deliver the plant in accordance with the specification and performance requirements contained therein and the Defendant to certify provisional and final handover. (Article 29.7).

2.2 The plant was delivered to the Defendant and, by its President and agent Professor Sidi Handani, it certified provisional handover on 1 February 1988 and final handover on 1 April 1988.

2.3 The contract required payment of 80% of the contract price 28 days after provisional handover and the balance 28 days after final handover. (Article 30.10.7).

2.4 Article 32.3.2 of the contract provided that payment under the contract should not be held up and any dispute between the Parties should be promptly referred for resolution in accordance with Article 35 set out in Section II above

2.5 The Defendant has paid the contract price less the sum of US$2,500.00.

2.6 At the end of 1987 it was recognised by the Parties that the plant would not operate at maximum capacity as laid down in the contract.

2.7 The Parties are in dispute as to the cause of the plant's insufficiency. The claimant contended that it was due to local feed supply problems for which it was not responsible and the Defendant denied this and claimed that the plant itself was defective.

2.8 The Defendant threatened to call the performance bond of US$2,500.00.

2.9 At a meeting attended by the President of GAT on 5th January 1988 the Defendant undertook not to call the bond as the Claimant agreed to make certain modifications to the plant and if necessary to consider the question of compensation. The Defendant agreed to accept the plant when the modifications had been carried out.

3. Submissions and Findings

Jurisdiction

3.1. The Defendant contended that there was no dispute because the Parties had agreed that the plant could not reach its specification, that US$2,500.00 was the minimum compensation to which the Defendant was entitled and that the handover certificates would be issued on this basis. Alternatively, it was contended that if there was a dispute Article 35 required it to be first referred to the President of GAT as a condition precedent to arbitration and the matter had not been so referred.

3.2 The Claimant argued that Article 35 did not contain a condition precedent. Inter alia, it was said that the wording was not sufficiently precise, but that in any event the matter had been referred to the President and further the Defendant had waived its ability to rely upon a condition precedent by electing to make a counterclaim in this arbitration.

Partial Award

3.3. The Claimant relied upon (a) Article 32.3.2 which it is said requires prompt payment notwithstanding the existence of a dispute or counterclaim and also

(b) upon Article 30.10.7 which it is said requires payment to be made automatically upon certification. Moreover the Claimant denied that there was any compromise and contended alternatively that the compromise alleged would be a variation of the contract, which could only be effective if it was in writing and had been submitted to a Notary Public as required by Article 32.2, which was not the case.

3.4. The Defendant relied upon the alleged compromise and said that writing was not necessary as the compromise was not a variation of the contract, but a settlement of a dispute as to breach of the contract unvaried. Further it was said that it was inappropriate to make a partial award until the counterclaim had been decided.

3.5 Although the contract provided by Article 32.5 that the contract should be interpreted and governed by the laws of France no evidence was called as to the laws of France and Counsel agreed that we should assume that the laws of France and England were the same.

4. *The Tribunal's Determination*

Jurisdiction

4.1 We hold unanimously that Article 35 contains a condition precedent to the effect that a dispute or difference shall first be referred to the President of GAT before the matter may be referred to arbitration. Furthermore, only when the referral produces no resolution may the matter be settled by arbitration.

4.2 We reject the Claimant's arguments to the effect that the Article is not sufficiently specific to require the procedure stated therein to be compulsory before arbitration can take place. We reach this conclusion because the words of the Article seem to us to demand it.

4.3 While it is always possible for parties to express only a willingness to consider other forms of resolution of a dispute before resorting to arbitration Article 35 is couched in imperative terms: "any dispute ..... shall first be referred...." and then "only in the event.". This imperative wording leads us to conclude that a reference to the President must precede arbitration in relation to a dispute.

4.4 However we are not unanimous as to whether there was such a reference. The majority find that there was a reference for the following reasons. When the parties are in contention many points arise for discussion and claims may be variously formulated as being consequent upon matters of the dispute. In one sense the subject matter of the dispute may be crystallized into a simple proposition "Is there liability to pay?". However that liability depends upon other disputed matters. It is necessary first to determine the real nature of the dispute and then to ask if this has been referred.

4.5 The real nature of the dispute was whether or not the admitted inability of the plant to achieve the contractual standard of performance was the fault of the Claimant. Dependent upon this dispute was the ultimate amount of the contract price. Payment consequent upon the certificates would not be final but subject to arbitration.

4.6 The President of GAT was called upon to consider this dispute. In his presence the Parties agreed to follow the solution approved by him, namely further adjustments to the plant and an attempt to arrive at a figure for compensation. This, however, did not resolve the problem. The Parties are still in dispute as to the cause of the plant being unable to perform according to original expectations and requirements. It is this dispute which is now referred to arbitration and consequent upon its resolution will depend the validity of the Claimants claim for US$2,500.00. The majority therefore hold that the Tribunal has jurisdiction.

Waiver

4.7 We do not consider that there was waiver. The counterclaim did not initiate the proceedings. It is *pro tanto* a defence but to a claim where jurisdiction is denied. The Defendant intends to counterclaim only if we decide that we have jurisdiction.

Partial Award

4.8 The matters raised in the answer and counterclaim, namely the alleged compromise, the allegation that the Claimant was in breach of contract and the counterclaim for damages, would, if substantiated, defeat the claim completely. If there was a compromise as alleged and/or the certification was agreed to be subject to conditions which were not fulfilled, which is alleged, then the Claimants could not rely upon the provision of Article 30.10.7 to demand payment within 28 days.

4.9 We do not accept the argument that the compromise alleged must be in writing by virtue of Article 32.2. The alleged compromise seeks to resolve a dispute between the parties as to their rights and obligations based upon the original contract. They do not seek to vary it but to compromise the dispute arising from it.

4.10 In these circumstances it is impossible to determine whether or not any monies are due to the Claimant until we have heard the whole case. We therefore refuse to order any payment by Interim partial award.

5. Appointment of an Expert

Until we know what the precise differences are between the Parties as to the technical or engineering problems in this case it is premature to consider the appointment of an expert and we reach no final conclusion on this matter.

6. Award

Having reviewed and considered the memoranda presented on behalf of the Parties together with the evidence and argument at the hearing we hereby award as follows.

It is declared and ordered that the Tribunal has jurisdiction to determine the Claimant's claim.

Award made in London this 10th day of December 1989

....	....	....
Arbitrator	Chairman	Arbitrator

APPENDIX II

ICC RULES OF CONCILIATION AND ARBITRATION

New Conciliation Rules and amended Arbitration Rules in force as from January 1, 1988

RULES OF OPTIONAL CONCILIATION

Preamble

Settlement is a desirable solution for business disputes of an international character.

The International Chamber of Commerce therefore sets out these Rules of Optional Conciliation in order to facilitate the amicable settlement of such disputes

Article 1

All business disputes of an international character may be submitted to conciliation by a sole conciliator appointed by the International Chamber of Commerce.

Article 2

The party requesting conciliation shall apply to the Secretariat of the International Court of Arbitration of the International Chamber of Commerce setting out succinctly the purpose of the request and accompanying it with the fee required to open the file, as set out in Appendix III hereto.

Article 3

The Secretariat of the International Court of Arbitration shall, as soon as possible, inform the other party of the request for conciliation. That party will be given a period of 15 days to inform the Secretariat whether it agrees or declines to participate in the attempt to conciliate.

If the other party agrees to participate in the attempt to conciliate it shall so inform the Secretariat within such period.

In the absence of any reply within such period or in the case of a negative reply the request for conciliation shall be deemed to have been declined. The Secretariat shall, as soon as possible, so inform the party which had requested conciliation.

Article 4

Upon receipt of an agreement to attempt conciliation, the Secretary General of the International Court of Arbitration shall appoint a conciliator as soon as possible. The conciliator shall inform the parties of his appointment and set a time-limit for the parties to present their respective arguments to him.

Article 5

The conciliator shall conduct the conciliation process as he thinks fit, guided by the principles of impartiality, equity and justice.
With the agreement of the parties, the conciliator shall fix the place for conciliation.

The conciliator may at any time during the conciliation process request a party to submit to him such additional information as he deems necessary.
The parties may, if they so wish, be assisted by counsel of their choice.

Article 6

The confidential nature of the conciliation process shall be respected by every person who is involved in it in whatever capacity.

Article 7

The conciliation process shall come to an end:

(a) Upon the parties signing an agreement. The parties shall be bound by such agreement. The agreement shall remain confidential unless and to the extent that its execution or application require disclosure.

(b) Upon the production by the conciliator of a report recording that the attempt to conciliate has not been successful. Such report shall not contain reasons.

(c) Upon notification to the conciliator by one or more parties at any time during the conciliation process of an intention no longer to pursue the conciliation process.

Article 8

Upon termination of the conciliation, the conciliator shall provide the Secretariat of the International Court of arbitration with the settlement agreement signed by the parties or with his report of lack of success or with a notice from one or more parties of the intention no longer to pursue the conciliation process.

Article 9

Upon the file being opened, the Secretariat of the International Court of Arbitration shall fix the sum required to permit the process to proceed, taking into consideration the nature and importance of the dispute. Such sum shall be paid in equal shares by the parties.

This sum shall cover the estimated fees of the conciliator, expenses of the conciliation, and the administrative expenses as set out in Appendix III hereto.

In any case where, in the course of the conciliation process, the Secretariat of the Court shall decide that the sum originally paid is insufficient to cover the likely total costs of the conciliation, the Secretariat shall require the provision of an additional amount which shall be paid in equal shares by the parties.

Upon termination of the conciliation, the Secretariat shall settle the total costs of the process and advise the parties in writing.

All the above costs shall be borne in equal shares by the parties except and insofar as a settlement agreement provides otherwise.

A party's other expenditures shall remain the responsibility of that party.

Article 10

Unless the parties agree otherwise, a conciliator shall not act in any judicial or arbitration proceeding relating to the dispute which has been the subject of the conciliation process whether as an arbitrator, representative or counsel of a party.

The parties mutually undertake not to call the conciliator as a witness in any such proceedings, unless otherwise agreed between them.

Article 11

The parties agree not to introduce in any judicial or arbitration proceeding as evidence or in any manner whatsoever.

(a) any views expressed or suggestions made by any party with regard to the possible settlement of the dispute;
(b) any proposals put forward by the conciliator;
(c) the fact that a party had indicated that it was ready to accept some proposal for a settlement put forward by the conciliator.

RULES OF ARBITRATION

Article 1

International Court of Arbitration

1. The International Court of Arbitration of the International Chamber of Commerce is the arbitration body attached to the International Chamber of Commerce. Members of the Court are appointed by the Council of the International Chamber of Commerce. The function of the Court is to provide for the settlement by arbitration of business disputes of an international character in accordance with these Rules.
2. In principle, the Court meets once a month. It draws up its own internal regulations.
3. The Chairman of the International Court of Arbitration or his deputy shall have power to take urgent decisions on behalf of the Court, provided that any such decision shall be reported to the Court at its next session.
4. The Court may, in the manner provided for in its internal regulations, delegate to one or more groups of its members the power to take certain decisions provided that any such decision shall be reported to the Court at its next session.
5. The Secretariat of the International Court of Arbitration shall be at the Headquarters of the International Chamber of Commerce.

Article 2

The Arbitral Tribunal

1. The International Court of arbitration does not itself settle disputes. Insofar as the parties shall not have provided otherwise, it appoints, or confirms the appointments of, arbitrators in accordance with the provisions of this Article. In making or confirming such appointment, the Court shall have regard to the proposed arbitrator's nationality, residence and other relationships with the countries of which the parties or the other arbitrators are nationals.
2. The disputes may be settled by a sole arbitrator or by three arbitrators. In the following Articles the word "arbitrator" denotes a single arbitrator or three arbitrators as the case may be.
3. Where the parties have agreed that the disputes shall be settled by a sole arbitrator, they may, by agreement, nominate him for confirmation by the Court. If the parties fail so to nominate a sole arbitrator within 30 days from the date when the Claimant's Request for Arbitration has been communicated to the other party, the sole arbitrator shall be appointed by the Court.
4. Where the dispute is to be referred to three arbitrators, each party shall nominate in the Request for Arbitration and the Answer thereto respectively one arbitrator for confirmation by the Court. Such person shall be independent of the party nominating him. If a party fails to nominate an arbitrator, the appointment shall be made by the Court.

   The third arbitrator, who will act as chairman of the arbitral tribunal, shall be appointed by the Court, unless the parties have provided that the arbitrators nominated by them shall agree on the third arbitrator within a fixed time-limit. In such a case the Court shall confirm the appointment of such third arbitrator.

Should the two arbitrators fail, within the time-limit fixed by the parties or the court, to reach agreement on the third arbitrator, he shall be appointed by the Court.

5. Where the parties have not agreed upon the number of arbitrators, the Court shall appoint a sole arbitrator, save where it appears to the Court that the dispute is such as to warrant the appointment of three arbitrators. In such a case the parties shall each have a period of 30 days within which to nominate an arbitrator.
6. Where the Court is to appoint a sole arbitrator or the chairman of an arbitral tribunal, it shall make the appointment after having requested a proposal from a National Committee of the ICC that it considers to be appropriate. If the Court does not accept the proposal made, or if said National Committee fails to make the proposal requested within the time-limit fixed by the Court, the court may repeat its request or may request a proposal from another appropriate National Committee.

   Where the Court considers that the circumstances so demand, it may choose the sole arbitrator or the chairman of the arbitral tribunal from a country where there is no National Committee, provided that neither of the parties objects within the time-limit fixed by the Court.
   The sole arbitrator or the chairman of the arbitral tribunal shall be chosen from a country other than those of which the parties are nationals. However, in suitable circumstances and provided that neither of the parties objects within the time-limit fixed by the Court, the sole arbitrator or the chairman of the arbitral tribunal may be chosen from a country of which any of the parties is a national.

   Where the Court is to appoint an arbitrator on behalf of a party which has failed to nominate one, it shall make the appointment after having requested a proposal from the National Committee of the country of which the said party is a national. If the Court does not accept the proposal made, or if said National Committee fails to make the proposal requested within the time-limit fixed by The Court, or if the country of which the said party is a national has no National Committee, the Court shall be at liberty to choose any person whom it regards as suitable, after having informed the National Committee of the country of which such person is a national, if one exists.
7. Every arbitrator appointed or confirmed by the Court must be and remain independent of the parties involved in the arbitration.

   Before appointment or confirmation by the Court, a prospective arbitrator shall disclose in writing to the Secretary General of the Court any facts or circumstances which might be of such a nature as to call into question the arbitrator's independence in the eyes of the parties. Upon receipt of such information, the Secretary General of the Court shall provide it to the parties in writing and fix a time-limit for any comments from them.

   An arbitrator shall immediately disclose in writing to the Secretary General of the Court and the parties any facts or circumstances of a similar nature which may arise between the arbitrator's appointment or confirmation by the Court and the notification of the final award.
8. A challenge of an arbitrator, whether for an alleged lack of independence or otherwise, is made by the submission to the Secretary General of the Court of a written statement specifying the facts and circumstances on which the challenge is based.

   For a challenge to be admissible, it must be sent by a party either within 30 days from receipt by that party of the notification of the appointment or confirmation of the arbitrator by the Court; or within 30 days from the date when the party making the challenge was informed of the facts and circumstances on which the challenge is based, if such date is subsequent to the receipt of the aforementioned notification.

9. The Court shall decide on the admissibility, and at the same time if need be on the merits, of a challenge after the Secretary General of the Court has accorded an opportunity for the arbitrator concerned, the parties and any other members of the arbitral tribunal to comment in writing within a suitable period of time.
10. An arbitrator shall be replaced upon his death, upon the acceptance by the Court of a challenge, or upon the acceptance by the Court of the arbitrator's resignation.
11. An arbitrator shall also be replaced when the court decides that he is prevented *de jure* or *de facto* from fulfilling his functions, or that he is not fulfilling his functions in accordance with the Rules or within the prescribed time-limits.

    When, on the basis of information that has come to its attention, the Court considers applying the preceding sub-paragraph, it shall decide on the matter after the Secretary General of the Court has provided such information in writing to the arbitrator concerned, the parties and any other members of the arbitral tribunal, and accorded an opportunity to them to comment in writing within a suitable period of time.
12. In each instance where an arbitrator is to be replaced, the procedure indicated in the proceeding paragraphs 3, 4, 5 and 6 shall be followed. Once reconstituted, and after having invited the parties to comment, the arbitral tribunal shall determine if and to what extent prior proceedings shall again take place.
13. Decisions of the Court as to the appointment, confirmation, challenge or replacement of an arbitrator shall be final.

The reasons for decisions by the Court as to the appointment, confirmation, challenge, or replacement of an arbitrator on the grounds that he is not fulfilling his functions in accordance with the Rules or within the prescribed time-limits, shall not be communicated.

Article 3

Request for Arbitration

1. A party wishing to have recourse to arbitration by the International Chamber of Commerce shall submit its Request for Arbitration to the Secretariat of the International Court of Arbitration, through its National Committee or directly. In this latter case the Secretariat shall bring the Request to the notice of the National Committee concerned.

   The date when the Request is received by the Secretariat of the Court shall, for all purposes, be deemed to be the date of commencement of the arbitral proceedings.
2. The Request for Arbitration shall inter alia contain the following information:
   (a) names in full, description, and addresses of the parties,
   (b) a statement of the Claimant's case,
   (c) the relevant agreements, and in particular the agreement to arbitrate, and such documentation or information as will serve clearly to establish the circumstances of the case,
   (d) all relevant particulars concerning the number of arbitrators and their choice in accordance with the provisions of Article 2 above.
3. The Secretariat shall send a copy of the Request and the documents annexed thereto to the Defendant for his Answer.

Article 4

Answer to the Request

1. The Defendant shall within 30 days from the receipt of the documents referred to in paragraph 3 of Article 3 comment on the proposals made concerning the number of arbitrators and their choice and, where appropriate, nominate an arbitrator. He shall at the same time set out his defence and supply relevant documents. In exceptional circumstances the Defendant may apply to the Secretariat for an extension of time for the filing of his defence and his documents. The application must, however, include the Defendant's comments on the proposals made with regard to the number of arbitrators and their choice and also, where appropriate, the nomination of an arbitrator. If the Defendant fails so to do, the Secretariat shall report to the International Court of Arbitration, which shall proceed with the arbitration in accordance with these Rules.
2. A copy of the Answer and of the documents annexed thereto, if any, shall be communicated to the claimant for his information.

Article 5

Counter-claim

1. If the Defendant wishes to make a counter-claim, he shall file the same with the Secretariat, at the same time as his Answer as provided for in Article 4.
2. It shall be open to the Claimant to file a Reply with the Secretariat within 30 days from the date when the counter-claim was communicated to him.

Article 6

Pleadings and written statements, notifications or communications

1. All pleadings and written statements submitted by the parties, as well as all documents annexed thereto, shall be supplied in a number of copies sufficient to provide one copy for each party, plus one for each arbitrator, and one for the Secretariat.
2. All notifications or communications from the Secretariat and the arbitrator shall be validly made if they are delivered against receipt or forwarded by registered post to the address or last known address of the party for whom the same are intended as notified by the party in question or by the other party as appropriate.
3. Notification or communication shall be deemed to have been effected on the day when it was received, or should, if made in accordance with the preceding paragraph, have been received by the party itself or by its representative.
4. Periods of time specified in the present Rules or in the Internal Rules or set by the International Court of Arbitration pursuant to its authority under any of these Rules shall start to run on the day following the date a notification or communication is deemed to have been effected in accordance with the preceding paragraph. When, in the country where the notification or communication is deemed to have been effected, the day next following such date is an official holiday or a non-business day, the period of time shall commence on the first following working day. Official holidays and non-working days are included in the calculation of the period of time. If the last day of the relevant period of time granted is an official holiday or a non-business day in the country where the notification or communication is deemed to have been effected, the period of time shall expire at the end of the first following working day.

Article 7

Absence of agreement to arbitrate

Where there is no prima facie agreement between the parties to arbitrate or where there is an agreement but it does not specify the International Chamber of Commerce, and if the Defendant does not file an Answer within the period of 30 days provided by paragraph 1 of Article 4 or refuses arbitration by the International Chamber of Commerce, the Claimant shall be informed that the arbitration cannot proceed.

Article 8

Effect of the agreement to arbitrate

1. Where the parties have agreed to submit to arbitration by the International Chamber of Commerce, they shall be deemed thereby to have submitted *ipso facto* to the present Rules.
2. If one of the parties refuses or fails to take part in the arbitration, the arbitration shall proceed notwithstanding such refusal or failure.
3. Should one of the parties raise one or more pleas concerning the existence or validity of the agreement to arbitrate, and should the International Court of Arbitration be satisfied of the prima facie existence of such an agreement, the Court may, without prejudice to the admissibility or merits of the plea or pleas, decide that the arbitration shall proceed. In such a case any decision as to the arbitrator's jurisdiction shall be taken by the arbitrator himself.
4. Unless otherwise provided, the arbitrator shall not cease to have jurisdiction by reason of any claim that the contract is null and void or allegation that it is inexistent provided that he upholds the validity of the agreement to arbitrate. He shall continue to have jurisdiction, even though the contract itself may be inexistent or null and void, to determine the respective rights of the parties and to adjudicate upon their claims and pleas.
5. Before the file is transmitted to the arbitrator, and in exceptional circumstances even thereafter, the parties shall be at liberty to apply to any competent judicial authority for interim or conservatory measures, and they shall not by so doing be held to infringe the agreement to arbitrate or to affect the relevant powers reserved to the arbitrator.

   Any such application and any measures taken by the judicial authority must be notified without delay to the Secretariat of the International Court of Arbitration. The Secretariat shall inform the arbitrator thereof.

Article 9

Advance to cover costs of arbitration

1. The International Court of Arbitration shall fix the amount of the advance on costs in a sum likely to cover the costs of arbitration of the claims which have been referred to it.

   Where, apart from the principal claim, one or more counter-claims are submitted, the Court may fix separate advances on costs for the principal claim and the counter-claim or counter-claims.
2. The advance on costs shall be payable in equal shares by the Claimant or Claimants and the Defendant or Defendants. However, any one party shall be free to pay the whole of the advance on costs in respect of the claim or the counter-claim should the other party fail to pay its share.
3. The Secretariat may make the transmission of the file to the arbitrator conditional upon the payment by the parties or one of them of the whole or part of the advance on costs to the International Chamber of Commerce.
4. When the Terms of Reference are communicated to the court in accordance with the provisions of Article 13, the court shall verify whether the requests for the advance on costs have been complied with.

   The Terms of Reference shall only become operative and the arbitrator shall only proceed in respect of those claims for which the advance on costs has been duly paid to the International Chamber of Commerce.

Article 10

Transmission of the file to the arbitrator

Subject to the provisions of Article 9, the Secretariat shall transmit the file to the arbitrator as soon as it has received the Defendant's Answer to the Request for Arbitration, at the latest upon the expiry of the time-limits fixed in Articles 4 and 5 above for the filing of these documents.

Article 11

Rules governing the proceedings

The rules governing the proceedings before the arbitrator shall be those resulting from these Rules and, where these Rules are silent, any rules which the parties (or, failing them, the arbitrator) may settle, and whether or not reference is thereby made to a municipal procedural law to be applied to the arbitration.

Article 12
Place of arbitration

The place of arbitration shall be fixed by the International Court of Arbitration, unless agreed upon by the parties.

Article 13

Terms of Reference

1. Before proceeding with the preparation of the case, the arbitrator shall draw up, on the basis of the documents or in the presence of the parties and in the light of their most recent submissions, a document defining his Terms of Reference. This document shall include the following particulars:
   (a) the full names and description of the parties,
   (b) the addresses of the parties to which notifications or communications arising in the course of the arbitration may validly be made,
   (c) a summary of the parties' respective claims,
   (d) definition of the issues to be determined,
   (e) the arbitrator's full name, description and address,
   (f) the place of arbitration,
   (g) particulars of the applicable procedural rules and, if such is the case, reference to the power conferred upon the arbitrator to act as amiable compositeur,
   (h) such other particulars as may be required to make the arbitral award enforceable in law, or may be regarded as helpful by the International Court of Arbitration or the arbitrator.
2. The document mentioned in paragraph 1 of this Article shall be signed by the parties and the arbitrator. Within two months of the date when the file has been transmitted to him, the arbitrator shall transmit to the Court the said document signed by himself and by the parties. The Court may, pursuant to a reasoned request from the arbitrator or if need be on its own initiative, extend this time-limit if it decides it is necessary to do so.

   Should one of the parties refuse to take part in the drawing up of the said document or to sign the same, the Court, if it is satisfied that the case is one of those mentioned in paragraphs 2 and 3 of Article 8, shall take such action as is necessary for its approval. Thereafter the Court shall set a time-limit for the signature of the statement by the defaulting party and on expiry of that time-limit the arbitration shall proceed and the award shall be made.

3. The parties shall be free to determine the law to be applied by the arbitrator to the merits of the dispute. In the absence of any indication by the parties as to the applicable law, the arbitrator shall apply the law designated as the proper law by the rule of conflict which he deems appropriate.
4. The arbitrator shall assume the powers of an amiable compositeur if the parties are agreed to give him such powers.
5. In all cases the arbitrator shall take account of the provisions of the contract and the relevant trade usages.

Article 14

The arbitral proceedings

1. The arbitrator shall proceed within as short a time as possible to establish the facts of the case by all appropriate means. After study of the written submissions of the parties and of all documents relied upon, the arbitrator shall hear the parties together in person if one of them so requests; and failing such a request he may of his own motion decide to hear them.

   In addition, the arbitrator may decide to hear any other person in the presence of the parties or in their absence provided they have been duly summoned.
2. The arbitrator may appoint one or more experts, define their Terms of Reference, receive their reports and/or hear them in person.
3. The arbitrator may decide the case on the relevant documents alone if the parties so request or agree.

Article 15

1. At the request of one of the parties or if necessary on his own initiative, the arbitrator, giving reasonable notice, shall summon the parties to appear before him on the day and at the place appointed by him and shall so inform the Secretariat of the International Court of Arbitration.
2. If one of the parties, although duly summoned, fails to appear, the arbitrator, if he is satisfied that the summons was duly received and the party is absent without valid excuse, shall have power to proceed with the arbitration, and such proceedings shall be deemed to have been conducted in the presence of all parties.
3. The arbitrator shall determine the language or languages of the arbitration, due regard being paid to all the relevant circumstances and in particular to the language of the contract.
4. The arbitrator shall be in full charge of the hearings, at which all the parties shall be entitled to be present. Save with the approval of the arbitrator and of the parties, persons not involved in the proceedings shall not be admitted.
5. The parties may appear in person or through duly accredited agents. In addition, they may be assisted by advisers.

Article 16

The parties may make new claims or counter-claims before the arbitrator on condition that these remain within the limits fixed by the Terms of Reference provided for in Article 13 or that they are specified in a rider to that document, signed by the parties and communicated to the International Court of Arbitration.

Article 17

Award by consent

If the parties reach a settlement after the file has been transmitted to the arbitrator in accordance with Article 10, the same shall be recorded in the form of an arbitral award made by consent of the parties.

Article 18

Time-limit for award

1. The time-limit within which the arbitrator must render his award is fixed at six months. Once the terms of Article 9(4) have been satisfied, such time-limit shall start to run from the date of the last signature by the arbitrator or of the parties of the document mentioned in Article 13, or from the expiry of the time-limit granted to a party by virtue of Article 13(2), or from the date that the Secretary General of the International Court of Arbitration notifies the arbitrator that the advance on costs is paid in full, if such notification occurs later.
2. The Court may, pursuant to a reasoned request from the arbitrator or if need be on its own initiative, extend this time-limit if it decides it is necessary to do so.
3. Where no such extension is granted and, if appropriate, after application of the provisions of Article 2(11), the Court shall determine the manner in which the dispute is to be resolved.

Article 19

Award by three arbitrators

When three arbitrators have been appointed, the award is given by a majority decision. If there be no majority, the award shall be made by the Chairman of the arbitral tribunal alone.

Article 20

Decisions as to costs of arbitration

1. The arbitrator's award shall, in addition to dealing with the merits of the case, fix the costs of the arbitration and decide which of the parties shall bear the costs or in what proportions the costs shall be borne by the parties.
2. The costs of the arbitration shall include the arbitrator's fees and the administrative costs fixed by the International Court of Arbitration in accordance with the scale annexed to the present Rules, the expenses, if any, of the arbitrator, the fees and expenses of any experts, and the normal legal costs incurred by the parties.
3. The Court may fix the arbitrator's fees at a figure higher or lower than that which would result from the application of the annexed scale if in the exceptional circumstances of the case this appears to be necessary.

Article 21

Scrutiny of award by the Court

Before signing an award, whether partial or definitive, the arbitrator shall submit it in draft form to the International Court of Arbitration. The Court may lay down modifications as to the form of the award and, without affecting the arbitrator's liberty of decision, may also draw his attention to points of substance. No award shall be signed until it has been approved by the Court as to its form.

Article 22

Making of award

The arbitral award shall be deemed to be made at the place of the arbitration proceedings and on the date when it is signed by the arbitrator.

Article 23

Notification of award to parties

1. Once an award has been made, the Secretariat shall notify to the parties the text signed by the arbitrator; provided always that the costs of the arbitration have been fully paid to the International Chamber of Commerce by the parties or by one of them.
2. Additional copies certified true by the Secretary General of the International Court of Arbitration shall be made available, on request and at any time, to the parties but to no one else.
3. By virtue of the notification made in accordance with paragraph 1 of this article, the parties waive any other form of notification or deposit on the part of the arbitrator.

Article 24

Finality and enforceability of award

1. The arbitral award shall be final.
2. By submitting the dispute to arbitration by the International Chamber of Commerce, the parties shall be deemed to have undertaken to carry out the resulting award without delay and to have waived their right to any form of appeal insofar as such waiver can validly be made.

Article 25

Deposit of award

An original of each award made in accordance with the present Rules shall be deposited with the Secretariat of the International court of Arbitration.

The arbitrator and the Secretariat of the Court shall assist the parties in complying with whatever further formalities may be necessary.

Article 26

General rule

In all matters not expressly provided for in these Rules, the International Court of Arbitration and the arbitrator shall act in the spirit of these rules and shall make every effort to make sure that the award is enforceable at law.

Appendix I – Statutes of the International Court of Arbitration

Article 1

Appointment of members

The members of the International Court of Arbitration of the International Chamber of Commerce are appointed for a term of three years by the Council of that Chamber pursuant to Article 5.3i of the Constitution, on the proposal of each National Committee.

Article 2

Composition

The International Court of Arbitration shall be composed of a Chairman, of eight Vice-Chairmen, of a Secretary General and of one or several Technical Advisers chosen by the Council of the International Chamber of Commerce either from among the members of the Court or apart from them, and of one member for, and appointed by, each National Committee.

The chairmanship may be exercised by two Co-Chairmen; in this case, they shall have equal rights, and the expression "the Chairman", used in the Rules of Conciliation and Arbitration, shall apply to either of them equally.

When a member of the Court does not reside in the city where International Headquarters of the International Chamber of Commerce is situated, the Council may appoint an alternate member.

If the Chairman is unable to attend a session of the Court, he shall be replaced by one of the Vice-Chairmen.

Article 3

Function and powers

The function of the International Court of Arbitration is to ensure the application of the Rules of Conciliation and Arbitration of the International Chamber of Commerce, and the Court has all the necessary powers for that purpose. It is further entrusted, if need be, with laying before the commission on International Arbitration any proposals for modifying the Rules of Conciliation and Arbitration of the International Chamber of Commerce which it considers necessary.

Article 4

Deliberations and quorum

The decisions of the International Court of Arbitration shall be taken by a majority vote, the Chairman having a casting vote in the event of a tie. The deliberations of the Court shall be valid when at least six members are present.

The Secretary General of the International Chamber of Commerce, the Secretary General of the Court and the Technical Adviser or Advisers shall attend in an advisory capacity only.

Appendix II – Internal Rules of the International Court of Arbitration

Rules of the International Court of Arbitration

1. The International Court of Arbitration may accept jurisdiction over business disputes not of an international business nature, if it has jurisdiction by reason of an arbitration agreement.

   Confidential character of the work of the International Court of Arbitration

2. The work of the International Court of arbitration is of a confidential character which must be respected by everyone who participates in that work in whatever capacity.
3. The sessions of the International Court of Arbitration, whether plenary or those of a Committee of the Court, are open only to its members and to the Secretariat.

   However, in exceptional circumstances and, if need be, after obtaining the opinion of members of the Court, the Chairman of the International Court of Arbitration may invite honorary members of the Court and authorize observers to attend. Such persons must respect the confidential character of the work of the Court.
4. The documents submitted to the Court or drawn up by it in the course of the proceedings it conducts are communicated only to the members of the Court and to the Secretariat.

   The Chairman or the Secretary General of the Court may nevertheless authorize researchers undertaking work of a scientific nature on international trade law to acquaint themselves with certain documents of general interest, with the exception of memoranda, notes, statements and documents remitted by the parties within the framework of arbitration proceedings.

   Such authorization shall not be given unless the beneficiary has undertaken to respect the confidential character of the documents made available and to refrain from any publication in their respect without having previously submitted the text for approval to the Secretary General of the Court.

   Participation of members of the International Court of Arbitration in ICC arbitration
5. Owing to the special responsibilities laid upon them by the ICC Rules of Arbitration, the Chairman, the Vice-Chairmen and the Secretariat of the International Court of Arbitration may not personally act as arbitrators or as counsel in cases submitted to ICC arbitration.

   The members of the International Court of Arbitration may not be directly appointed as co-arbitrators, sole arbitrator or Chairman of an arbitral tribunal by the International Court of Arbitration. They may however be proposed for such duties by one or more of the parties, subject to confirmation by the Court.
6. When the Chairman, a Vice-Chairman or a member of the Court is involved, in any capacity whatsoever, in proceedings pending before the Court, he must inform the Secretary General of the Court as soon as he becomes aware of such involvement.

   He must refrain from participating in the discussions or in the decisions of the Court concerning the proceedings and he must be absent from the court-room whenever the matter is considered.

   He will not receive documentation or information submitted to the Court during the proceedings.

   Relations between the members of the Court and the ICC National Committees
7. By virtue of their capacity, the members of the International Court of Arbitration are independent of the ICC National Committees which proposed them for nomination by the ICC Council.

   Furthermore, they must regard as confidential, vis-a-vis the said National Committees, any information concerning individual disputes with which they have become acquainted in their capacity as members of the Court except when they have been requested, by the Chairman of the Court or by its Secretary

General, to communicate that information to their respective National Committees.

Committee of the Court

8. In accordance with the provisions of Article 1(4) of the ICC Rules of Arbitration, the International Court of Arbitration hereby establishes a Committee of the Court composed as follows, and with the following powers.
9. The Committee consists of a Chairman and two members. The Chairman of the International Court of Arbitration acts as the Chairman of the Committee. He may nevertheless designate a Vice-Chairman of the Court to replace him during a session of the Committee.

   The other two members of the Committee are appointed by the Court from among the Vice-Chairmen or the other members of the Court. At each meeting of the Court it appoints the members who are to attend the meeting of the Committee to be held before the next plenary session of the Court.
10. The Committee meets when convened by its Chairman, in principle twice a month.
11. (a) The Committee is empowered to take any decision within the jurisdiction of the Court, with the exception of decisions concerning challenges of arbitrators (Arts. 2(8) and 2(9) of the ICC Rules of Arbitration), allegations that an arbitrator is not fulfilling his functions (Art 2(11) of the ICC Rules of Arbitration) and approval of draft awards other than awards made with the consent of the parties.
    (b) The decisions of the Committee are taken unanimously.
    (c) When the Committee cannot reach a decision or deems it preferable to abstain, it transfer the case to the next plenary session of the Court, making any suggestions it deems appropriate.
    (d) The Committee's proceedings are brought to the notice of the Court at its next plenary session.

Absence of an arbitration agreement

12. Where there is no prima facie arbitration agreement between the parties or where there is an agreement but it does not specify the ICC, the Secretariat draws the attention of the Claimant to the provisions laid down in Article 7 of the Rules of Arbitration. The Claimant is entitled to require the decision to be taken by the International Court of Arbitration.

    This decision is of an administrative nature. If the Court decides that the arbitration solicited by the Claimant cannot proceed, the parties retain the right to ask the competent jurisdiction whether or not they are bound by an arbitration agreement in the light of the law applicable.

    If the Court considers prima facie that the proceedings may take place, the arbitrator appointed has the duty to decide as to his own jurisdiction and, where such jurisdiction exists, as to the merits of the dispute.

Joinder of claims in arbitration proceedings

13. When a party presents a Request for Arbitration in connection with a legal relationship already submitted to arbitration proceedings by the same parties and pending before the International Court of Arbitration, the Court may decide to include that claim in the existing proceedings, subject to the provisions of Article 16 of the ICC Rules of Arbitration.

Advances to cover costs of arbitration

14. When the International Court of Arbitration has set separate advances on costs for a specific case in accordance with Article 9 (1)(sub para. 2) of the ICC Rules

of Arbitration, the Secretariat requests each of the parties to pay the said advances on costs in equal shares, if they deem it advisable.

15. When a request for an advance on costs has not been complied with, the Secretariat may set a time-limit, which must not be less than 30 days, on the expiry of which the relevant claim, whether principal claim or counter-claim, shall be considered as withdrawn. This does not prevent the party in question from lodging a new claim at a later date.

    Should one of the parties wish to object to this measure, he must make a request, within the aforementioned period, for the matter to be decided by the Court.

16. If one of the parties claims a right to a set-off with regard to either a principal claim or counter-claim, such set-off is taken into account in determining the advance to cover the costs of arbitration, in the same way as a separate claim, insofar as it may require the arbitrators to consider additional matters.

Arbitral awards : form

17. When it scrutinizes draft arbitral awards in accordance with Article 21 of the ICC Rules of Arbitration, the International Court of Arbitration pays particular attention to the respect of the formal requirements laid down by the law applicable to the proceedings and, where relevant, by the mandatory rules of the place of arbitration, notably with regard to the reasons for awards, their signature and the admissibility of dissenting opinions.

Arbitrators' fees

18. In setting the arbitrators' fees on the basis of the scale attached to the ICC Rules of Arbitration, the International Court of Arbitration takes into consideration the time spent, the rapidity of the proceedings and the complexity of the dispute, so as to arrive at a figure within the limits specified or, when circumstances require, higher or lower than those limits (Art. 20(3) of the ICC Rules of Arbitration).

Appendix III – Schedule of Conciliation and Arbitration Costs

1. Costs of conciliation

a) The administrative expenses for a conciliation procedure shall be fixed at one-quarter of the amount calculated in accordance with the scale of administrative expenses hereinafter set out. Where the sum in dispute in a conciliation procedure is not stated, the Secretary General of the International Court of Arbitration shall fix the administrative expenses at his discretion.
b) The fee of the conciliator to be paid by the parties shall be fixed by the Secretary General of the Court. Such fee shall be reasonable in amount, taking into consideration the time spent, the complexity of the dispute and any other relevant circumstances.

2. Costs of arbitration

a) The advance on costs fixed by the International Court of Arbitration comprises the fee(s) of the arbitrator(s), any personal expenses of the arbitrator(s) and the administrative expenses.

b) The submission of any claim or counter-claim to the arbitrator(s) shall be made only after at least half of the advance on costs fixed by the Court has been satisfied. Terms of Reference shall only become operative and the arbitrator(s) shall only proceed in respect of those claims and counter-claims for which the totality of the advance on costs fixed by the Court has been satisfied.

c) The Court shall fix the administrative expenses of each arbitration in accordance with the scale hereinafter set out or, where the sum in dispute is not stated, at its discretion. If exceptional circumstances so require, the Court may fix the administrative expenses at a lower figure than that which would result from application of said scale.

d) Subject to Article 20(3) of the ICC Rules of Arbitration, the Court shall fix the fee(s) of the arbitrator(s) in accordance with the scale hereinafter set out or, where the sum in dispute is not stated, at its discretion.

e) When a case is submitted to more than one arbitrator, the Court, at its discretion, shall have the right to increase the total fees up to a maximum of three times the fee payable to one arbitrator.

f) When arbitration is preceded by attempted conciliation, one-half of the administrative expenses paid in respect of the said attempt shall be credited to the administrative expenses of the arbitration.

g) Before any expertise can be commenced, the parties, or one of them, shall pay an advance on costs fixed by the arbitrator(s) sufficient to cover the expected fee and expenses of the expert as determined by the arbitrator(s).

3. Advance on administrative expenses

a) Each party to a dispute submitted to conciliation under the Rules of Optional Conciliation of the ICC is required to make an advance payment of US $500 on the administrative expenses.

b) Each request to open an arbitration pursuant to the ICC Rules of Arbitration must be accompanied by an advance payment of US $2,000 on the administrative expenses.

c) No request for conciliation or arbitration will be entertained unless accompanied by the appropriate payment. This payment is not recoverable and becomes the property of the ICC. Such payment by a party shall be credited to its portion of the administrative expenses for the conciliation or arbitration, as the case may be.

4. Appointment of arbitrators

A registration fee of US $1,000 is payable by the requesting party in respect of each request made to the ICC to appoint an arbitrator for any arbitration not conducted under the ICC Rules of Arbitration. No request for appointment of an arbitrator will be entertained unless accompanied by said fee, which is not recoverable and becomes the property of the ICC.
Such fee shall cover any additional services rendered by the ICC regarding the appointment, such as decisions on a challenge of the arbitrator and the appointment of a substitute arbitrator.

5. Scales of administrative expenses and arbitrator's fees

[not printed]

APPENDIX III

ICC DRAFT UNIFORM RULES FOR GUARANTEES (JUNE 1989)

Section A: Scope and Application

Section B: Definitions

Section C: General Provisions

Section D: Liabilities and Responsibilities of Guarantors

Section E: Claims

Section F: Submission of Claims

Section G: Expiry Provisions

Section H: Governing Law and Jurisdiction

A. Scope and Application of the Rules

Article I

These Rules apply to any guarantee, however named or described (hereinafter "Guarantee") and amendment thereto which a Guarantor (as hereinafter described) has been instructed to issue and which states that it is subject to the Uniform Rules for Guarantees of the International Chamber of Commerce (Publication No. XXX) and are binding on all parties thereto unless otherwise expressly stated in the Guarantee or any amendment thereto.

B. Definitions

Article 2

a) For the purposes of these Rules a Guarantee means an undertaking by a bank, insurance company or other body or person (hereinafter "the Guarantor") given in writing for the payment of money, subject to compliance with the terms and conditions of the Guarantee
   i) at the request, or on the instructions and under the liability of a Party (hereinafter called "the Principal"); or
   ii) at the request, or on the instructions and under the liability of a bank, insurance company or any other body or person (hereinafter "the instructing Party") acting on the instruction of a Principal

   to another party (hereinafter the "Beneficiary").
b) A Guarantee is independent of any underlying transaction and the terms of any such transaction shall in no way affect the Guarantor's rights and obligations under a Guarantee notwithstanding any reference thereto in the Guarantee. A Guarantor's obligation of performance under a Guarantee is to pay the sum or sums specified.
c) For the purpose of these Rules "Counter-Guarantee" means the written undertaking of the instructing Party to effect payment to the Guarantor on receipt of his notification that he has been called upon to pay in accordance with the terms and conditions of his Guarantee.

The Counter-Guarantee is independent of the Guarantee itself and of any underlying transaction.

d) The expression "writing" shall include an authenticated teletransmission or tested electronic data interchange ("EDZ") message equivalent thereto

C. General Provisions

Article 3

All instructions for the issue of Guarantees and amendments thereto and Guarantees and amendments themselves should be clear, precise and avoid excessive detail. Accordingly, all Guarantees should stipulate:

a) the Principal;
b) the Beneficiary;
c) the Guarantor;
d) the underlying transaction requiring the issue of the Guarantee;
e) the maximum amount payable and the currency in which it is payable;
f) the expiry date and/or expiry event of the Guarantee;
g) the terms and conditions for claiming payment;
h) any provision for reduction of the guarantee amount.

Article 4

The Beneficiary's right to claim under a Guarantee is not assignable unless he and the Principal expressly agree thereto in the Guarantee wording itself or in an amendment thereto.

This rule shall not, however, affect the Beneficiary's right to assign any proceeds to which he may be, or may become, entitled under the Guarantee.

Article 5

All Guarantees are irrevocable.

Article 6

A Guarantee enters into effect as from the date of its issue unless its terms expressly provide that such entry into effect is subject to conditions specified in the Guarantee and determinable by the Guarantor.

Article 7

Where a Guarantor has been given instructions for the issue of a Guarantee but the instructions are such that, if they were to be carried out, the Guarantor would by reason of law or regulation in the country of issue be unable to fulfil the terms and conditions of the Guarantee, the instructions shall not be executed and the Guarantor shall immediately inform the party which gave the Guarantor its instructions by telecommunication or if that is not possible by the most expeditious means of the reasons for such inability and request appropriate instructions from that party.

Article 8

A Guarantee may contain express provision for reduction by a specified or determinable amount or amounts on a specified date or dates or upon presentation to the Guarantor of the document(s) specified for this purpose in the Guarantee.

D. Liabilities and Responsibilities of Guarantors

Article 9

All documents presented under a Guarantee, including the claim, shall be examined by the Guarantor with reasonable care to ascertain whether or not they appear on their face to conform with the terms or conditions of the Guarantee. Where such documents do not appear so to conform or appear on their face to be inconsistent with one another, they shall be refused.

a) A Guarantor shall have reasonable time in which to examine a claim under a Guarantee and to decide whether to pay or to refuse the claim.
b) If the Guarantor decides to refuse a claim, it shall immediately give notice thereof to the Beneficiary by teletransmission or, if that is not possible, by other expeditious means. Any documents shall be put at the disposal of the Beneficiary.

Article 11

Guarantors and instructing Parties assume no liability or responsibility for the form, sufficiency, accuracy, genuineness, falsification, or legal effect of any document presented to them or for the general and/or particular statements made therein, or for the good faith or acts and/or omissions of any person whomsoever.

Article 12

Guarantors and Instructing Parties assume no liability or responsibility for the consequences arising out of delay and/or loss in transit of any messages, letters, claims or documents, or for delay, mutilation or other errors arising in the transmission of any telecommunication. Guarantors and Instructing Parties assume no liability for errors in translation or interpretation of technical terms and reserve the right to transmit Guarantee texts or any parts thereof without translating them.

Article 13

Guarantors and Instructing Parties assume no liability or responsibility for consequences arising out of the interruption of their business by acts of God, riots, civil commotions, insurrections, wars or any other causes beyond their control or by strikes, lock-outs or industrial action of whatever nature.

Article 14

b) Guarantors and instructing Parties assume no liability or responsibility should the instructions they transmit not be carried out even if they have themselves taken the initiative in the choice of such other party.
c) The Principal shall be liable to indemnify the Guarantor or the Instructing Party, as appropriate, against all obligations and responsibilities imposed by foreign laws and usages.

Article 15

Guarantors and Instructing Parties shall not be excluded from liability or responsibility under the terms of Articles 11, 12 and 14 above for their failure to act in good faith and with reasonable care.

Article 16

A Guarantor is liable to the Beneficiary only in accordance with the terms and conditions specified in the Guarantee and any amendment thereof, and in these Rules, and up to an amount not exceeding that stated in the Guarantee and any amendment thereof.

E. Claims

Article 17

Without prejudice to the terms of Article 10, in the event of a claim the Guarantor shall without delay so inform the principal or its Instructing Party and where applicable the Instructing Party shall so inform the Principal.

Article 18

The amount payable under a Guarantee shall be reduced by the amount of any payment made by the Guarantor in satisfaction of a claim in respect thereof and, where the maximum amount payable under Guarantee has been satisfied by payment and/or reduction, the Guarantee shall thereupon terminate whether or not the Guarantee or any amendment thereto are returned.

F. Submission of Claims

Article 19

A claim shall be made in accordance with the terms and conditions of the Guarantee on or before its expiry and, in particular, all documents specified in the Guarantee shall be presented to the Guarantor on or before its expiry at its place of issue, otherwise the claim shall be refused.

Article 20

A Guarantee shall provide for any claim for payment presented to the Guarantor to be made by the Beneficiary in writing and supported by either:

a) the Beneficiary's written statement that and in what respect the Principal is in breach of his specified obligation(s); or
b) the Beneficiary's written statement that and in what respect the Principal is in breach of his specified obligation(s) together with any other document(s) specified in the Guarantee.

Sub-sections a) and b) shall not apply when the payment of the Guarantee is to be made on (first) demand without supporting statements or documents (i.e. simple demand) or on any other conditions specified in the Guarantee.

Article 21

After having paid a claim and received reimbursement, the Guarantor shall without delay transmit the Beneficiary's claim and any related documents to the Principal or to the Instructing Party for transmission to the Principal.

G. Expiry Provisions

Article 22

Expiry of a Guarantee for the presentation of claims shall be upon a specified calendar date ("Expiry Date") or upon presentation to the Guarantor of the document(s) specified for the purpose of expiry ("Expiry Event"). If both an Expiry Date and an Expiry Event are specified in a Guarantee, the Guarantee shall expire on whichever of the Expiry Date or Expiry Event occurs first. Claims received after the Expiry Date or Expiry Event shall be rejected by the Guarantor.

Article 23

Irrespective of any expiry provision contained therein, a Guarantee shall be cancelled prior to the Expiry Date or Expiry Event on presentation to the Guarantor of the Guarantee itself or the Beneficiary's authenticated statement of release from liability under the Guarantee, whether or not the Guarantee or any amendments thereto are returned.

Article 24

Where a Guarantee has terminated by payment, expiry, cancellation or otherwise, retention of the Guarantee or of any amendments thereto shall not preserve any rights of the Beneficiary under the Guarantee.

Article 25

Where a Guarantee has terminated by payment, expiry, cancellation or otherwise or there has been a reduction of the total amount payable thereunder a Guarantor shall without delay so notify the Instructing Party or Principal and, where applicable, the Instructing Party shall so notify the Principal.

Article 26

If the Beneficiary requests an extension of the validity of the Guarantee as an alternative to a claim for payment submitted in accordance with the Guarantee, the Guarantor shall then suspend payment of the claim for such time as he considers reasonable to permit the Principal and the Beneficiary to reach agreement on the granting of such extension and for the Principal to arrange for such extension to be issued.

Unless an extension is granted, the Guarantor is obliged to pay the Beneficiary's conforming claim without requiring any further action on the Beneficiary's part. The Guarantor shall incur no liability (for interest or otherwise) should any payment to the Beneficiary be delayed as a result of the above-mentioned procedure. Even if the Principal agrees to or requests such extension, it shall not be granted unless the Guarantor and Instructing Party(ies) also agree thereto.

H. Governing Law and Jurisdiction

Article 27

Unless otherwise provided in the Guarantee, its governing law shall be that of the Guarantor's place of business or, if the Guarantor has more than one place of business, that of the branch which issued the Guarantee.

Article 28

Unless otherwise provided in the Guarantee, any dispute between the Guarantor and the Beneficiary relating to the Guarantee shall be settled exclusively by the competent court of the country of the Guarantor's place of business or, if the Guarantor has more than one place of business, by the competent court of the country of the branch which issued the Guarantee.

APPENDIX IV

ICC DRAFT UNIFORM RULES FOR GUARANTEES (SEPTEMBER 1989)

Introduction

These Uniform Rules have been drawn up by an ICC Joint Working Party of memebers representing the Commission on Banking Technique and Practice to apply to the use of guarantees worldwide. Their purpose is to provide a basis for consistency of treatment by the parties to these engagements and the resolution of problems notably in relation to claims and expiry.

These Uniform Rules replace the ICC's Uniform Rules for Contract Gurantees, Publication No. 325, dated 1978, which are hereby cancelled. ICC's Publication No. 325 did not find acceptability in certain quarters for various reasons, and one of the main purposes for making the changes incorporated in these new Rules is to recognise the different interests of the parties involved in a guarantee transaction. Existing obligatiions contracted uinder Publication 325 are not affected.

Stand-by letters of credit cannot be governed by these Rules since they are governed by UCP 400.

The Beneficiary. The beneficiary wishes to be secured against the risk of the principal not fulfilling his obligations towards the beneficiary in respect of whatever transaction is the subject of the guarantee. The guarantee accomplishes this by providing the beneficiary with quick access to a sum of money if these obligations are not fulfilled.

The Principal. Whilst recognising the needs of the beneficiary, the principal can expect on the grounds of equity and good faith to be informed in writing, that, and in what respect, it is claimed he is in breach of his obligations. This should help to eliminate a certain level of abuse of guarantees through unfair claims by beneficiaries.

The Guarantor. The terms of the guarantee should not require the guarantor to decide whether the beneficiary and principal have or have not fulilled their obligations under their underlying transaction as the guarantee is wholly independent of it. Guarantee wording should be clear and unambiguous.

The Instructing Party. The new Rules recognise the existing widespread practice whereby an instructing party may forward to the guarantor instructions received from or on behalf of the principal and counter-guarantee such instructions.

General. The ICC wishes to encourage good guarantee practice which is equitable to all concerned, and believes that these Rules will result in a fair balance of interests, recognising the rights and obligations of all parties.

Compared with the ICC Rules published in 1978, these Rules incorporate a major change favourable to beneficiaries in that they no longer have necessarily to present an arbitration award or other independent documentary evidence in support of any claim. However, guarantees including requirements for such evidence, and other forms of guarantees, are still within the scope of these Rules if the parties agree to them in appropriate cases.

There is a certain degree of confusion about the meaning of "first demand guarantees", "on-demand guarantees", "simple demand guarantees", and so on.

To clarify this it should be borne in mind that all guarantees covered by these Rules are by their nature "payable on first demand" which in international practice simply stresses the independent (abstract/autonomous) character of the guarantee undertaking and means in effect that the guarantor has waived all rights of objection and defence based on the underlying transaction. The term "on-demand guarantee" is identical.

There are various types of "first-demand" or "on-demand" guarantees, for example: (1) a so-called "simple demand guarantee" where the beneficiary when claiming the guarantee amount has to do just that, i.e. he need not give a written statement or supply supporting documents; (2) the beneficiary when claiming payment simultaneously states that and in what respect the principal is in breach of his specified obligation(s); (3) in addition to the claim and statement the beneficiary has to supply certain supporting documents specified in the guarantee.

The ICC considers simple demand guarantees as undesirable commercial practice, since they appear to give scope for unjustifiable claims, whereas it is to be supposed that any claim will be made in good faith as to its reasons and as to the amount. Such guarantees, therefore, should not be necessary or appropriate; it is reasonable to expect that the guarantee conditions should provide, as a minimum requirement, that the beneficiary is to support the legitimacy of his claim with a written statement indicating the principal's alleged default. Accordingly, the ICC opposes simple demand guarantees and wishes to discourage their use.

As with the Uniform Customs and Practice for Documentary Credits (ICC Publication No.400), this is a voluntary set of rules which does not confront the difficulties and conflicts arising from different national systems of law. It is acknowledged that for a period of time there may remaim situations in which some guarantees will not by their terms or because of the specific requirements of certain countries fall within all the articles hereafter, but the frequency of such cases would be expected to diminish. The new Rules will largely depend for their eventual success, as did the Uniform Customs and Practice for Documentary Credits, upon their adoption and employment by the international business community. The ICC, through its National Committees and international fora, will strongly encourage industrial and financial circles to adhere to these rules.

A. Scope and Application of the Rules

Article 1

These Rules apply to any guarantee, however, named or described (hereinafter "Guarantee") and amendment thereto which a Guarantor (as hereinafter described) has been instructed to issue and which states that it is subject to the Uniform Rules for Guarantees of the International Chambers of Commerce (Publication No. XXX) and are binding on all parties thereto unless otherwise expressly stated in the Guarantee or any amendment thereto.

B. Definitions

Article 2

(a) For the purposes of these Rules a Guarantee means an undertaking by a bank, insurance company or other body or person (hereinafter "the Guarantor") given in writing for the payment of money, subject to compliance with the terms and conditions of the Guarantee
   (i) at the request or on the instructions and under the liability of a Party (hereinafter called "the Principal"); or
   (ii) at the request or on the instructions and under the liability of a bank, insurance company or any other body or person (hereinafter called "the Instructing Party") acting on the instruction of a Principal

to another party (hereinafter called "the Beneficiary")"

(b) A Guarantee is independent of any underlying transaction and the terms of any such transaction shall not affect the Guarantor's rights and obligations under a Guarantee notwithstanding any reference thereto in the Guarantee, A Guarantor's obligation of performance under a Guarantee is to pay the sum, or sums specified therein, subject to compliance with the terms and conditions of the Guarantee.

(c) For the purpose of these Rules "Counter-Guarantee" means the written undertaking of the Instructing Party to effect payment to the Guarantor in accordance with the terms of the Counter-Guarantee on receipt of the Guarantor's notification that it has been called upon to pay in accordance with terms of the Guarantee.
   The Counter-Guarantee is independent of the Guarantee itself and of any underlying transaction.

(d) The expression "writing" shall include an authenticated teletransmission or tested electronic data interchange ("EDI") messge equivalent thereto.

C. General Provisions

Article 3

All instructions for the issue of Guarantees and amendments thereto and Guarantees and amendments themselves should be clear, precise and avoid excessive detail. Accordingly, all Guarantees should stipulate:

(a) the Principal;
(b) the Beneficiary)
(c) the Guarantor;
(d) the underlying transaction requiring the issue of the Guarantee;
(e) the maximum amount payable and the currency in which it is payable;
(f) the expiry date and/or expiry event of the Guarantee;
(g) the terms and conditions for claiming payment;
(h) any provision for reduction of the guarantee amount.

Article 4

The Beneficiary's right to claim under a Guarantee is not assignable unless expressly stated in the Guarantee wording itself or in an amendment thereto.

This article shall not, however, affect the Beneficiary's right to assign any proceeds to which he may be, or may become, entitled under the Guarantee.

Article 5

All Guarantees and Counter-Guarantees are irrevocable.

Article 6

A Guarantee enters into effect as from their date of its issue unless its terms expressly provide that such entry into effect is subject to conditions specified in the Guarantee and determinable by the Guarantor.

Article 7

Where a Guarantor has been given instructions for the issue of a Guarantee but the instructions are such that, if they were to be carried out, the Guarantor would by reason of law or regulation in the country of issue be unable to fulfill the terms and conditions of the Guarantee, the instructions shall not be executed and the Guarantor shall immediately inform the party which gave the Guarantor its instructions by telecommunication or if that is not possible by other expeditious means of the reasons for such inability and request appropriate instructions from that party.

Article 8

A Guarantee may contain express provision for reduction by a specified or determinable amount or amounts on a specified date or dates or upon presentation to the Guarantor of the document(s) specified for this purpose in the Guarantee.

D. Liabilities and Responsibilities

Article 9

All document(s) specified and presented under a Guarantee,including the claim, shall be examined by the Guarantor with reasonable care to ascertain whether or not they appear on their face to conform with the terms of the Guarantee. Where such document(s) do not appear so to conform or appear on their face to be inconsistent with one other, they shall be refused.

Article 10

(a) A Guarantor shall have reasonable time in which to examine a claim under a Guarantee and to decide whether to pay or to refuse the claim.
(b) If the Guarantor decides to refuse a claim, it shall immediately give notice thereof to the Beneficiary by teletransmissionn or, if that is not possible, by other expeditious means. Any documents shall be held at the disposal of the Beneficiary.

Article 11

Guarantors and Instructing Parties assume no liability or responsiblity for the form, sufficiency, accuracy, genuineness, falsification, or legal effect of any document presented to them or for the general and/or particular statements made therein, or for the good faith or acts and/or omissions of any person whomsoever.

Article 12

Guarantors and Instructing Parties assume no liability or responsibility for the consequences arising out of delay and/or loss in transit of any messages, letters, claims or documents, or for delay, mutilation or other errors arising in the transmission of any telecommunication. Guarantors and Instructing Parties assume no liability for errors in translation or interpretation of technical terms and reserve the right to transmit Guarantee texts or any parts thereof without translating them.

Article 13

Guarantors and Instructing Parties assume no liability or responsibility for consequences arising out of the interruption of their business by acts of God, riots, civil commotions, insurrections, wars or any other causes beyond their control or by strikes, lock-outs or industrial action of whatever nature.

Article 14

(a) Guarantors and Instructing Parties utilising the services of another party for the purpose of giving effect to the instructions of a Principal do so for the account and at the risk of that Principal.
(b) Guarantors and Instructing Parties assume no liability or responsibility should the instructions they transmit not be carried out even if they have themselves taken the initiative in the choice of such other party.
(c) The Principal shall be liable to indemnify the Guarantor or the Instructing Party, as the case may be, against all obligations and responsibilities imposed by foreign laws and usages.

Article 15

Guarantors and Instructing Parties shall not be excluded from liability or responsibility under the terms of Articles 11, 12 and 14 above for their failure to act in good faith and with reasonable care.

Article 16

A Guarantor is liable to the Beneficiary only in accordance with the terms specified in the Guarantee and any amendment thereof and in these Rules and up to an amount not exceeding that stated in the Guarantee and any amendment thereof.

E. Claims

Article 17

Without prejudice to the terms of Article 10, in the event of a claim the Guarantor shall without delay so inform the Principal or where applicable its Instructing Party and in that case the Instructing Party shall so inform the Principal.

Article 18

The amount payable under a Guarantee shall be reduced by the amount of any payment made by the Guarantor in satisfaction of a claim in respect thereof and, where the maximum amount payable under a Guarantee has been satisfied by payment and/or reduction, the Guarantee shall thereupon terminate whether or not the Guarantee or any amendment thereto are returned.

F. Submission of Claims

Article 19

A claim shall be made in accordance with the terms of the Guarantee on or before its expiry and, in particular, all documents specified in the Guarantee for the purpose of claiming shall be presented to the Guarantor on or before its expiry at its place of issue, otherwise the claim shall be refused.

Article 20

After having paid a claim and received reimbursement the Guarantor shall without delay transmit the Beneficiary's claim and any related documents to the Principal or where applicable to the Instructing Party for transmission to the Principal.

G. Expiry Provisions

Article 21

Expiry of a Guarantee for the presentation of claims shall be upon a specified calendar date ("Expiry Date") or upon presentation to the Guarantor of the document(s) specified for the purpose of expiry ("Expiry Event"). If both an Expiry Date and an Expiry Event are specified in a Guarantee, the Guarantee shall expire on whichever of the Expiry Date or Expiry Event occurs first. Claims received ater the Expiry Date or Expiry Event shall be refused by the Guarantor.

Article 22

Irrespective of any provision contained therein, a Guarantee shall be cancelled prior to the Expiry Date or Expiry Event on presentation to the Guarantor of the Gurantee itself or the Beneficiary's authenticated statement of release from, liability under the Guarantee, whether or not the Guarantee or any amendments thereto are returned.

Article 23

Where a Guarantee has terminated by payment, expiry, cancellation or otherwise, retention of the Guarantee or of any amendments thereto shall not preserve any rights of the Beneficiary under the Guarantee.

Article 24

Where a Guarantee has terminated by payment, expiry, cancellation or otherwise or there has been a reduction of the total amount payable thereunder a Guarantor shall without delay so notify the Principal or where applicable the Instructing Party and, in that case, the Instructing Party shall so notify the Principal.

Article 25

If the Beneficiary requests an extension of the validity of the Guarantee as an altenative to a claim for payment submitted in accordance with the terms and conditions of the Guarantee, the Guarantor shall without delay so inform the party which gave the Guarantor its instructions. The Guarantor shall then suspend payment of the claim for such time as he considers reasonable to permit the Principal and the Beneficiary to reach agreement on the granting of such extension and for the Principal to arrange for such extension to be issued.

Unless an extension is granted, the Guarantor is obliged to pay the Beneficiary's conforming claim without requiring further action on the Beneficiary's part. The Guarantor shall incur no liability (for interest or otherwise) should any payment to the Beneficiary be delayed as a result of the above-mentioned procedure.

Even if the Principal agrees to or requests such extension, it shall not be granted unless the Guarantor and the Instructing Party(ies) also agree thereto.

H. Governing Law and Jurisdiction

Article 26

Unless otherwise provided in the Guarantee, its governing law shall be that of the Guarantor's place of business or, if the Guarantor has more than one place of business, that of the branch which issued the Guarantee.

Article 27

Unless otherwise provided in the Guarantee, any dispute between the Guarantor and the Beneficiary relating to the Guarantee shall be settled exclusively by the competent court of the country of the Guarantor's place of business or, if the Guarantor has more than one place of business, by the competent court of the country of the branch which issued the Guarantee.

APPENDIX V

LONDON COURT OF INTERNATIONAL ARBITRATION RULES

(effective from 1 January 1985)

London Court of International Arbitration

30–32 St. Mary Axe London EC3A 8ET England

Index

Article

LONDON COURT OF INTERNATIONAL ARBITRATION RULES

adopted to take effect from 1 January 1985

Where any agreement, submission or reference provides for arbitration under the Rules of the London Court of International Arbitration (formerly called the London Court of Arbitration) (the LCIA), the parties shall be taken to have agreed that the arbitration shall be conducted in accordance with the following Rules, or such amended Rules as the Court may have adopted to take effect before the commencement of the arbitration.

The Arbitration Court of the LCIA, in these Rules called "The Court", has the function of ensuring the application of the Rules.

Article 1 Request for Arbitration

Any party wishing to commence an arbitration under these Rules ('the Claimant') shall send to the Registrar of the Court ('the Registrar') a written request for arbitration ('the Request') which shall include, or be accompanied by:

(a) the names and addresses of the parties to the arbitration;

(b) copies of the contractual documents in which the arbitration clause is contained or under which the arbitration arises;

(c) a brief statement describing the nature and circumstances of the dispute, and specifying the relief claimed;
(d) a statement of any matters (such as the place or language of the arbitration, or the number of arbitrators, or their qualifications or identities) on which the parties have already agreed in relation to the conduct of the arbitration, or with respect to which the requesting party wishes to make a proposal;
(e) if the arbitration agreement calls for party nomination of arbitrators, the name and address (and telephone number and telex numbers, if known) of the Claimant's nominee;
(f) the fee prescribed in the Schedule of Costs;

and shall confirm to the Registrar that copies have been served on the other parties. The date of receipt by the Registrar of the Request for Arbitration shall be deemed to be the date on which the arbitration has commenced.

Article 2 Response by Respondent

2.1 For the purpose of facilitating the choice of arbitrators within 30 days of receipt of its copy of the Request for Arbitration the Respondent may send to the Registrar a Response containing:
(a) confirmation or denial of all or part of the claims;
(b) a brief statement of the nature and circumstances of any envisaged counterclaims;
(c) comment in response to any statements contained in the Request, as called for under Article 1(d), on matters relating to the conduct of the arbitration;
(d) if the arbitration agreement calls for party nomination of arbitrators, the name and address (and telephone and telex numbers if known) of the Respondent's nominee;

and shall confirm to the Registrar that copies have been served on the other parties.

2.2 Failure to send a Response shall not preclude the Respondent from denying the claim nor from setting out a counterclaim in its Statement of Defence. However, if the arbitration agreement calls for party nomination of arbitrators, failure to send a Response or to nominate an arbitrator in it shall constitute a waiver of the opportunity to nominate an arbitrator.

Article 3 The Arbitral Tribunal

3.1 In these Rules, the expression 'the Tribunal' includes a sole arbitrator or all the arbitrators where more than one is appointed. All arbitrators (whether or not nominated by the parties) conducting an arbitration under these Rules shall be and remain at all times wholly independent and impartial, and shall not act as advocates for any party. Before appointment by the Court, if the Registrar so requests, any arbitrator shall furnish a resume of his past and present professional positions (which will be communicated to the parties). In any event every arbitrator shall sign a declaration to the effect that there are no circumstances likely to give rise to any justified doubts as to his impartiality or independence, and that he will forthwith disclose any such circumstances to the Court and to all the parties if they should arise after that time and before the arbitration is concluded.

3.2 The Court will appoint the Tribunal to determine the dispute as soon as practicable after receipt by the Registrar of the Response, or after the expiry of 30 days following receipt by the Respondent of the Request if no Response is received, provided that the Registrar is satisfied that the Request has been properly served. A sole arbitrator will be appointed unless the parties have agreed otherwise, or unless the Court determines that in view of the circumstances of the case a three-member tribunal is appropriate.

3.3 The Court alone is empowered to appoint arbitrators and such appointment will be made in the name of the Court by the President or any Vice President of the Court. The Court will appoint arbitrators with due regard for any particular method or criteria of selection agreed by the parties. In selecting arbitrators consideration will be given, so far as possible, to the nature of the contract, the nature and circumstances of the dispute, and the nationality, location and language of the parties. Where the parties are of different nationalities, then unless they have agreed otherwise, sole arbitrators or chairmen are not to be appointed if they have the same nationality as any party (the nationality of the parties being understood to include that of controlling shareholders or interests). If the parties have agreed that they are to nominate arbitrators themselves, or to allow two arbitrators, or a third party, to nominate an arbitrator, the Court may refuse to appoint such nominees if it determines that they are not suitable or independent or impartial. In the case of a three-member Tribunal the Court will designate the Chairman, who will not be a party-nominated arbitrator.

3.4 If the arbitration agreement calls for party nominations, and the Respondent fails to make such a nomination within the time limit established by Article 2, the Court will forthwith appoint an arbitrator in place of the arbitrator to be nominated by the Respondent. If the Request does not contain a nomination by the Claimant, and the Claimant fails to make such a nomination with the same time limit, the Court will likewise make that appointment.

3.5 In the event that the Court determines that a nominee is not suitable or independent or impartial, or if an appointed arbitrator is to be replaced, the Court shall have discretion to decide whether or not to follow the original nominating process. If it so decides any opportunity for renomination shall be waived if not exercised within 30 days, after which the Court shall appoint the replacement as soon as practicable.

3.6 If any arbitrator, after appointment dies, refuses, or in the opinion of the Court becomes unable or unfit to act, the Court will, upon request by a party or by the remaining arbitrators, appoint another arbitrator in accordance with the provisions of Article 3.5. If in the opinion of the Court an arbitrator acts in manifest violation of these Rules, or does not conduct the proceedings with reasonable diligence, he will be considered unfit.

3.7 An arbitrator may be challenged if circumstances exist that give rise to justifiable doubts as to his impartiality or independence. A party may challenge an arbitrator it has nominated, or in whose appointment it has participated, only for reasons of which it becomes aware after the appointment has been made.

3.8 A party who intends to challenge an arbitrator shall, within fifteen days of the constitution of the Tribunal or after becoming aware of any circumstances referred to in Article 3.6 or 3.7, whichever is the later, send a written statement of the reasons for the challenge to the Court. Unless the challenged arbitrator withdraws or the other party agrees to the challenge within 15 days of receipt of the written statement of challenge, the Court shall decide on the challenge.

3.9 The decision of the Court with respect to all matters referred to in this Article shall be final. Such decisions are deemed to be administrative in nature, and the Court shall not be required to give reasons for them. To the extent permitted by the law of the place of arbitration the parties shall be taken to have waived any right of appeal in respect of any such decisions to a court of law or other judicial authority. If such appeals remain possible due to mandatory provisions of the law of the place of arbitration, the Court shall, subject to the provisions of the applicable law, decide whether the arbitral proceedings are to continue notwithstanding an appeal.

Article 4 Communication between Parties and the Tribunal

4.1 Until the Tribunal is finally constituted and the Court determines that it would be appropriate for the parties and the Tribunal to communicate directly, all communications between parties and arbitrators shall be made through the Registrar. If and when the Court directs that communication shall take place directly between the Tribunal and the parties (with simultaneous copies to the Registrar) all further reference in these Rules to the Registrar shall thereafter be read as references to the Tribunal.
4.2 Where the Registrar, on behalf of the Tribunal, sends any communication to one party, he shall send a copy to each of the other parties.
4.3 Where any party sends any communication (including Statements under Article 6) to the Registrar, it shall include a copy for each arbitrator, and it shall also send copies to all the other parties and confirm to the Registrar in writing that it has done so.
4.4 The addresses of the parties for the purpose of all communications during the proceedings shall be those set out in the Request, or as any party may at any time notify to the Registrar and to the other parties.

Article 5 Conduct of the Proceedings

5.1 The parties may agree on the arbitral procedure, and are encouraged to do so.
5.2 In the absence of procedural rules agreed by the parties or contained herein, the Tribunal shall have the widest discretion allowed under such law as may be applicable to ensure the just, expeditious, economical, and final determination of the dispute.
5.3 In the case of a three-member tribunal the Chairman may, after consulting the other arbitrators, make procedural rulings alone.

Article 6 Submission of Written Statements and Documents

6.1 Subject to any procedural rules agreed by the parties or determined by the Tribunal under Article 5, the written stage of the proceedings shall be as set out in this Article.
6.2 Within 30 days of receipt of notification from the Court of the appointment of the Tribunal, the Claimant shall send to the Registrar a Statement of Case setting out in sufficient detail the facts and any contentions of law on which it relies, and the relief claimed.
6.3 Within 40 days of receipt of the Statement of Case, the Respondent shall send to the Registrar a statement of defence stating in sufficient detail which of the facts and contentions of law in the Statement of Case it admits or denies, on what grounds, and on what other facts and contentions of law it relies. Any counterclaims shall be submitted with the Statement of Defence in the same manner as claims are set out in the Statement of Case.
6.4 Within 40 days of receipt of the Statement of Defence, the Claimant may send to the Registrar a Statement of Reply which, where there are counterclaims, shall include a Defence to Counterclaims.
6.5 If the Statement of Reply contains a Defence to Counterclaims, the Respondent has a further 40 days to send to the Registrar a Statement of Reply regarding Counterclaims.
6.6. All Statements referred to in this Article shall be accompanied by copies (or, if they are specially voluminous, lists) of all essential documents on which the party concerned relies and which have not previously been submitted by any party, and (where appropriate) by any relevant samples.
6.7 As soon as practicable following completion of the submission of the Statements specified in this Article, the Tribunal shall proceed in such manner as has been

agreed by the parties, or pursuant to its authority under these Rules. If the Respondent fails to submit a Statement of Defence, or if at any point any party fails to avail itself of the opportunity to present its case in the manner directed by the Tribunal, the Tribunal may nevertheless proceed with the arbitration and make the award.

Article 7 Place of Arbitration

7.1 The parties may choose the place of arbitration. Failing such a choice, the place of arbitration shall be London, unless the Tribunal determines in view of all the circumstances of the case that another place is more appropriate.

7.2 The Tribunal may hold hearings and meetings anywhere convenient, subject to the provisions of Article 10.2, and provided that the award shall be made at the place of arbitration.

Article 8 Language of Arbitration

8.1 The language(s) of the arbitration shall be that of the document(s) containing the arbitration agreement, unless the parties have agreed otherwise.

8.2 If a document is drawn up in a language other than the language of the arbitration, and no translation of such document is submitted by the party producing the document, the Tribunal, or if the Tribunal has not been appointed the Court, may order that party to submit a translation in a form to be determined by the Tribunal or the Court.

Article 9 Party Representatives

Any party may be represented by legal practitioners or any other representatives, subject to such proof of authority as the Tribunal may require.

Article 10 Hearings

10.1 Any party has the right to be heard before the Tribunal, unless the parties have agreed on documents-only arbitration

10.2 The Tribunal shall fix the date, time and place of any meetings and hearings in the arbitration, and the Registrar shall give the parties reasonable notice thereof.

10.3 The Tribunal may in advance of hearings submit to the parties a list of questions which it wishes them to treat with special attention.

10.4 All meetings and hearings shall be in private unless the parties agree otherwise.

Article 11 Witnesses

11.1 Before any hearing, the Tribunal may require any party to give notice of the identity of witnesses it wishes to call, as well as the subject matter of their testimony and its relevance to the issues.

11.2 The Tribunal has discretion to allow, refuse or limit the appearance of witnesses, whether witnesses of fact or expert witnesses.

11.3 Any witness who gives oral evidence may be questioned by each of the parties or their legal practitioners, under the control of the Tribunal. The Tribunal may put questions at any stage of the examination of the witnesses.

11.4 The testimony of witnesses may be presented in written form, either as signed statements or by duly sworn affidavits. Subject to Article 11.2 any party may request that such a witness should attend for oral examination at a hearing. If he fails to attend, the Tribunal may place such weight on the written testimony as it thinks fit, or exclude it altogether.

11.5 Subject to the mandatory provisions of any applicable law it shall be proper for any party or its legal practitioners to interview any witness or potential witness prior to his appearance at any hearing.

Article 12 Experts Appointed by Tribunal

12.1 Unless otherwise agreed by the parties, the Tribunal:
(a) may appoint one or more experts to report to the Tribunal on specific issues;
(b) may require a party to give any such expert any relevant information or to produce, or to provide access to, any relevant documents, goods or property for inspection by the expert.

12.2 Unless otherwise agreed by the parties, if a party so requests or if the Tribunal considers it necessary, the expert shall, after delivery of his written or oral report, participate in a hearing at which the parties shall have the opportunity to question him, and to present expert witnesses in order to testify on the points at issue.

Article 13 Additional Powers of the Tribunal

13.1 Unless the parties at any time agree otherwise, and subject to any mandatory limitation of any applicable law, the Tribunal shall have the power, on the application of any party or of its own motion, but in either case only after giving the parties a proper opportunity to state their views, to:
(a) determine what are the rules of law governing or applicable to any contract, or arbitration agreement or issue between the parties;
(b) order the correction of any such contract or arbitration agreement, but only to the extent required to rectify any mistake which it determines to be common to all the parties and then only if and to the extent to which the rules of law governing or applicable to the contract permit such correction;
(c) allow other parties to be joined in the arbitration with their express consent, and make a single final award determining all disputes between them;
(d) allow any party, upon such terms (as to costs and otherwise) as it shall determine, to amend claims or counterclaims;
(e) extend or abbreviate any time limits provided by these Rules or by its directions;
(f) conduct such enquiries as may appear to the Tribunal to be necessary or expedient;
(g) order the parties to make any property or thing available for inspection, in their presence, by the Tribunal or any expert;
(h) order the preservation, storage, sale or other disposal of any property or thing under the control of any party;
(i) order any party to produce to the Tribunal, and to the other parties for inspection, and to supply copies of, any documents or classes of documents in their possession or power which the Tribunal determines to be relevant.

13.2 By agreeing to arbitration under these Rules the parties shall be taken to have agreed to apply only to the Tribunal, and not to any court of law or other judicial authority, for an order under paragraphs (g) (h) or (i) of Article 13.1.

Article 14 Jurisdiction of the Tribunal

14.1 The Tribunal shall have the power to rule on its own jurisdiction, including any objections with respect to the existence or validity of the arbitration agreement. For that purpose, an arbitration clause which forms part of a contract shall be treated as an agreement independent of the other terms of the contract. A decision by the Tribunal that the contract is null and void shall not entail *ipso jure* the invalidity of the arbitration clause.

14.2 A plea that the Tribunal does not have jurisdiction shall be raised not later than in the Statement of Defence. A plea that the Tribunal is exceeding the scope of its authority shall be raised promptly after the Tribunal has indicated its intention to decide on the matter alleged to be beyond the scope of its authority. In either case the Tribunal may nevertheless admit a late plea under this paragraph if it considers the delay justified.

14.3 In addition to the jurisdiction to exercise the powers defined elsewhere in these Rules, the Tribunal shall have jurisdiction to determine any question of law arising in the arbitration; proceed in the arbitration notwithstanding the failure or refusal of any party to comply with these Rules or with the Tribunal's orders or directions, or to attend any meeting or hearing, but only after giving that party written notice that it intends to do so; and to receive and take into account such written or oral evidence as it shall determine to be relevant, whether or not strictly admissible in law.

Article 15 Deposits and Security

15.1 The Tribunal may direct the parties, in such proportions as it deems just, and subject to the confirmation of the Court that the amounts are in conformity with the Schedule of Costs, to make one or several interim or final payments on account of the costs of the arbitration. Such deposits shall be made to and held by the Court to the order of the Chairman of the Tribunal or sole arbitrator, and may be drawn from as required by the Tribunal. Interest on sums deposited, if any, shall be accumulated to the deposits.

15.2 The Tribunal shall have the power to order any party to provide security for the legal or other costs of any other party by way of deposit or bank guarantee or in any other manner the Tribunal thinks fit.

15.3 By agreeing to arbitration under these Rules the parties shall be taken to have agreed to apply only to the Tribunal, and not to any court of law or other judicial authority, for an order under Article 15.1, or for an order for security of costs under Article 15.2.

15.4 Without prejudice to the right of any party to apply to a competent court for pre-award conservatory measures (except those referred to in Articles 15.1 and 15.2), the Tribunal shall also have the power to order any party to provide security for all or part of any amount in dispute in the arbitration.

15.5 In the event that orders under paragraphs 1, 2 and 4 of this Article are not complied with, the Tribunal may disregard claims or counterclaims by the non-complying party, although it may proceed to determine claims or counterclaims by complying parties.

Article 16 The Award

16.1 The Tribunal shall make its award in writing and, unless all the parties agree otherwise, shall state the reasons upon which its award is based. The award shall state its date and shall be signed by the arbitrator or arbitrators.

16.2 If any arbitrator refuses or fails to comply with the mandatory provisions of any applicable law relating to the making of the award, having been given a reasonable opportunity to do so, the remaining arbitrators shall proceed in his absence.

16.3 Where there is more than one arbitrator and they fail to agree on any issue, they shall decide by a majority. Failing a majority decision on any issue, the Chairman of the Tribunal shall make the award alone as if he were sole arbitrator. If an arbitrator refuses or fails to sign the award, the signatures of the majority shall be sufficient, provided that the reason for the omitted signature is stated.

16.4 The sole arbitrator or chairman shall be responsible for delivering the award to the Court, which shall transmit certified copies to the parties provided that the costs of the arbitration have been paid to the Court in accordance with Article 18.

16.5 Awards may be expressed in any currency, and the Tribunal may award that simple or compound interest shall be paid by any party on any sum which is the subject of the reference at such rates as the Tribunal determines to be appropriate, without being bound by legal rates of interest, in respect of any period which the Tribunal determines to be appropriate ending not later than the date upon which the award is complied with.

16.6 The Tribunal may make separate final awards on different issues at different times, which shall be subject to correction under the procedure specified in Article 17. Such awards shall be enforceable.

16.7 In the event of a settlement, the Tribunal may render an award recording the settlement if any party so requests. If the parties do not require a consent award, then on confirmation in writing by the parties to the Court that a settlement has been reached the Tribunal shall be discharged and the reference to arbitration concluded, subject to payment by the parties of any outstanding costs of the arbitration in accordance with Article 18.

16.8 By agreeing to arbitration under these Rules, the parties undertake to carry out the award without delay, and waive their right to any form of appeal or recourse to a court of law or other judicial authority, insofar as such waiver may be validly made. Awards shall be final and binding on the parties as from the date they are made.

Article 17 Correction of Awards and Additional Awards

17.1 Within thirty days of receipt of the award, unless another period of time has been agreed upon by the parties, a party may by notice to the Registrar request the Tribunal to correct in the award any errors in computation, any clerical or typographical errors or any errors of a similar nature. If the Tribunal considers the request to be justified, it shall make the corrections within thirty days of receipt of the request. Any correction, which shall take the form of a separate memorandum, shall become part of the award.

17.2 The Tribunal may correct any error of the type referred to in Article 17.1 on its own initiative within thirty days of the date of the award.

17.3 Unless otherwise agreed by the parties, a party may, within thirty days of receipt of the award, and with notice to the other party or parties, request the Tribunal to make an additional award as to claims presented in the arbitral proceedings but not dealt with in the award. If the Tribunal considers the request to be justified, it shall make the additional award within sixty days.

17.4 The provisions of Article 16 shall apply *mutatis mutandis* to a correction of the award and to any additional award.

Article 18 Costs

18.1 The costs of the arbitration (other than the legal or other costs incurred by the parties themselves) shall be in accordance with the schedule of Costs applicable to these Rules as of the date of the Request for Arbitration.

18.2 The Tribunal shall specify in the award the total amount of the costs of the arbitration, subject to the confirmation of the Court that the amount is in conformity with the Schedule of Costs. Unless the parties shall agree otherwise, the Tribunal shall determine the proportions in which the parties shall pay all or part of them to the Court. If the Tribunal has determined that all or any part of the costs of the arbitration shall be paid by any party other than a party which has already paid them to the Court, the latter shall have the right to recover the appropriate amount from the former.

18.3 The Tribunal shall have the authority to order in its award that all or a part of the legal or other costs of a party (apart from the costs of the arbitration) be paid by another party.

18.4 If the arbitration is abandoned, suspended or concluded, by agreement or otherwise, before the final award is made, the parties shall be jointly and severally liable to pay to the Court the costs of the arbitration as determined by the Tribunal, subject to the confirmation by the Court that the amount is in conformity with the Schedule of Costs. In the event that the costs so determined are less than the deposits made, there shall be a refund in such proportions as the parties may agree, or, failing agreement, by the same proportions as the deposits were made.

Article 19 Exclusion of Liability

19.1 Neither the court nor any arbitrator shall be liable to any party for any act or omission in connection with any arbitration conducted under these Rules, save that arbitrators (but not the Court) may be liable for the consequences of conscious and deliberate wrongdoing.

19.2 After the award has been made and the possibilities of correction and additional awards referred to in Article 17 have lapsed or been exhausted, neither the Court nor any arbitrator shall be under any obligation to make any statement to any person about any matter concerning the arbitration, nor shall any party seek to make any arbitrator or any officer of the Court a witness in any legal proceedings arising out of the arbitration.

Article 20 General Rules

20.1 A party who knows that any provision of, or requirements under, these Rules has not been complied with and yet proceeds with the arbitration without promptly stating its objection to such non-compliancc, shall be deemed to have waived its right to object.

20.2 In all matters not expressly provided for in these Rules, the Court and the Tribunal shall act in the spirit of these rules and shall make every reasonable effort to ensure that the award is legally enforceable.

APPENDIX VI

CLAUSE 67
OF THE FIDIC CONDITIONS OF CONTRACT
3RD EDITION 1974
SETTLEMENT OF DISPUTES

67. If any dispute or difference of any kind whatsoever shall arise between the Employer and the Contractor or the Engineer and the Contractor in connection with, or arising out of the Contract, or the execution of the Works, whether during the progress of the Works or after their completion and whether before or after the termination, abandonment or breach of the Contract, it shall, in the first place, be referred to and settled by the Engineer who shall, within a period of ninety days after being requested by either party to do so, give written notice of his decision to the Employer and the Contractor. Subject to arbitration, as hereinafter provided, such decision in respect of every matter so referred shall be final and binding upon the Employer and the Contractor and shall forethwith be given effect to by the Employer and by the Contractor, who shall proceed with the execution of the Works with all due diligence whether he or the Employer requires arbitration, as hereinafter provided, or not. If the Engineer has given written notice of his decision to the Employer and the Contractor and no claim to arbitration has been communicated to him by either the Employer or the Contractor within a period of ninety days from receipt of such notice, the said decision shall remain final and binding upon the Employer and the Contractor. If the Engineer shall fail to give notice of his decision, as aforesaid, within a period of ninety days after being requested as aforesaid, or if either the Employer or the Contractor be dissatisfied with any such decision, then and in any such case either the Employer or the Contractor may within ninety days after receiving notice of such decision, or within ninety days after the expiration of the first-named period of ninety days, as the case may be, require that the matter or matters in dispute be referred to arbitration as hereinafter provided. All disputes or differences in respect of which the decision, if any, of the Engineer has not become final and binding as aforesaid shall be finally settled under the Rules of Conciliation and Arbitration of the International Chamber of Commerce by one or more arbitrators appointed under such Rules. The said arbitrator/s shall have full power to open up, revise and review any decision, opinion, direction, certificate or valuation of the Engineer. Neither party shall be limited in the proceedings before such arbitrator/s to the evidence or arguments put before the Engineer for the purpose of obtaining his said decision. No decision given by the Engineer in accordance with the foregoing provisions shall disqualify him from being called as a witness and giving evidence before the arbitrator/s on any matter whatsoever relevant to the dispute or difference referred to the arbitrator/s as aforesaid. The reference to arbitration may proceed notwithstanding that the Works shall not then be or be alleged to be complete, provided always that the obligations of the Employer, the Engineer and the Contractor shall not be altered by reason of the arbitration being conducted during the progress of the Works.

CLAUSE 67 OF THE FIDIC CONDITIONS OF CONTRACT 4TH EDITION, 1987

SETTLEMENT OF DISPUTES

Engineer's Decision

67.1. If a dispute of any kind whatsoever arises between the Employer and the Contractor in connection with, or arising out of, the Contract or the execution of the Works, whether during the execution of the Works or after the completion and whether before or after repudiation or other termination of the Contract, including any dispute as to any opinion, instruction, determination, certificate or valuation of the Engineer, the matter in dispute shall, in the first place, be referred in writing to the Engineer, with a copy to the other party. Such reference shall state that it is made pursuant to this Clause. No later than the eighty-fourth day after the day on which he received such reference the Engineer shall- give notice of his decision to the Employer and the Contractor. Such decision shall state that it is made pursuant to this Clause.

Unless the Contract has already been repudiated or terminated, the Contractor shall, in every case, continue to proceed with the Works with all due diligence and the Contractor and the Employer shall give effect forthwith to every such decision of the Engineer unless and until the same shall be revised, as hereinafter provided, in an amicable settlement or an arbitral award.

If either the Employer or the Contarctor be dissatisfied with any decision of the Engineer, or if the Engineer fails to give notice of his decision on or before the eighty-fourth day after the day on which he received the reference, then either the Employer or the Contractor may, on or before the seventieth day after the day on which he received notice of such decision, or on or before the seventieth day after the day on which the said period of 84 days expired, as the case may be, notify the other party, with a copy for information to the Engineer, of his intention to commence arbitration, as hereinafter provided as to the matter in dispute. Such notification shall establish the entitlement of the party giving the same to arbitrate such matter.

If the Engineer has given notice of his decision to the Employer and the Contractor and no notification of intention to commence arbitration has been given by either the Employer or the Contarctor on or before the seventieth day after the day on which the parties received such notice from the Engineer, the said decision shall become final and binding upon the Employer and the Contractor.

Amicable Settlement

67.2. Where notice of intention to commence arbitration as to a dispute has been given in accordance with Sub-clause 67.1, arbitration of such dispute shall not commence unless an attempt has first been made by the parties to settle such dispute amicably. Provided that, unless the parties otherwise agree, arbitration may commence on or after the fifty-sixth day after the day on which notice of intention to commence arbitration of such dispute was given, whether or not any attempt at amicable settlement thereof has been made.

Arbitration

67.3. Any dispute in respect of which:

(a) the decision, if any, of the Engineer has not become final and binding pursuant to Sub-Clause 67.1, and

(b) amicable settlement has not been reached

shall be finally settled, unless otherwise specified in the Contract, under the Rules of Conciliation and Arbitration of the International Chamber of Commerce by one or more arbitrators appointed under such Rules. The said arbitrator/s shall have full power to open up, review and revise any decision, opinion, instruction, determination, certificate or valuation of the Engineer related to the dispute.

Neither party shall be limited in the proceedings before such arbitrator/s to the evidence or arguments put before the Engineer for the purpose of obtaining his said decision pursuant to Sub-clause 67.1. No such decision shall disqualify the Engineer from being called as a witness and giving evidence before the arbitrator/s on any matter whatsoever relevant to the dispute.

Arbitration may be commenced prior to or after completion of the Works, provided that the obligations of the Employer, the Engineer and the Contractor shall not be altered by reason of the arbitration being conducted during the progress of the Works.

Notwithstanding any other provision of the Contract, arbitration of any dispute must be commenced on or before the last day for the institution of legal proceedings in respect of such dispute under the applicable law (if any).

Failure to Comply with Engineer's Decision

67.4. Where neither the Employer nor the Contractor has given notice of his intention to commence arbitration of a dispute within the period stated in Sub-clause 67.1 and the related decision has become final and binding, either party may, if the other party fails to comply with such decision, and without prejudice to any other rights it may have, refer the failure to arbitration in accordance with Sub-clause 67.3. The provisions of Sub-clause 67.1 shall not apply to such reference.

Index